SHAWNEE!

Discarded

SHAWNEE!

The Ceremonialism
of a Native Indian Tribe
and Its Cultural Background

JAMES H. HOWARD

 **Ohio University Press**
Athens

Ohio University Press books are printed on acid-free paper ∞

Library of Congress Cataloging-in Publication Data

Howard, James Henri, 1925–
        Shawnee!: The ceremonialism of a native Indian tribe and its cultural back-
ground.
        Bibliography: p.
        Includes index.
        1. Shawnee Indians. 2. Shawnee Indians–Rites and ceremonies.
3. Indians of North America–Rites and ceremonies. I. Title.
E99.S35H68   970.004'97
ISBN 0-8214-0614-0 pbk.   80-23752
                                                                CIP

Contents

Figures

Plates

Preface

In spite of the important role that it played during the colonial period and the early years of the American republic, the Shawnee tribe of American Indians has been largely ignored by the scholarly world. Anthropologists, particularly, have slighted the Shawnees despite the tribe's rich culture and pivotal position among groups in eastern North America. Only rarely do they figure in those cultural-historical summaries of American Indians that appear as college textbooks or coffee-table books for the general reading public. Ask an anthropology undergraduate about the Iroquois, Cherokees, or even the Natchez and you will probably elicit some information. Ask about the Shawnees and you will probably get a blank stare, perhaps followed by "Did you say *Shawnees* or *Pawnees*?" Clearly at present the Shawnees are one of the least known groups of Native Americans.

Several possible explanations for this neglect can be offered. Undoubtedly important was the transfer of interest from the Indian groups of the eastern seaboard to those of the High Plains and the Southwest as the frontier advanced. By the time scientific interest in the American Indian was aroused, attention had already shifted to the more colorful and less acculturated Pueblo groups and the bison hunters of the Plains.

Within the infant discipline of anthropology the rigidities built into the popular "culture area" approach may be partly responsible for an almost systematic neglect of the Shawnees. Anthropologists accustomed to this approach tend to think in terms of absolutes. Thus, for descriptive and comparative purposes in the discipline, "typical" Plains tribes, and "typical"

Woodland tribes, in terms of the culture-area concept, are invariably selected for exposition and study. Descriptions of these "typical" groups have, by repetition, become known to several generations of scholars, serving to generate further interest and study of these same groups. With no overall anthropological planning agency to assure balanced coverage, this has led to the popularization of certain groups that have become considered to be "typical" of the classic culture areas to the virtual neglect of other groups whose tribal domain happened to embrace two or more culture areas or who happened to move from one area to another. The Shawnees are an excellent case in point. Most anthropologists are not quite certain whether the Shawnees belong in the Northeast, the Southeast, or the Prairie area. Thus, for most anthropologists, the Shawnees simply do not come to mind, or if they do, they appear as a vague afterthought.

Historians, on the other hand, although they are more apt to acknowledge the existence of the Shawnees, almost invariably limit themselves to a chronicling of political decisions affecting white-Indian relations and to accounts of military conflicts between Shawnees and the advancing frontiersmen. Only rarely does a historian give real consideration to the Indian viewpoint or seem to have any glimmering of the notion that Shawnee culture, though technologically less complex than that of the white man, might contain something of value. Usually to the white "frontier historian" the Shawnees are merely an obstacle that had to be surmounted in settling the Midwest, their history becoming a savage backdrop against which the brave deeds of a Daniel Boone or a Simon Kenton show to best advantage. Certain of the numerous captivity accounts, which were written from a very subjective point of view, give us fleeting glimpses of Shawnee culture; but a recent analysis of several such captivities that deal with the Shawnees indicates that the material contained in them is fragmentary, and in some cases, unreliable (D. L. Smith "Shawnee Captivity Ethnography,": p. 31).

In spite of this neglect and distortion of Shawnee culture, a few excellent studies have appeared through the years. Unfortunately most of them are available only in the largest libraries. C. C. Trowbridge's *Shawnese Traditions* (1939), penned in the early nineteenth century, remains a good point of departure for Shawnee studies, as do Henry Harvey's *History of the Shawnee Indians* (1855), and Lewis Henry Morgan's Shawnee data in *The Indian Journals, 1859-62* (1959).* Likewise Joab Spencer's *The*

Shawnee Indians (1908) contains material that is not available elsewhere. The best modern accounts are Thomas W. Alford's *Civilization* (1936)** and the various papers stemming from the fieldwork of C. F. and E. W. Voegelin between 1933 and 1935. To date there has been no comprehensive study of Shawnee culture, and it was with this objective in mind that I have undertaken this work. The ceremonialism of the Shawnees, in particular, has been neglected. It is a rich field, because in this regard the tribe is one of the most conservative in North America. In this respect, especially, this book must be viewed as a pioneering work.

My approach has been simply to assemble as much cultural data regarding the Shawnees as possible from published accounts, documents, and Shawnee informants. I have attempted to weigh this information, digest it, and then present it in an orderly and interesting fashion so that the culture of the Shawnees, whom Lewis Henry Morgan termed "this remarkable and highly advanced tribe, one of the highest representatives of the Algonkin stock . . . (*Ancient Society*: p. 172-3)" will attain the prominence it deserves. In my presentation I have followed the scheme embodied in the *Outline of Cultural Materials* (G.P. Murdock et al 3rd rev. ed.), though I have omitted certain categories and combined others in conformity with my Shawnee data.

Customarily, the author of a tribal ethnography tends to treat his or her group as an isolated unit for purposes of study and explication. This "in vacuo" kind of approach gives the reader the false impression that most American Indian tribes had little to do with others. By departing somewhat from this usual model, within the limits of space, this book points up the close interrelationships of the Shawnees and certain neighboring tribes. Intertribal cooperation is particularly evident in the area of ceremonialism. Thus present-day Shawnee ritualists often attend and assume prominent roles in the ceremonies of certain other tribes, and key personnel from these groups reciprocate by assisting in Shawnee rites. I have attempted to illuminate this very interesting phenomenon, which reflects the long-standing friendships between the Eastern and Loyal Shawnee bands and the Oklahoma Delawares, the Oklahoma Seneca-Cayugas (the modern descendants of the Mingo Iroquois), and the Quapaws; and the Absentee Shawnee band with the Absentee or "Caddo" Delawares, the Caddoes, the Kickapoos, the Creeks, and the Seminoles.

My field work among the Shawnees in Oklahoma was supported by the American Philosophical Society (Grant No. 5834, Penrose Fund) and by the College of Arts and Sciences, Oklahoma State University. The bulk of this fieldwork, in the form of short trips of a day or two in length from my home in Stillwater to the various Shawnee communities, took place during the period from 1969 to 1974. Transcriptions of Shawnee songs were made from tapes by Sandra Wilbur who was at that time associated with the Institute of Ethnomusicology at the University of California. The assistance of the various members of the Shawnee tribe, whose specific contributions are noted in the text, is gratefully acknowledged. Special mention must be made of the late Ranny Carpenter (he was seventy-seven years of age at the time of his death in 1973), who took me as his "brother" in the Indian manner early on in my visits to his people, and to his singing partner William Shawnee (age seventy-four at the time of his death in 1978), a prominent ritualist of this group. Affectionate thanks also to Mrs. Ranny (Emmaline) Carpenter, who was chief matron of the Loyal band during the period of my study, and to the late Esther Dixon (she was seventy-eight years of age at the time of her death in 1973) of Eastern Shawnee and Delaware descent who attended ceremonials of the Loyal band at Whiteoak. In the Absentee band my special thanks go to the late Mary Spoon (seventy-six years of age at the time of her death in 1975) of Tecumseh, Oklahoma; Alfred Switch (age seventy-seven) of Shawnee, Oklahoma; Richard Gibson (age fifty-six) of Little Axe, Oklahoma; George Whitewater (a Kickapoo of part Shawnee background, age sixty) Shawnee, Oklahoma; Bill Johnson (age fifty-one) and his brother Henry (age fifty-six) both of Norman, Oklahoma; Clifton Blanchard (age fifty) of Little Axe; John Ellis (age sixty-three) and his wife Lillie (age seventy) of Tecumseh; and Cody and Agnes Mack (both age sixty) of Shawnee. The ages of these informants, unless otherwise noted, are as of September, 1979.

Scholars who have read and commented upon earlier drafts of this monograph include Charles Callender, William A. Hunter, Erminie Wheeler Voegelin, and John Witthoft. Their helpful suggestions are gratefully acknowledged. I alone am responsible for any errors or misinterpretations that may remain.

Shawnee words in the text are transcribed using a slight modification of the system of phonemic symbols employed by C.

F. Voegelin ("Shawnee Phonemes": p. 23). His table of phonemes is reproduced here:

Tables of Phonemes

	Labial	Dental tongue-tip	Dental tongue-blade	Velar	Laryngal
Voiceless Consonants					
stops and affricate	p	t(T)	č	k(K)	
fricatives		θ	š		?
glottalic phoneme					
Voiced Consonants					
nasals and lateral	m	n,l			
semivowels	w		y		
Vowels					
high i o					
low e a					

To save typesetting costs I have modified this as follows: For the dental fricative *θ* I have used *th*, for *č*, *ch*, and for *š*, *sh*. It is suggested that Voegelin's paper be consulted for a detailed consideration of the subject. For the casual reader interested in roughly approximating the pronunciation of the Shawnee terms used in this work, I might note that *p, t, (T), k, (K), m, n, l, w,* and *y* have roughly the same sounds as in English. *Ch* has much the same sound as *ch* in the English word *church*; *th* the sound of *th* in the English *thin*; and *sh* the sound of *sh* in the English *ship*. Voegelin has reduced the vowels in Shawnee to four, *i, e, o,* and *a.* These vowel phonemes range phonetically within the following limits (ibid.: p. 35).

Vowels

```
                    front        close              back
                      i                              u
                 (cp. Eng. eat)                 (cp. Eng soup)
                                                                         o
    i                                                                 phoneme
  phoneme
                      (                            o
                 (cp. Eng. it)                (cp. Eng. soap)
                      ε
                 (cp. Eng. met)
    e
  phoneme             ä
                 (cp. Eng mad)
                                                  ɔ
                                          (cp. London Eng. hot)
                                                                         a
                                                                      phoneme
                                              a
                                     (cp. New York Eng. hot)
                    open
```

Which limit a variant will approach is determined by a number of factors, including juxtaposed phonemes, stress, and style of speech (ibid.: pp. 35-36). The vowels in Shawnee may appear doubled (ii, ee, aa, oo). Three of the voiceless consonants also appear doubled (kk, ss, ??) (ibid.: p. 24).

The Shawnee language belongs to the Algonkian linguistic stock. There are three dialects, corresponding to the Eastern, Loyal, and Absentee bands. These dialects show some lexical differences, very few phonetic, and no phonemic differences (ibid.: p. 23).

* *Civilization as Told to Florence Drake*, by Thomas Wildcat Alford © 1936 by the University of Oklahoma Press.

** *The Indian Journals, 1859-62* by Lewis H. Morgan, Leslie A. White Editor University of Michigan Press 1959.

1

Historical Summary

The origins and early history of the Shawnees are not the main thrust of this book, but a short summary of these matters may help to place my account of historical Shawnee culture and the tribe's present situation in proper context. In Sauk, Fox, and many other Algonkian languages the name for the Shawnees, *Shawunogi*, and its variants, means "Southerners" (J. Mooney "Shawnee": pp. 530-537). Earlier students of the Shawnees usually accepted this name at face value and assigned the tribe a southeastern homeland. Because some Shawnee bands were, indeed, living in the Southeast in the early colonial period, this theory was unchallenged for many years. More recently, however, scholars have placed the Shawnees in the Ohio country just prior to European contact (C.C. Royce "An Inquiry into the Identity and History of the Shawnee Indians" pp. 177-189; C. A. Hanna *The Wilderness Trail*, I: p. 126; J. B. Griffin *Archeology of Eastern United States*: p. 364; J. Witthoft and W.A. Hunter "The Seventeenth Century Origin of the Shawnee" pp. 42-57). Griffin (*Archeology of Eastern United States*: p. 364) and Witthoft and Hunter ("Seventeenth Century Origin": p. 42) are of the opinion that the Shawnees can be equated with at least a part of the Fort Ancient Aspect, an archeological culture dated from about A.D. 1400 to 1650, but not all scholars who have worked with the relevant archeological and ethnohistorical data agree (cf. Richard G. Morgan in Griffin *Archeology of Eastern United States*: p. 95; E.W. Voegelin and H.H. Tanner *Indians of Ohio and Indiana Prior to 1795*: pp. 172-3).

The Fort Ancient Aspect has been described in detail by Griffin (*The Fort Ancient Aspect*). The Fort Ancient people occupied an area embracing southern Ohio, southern Indiana, northern Kentucky, and western West Virginia. Their villages were situated near streams or rivers and were composed of rows of circular or rectangular structures built of poles and probably covered with wattle and daub, bark, or sewn mats made of split cattails. Inside or near the dwellings were basin-shaped firepits sometimes made of puddled clay. Larger structures similar to the dwellings are probably the prehistoric antecedent of the historic Shawnee council houses, which combined legislative and religious functions.

The economy of the Fort Ancient people combined hunting, fishing and gathering with horticulture. Their principal crops were corn, beans, squash, and sunflowers. Most of the native animals and birds of the region were hunted, with elk being one of the most important game animals. Pottery was unpainted with either grit or crushed shell temper and was tan, gray to black, and brown to reddish brown in color. Most of the vessels are squat and globular, with rounded bottoms, broad mouths, a slight constriction of the neck and upper shoulder area, and slightly flaring rims. Strap handles are commonly found on these vessels; lugs on the rims are found less frequently. Sometimes the lugs are in the form of a small lizard, bird, or fish's head. Vessel surfaces are cord-marked or smooth. Many vessels show decoration on the rim or shoulder produced by incising or punctating the vessel before firing. Characteristic patterns are guilloches (intertwined wavy lines), rows or areas of puctates, and line-filled angular plats in bands. Vessel lips are sometimes notched in an ornamental fashion. In addition to jars for cooking and food storage there were colanders and thick basins used for evaporating salt from saline water. The Fort Ancient Indians also made ceramic animal effigies, a trait that was common in the Mississippian archeological culture and among the historic Yuchi, Oto, and Ponca Indians (Griffin *The Fort Ancient Aspect*: Pl. LXXI; T.M.N. Lewis and M. Kneberg *Tribes That Slumber*: pp. 148, 149; J.H. Howard *The Ponca Tribe*: p. 80). In addition to pottery vessels there were wooden bowls and conch-shell containers. Spoons were made of shell or turtle carapaces, and probably of wood and bison horn as well. Picks, hoes, and tools for flint knapping were made of antler.

These people planted their fields with the aid of digging sticks and cultivated with shell or stone hoes lashed to a wooden handle. Some hoes were made of elk scapulae fastened to wooden handles. Flat stone slabs and small biscuit-shaped manos were used to grind corn into meal. Although they are not found archeologically one suspects that wooden mortars and pestles were also in use. The bow and arrow was the chief hunting weapon. Long, narrow, triangular points of chipped flint were commonly used. Other arrow points were made of antler and even of deer toe bones. Shaft wrenches and grooved sandstone shaft smoothers were also a part of the archer's kit. Knives were made from clamshells, chipped flint, and long unworked flint blades. Chipped flint "swords" also occur but are rare and undoubtedly served only as ceremonial weapons.

Fish were taken with bone hooks and gorges, antler or bone harpoons, and in nets weighted with notched stone sinkers. Celts of chipped flint or ground stone are more common at Fort Ancient sites than grooved axes. Other woodworking tools were various styles of chipped stone drills, ground stone adzes, bone awls in a variety of forms, and various chipped stone scrapers and hammerstones. Stone plummets, of indeterminate use, also occur at Fort Ancient sites. Awls, scrapers, needles, and bone beaming tools were used in the preparation of animal skins for clothing.

Both stone and clay were used in making pipes, which appear in many shapes. The most common forms are rectanguloid or conoidal pipes with stone bowls and wooden stems, effigy pipes, equal-armed elbow pipes, pipes with projecting "prows" at the front (to provide a cool handhold for the smoker), and platform pipes. Ornaments were fashioned from bone, shell, and a variety of other materials. Beads were made of shell, freshwater pearl, and decorated bone. Circular and crescent-shaped gorgets were made of shell. Antler combs, shell earpins, and the bone spreaders used with the roach headdress (presumably together with the headdress itself, which has not survived archeologically) adorned Fort Ancient heads. Pendants were made of animal teeth, shells, and bone, as well as cut animal jaws. Musical instruments included drums, musical rasps of bone, turtle-shell and turkey-skull rattles, and bone flutes.

Many Fort Ancient objects indicate that these people participated in the Southeastern Ceremonial Complex, a religious expression centering in the Southeast and usually associated with the Mississippian archeological culture (cf. J.H. Howard *The Southeastern Ceremonial Complex and Its Interpretation*). These objects include masklike and engraved conch-shell gorgets, large, cylindrical shell beads; copper ornaments, and the aforementioned flint "swords." Discoidals (probably gaming stones used in the game of chunkey) and circular engraved stones should probably be included in this category as well.

The dead were buried beneath the floors of houses in some instances; in other cases they were placed in refuse pits, in specially dug graves in the village, in subfloor pits beneath mounds of earth, or within funerary mounds composed of alternate layers of earth and layers of bodies. Some of the graves in mounds or cemetaries were lined with stone slabs. Bodies were generally fully extended in the graves or extended with the knees bent. Many were flexed, and some secondary burials made up of bundles of disarticulated bones have been found. Pottery and other offerings often accompanied burials.

It is extremely risky to assign the names of historic tribal groups to archeological manifestations, but there is good reason for believing that the Fort Ancient Aspect, as summarized above, represents at least in part the ancestors of the Shawnees. The peculiar and distinctive combination of Northeastern, Iroquois-like traits with Southeastern (Mississippian) and Midwestern (Oneota) features in Fort Ancient sites fits exactly our picture of historic Shawnee culture, which had a similar composition. The location of Fort Ancient sites in the territory that ethnohistorical data indicates was occupied by the Shawnees in the early historic period adds further weight to such speculations. It would certainly appear that the most economical explanation in terms of available archeological, linguistic, and ethnohistorical data is to equate the prehistoric Shawnees with at least part of the Fort Ancient archeological culture, though other groups were probably involved as well. Griffin (*Archeology of Eastern United States*: p. 364) would include the northern tribes of the Illinois confederacy and E.W. Voegelin would include the now extinct Mosopeleas, particularly in regard to the Madisonville Focus (Voegelin and Tanner *Indians of Ohio and Indiana Prior to 1795*: p. 190).

The earliest historical mentions of the Shawnees tend to reinforce the archeological data by placing them in the upper Ohio Valley and in the valley of the Cumberland River, one of its major tributaries from the south. Thus in 1673 Marquette, descending the Mississippi, reached the mouth of the "Waboukigou" (the Wabash-Ohio) and writes, "This river flows from the lands of the East, where dwell the people called Chaouanons in so great numbers that in one district there are as many as 23 villages, and 15 in another, quite near one another" (E. Kenton *Indians of North America*: p. 208). This same location is echoed on Franquelin's 1681 map, which places "Chaouanons, fifteen villages" south of the Wabash-Ohio (Hanna *The Wilderness Trail*, I: p. 119) and a similar interpretation may be drawn from Marquette's map (Griffin *The Fort Ancient Aspect*: p. 14). Much more information is provided by Franquelin's map of 1684, based on La Salle's Indian data and perhaps on the testimony of two Shawnees who were with La Salle in Paris when it was drawn (Hanna *The Wilderness Trail*, II: opp. p. 92). This map shows the upper half of what we know now as the Ohio river with the legend "Ohio als Mosopeleacipi als Olighin" (Ohio alias Mosopeleacipi alias Olighin). North of the upper Ohio are depicted and legended "Mosopelea 8 Vil détruits" (Mosopelea 8 villages destroyed). E.W. Voegelin (Voegelin and Tanner *Indians of Ohio and Indiana Prior to 1795*: p. 183) points out that the name *Mosopelea* is translatable as "Big Turkey" in Shawnee, and *Mosopeleacipi* as "Big Turkey river", therefore these people may have been Shawnees or a closely related Shawnee-speaking group. The branch of the Fleuve St. Louis (lower Ohio) on this map which is south and east of that where the Mosopelea villages are placed has the legend "Skipakicipi ou la riviere bleue." *Skipakicipi* translates "Blue river" in Shawnee and confirms the French translation of the term. *Shkipakithithipi*, "Blue river" is to this day the name the Shawnees apply to the Cumberland (W.A. Galloway *Old Chillicothe*: pp. 18–19; Voegelin and Tanner *Indians of Ohio and Indiana Prior to 1795*: p. 184). North of this branch, almost intermediately between it and the Mosopeleacipi are the "Chaskepe," (possibly the Kishpoko division of the Shawnees), and on its banks the "Meguatchaiki" (probably the Mekoche division of the tribe). South of the river are the "Cisca" which were possibly another Shawnee group. This same map also traces a route from the Chaskepe; Meguatchaiki; and Cisca to St. Augustine, Florida, identified as "Chemin par les Casquinampo et les Chaouanons vont en traite aux Espagnols" ("route traveled by the Casquinampo and the Shawnees in trading with the Spanish"). This Spanish trade is verified by Marquette's Illinois informants who in 1669 described their Shawnee visitors as "laden with glass beads" (Kenton *Indians of North America*: p. 208). The Spanish trade may account for the presence of European trade materials at the Fort Ancient Madisonville site.

The Cumberland river is frequently referred to as "la riviere des Chaouesnons" or "River of the Shawnees" on early maps and documents. Thus La Salle (P. Margry *Decouvertes et É tablissements des Francais dans L'Ouest*, II: p. 96) describes the Ohio as receiving two considerable branches before falling into the Mississippi, the "Agouassake" from the north and "la riviere des Chaouesnons" from the south. He also refers, in 1681, to a Shawnee captain who lived "on a large river that falls into the Ohio" (ibid., I: p. 529). In 1742 (Public Archives of Canada, Arch. des Colonies, Ser C11A, Corresp. gen., F-77, f. p. 259) Shawnees informed Governor Beauharnois of their intention to remove from two villages on the Allegheny to "la Riviere des Cha8anons" near the Wabash and the River of the Cherokees (Tennessee): stating "these are positively the lands where we were born," and in 1760 (Ibid. 105, ff, pp. 189-90) Vaudreuil reports forty cabins of Shawnees on "la riviere de leur nom". Although identification of the Cumberland as the "River of the Shawnees" cannot be directly established from the earliest maps because of their vagueness and inaccuracy, it can be done indirectly by comparing the John Mitchell map of 1755 with the Bellin Carte de l'Amerique Septentrionale of the same year. The "Cumberland R." of the English map is clearly identical with the "Riv. des Anciens Chaenons" of its French counterpart. Very likely there were two concentrations of Shawnees in the late seventeenth century, one on the upper Ohio, the other on the Cumberland, and these may represent divisions of the tribe. Two seventeenth century references seem to indicate such a division. La Salle, in 1680 (Margry *Decouvertes et Etablissements*, I: pp. 506-7) reports that 100 Shawnees, armed with bows, joined an Iroquois war party but the following year (ibid.: p. 529, and II: pp. 142-3) he reports a Shawnee captain of 150 warriors asking protection from the Iroquois.

Accounts falling into the years between 1662 and 1673 (Galinée in Margry *Decouvertes et Etablissements*, I: pp. 133-7; Marquette in Kenton *Indians of North America*: p. 277: N. Perrot *Memoirs on the Manners, Customs and Religion of the Savages of North America*: p. 226; B. de la Potherie *History of the Savage Peoples*

Who are Allies of New France: p. 348) document a pattern of
Iroquois expansionism and aggression toward neighboring
tribes, particularly the Shawnees. These attacks gain in intensity
and ultimately result in the Shawnees being driven out of the Ohio
and Cumberland valleys. To save themselves the Shawnees split
into a number of fragments, probably on the basis of their five
traditional divisions, and moved off in various directions. In 1683
several hundred Shawnees came to La Salle's post at Starved
Rock (Fort St. Louis) in Illinois, remaining there until 1688 or 1689
(P. Liette *The Western Country in the 17th Century*: p. 92; La Salle
in Margry *Decouvertes et Etablissements*, II: p. 314; Tonty in L.P.
Kellogg *Early Narratives of the Northwest, 1634-1699*: p. 309).

Other Shawnees moved into the Southeast, reaching the
Savannah river opposite what is now Augusta, Georgia. About
1680 these Shawnees evicted the Westo tribe and for a time
established themselves as a dominant tribe in the area. For a
decade or so the Carolinians regularly supplied the Shawnees
with arms and purchased slaves taken by them in raids upon
fugitive Westos, Winyahs, Appomattoxes, Cherokees, and
Chatots (V.W. Crane *The Southern Frontier, 1670-1732*: pp.
20-21). Lawson, who traveled through Carolina in 1701, mentions
the Shawnees as the "Savannas, a famous, warlike, friendly
nation of Indians living to the south end of Ashley r." (Mooney
"Shawnee": p. 532). In 1707, under attack by Carolina, some of the
Savannah River Shawnees moved to Pennsylvania. In 1715, after
involvement in the Yamasee War, the rest, sixty-seven men, left
(W.R. Jacobs *The Appalachian Indian Frontier*: p. 66). Some
fugitives from the Savannah River settled on the Chattahoochee
near what is presently Mobile, Alabama, in 1716, and later moved
to the Tallapoosa and were incorporated into the Creek nation
(ibid.: p. 65).

In 1692 some of the western Shawnees living under French
protection at Fort St. Louis were persuaded by some Munsee
Indians (who made up the northern division of the Delawares)
from the upper Delaware River to come east (D'Iberville in Margry
Decouvertes et Etablissements, IV: pp. 341-2). This group,
consisting of seventy-two men and one hundred women and
children, together with a French trader named Martin Chartier
who was married to a Shawnee woman, appeared at the mouth of
the Susquehanna in the summer of that year (Maryland Archives
1890 VIII: pp. 341-5). Chartier was brought before the Maryland

Council for examination, through an interpreter, as it was
thought he might be a " . . . spie, or party concerned with them
in designs of mischief." Chartier, who described himself as a
deserter from Fort St. Louis, was held prisoner for two and a half
months, then released by order of the council (ibid.: p. 345).
Chartier continued to reside with the Shawnees and afterwards
became well known as an Indian trader at their village named
Pequea, in what is now Lancaster, Pennsylvania. From the name
of their village it would appear that these Shawnees were of the
Pekowi division of the tribe. Another Shawnee band, apparently
coming directly from the Ohio country, was brought into eastern
Pennsylvania in 1694 by Arnold Viele (P. Wraxall *An Abridge-
ment of the Indian Affairs . . . Transacted in the Colony of New
York, From the Year 1678 to the Year 1751*: p. 22). Pennsylvania
became the major Shawnee center in the early eighteenth century
as small groups from the Savannah River migrated to that
colony.

It would appear that those Shawnees who settled in Pennsylvania, like their Susquehannock hosts and other groups in the
area, such as the Munsees, Nanticokes, Delawares, and Conoys,
were clearly under the domination of the Iroquois. In 1697
Captain John Tillman reported that: " . . . Shevanoo [Shawnee]
Indians being about thirty men beside women & children live
within foure miles of Caristauga [the town of Conestoga on the
Susquehanna River] lower downe & submit themselves & pay
tribute to the Susquehannocks & Senecas," (Maryland Archives
1899, XIX: p. 520). In 1700 the Shawnees of the Pekowi division,
under their sachem Opessa [Wapaththa] made a treaty with
Maryland (ibid. 1905, XXV: pp. 103-6) and the following year
made one with William Penn (Hanna *The Wilderness Trail*, I: p.
150). The Iroquois continued to insist upon their position as
overlords of the Shawnees, and when possible made the
Shawnees toe the mark. Thus in 1711 the Iroquois forced Opessa
to abdicate his position and appointed the Oneida chief Caron-
dawana to govern this group in his stead (F. Jennings "The
Constitutional Evolution of the Convenant Chain": p. 91).

Robert Rogers, the famous New Hampshire ranger of the
French and Indian War, greatly admired the Iroquois, and reflects
their view of their relationship with the Shawnees in the following
anecdote: "They [the Mohawks] also took prisoners the whole
nation of the Shawnees, who lived upon the Wabash, and

afterwards, by the mediation of Mr. Penn, at the first settlement of Pensilvania, gave them liberty to settle in the westerly parts of that province; but obliged them, as a badge of their cowardice, to wear petticoats for a long time. They gave them, however, the appellation of cousins, and allowed them to claim kindred with the Five Nations, as their uncles," (R. Rogers *A Concise Account of North America*: p. 207). Rogers is an unreliable historical source, yet his statement here accurately reflects not only the Iroquois view, but the "official" view of the colonial authorities, who for many years found it to their convenience to deal with the Shawnees, Delawares, and other western tribes through the Iroquois. In 1731 James Logan, Provincial Secretary of Pennsylvania, proposed a council to be held with the Six Nations, who for several years had not visited Philadelphia, but "have absolute authority as well over the Shawanese as all our Indians, that by their means the Shawanese may not only be kept firm to the English [Pennsylvania] Interest, but likewise be induced to remove from Allegheney nearer to the English Settlement," (Minutes of the Pennsylvania Provincial Council III, quoted in Voegelin and Tanner *Indians of Ohio and Indiana Prior to 1795*: p. 263). Needless to say, this official Iroquois-colonial government view was a distortion of the facts and neither the Shawnees nor the Delawares viewed their situation in this manner. Whenever possible they ignored agreements forced upon them by Iroquois conquest or military threat. This behavior infuriated both the Iroquois and the colonial governments. Again, Major Rogers reflects the views of his Mohawk friends and the English colonial governments when he writes: "The Delawares and Shawnees are remarked for their deceit and perfidy, paying little or no regard to their word and most solemn engagements" (Rogers *A Concise Account of North America*: p. 237).

The influence of the Iroquois on both the Shawnees and the Delawares was nevertheless strong until the outbreak of the French and Indian War, when both groups disregarded the Six Nations of the Iroquois and allied themselves with the French. Even after they ceased to be politically dominated by the Iroquois League, both Shawnees and Delawares continued to associate with and exchange cultural elements with the Mingo Iroquois. These Mingoes were young Iroquois people who had gone to the Ohio and Indiana country to hunt for meat and peltry, found the country to be agreeable, and settled down on the Ohio. Though drawn from all six tribes of the league, they were mostly Senecas and Cayugas. They had gradually dissociated themselves from their eastern kinsmen and did not feel bound by the agreements between the League and the English, who were constantly calling for them to return to their "original homes" in the East. The League, in fact, often gave their Mingo kinsmen the same shabby treatment which they meted out to the Shawnees and Delawares (R.C. Downes *Council Fires on the Upper Ohio*: pp. 134-5 et seq. cf. also Voegelin and Tanner *Indians of Ohio and Indiana Prior to 1795*).

It was not a desire to escape Iroquois domination, however, but rather the increasing pressure of white settlement that caused the Susquehanna Shawnees to begin a general movement west in the early years of the eighteenth century. Their village at Pequa Creek on the Susquehanna was disturbed in 1710 or 1711 by Swiss Mennonite immigrants. The Shawnees moved farther upstream on the Susquehanna but were disturbed again. Finally they gave up the whole business about 1728 to go off to the west again, where they were forced to place themselves under French protection (Jennings "Constitutional Evolution of the Convenent Chain": p. 93).

In 1731 about twelve hundred Shawnees lived on the headwaters of the Ohio, with others on the Juniata and Susquehanna and some in the Wyoming Valley (Hanna *The Wilderness Trail*, I: pp. 154, 187, 296). The Wyoming group moved west about 1743, founding Logstown on the Ohio (ibid., I: pp. 154, 187, 354-6). The settlement later called the Lower Shawnee Town was established at the mouth of the Scioto sometime before 1739, perhaps by members of the Hathawikila division who fled down the Ohio in 1735 after killing an Iroquois chief (ibid., I: pp. 302-3; II: p. 109).

The flight of the Hathawikila foreshadowed a new hegira for the Shawnees. Its ultimate causes were abuses in the fur trade. Unlicensed traders used rum to obtain furs cheaply, leaving the Shawnees impoverished and in debt to the licensed traders who had provided them goods on credit (Downes *Council Fires on the Upper Ohio*: pp. 20-25; 30-41). Repeated requests were made to the Pennsylvania government to regulate trade and enforce the anti-rum laws, but these requests were ignored. Finally in 1745 the Indians turned on their tormentors, pillaging several unlicensed traders and leaving Pennsylvania with Peter Chartier, the half-

Shawnee son of Martin Chartier mentioned earlier. Some went to Lower Shawnee town, others to Logstown, and the main body founded a new settlement in northern Kentucky (Hanna *The Wilderness Trail*, I: pp. 311-12; II: p. 134, 138, 240).

In 1747 they abandoned this town and moved south, where, after a war with the Chickasaws, they settled among the Creeks. By 1752 a large group had returned to Lower Shawnee Town, which became the tribal center for this part of the Shawnees. Another section moved to the Cumberland, settling near the site of present day Nashville, Tennessee. The Chickasaws drove them from this location in 1756 and they moved to the lower Ohio (J. Adair *The History of the American Indian*, II: p. 409; Draper in Hanna *The Wilderness Trail*, II: pp. 240-2).

As the French and English competition for control of the North American continent moved into the Ohio Valley in the 1730s and 1740s, the Shawnees found themselves in an increasingly uncomfortable geographic position. Under pressure from both English and French to choose sides, the Shawnees fully realized that no matter which side triumphed they themselves would be the ultimate losers. Thus Shawnee history during this period and throughout the French and Indian Wars (1754-63) can best be understood as an attempt by the Shawnees to accomplish three things: maintain their ancient hunting grounds for their own use; avoid dangerous involvement as shock troops by either the French or the English; and assure themselves of a continued supply of trade goods from either French or English sources, particularly the firearms and gunpowder upon which they had come to rely for hunting and self-defense.

The French, alarmed by the infiltration of the English into an area that they claimed as their own, and seemingly unable to compete with the English in the amount and quality of trade goods offered to the Indians, warned the Ohio tribes to expel the Englishmen from their villages. When the tribes ignored this warning the French resorted to strong-arm tactics. In 1750 the Shawnees suffered an attack on one of their villages, probably on the Scioto, by a combined force of French and northern Indians, in which one Shawnee warrior was killed and three noncombatants were captured (Downes *Council Fires on the Upper Ohio*: p. 57). In the pursuit that followed five Frenchmen and several of their Indian allies were captured. The Shawnees refused to be intimidated by this attack and sent a message to Governor

Hamilton of Pennsylvania, dated 8 February, 1752, stating that they were going to strike the French "and not suffer ourselves to be insulted any more." They asked the English for support in their endeavor (ibid.: p. 57).

Unfortunately at the time when the Indians looked to the English for leadership and supplies the colonists demonstrated their chronic disunity. Virginians were at odds with Pennsylvanians over trade in the Ohio Valley. The situation was further aggravated by the haughty attitude of British military officers like General Braddock who, when questioned by Indians in council concerning what treatment they might expect if British arms prevailed in the impending hostilities, informed them that "No Savage Shoud Inherit the Land" (ibid.: p. 78). Refused supplies and military support by the English and colonial governments, and treated with contempt by British officers, the Shawnees and Delawares living in Ohio began to waver in their loyalty to the English, and when Braddock was defeated in 1755 they reluctantly took sides with the victorious French. Those Shawnees at Wyoming (present-day Wilkes-Barre) remained neutral at first, but when it appeared certain that the English were losing, they too espoused the French cause. In 1756 they moved to join their relatives on the Ohio. This worked to their ultimate disadvantage, as it led to attacks by both the British and their Iroquois allies, and the destruction of the new Shawnee settlements on the Ohio River. In 1758 the fall of Fort Duquesne (now Pittsburgh) restored the British presence, and in the final years of the French wars the Shawnees fought as English allies (ibid.: pp. 101–2).

The end of the French and Indian wars in 1763 offered no relief for the Shawnees, for with the French no longer a menace, the great eruption of white settlers into their Kentucky and Ohio hunting grounds began. At first the Shawnees handled such intrusions with restraint and even generosity as in the case when in 1769, they learned that a hunting and exploring party led by Daniel Boone had invaded their territory. These frontiersmen were killing game in a profligate manner, saving only the furs and hides and leaving the meat to rot. Boone himself was captured, and the Shawnees forced him to lead them to the individual camps of his men. These camps were surprised one by one, and the accumulated pelts, guns, ammunition, horses, and all other property of the white interlopers were either destroyed or confiscated. Having rendered Boone's expedition fruitless, the Shawnees, with typical Indian generosity and consideration, freed their captives and sent them home unharmed, presenting each with two pairs of moccasins, a doeskin for patch leather, a little trading gun, and a few loads of powder so that they would not starve on their way back to the settlements. They also warned Boone never to return, saying "Don't come here any more, for this is the Indians' hunting ground, and all the animals, skins, and furs are ours; and if you are so foolish as to venture here again, you may be sure the wasps and yellow-jackets will sting you severely" (ibid.: p. 12).

The frontiersmen, however, considered their treatment at the hands of the Shawnees an outrage. Recognizing no Indian rights to the country or the game in it, their only thought was to return as soon as possible and retaliate upon the Shawnees for their wanton destruction of seven months' hunting. Encouraged by Boone's discoveries in the hunting field, new parties crossed the mountains into Kentucky to continue the slaughter. Boone himself returned in 1770 for a winter hunt and again in 1771, when he was again captured and plundered but released unharmed. Thus the stage was set for the Shawnee war of 1774, better known to historians as Lord Dunmore's War, in which the main bone of contention was the Kentucky country. The pattern in this conflict and most of those that followed was the same: white frontiersmen and land speculators invaded the Shawnee country, slaughtering the game and surveying the land. They were shortly followed by actual settlers, who proceeded to erect cabins and fences. Shawnees who objected were killed, and when other Shawnees retaliated by attacking settlements, the frontiersmen clamored for government protection against the Indians.

The particular event that led to Dunmore's War was the wanton killing of thirteen Shawnees and Mingo Iroquois in a particularly brutal series of unprovoked murders by drunken frontier ruffians (ibid.: pp. 161–178). Unable to secure allies, the Shawnee chiefs decided against war, but relatives of the victims joined a group of Mingoes to kill 13 settlers in retaliation. The Virginia government, of which Dunmore was governor, responded by supporting the frontiersmen, and a Virginia army destroyed a Shawnee town in the Muskingum Valley. After unsuccefully trying to block an invasion of the Scioto valley, the Shawnees made peace and accepted the Ohio River as their southern boundary (ibid.: p. 184).

Occasionally a white intellectual would admit that the Indians had just cause for their hostile behavior. One such was Richard Butler, who was later Indian commissioner and agent of the United States and first superintendent of Indian affairs. Butler wrote, at the close of his *Account of the Rise of the Indian War, 1774*; "These facts I think was sufficient to bring on a war with a Christian instead of a Savage People, and I do declare it as my opinion that the Shawanese did not intend a war this Season, let their future Intentions be what they might; and I do likewise declare that I am afraid . . . that they will bring on a general war, as there is so little pains taken to restrain the common People whose prejudice leads them to greater lengths than ought to be shown by civilized People, and their Superiors take too little if any pains, and I do really think is much to blame themselves in the whole Affair" (quoted in ibid.: pp. 152-3).

The frontiersmen, however, operated under a philosophy that had no place for Indian rights. It seemed inevitable to most whites on the Indian frontier, and to most politicians behind it, that Indians, being savage, would resist savagely; that they would have to be beaten down savagely; that some whites would have to make the sacrifice of meeting them on their own terms. Some of the whites, and all of the Indians, would be destroyed in the process but in the end civilization, as defined by the whites, would triumph. (See R.H. Pearce "The Metaphysics of Indian-Hating": pp. 31-2). An understanding of this philosophy makes quite clear what treatment the Shawnees and other Native Americans received throughout the eighteenth and nineteenth centuries. Even today, in a period when one reads and hears much about equal rights and equal access to "the good life" for ethnic minorities it is this philosophy which lurks behind most government decisions relating to Indians—decisions as to whose land will be flooded by a certain dam, or whose age-old pattern of land use will be altered to provide a new source of fuel or recreation for the white man.

The American Revolution (1775-83) was for the Shawnees merely a continuation of their earlier struggles to retain their country. They first adopted a policy of neutrality and moved from the Scioto to the headwaters of the Miami and its tributaries (ibid.: pp. 189-90, 194). In 1777 part of the tribe entered the war and joined the Mingoes in attacking American settlements (ibid.: pp. 197-200). Later the murder of chief Cornstalk by the Americans while he was a hostage at Fort Randolph brought the peace party into the war as well (ibid.: pp. 204–210). Choosing the British side in the Revolution was, like their espousal of the French cause two decades earlier, simply a matter of choosing the lesser of two evils. Supplied with arms and assistance by the British, they struck hard at the forts and settlements of the Americans and brought to a temporary standstill the incursions of the frontiersmen. Most of the expeditions sent across the Ohio during the war were directed at the Shawnees, and most of the destruction on the Kentucky frontier was due to their efforts, but their own towns were repeatedly destroyed by American armies, and they were forced north to the Auglaize (Galloway *Old Chillicothe*: pp. 43-4; Downes *Council Fires on the Upper Ohio*: pp. 278-9; 298).

Even before the end of the Revolution there was a major split in the Shawnee tribe concerning the issue of active participation in the hostilities. Most of the Thawikila, Pekowi, and Kishpoko divisions believed that further conflict with the Americans was useless. This group began moving westward in 1780, and by 1790 they had crossed the Mississippi, settling in what is now Cape Girardeau County in eastern Missouri. This was at that time a part of Spanish Louisiana, and the Shawnees were welcomed by the Spanish governor, Baron de Carondelet (Mooney "Shawnee": pp. 535-6). The Thawikila division probably formed the vanguard in this movement west. According to a biography of Kishkalwa, a notable Shawnee war chief, this man, after the battle of Point Pleasant in Lord Dunmore's War, was: " . . . unwilling to become again embroiled with the Americans, towards whom he was well disposed, or take any part in the contest which was about to be commenced between Great Britain and her colonies . . . removed with a part of the tribe called the Sawekela band [*Thawikila* division] to the south, in 1774, and settled among the Creeks. This band returned again to the shores of the Ohio in 1790, but took no part in the war of 1794, nor in that of 1812, nor has this portion of the tribe ever been engaged against the Americans, since the decisive battle of Point Pleasant" (T.L. McKenny and J. Hall *History of the Indian Tribes of North America*, I: p. 39).

These Missouri Shawnees were joined shortly by some of the Delawares. Most of the Chalakaatha and Mekoche, plus a few families from the other Shawnee divisions, were in favor of continued hostilities. Some of this latter group remained in Ohio and following the treaty of 1782 are henceforth known as the Ohio

Shawnees. Still others joined the hostile Cherokees and Creeks in the South (Mooney "Shawnee": p. 535).

The end of the Revolutionary War left the Shawnees and other Indian allies of the British high and dry. Despite their sacrifices for the common cause no provision was made for them in the treaty that ended the hostilities. To their dismay they learned that the English had granted the Americans title to a vast territory extending from the Great Lakes on the north to Spanish Florida on the south, and west to the Mississippi. The Indian inhabitants of this territory included, in addition to the Shawnees, the Delawares, Munsees, Ottawas, Wyandots, Mingo Iroquois, Kickapoos, Potawatomis, Ojibwas, Miamis, Peorias, Kaskaskias, Weas, Piankeshaws, Sauks, and Foxes. The settlers and land speculators regarded the end of the fighting as they had regarded the end of the French and Indian Wars—as a signal to move the frontier deeper into Indian territory. One frontiersman argued that "all mankind . . . have an undoubted right to pass into every vacant country." A spokesman for western Pennsylvania denied that "the animals vulgarly called the Indians" had any natural rights in the land (W.T. Hagan *American Indians* : pp. 38–39).

Deprived of their British allies, the various tribes of the Ohio country met on the Sandusky River in 1783 to form an Indian confederacy "to defend their country against all invaders." The confederacy insisted that the boundary between whites and Indians was the Ohio River, a line which had been established by the second Fort Stanwix Treaty of 1768. This treaty was not recognized by the United States government because it antedated the Revolution. Thus the Shawnees and other tribes took up their weapons once again to attack the wagon trains moving west from Fort Pitt and the supply boats moving down the Ohio (C.A. Weslager *The Delaware Indians, A History*: pp. 320-1).

The United States took retaliatory action by sending an expedition under General Josiah Harmar in 1789 and a second under General St. Clair in 1791. Both suffered crushing defeats by the allied forces of Little Turtle and his Miamis, Blue Jacket and his Shawnees, and Buckongahelas and his Delaware warriors. St. Clair's defeat, in which his army dissolved in panic and fled south after suffering over nine hundred casualties has been called the worst defeat ever inflicted by Indians on a white army (Hagan *American Indians*: p. 51). The third expedition, however, was led

by General "Mad" Anthony Wayne, who was a brilliant tactician.
Wayne advanced methodically into the Indian country, building
a chain of forts along his route. He purposely delayed engaging
the Indian force which assembled to meet him until their food
supply had run short and several hundred left to hunt or beg food
from the British post four miles away. He then launched his
attack and dealt the Indians a crushing defeat at what has come
to be known as the Battle of Fallen Timbers. Following the battle
Wayne's army proceeded to lay waste to all crops and property
within several miles. Wayne's campaign broke the back of the
Indian confederacy. Following his victory, Wayne concluded an
important treaty at Greenville, Ohio, on August 3rd, 1795. The
Greenville treaty opened up the Northwest Territory, and as the
Indians withdrew the Americans seized control of the Ohio
Valley. As a result of the treaty the Shawnees were obliged to give
up their territory on the Miami in Ohio, and retired to the
headwaters of the Auglaize. The more hostile part of the tribe
crossed the Mississippi and joined those who were living at Cape
Girardeau. In 1798 a part of those in Ohio settled on the White
River in Indiana by invitation of the Delawares (Mooney
"Shawnee": p. 536).

In the early 1800s both the Ohio Shawnees and those in Spanish
Louisiana again divided. Most of the Ohio Shawnees dropped
their hostilities against the United States and removed to
Wapakoneta, Ohio. A part of this group, however, headed by the
war chief Tecumseh and his brother Tenskwatawa or "Open
Door," who was also known as the Shawnee Prophet, were still
definitely anti-American and sought to form an alliance of all
tribes against the Americans. Their resistance movement had
both political and religious aspects and constitutes a classic
example of a "revitalization movement" in the anthropological
sense (cf. A.F.C. Wallace "Revitalization Movements"). Tenskwatawa, the Prophet, a man as remarkable in his own way as the
brilliant and eloquent Tecumseh, was the spiritual leader of the
movement. His brother Tecumseh, who is better known to
historians, was its political and military head.

The Prophet claimed that while in a trance he had been
conducted to the afterworld and learned the secrets of the spirits.
He claimed that he could read men's minds and perform
supernatural feats. He drew large crowds when he preached of his
visions and taught that the Indians should return to aboriginal

ways, by doing such things as giving up the raising of cattle and returning to native garb and face paint. He also preached against the use of whiskey and the practice of witchcraft. Tenskwatawa developed a large following among both his own people and the Delawares living on the White River (B. Drake *Life of Tecumseh and of His Brother the Prophet*; J. Mooney "Tenskwatawa": p. 730).

While the Prophet was preaching in Indiana, Tecumseh was traveling widely from the Great Lakes to Florida and from Ohio west to the Missouri, trying to unite the various tribes against the usurpation of their lands by the whites. His dream was to weld the tribes into a great Indian confederacy occupying a separate Indian state. Though called the greatest Indian leader who ever lived, Tecumseh was nevertheless doomed to failure. The westward drive of the expanding United States would not be halted by "mere Indians," and even Tecumseh's eloquence and charisma could not weld a congeries of jealous rival tribes into an effective political or military force. Since he found some of his own people resistant to his doctrines, Tecumseh lived in Indiana between 1798 and 1805. In 1805 he and the Prophet and their followers removed to Greenville, Ohio, and in 1808 founded what the whites called the "Prophet's Town" at the mouth of the Tippecanoe River in Indiana (Drake *Life of Tecumseh*; Mooney "Tenskwatawa": p. 730).

The settlement at the Prophet's Town was regarded as a threat by the United States, and an army was assembled to march against it. While Tecumseh and several of his warriors were absent, United States troops under the command of William Henry Harrison attacked and defeated the Shawnees remaining at the Prophet's Town in 1811. Because the Prophet had predicted supernatural assistance for the Indians in the battle and an easy victory over the Americans, he and his religious movement were largely discredited by Harrison's victory (Drake *Life of Tecumseh*: p. 221).

Tecumseh still retained a considerable following, and at the outbreak of the War of 1812 he and his remaining forces threw in their lot with the British. Tecumseh was rewarded with a regular commission as brigadier general and commanded some two thousand warriors of the allied tribes. He and his warriors fought gallantly at the battles of Frenchtown, the Raisin River, and Fort Meigs and Fort Stephenson, and covered Proctor's retreat after

Perry's victory at Lake Erie. Throughout the war Tecumseh was angered and disgusted at the half-hearted British effort, and before the final retreat publicly accused General Proctor, the British commander, of cowardice. Finally, refusing to retreat further, he compelled Proctor to make a stand on the Thames river, near what is today Chatham, Ontario. In the battle that ensued the allied British and Indians were completely defeated by the Americans. Here Tecumseh, still revered as the greatest Shawnee chief, lost his life at the front of his warriors on 5 October 1813. Prophesying his death in the impending conflict, Tecumseh discarded his general's uniform before the battle and dressed himself in native buckskin garb. Following the War of 1812 the remainder of Tecumseh's group, under the leadership of the Prophet, settled for a time at Fort Malden, at the mouth of the Detroit River on the Ontario side (Drake *Life of Tecumseh*; J. Mooney "Tecumsch"; "Tenskwatawa": p. 730).

The Missouri Shawnees, in the meantime, remained in scattered groups in eastern Missouri until 1822 when a part of them, in company with portions of the Cherokees, Delawares, Kickapoos, Quapaws, Choctaws, Biloxis, Yowanis or Hainais (in either case a division of the Caddoes), Anadarkos (another Caddo division), "Tahookatookies" (said to be a band of Cherokees), Alabamas, and Koasatis, moved to east Texas, which was then a part of Mexico (D.H. Winfrey "Chief Bowles of the Texas Cherokee": p. 31). This mixed group looked to the Cherokees, who composed the largest tribal element among them, for their leadership. The remainder of the Missouri Shawnees stayed near Cape Girardeau for a short time but in 1825 began to emigrate farther west, reaching a new reservation provided for them on the Kansas or Kaw River in eastern Kansas in 1826. With the advent of the Jackson administration in 1829, the Indian removal policy became more relentless. On 28 May 1830, Congress enacted the Removal Act. Pursuant to the provisions of this act, treaties were negotiated with the mixed band of Senecas and Shawnees that had been living at Lewistown, Ohio, on 20 July 1831, and the Shawnees of Wapakoneta and Hog Creek on 8 August. The Lewistown Shawnees and Senecas removed to what is now northeastern Oklahoma in 1832 and the Shawnees from Wapakoneta and Hog Creek removed to the Kansas reservation the same year. Great hardships were endured by these Shawnees on the trip west. Whiskey traders, government bungling of supply deliveries, and illness augmented the difficulties. A final twelve families of the Hog Creek band, consisting of 84 persons who had refused to migrate in 1832 finally arrived in Kansas in 1833 (C.G. Klopfenstein "Westward Ho: Removal of Ohio Shawnees, 1832-1833"; G. Foreman *The Last Trek of the Indians*).

Those Shawnees who had gone to east Texas were allies of the great Cherokee chief "The Bowl" or "Bowles". Bowles had been promised a tract of land by the Mexican government but was never able to secure a firm commitment. He therefore supported the movement for Texas' independence. The Texas Shawnees, together with Bowles and his Cherokees, signed the "Sam Houston Treaty" of 23 February 1835, with the Texas Republic. Houston, himself an adopted Cherokee, was friendly with the Indians but was unable to secure them the land which had been promised. Houston's successor, the notorious Indian hater Mirabeau Lamar, actively harassed the Indians, and provoked Bowles and his Cherokees to battle on 15 and 16 July, 1839. Bowles was killed in the engagement and the Indians defeated, whereupon the Cherokees, Shawnees, and most of the other Cherokee allies were forced to leave Texas (Winfrey "Chief Bowles of the Texas Cherokee").

The Shawnee element of this group settled on the Canadian River in Oklahoma and became the nucleus of the present Absentee band of Shawnees. In 1846 they were joined by a large segment of the Kansas group, mostly members of the Thawikila, Pekowi, and Kishpoko divisions. By the early 1850's there was already a thriving community of Shawnees living on the Canadian at the mouth of Little River. (F.C. Smith "Pioneer Beginnings of Emmanuel, Shawnee": p. 8). Some other Shawnees remained in Texas, living with other tribes on the Brazos river reserve until 1859 when they, too, were forced to leave the state (ibid.: p. 8). This group of Shawnees also joined the Absentee band on the Canadian River.

The Absentee band of Shawnees takes its name from a provision of the treaty of 10 May 1854, concluded with those Shawnees who were remaining in Kansas. This treaty granted individual sections of 200 acres of land to tribal members. If other Shawnees, who were absent from the tribe at that time, returned within five years, they would also receive 200 acres (B.B. Chapman "The Potawatomie and Absentee Shawnee Reservation": p. 301). These "Absentee" Shawnees were, of course, those who were living in the Indian Territory. As I have noted above, they were mostly members of the Thawikila, Pekowi and Kishpoko divisions of the tribe, while those remaining in Kansas were Chalakaatha and Mekoche.

During the American Civil War both groups of Shawnees suffered many hardships. Those in Kansas were harassed by Confederate guerillas operating out of Missouri. The members of the Absentee band, early in the war, were pressured by pro-Southern Creeks to place themselves under the protection of the Confederacy. The Absentee chiefs temporized with the Confederate Creek officers who refused to allow them to remain neutral. In sentiment the Shawnees of both bands were almost unanimously pro-Union (Letter of Geogre A. Cutter, Creek Agent, to Commissioner William P. Dole, 4 Nov. 1861). Finally, fearing retribution at the hands of Confederate troops, the Absentees fled to their brethren of the Ohio band in their settlement near Bellemont, Kansas. They remained in this location for the remainder of the war. Here many of the young Shawnee men enlisted in the Union army, some as members of a mixed Delaware-Shawnee company in the Indian Expedition or Indian Home Guard (A.H. Abel *The American Indian as Participant in the Civil War*: p. 113) and others in Company M, 15th Kansas cavalry (T.W. Alford *Civilization*: p. 12).

The Shawnees negotiated treaties with the federal government, concerning permanent reservations on 18 March 1864; 1 March 1866; and 4 March 1867. None of these treaties was ratified by Congress. This meant that the Absentee Shawnees, when they returned to their homes in the Indian Territory in 1868, had no title to their lands or improvements. To complicate matters, certain members of the Potawatomi tribe, whose reservation had been in Kansas, gave up their lands in that state and were assigned tracts in the area that was already occupied by the Absentee Shawnees. The Potawatomis began to arrive in 1870, and bad feeling that nearly grew into tribal warfare developed when the Potawatomis began to select homesites in the area that had been settled by the Shawnees. Finally, in 1872, Commissioner Walker directed that the Absentee Shawnees be permitted to remain in undisturbed possession of their lands and improvements (Chapman "The Potawatomie and Absentee Shawnee Reservation": p. 314).

Those Shawnees who had been a part of the mixed Seneca-

Shawnee group of Lewistown, Ohio, and who had removed to the
Indian Territory in 1832, separated from their Seneca partners in
1867. They are now known as the Eastern Shawnees. In 1869 the
main body of Chalakaatha and Mekoche in Kansas were
incorporated with the Cherokee Nation and moved to the vicinity
of what is now Whiteoak, Oklahoma, where they are now known
as the Loyal or Cherokee Shawnees. The assignment of Cherokee
lands to the Shawnees was designed to reward the Shawnees, who
had remained loyal to the Union, and at the same time to punish
the Cherokees, many of whom had supported the Confederacy.
The Absentee band was joined that same year by Black Bob's
band (Chalakaatha division) which had refused to be removed
from Kansas but were finally induced to do so in 1869.

In 1875 there was a division in the Absentee band over the
question of allotments. The "progressive" party, under the
leadership of chiefs John Sparney and Joe Ellis accepted the
allotments, but the conservatives, under chiefs Big Jim and Sam
Warrior, refused to do so and moved in the spring of 1876 to the
Kickapoo reservation, which was north of present-day Harrah,
Oklahoma. They resided there for ten years until they were
removed by the army in 1886. In 1884 Joe Ellis, one of the
progressive chiefs, died, and in the following year John Sparney,
the other progressive chief, passed on as well. The Absentee band
was thus left under the leadership of Big Jim and Sam Warrior,
who were both bitterly opposed to white culture in any form. In
1898 a group of white land speculators in the area, seeing a chance
to separate the Absentees from their land, formulated a scheme to
persuade the Shawnees to move to Mexico where, they told the
conservative Shawnee chiefs, they would be free of the pressures
of white settlement. Although they were unable to effect a
wholesale robbery, the gang did persuade Big Jim and some of his
followers to vacate their Oklahoma lands.

In 1900 Big Jim and a number of his braves set out to find a
place in Old Mexico where they might take their families and
make their homes. Arriving with his company among the friendly
Mexican Kickapoos at their village west of Nacimiento, Coahuila,
the party found an epidemic of smallpox raging. The chief and his
whole company were exposed to the disease before they knew it.
The Kickapoos offered to care for the Shawnees, but the party
elected to return to Oklahoma. The group was placed under
quarantine by Mexican authorities when they reached Sabinas,

and they were isolated in a camp on the bank of the river. Here all but two of the company died of the disease, including Big Jim, who succumbed on 29 September 1900. Sad as was this circumstance, it ended the work of the land speculators among the Absentee Shawnees (Alford *Civilization*: pp. 174-5.)

Various degrees of white acculturation are represented by the three named Shawnee bands, with the Eastern band being the most acculturated, the Absentee band the least, and the Loyal or Cherokee band occupying a middle status. Today's Shawnees, though proud of their Indian and tribal background, are fully integrated into the economic world of the white man. Some farm or raise cattle, while others are engaged in trades or professions. Almost all speak English, and most of those under twenty years of age do not speak Shawnee.

2

Tribal Name, Divisions, and Traditional History

Names are of great importance to American Indians, and they tend to persist over long periods of time with little change. Further, the names of tribes and their divisions often provide valuable clues about past locations of the groups and their relationships with other tribes; hence names should be considered carefully by those who are interested in Native Americans and their history. The Shawnee name for themselves is *Shaawanwa*, referring to the tribe as a whole or to an individual Shawnee. Plural forms are *Shaawanwaki* and *Shaawanooki*. According to C. F. Voegelin (*Shawnee Stems and the Jacob P. Dunn Miami Dictionary*, Part III: p. 318) this name derives from the Shawnee root *shawa-* (plus *-ni, -te*) meaning "moderate" or "warm." Thus *shawani*, "it is moderating," *sheeshawaniki*, "warm part of day," and *shawateni*, "it is moderating today," *sheeshawateki*, "warm day in winter" (C. F. Voegelin loc. cit.). I was personally unable to elicit any connotation for the name *Shaawanwa* from any of my informants. At the present time it appears to be used in a denotative sense only (i.e. "It just means Shawnee Indian, that's all."). I nevertheless suspect that the term originally referred to the southern (i.e. moderate, warm) habitat of the Shawnee tribe. Thus anthropologist William Jones, a native speaker of Sauk and Fox, derives the name from *shawŭn*, "south"; hence *shawŭnogi*, "southerners" (J. Mooney "Shawnee": pp. 530, 537). Likewise among the Ojibwa (F. Densmore *Chippewa Music II*: p. 129; author's Ojibwa field notes, 1960), Menomini (A. Skinner *Associations and Ceremonies of the Menomini Indians*: p. 212; F.

Densmore *Menominee Music*: p. 51) and Potawatomi (author's Potawatomi field notes, 1959) the name of the Shawnee dance of these tribes is alternatively translated "Dance of the South God," and "Southern Dance."

Whatever its connotations the name *Shaawanwa*, or its plural forms *Shaawanwaki* or *Shaawanoki*, in slightly variant forms, was used by many neighboring tribes to refer to the Shawnees. Thus Mooney records that the Cherokee name for the tribe is *Ani-Sawanugi*, "Shawnee men". The Teton Dakotas called them *Shawala*, a name also applied to a division of their own tribe supposedly descended from an adopted Shawnee chief. The Omahas, Poncas, Osages, Kansas, and Quapaws all called them *Shawana*. The Spanish form of the name is *Chaguanos*. The Ottawa name is *Oshawanoag*. The Tonkawa name was *Sa'wano*, a term used for both Shawnees and Delawares by the Tonkawas because the two tribes were so closely associated. The Creeks called them *Shawanogi* and the Tuscaroras *Sawa-nu-ha'ka* (Mooney "Shawnee": p. 536-8). The Delaware name is *Shaawanu*, *Shaawanuuwak* (E. W. Voegelin, C. Rafinesque, C. F. Voegelin, and E. Lilly *Walum Olum*: pp. 158-192). All of these apparently derive from the same Algonkian stem. Other tribal names for the Shawnees are not derived in this manner. The Iroquois (Onondaga) name for the tribe is *Ontwaganha*, or "one who utters unintelligible speech," an epithet applied to all Algonkian-speaking tribes, including the Shawnees (J.N.B. Hewitt "Ontwaganha": p. 136) and the Yuchi, according to Speck (F. G. Speck *Ethnology of the Yuchi Indians*, I: p. 11) call them yo^n*šta*, a term he does not translate.

As noted earlier the tribe is divided into five great divisions: *Chalaakaatha* ("Chillicothe"); *Mekoche* ("Mequache"), apparently also known as *Shpito* or *Shpitotha*; *Thawikila* or *Hathawikila*; *Pekowi* or *Pekowitha* ("Piqua"); and *Kishpoko* or *Kishpokotha* ("Kispokogi"). The various authors who have written on the Shawnees, as well as the Shawnees themselves, disagree as to the correct translations of the names of these divisions, all of which seem to be archaic forms.

The name of the first division, Chalaakaatha, was termed untranslatable by most of my informants, but Mary Spoon said that it meant "First Man," and was named after the Shawnee culture hero. Certainly a man of this name, Tshilikauthee in Trowbridge's orthography, appears as an important leader in the

Shawnee origin legend given to Trowbridge by the Shawnee prophet (C. C. Trowbridge *Shawnese Traditions*: p. 1-8). The principal chief of the entire Shawnee tribe was always chosen from either this or the Thawikila division (T. W. Alford in W. A. Galloway *Old Chillicothe*: p. 181; C. F. Voegelin *Shawnee Stems and the Jacob P. Dunn Miami Dictionary*, Part II: p. 199; Mary Spoon, informant, 1972). Mooney states that the members of this division always occupied a village having the same name as their division, (such as "Chillicothe Town"), and that this village was regarded as the chief town of the Shawnee tribe (J. Mooney (ed.) *Handbook of American Indians North of Mexico*: p. 267). Alford (in Galloway *Old Chillicothe*: p. 18) notes that the: ". . . two powerful clans [divisions], the Thawegila [Thawikila] and the Chalagawtha [Chalaakaatha] have charge of things political and all matters that affect the tribe as a whole. They are equal in power, and from one of them the principal chief must come, because of the Mee-saw-mi [sacred bundles] which are the potency of life. The chiefs of the other clans [divisions] are subordinate to the principal chief in all matters of great import to the tribe but their chief is independent, an authority in the matters pertaining to his own jurisdiction." Members of the Chalaakaatha division are now found mostly among the Eastern and Loyal bands of the Shawnees, although a few are in the Absentee band as well. The Eastern Shawnees, at present, live in Ottawa County, Oklahoma, in the city of Miami and in the area of their former reservation south and east of there. The Loyal or Cherokee Shawnees are concentrated in the vicinity of Whiteoak, Oklahoma.

The name of the second division, Mekoche, according to John Johnston (*Account of the Present State of the Indian Tribes Inhabiting Ohio*: p. 275) signifies "a fat man filled—a man made perfect, so that nothing is wanting." Hewitt, however, who gives the name in the form Mequachake, translates it as "Red Earth" (J. Mooney ed. *Handbook of American Indians*, I: p. 845). Johnston (loc. cit.) states that "this tribe has the priesthood. They perform the sacrifices and all the religious ceremonies of the nation. None but certain persons of this tribe are permitted to touch the sacrifices." Alford (in Galloway *Old Chillicothe*: p. 181) likewise notes that "the Maykujay [Mekoche] has charge of things pertaining to health, medicine and food." This preeminence of the Mekoche in religious matters, however, is negated by the origin legend that the Shawnee prophet recounted to Trowbridge. In this account a member of this division, and having the same name as the division, appears suddenly in the Shawnee council and claims the title of "great chief" belongs in his division, likewise that "to him was due the office of keeper of the medicine, because his heart was white & pure as the [white] paint on his body" (Trowbridge *Shawnese Traditions*: p. 6). On the basis of these presentations the Mekoche division is given half of the medicine kept by the Chalaakaatha. Later on, however, in a contest of power Chalaakaatha (the culture hero and founder of that division of the Shawnees) bests Mekoche, and he relinquishes his claim, whereupon he is appointed "counsellor for the whole nation" (Trowbridge *Shawnese Traditions*: p. 8).

From the fact that the name Mekoche is sometimes omitted from the lists of the Shawnee divisions and replaced by the name Shpitotha (Hough 1903, quoted in Mooney (ed.) *Handbook of American Indians*, II: p. 625; Mooney "Shawnee": p. 536; J. Spencer *The Shawnee Indians*: p. 320), I suspect that Mekoche and Shpitotha are alternate names for the same division, though some of my informants disagreed. Alfred Switch was one of these. He translated Shpitotha as "Big Toad", and said that this division is called the "Younger brother" of the tribe. The Mekoche, like the Chalaakaatha, are numbered among the present Eastern and Loyal Shawnee bands.

The name of the third division, Thawikila or Hathawikila is termed "of uncertain etymology" by Mooney ("Shawnee": p. 536) but was translated "an old word for eagle" by Alfred Switch. Switch termed it "the chief's clan [division] and said that it is termed the "elder brother" of the five groupings of the tribe. His neglecting to mention the Chalaakaatha as an alternate source of tribal chiefs probably reflects his Absentee Shawnee bias as well as his own membership in the Thawikila division. Mary Spoon, also a Thawikila, said the head chief of the Shawnees must be *either* a Chalaakaatha or a Thawikila. According to both Alfred and Mary, most of the members of the Thawikila division were included in the Absentee subband headed by Chief White Turkey, hence the terms Thawikila and "White Turkey band" are virtually synonymous.

It is interesting to note that the Shawnee prophet, speaking to Trowbridge in 1824, completely fails to mention the Thawikila as a division of the Shawnee tribe (Trowbridge *Shawnese Traditions*: p. 8). Chief Black Hoof, at the same date, considered the Thawikila completely extinct (ibid.: p. 62). Both statements indicate extremely poor communication between the Thawikila and the other Shawnee divisions during that period. It is also interesting to note that in Black Hoof's Shawnee origin legend both the Chalaakaatha and Thawikila, the two "chiefly" divisions, are credited with an overseas origin (ibid.: pp. 61-2). The Prophet's account, because it fails to note even the former existence of a Thawikila division, assigns an overseas origin to only the Chalaakaatha (ibid.: p. 3). Mooney ("Shawnee": p. 536) says that the Thawikila claimed to be the "elder brother" among the Shawnees by right of being "the first created of the tribe". He claims (Mooney ed. *Handbook of American Indians*; I: p. 150) that the band formerly under the leadership of Black Bob was a portion of this division, but it is our understanding that Black Bob and his following were Chalaakaatha.

The main concentration of the Thawikila division or White Turkey band until recent years was in the Sand Hill or Horseshoe Bend area, located about five miles north and three miles east of Shawnee, Oklahoma. The division has since dispersed to some extent, though most members still reside in the Shawnee-Tecumseh metropolitan and rural areas.

Johnston (*Account of the Present State of the Indian Tribes*: p. 275) gives an origin legend explaining the name of the fourth division, Pekowi or Pekowitha, sometimes rendered as "Piqua": "In ancient times they had a large fire, which being burned down, a great puffing and blowing were heard in the ashes; they looked, and behold a man stood up from the ashes!—hence the name Piqua—*a man coming out of the ashes*, or *made of ashes*." This same type of "phoenix" legend is given by Finley (in J. Spencer "Shawnee Folk-lore": p. 320). Mooney (*Handbook of American Indians*, II: p. 260) says that the name is "of indefinite meaning, but referring to ashes." Alfred Switch could not translate the name, but said "Sometimes we call them 'Dusty Feet' ". Both would appear to be correct as C. F. Voegelin notes (*Shawnee Stems and the Jacob P. Dunn Miami Dictionary, Part I*: p. 81): "*pekw-, pekow-* dust, ashes, rubbed to dust, worn out, sore. May function as occurent: *pekwi*, with plural, *pekowali* 'ashes, dust'): with animate formative, *pekowii θ a* 'political division of Shawnee'."

Switch said that the Pekowi division is termed the "second (oldest) brother" of the five Shawnee divisions, and that it was known as the "talking band" because it traditionally furnished the speaker who "talks for" or is the speaker for the tribal chief in the manner of Southeastern tribes. Alford strikes a similar note when he notes that (in Galloway *Old Chillicothe*: p. 18) ". . . the Peckuwe clan, or its chief, has charge of the maintenance of order and duty, and looks after the celebration of things pertaining to our religion or faith. . . ." Alfred Switch was of the opinion that the great nineteenth century Shawnee leader Tecumseh and his brother the Shawnee prophet were members of this division, but Johnston (*Account of the Present State of the Indian Tribes*: p. 275) indicates that they were Kishpokotha, and all of my other informants agreed that this was so. Members of the Pekowitha division are today included in the Absentee band of Shawnees. They were formerly concentrated at Tecumseh Junction, about two miles south of Shawnee, Oklahoma, and at Little Axe, between Tecumseh and Norman, Oklahoma. Richard Gibson, the present chief at the Little River ceremonial ground, which is located four miles north and a mile west of the Little Axe store, is largely of Pekowitha descent (though also part Kishpokotha), and so is Bill Johnson, the ceremonial leader of the Absentee "Old ground" which is located a mile west and a half mile south of the store.

The fifth and final division of the Shawnees is the Kishpoko or Kishpokotha. None of my informants could translate the name. J. Witthoft and W. A. Hunter (The Seventeenth Century Origin of the Shawnee": p. 52) note that the name was shared with the Creeks of Tuckabatchee town ". . . it is sometimes said that the Shawnee represent the original people of Tuckabatchee. They call themselves by the same name, ispogogi, among other terms." To the Tuckabatchee Creeks the Ispokogi were supernatural personages who once gave them a number of sacred brass plates and also moral instruction. Because the Absentee Shawnees and the Tuckabatchee Creeks maintained a special social and ceremonial alliance in the past century, considered themselves the same people, and had an arrangement whereby the sacred paraphernalia of the Busk or Green Corn Ceremony was to be turned over to the Shawnees at whatever time the people of Tuckabatchee neglected the rites, it is possible that the name Kishpoko or Kishpokotha is actually of Creek origin.

Whatever its derivation, this division of the Shawnees was universally dubbed the "war division" by my informants, echoing

Johnston's comment of 1820 that: "They were always inclined to war, and gave much trouble to the nation." (*Account of the Present State of the Indian Tribes*: p. 275; cf. also Alford in Galloway *Old Chillicothe*: p. 181). Today it is this division alone, among the Shawnees, which conducts the ceremonial "Ride-in" and War Dance each summer. At present, however, because few pure Kishpoko survive, a circumstance attributed to their losses in wars in the past, the actual officers of the War Dance are of mixed divisional background. Little Charley, the keeper of the Kishpokotha war bundle during the time of my fieldwork is of mixed Kishpoko and Pekowitha descent, as is Richard Gibson, the principal singer for the dance. This division is called the "third brother" of the five. The Kishpokotha are included among the Absentee band of Shawnees, and their main concentration is at Little Axe and Little River, between Tecumseh and Norman, Oklahoma.

All of the last three divisions named here, the Absentee Shawnee divisions, have maintained a close association for a long time. Alford (in Galloway *Old Chillicothe*: p. 181) writes, "The Thawegila, Peckuwe and Kispokotha clans have always been closely related, while the Chalahgawtha and Maykujay clans stood together . . . ."

It will come as no surprise to the reader, in view of their recorded history, to learn that most present-day Shawnees are not only of mixed divisional descent within the tribe, but also have strains of white and alien tribal background. Thus the Eastern and Loyal Shawnee bands number many persons of part white, Oklahoma Seneca-Cayuga, Delaware, and Quapaw descent, and many Absentee Shawnees are part Creek, Yuchi, "Absentee" Delaware and Caddo. So many of those Shawnees who gather for ceremonies at the "Old ground" south of the Little Axe store are of part-Delaware descent (particularly the Johnson family, the leading lineage) that the Shawnees themselves often term this ceremonial center the "Delaware ground".

C. F. Voegelin (*Shawnee Stems and the Jacob P. Dunn Miami Dictionary*, Pt. III: p. 318) gives the native names for the three governmentally recognized Shawnee bands. The Eastern Shawnees are called *Kchikamiwithiipi-wilenaweeki*, "Spring River people." The Loyal Shawnees are called *Shkipakaakamii-thaki*, or "Blue Water persons", a name probably referring to the eighteenth century home of this group on the Cumberland River, and also *Kaatheewithiipiiki-Shaawanwaki*, "Shawnees at the Kaw River" referring to their later residence in Kansas. The Absentee band are called *Kineetiwi-Shaawanwaki*, literally "Canadian [an English loan word] Shawnees", referring to their residence on the Canadian River in Oklahoma.

In his recent book, *The Invasion of America*, Francis Jennings argues convincingly that the pre-Columbian population estimates for North America in Mooney's widely quoted 1928 paper *The Aboriginal Population of America North of Mexico* (1928) are probably grossly in error (F. Jennings *The Invasion of America*: 15-31). For eastern North America, particularly, Jennings believes that the figures cited for most tribes probably represent no more than a tenth of the actual population. The rather small populations recorded for Eastern Woodland tribes in the seventeenth and early eighteenth centuries, he thinks, are the results of the catastrophic effects of European diseases, against which the Native Americans had no resistance. Jennings' remarks are particularly pertinent in regard to the Shawnees, for whom we have no really early population figures. In view of their part-agricultural economy and the extensive archeological remains of the Fort Ancient Aspect, a population of ten or twelve thousand Shawnees at the time of their first contact with Europeans would not appear excessive. Marquette's mention of the Shawnees as a people "in so great numbers that in one district there are as many as 23 villages, and 15 in another, quite near one another." (E. Kenton ed. *The Indians of North America*: p. 208) lends further weight to such an estimate. Though a population of ten or twelve thousand seems ridiculously small in terms of today's millions, one should recall that the total population of New England's white settlements as of 1670 was only about fifty-two thousand (United States Bureau of the Census 1960: p. 756).

Even in the early eighteenth century the tribe was quite large in comparison with many neighboring groups, and Lewis Henry Morgan, on the basis of interviews with Shawnee informants a few years earlier, wrote: "They once numbered three or four thousand persons, which was above the average among American Indian tribes" (*Ancient Society*: p. 173).

The scattering of the Shawnees following their wars with the Iroquois makes it difficult to estimate their population for most of the eighteenth century. A population of 1,440 can be arrived at for the Shawnees of western Pennsylvania in 1731 (C. A. Hanna *The*

Wilderness Trail, I: p. 296) but this does not include those living on the Susquehanna or in the Southeast. Those living in South Carolina in 1715 numbered 233 (J. R. Swanton *Early History of the Creek Indians and their Neighbors*: p. 317). In 1760 about four hundred lived among the Creeks, but a year later there were only 120 (Swanton op cit: p. 319). Mooney's estimates for the various eighteenth century dates are 1,750 (1732); 1,000 (1736); 1,500 (1759, 1765, 1778, 1783, and 1794) (Mooney (ed.) *Handbook of American Indians*: p. 536). These are almost certainly too low, though it is evident that the white man's diseases and the constant warfare of this period had taken their toll of the Shawnees. I would estimate that the total population at the time of the American Revolution was about 3,000.

By the beginning of the nineteenth century, when population figures began to become accurate, the Shawnees had shrunk to a pitiful fragment of their former strength. In a letter from John Johnston, United States Indian agent at Piqua (Ohio) to Caleb Atwater, dated 1819, figures are given for the Shawnees then resident in Ohio. At Wapaghkonetta, at the head of the Auglaize River, ten miles north of Piqua, there were 559 Shawnees, including 197 men, 178 women, and 184 children. At Hog Creek there were 72, 15 of whom were men, 22 women, and 35 children. Hog Creek was ten miles north of Wapaghkonetta. Finally there were 169 at Lewis Town, at the head of the Miami of the Ohio, thirty five miles northeast of Piqua. Fifty-three of these were men, 56 women, and 60 children. These numbers total 800 Shawnees in 1819, but do not include the larger Absentee group then living in Missouri. For this group, in 1824, 1,383 are reported (G. Foreman *Last Trek of the Indians*: p. 52). Two years later 500 left Ohio to join them, and in 1831, 600 still remained in the latter state (Foreman *Last Trek*: 65-6). These figures give, for 1824-31, a total of 2,483. Adding an estimated 2,400 living in Texas in 1827 (J. L. Berlandier *The Indians of Texas in 1830*: p. 142) gives 4,883, which is probably far too high a figure.

For 1869 Lewis H. Morgan, in his *Ancient Society* (p. 173) gives the total number of Shawnees as only 700. In his *Indian Journals*, however (p. 45) he states that there were 850 Shawnees located at the Friends Shawnee Mission in Kansas Territory in 1859 and 750 more "in the southern part of the state," giving a total of 1600, which is undoubtedly a more accurate figure for the mid-nineteenth century Shawnee population.

William E. Connelly (in Spencer *The Shawnee Indians*: p. 387) gives the following figures for the period just before the turn of the century:

Quapaw Agency	79	[Eastern band,]
Sac & Fox Agency	640	[Absentee band]
Incorporated w. Cherokees	800	[Loyal band,]
In Indian schools	40	
Total	1,559	

This total is very close to that given by Mooney (J. Mooney *The Aboriginal Population of America North of Mexico*: p. 11) who lists, as of 1900:

Cherokee Shawnees	790	[Loyal band]
Absentees of Sac & Fox Agency	509	
Absentees of Big Jim's band special agency	184	
Eastern Shawnees	93	
Total	1,576	

In 1902 allotment records show the following totals (M. H. Wright *A Guide to the Indian Tribes of Oklahoma*: p. 241):

Loyal Shawnees	820
Absentee Shawnees	563
Eastern Shawnees	84
Total	1,467

A part of this drop in population can be explained by the smallpox which carried off Big Jim and most of his followers in Mexico. In 1909, however, the population shows further decrease (Mooney "Shawnee": p. 536):

Eastern Shawnees	107
Cherokee Shawnees	800
Absentee Shawnees	481
Total	1,388

This steady decline continued for the next two decades, reaching an all-time low in 1930 with the following numbers (V. Kinietz and E. W. Voegelin in C. C. Trowbridge *Shawnese Traditions*: viii, p. 4):

Eastern Shawnees	221
Cherokee Shawnees	393
Absentee Shawnees	447
Total	1,061

I believe this disastrous decline in population, which was not limited to the Shawnees but rather paralleled in most other tribes at this period, to be largely the cumulative effect of Federal Indian policy in the period 1875–1933. During this time the official Federal Indian policy was to assimilate individual members of American Indian tribes even if their rights as members of tribes had to be breached. This pressure to individualize the tribes and dispose of the tribal land estate resulted in the passage of the General Allotment Act of 1887, better known as the Dawes Act, which divided the reservations up into allotments of 160 acres and assigned each Indian a piece of land for farming. The remainder of the tribal land was declared to be "surplus" and opened to settlement by non-Indians.

Before allotment was forced upon them there was little poverty on the reservations, as the tribes followed their age-old custom of sharing, and the land was held by the entire band or community. The effect of individualizing the tribal estate was the creation of extreme poverty with its attendant disease and apathy on many reservations. Individual Indians, unaccustomed to viewing land as a commodity, were easily swindled out of their allotments. Having nowhere else to go, they moved in with relatives who had not sold out, putting an even greater burden on already inadequate resources. This decline in the Indian land base, and the increase in poverty and disease, was not reversed until 1933, when the New Deal administration appointed John Collier as Indian Affairs Commissioner. Collier helped to write into law the basic charter of Indian rights called the Indian Reorganization Act of 1934. Under the provisions of this act tribes were given status as federal corporations, allotment was stopped, and efforts were made to rebuild a land base for Indian communities. Traditional ceremonies that had been banned by the government were also permitted once more, and the tribes began to have hope again.

It is undoubtedly this change in federal policy, together with a general improvement in the national and local economy following the depression and dust bowl conditions of the 1930s, that is reflected in the increase of population among the Shawnees beginning in the 1940s. In 1944 the total population was 2,139, including 308 Eastern Shawnees, 1,000 Loyal Shawnees, and 731 in the Absentee band (Wright *A Guide to the Indian Tribes of Oklahoma*: p. 241).

In 1950 the total was 2,252, broken down as follows (S. Stanley and R. K. Thomas *1950 Distribution of Descendants of the Aboriginal Population of Alaska, Canada and the United States* map).

Eastern Shawnees		440
Loyal Shawnees		1,100
Absentee Shawnees		712
	Total	2,252

These 1950 figures are undoubtedly too low, because in 1964 the membership roll of the Eastern Shawnee band listed 813 members. That same year the Cherokee or Loyal Shawnee payment roll listed 3,475 persons. Some of these were enrolled with other tribes but claimed eligibility to share in the payment as descendants of Loyal Shawnees. These are the latest available figures for both of these bands.

The Absentee Shawnee band had an enrolled membership of 1,543 as of June 1969. They are currently in the process of updating their tribal roll. It is anticipated that the new roll will have between 1,700 and 1,800 living members. The 1,543 population in 1969 showed 757 to reside within the jurisdiction of the Shawnee agency, 378 in Oklahoma but out of the agency area, 390 living out of state, and 18 unaccounted for. (Letter of John E. Taylor, Superintendent, Shawnee agency, 4 May 1973).

The remainder of this chapter is devoted to Shawnee traditional history. This is material concerning their own past preserved as a part of Shawnee tradition that, though it may be wholly or partially valid, is not supported independently by accounts of non-Indian historians. Because Shawnee traditional history has been preserved largely as an oral tradition, and because it is based upon totally different premises and criteria of validity than the accounts of non-Indian historians, this material is quite different from that which is presented in Chapter One. It is nevertheless, from the viewpoint of a traditional Shawnee interested in such matters, the *history* of the tribe as it has been passed down, orally, from one generation to the next. The material is of considerable interest in that it reflects the Shawnees' view of their past and their linguistic and cultural relationships with other tribes.

The most comprehensive body of Shawnee traditional history is contained in an origin legend supplied to Trowbridge by the Shawnee Prophet in 1824 (Trowbridge *Shawnese Traditions*: pp. 1–8). Because of its great importance I quote it here verbatim:

When the Great spirit made this island he thought it necessary to make also human beings to inhabit it, and with this view he formed an Indian. After making him he caused him to stand erect, and having surveyed him from head to foot he pronounced the work defective, and made another, which he examined in the same manner with great care and particularity and at length pronounced him well made & perfect. But previous to making the second he discovered that one of the principal defects in the other consisted in misplacing the privates to the forehead instead of the middle of the body, and seeing this he immediately took apart the limbs and reformed them. In this second formation he placed the privates under the arm of a man, and of a woman, whom he also made at the same time, and finding this would not do he became vexed and threw away the different members of the body. After some time employed in reflecting about the means necessary to accomplish the desired end, he set himself again to work to put them together, and at last made them as they now are, and was satisfied. Then his mind was a good deal troubled to know how this man & woman should commence to increase. He placed them together side by side & retiring a few paces seated himself to survey them. He thus changed their position to each other frequently, at each change seating himself to examine the effect, until they faced each other and by dint of changing and moving them became connected in the act of copulation. When he saw this he deemed it good, and having told them how to proceed left them to their will. After some time the woman was discovered to be pregnant & in about a year was delivered of a child. The great Spirit then told the man & woman that they should live, increase & multiply in that manner, that he had made them & thereafter they must make themselves. He then opened the door of the skies & the Indians looking down saw this Island. By this time there were 12 Indians at the residence of the Great Spirit. They were all Shawanese, but the roots of 12 tribes. He told them they must come down to live upon this Island, that it would take them 12 days, which days were equal to years of the Indians, and that in the mean time he would finish every thing to be created upon the earth. That means must be provided for their subsistence on the earth where they were to live and that as he had taken his time to make *them*, he must also proceed gradually in forming all things below. That he would give them a piece of his heart, which was good, and would *mix it* with the hearts which they had, so that a part of their hearts at least should be good. "Now" said the Gt. spirit, "I can hear, and will give you ears that you may distinguish the least noise. I can speak, & I will give you tongues that you may communicate with each other. I will also give you of my teeth to chew your food—which shall be corn, beans, cucumbers, squashes, melons—&Elk, Deer, Bear, Buffaloe, Turkey & Raccoon & small game. Of vegetables you shall have twelve kinds, and of meats twelve kinds. And now I have finished you and all things else. Remember who made you & these and do not at any time attribute the formation to any but me. Your age shall be 200 years, and then your head shall become white like mine, and you will drop down. When you become thus advanced you must tell your children all that I have told you that it may be transmitted to the latest posterity. You are now about to go to the Island which I have made for you, and which rests upon the back of a great turtle that carries it as a load. You must call this Turtle your grandfather. He will hear all your complaints & will treat you as his Grand Children. If any one of you should 'drop down' before 200 years, you will put upon him some of this medicine which I give you & he will get up again. As I shall not always be with you, you will require assistance from other sources. I therefore give you the sun to take care of you & give you light during the day, and the moon for the same purpose at night. I will also put some of my grey hairs upon one of you & he shall be an old man, & you shall call him your Grandfather." After having done this the Great spirit bethought himself that he had given a heart to every thing which he had made except to this Island, whereupon he made a heart for it of the old man. Then he told the Indians that the old man, being the first which he had formed, should be called, Kwee koo laa [Kwikule,] and that he would make another, who should be called Maakweekeelau [Mekwikila,]. That Kweekoolaa should be the head of the nation and Maakweekeelau the next in power.

The Great spirit then opened a door, and looking down they saw a white man seated upon the ground. He was naked, and destitute of hair upon his head or his body and had been circumcised. The great Spirit told them that this white man was not made by himself but by another spirit who made & governed the whites & over whom or whose subjects he had no control. That as soon as they reached their Island and had got comfortably situated, this great white spirit would endeavour to thwart his designs, and would certainly exert himself to change the period of their existence from 200 years to a shorter time.

After this the great Spirit put the twelve Indians & the two old men (he had created two to supply their place in the original number) in a large thing like a basket & told them he was going to put them on the Island. The old man first named carried with him all the good things entrusted to his care for the benefit of the Indians, in a pack, on his shoulders. The first earth they saw in their journey was on the other side of the great lake, and when they had arrived on the sea shore they stopped and rested. The old man told them that the place where his heart was, was in a northern direction from them and at a great distance. They could see nothing but water and knew not how they were to cross the great water to the Island. The old man then took from his pack a gourd and began to sing. They sung for a period of twelve days, during which time they ate nothing but a few roots. The old man then told the Indians that the Great spirit had promised to grant them all they desired and that they must pray to him to remove the water which impeded their journey to the Island. Soon after the water was dried up & they saw nothing but sand. The old man then observed that as he was too old to lead the party he would give his pack to one of the others, & he appointed Tshilikaūthee (Chilicothe) to be the leader & bearer of the pack, and told him that he (Kweekoolāā) would remain behind. So he seated himself on that which was the shore, and the young leader went forward with the band, which by this time had become quite numerous. When they had arrived on the opposite shore they encamped and remained for the period of twelve days employed in singing, during which time, as before, they abstained from eating. They then sent the waiting servant of Kweekoolāā, who had remained behind, to find out what course they had come, but he returned telling them that the waters had returned to their place & he could see nothing else. The Maakweekeelau made a speech to the Indians & told them he was satisfied of the power and justness of the great Spirit, and that *they* must remove farther to the north, but that he would remain on the shore to look back to his friend Kweekoolaa who remained on the opposite side of the sea. (These two old men have since turned into rocks and sit in their respective positions at this day, where they will remain so long as this Island stands.)

Tshilikaūthee then commenced his march to the north, followed by all the Indians; after travelling 12 days they thou' they must have arrived at the place of their destination, & stopped. Soon after, the Great spirit visited them & told them that they had reached the place where he had placed the heart of one of the old men, that they should thenceforth be called Shauwonoa and that the River upon whose banks they had encamped would bear the same name. (Shauwanoa wee Thēēppee). That he was going to leave them and would not be seen by them again, and that they must think for themselves & pray to their grand mother, the moon, who was present in the shape of an old woman.

The Prophet's legend, now in the period after the first creation,

continues, explaining the origins of some of the tribal divisions of
the Shawnees (Trowbridge *Shawnese Traditions*: pp. 5-8).

Four days after the departure of the Great Spirit, the old men sent out some of
the young men to hunt, telling them, that if they killed any game they must not
leave a single thing behind, but bring it all home. Accordingly the young men
hunted & killed an elk, but he was so large that they could not carry it all home
& so left the back bone on the ground, as the most valueless part. When they
returned & the old men saw that the back bone was missing they sent the
hunters after it, but these arriving at the place where they had killed the Elk
found the bone *moving*. They again found to their surprise that it had turned
into an Indian whose body was red. At the command of the old men they led him
into the camp where he was asked whence he came, but he could give no account
of himself. From this man sprung the Piccaway [Pekowitha] family. As this
man derived his existence neither from the Great spirit or from human beings,
but from an animal, he was appointed head of the warriors of the Shawanese
nation, and they called him Waaskoomisāū [Weskumisa] because he was red. It
became necessary now to appoint some person to take care of the great
medecine which had been given them by the Great spirit, and accordingly they
assembled in council to make the choice, but being divided in opinion they
spent seven days in fruitless efforts to elect some one to the distinguished office.
At last a man unknown to them all appeared suddenly in the council, entirely
naked. As none knew him he passed the first day unnoticed. On the day
following he came again, covered all over with white paint or clay, and during
the contest he rose and told the members that he was of the Maakoatshaa
[Mekoche] family or tribe of Shawanoa's, that the title of great chief was to be
held in his family, and that to him was due the office of keeper of the medecine,
because his heart was as white & pure as the paint on his body. He left the
Council & remained absent until the next day when he came again to urge upon
them his claims to the office, which were founded upon the fact of his being a
great chief, of his being without blood in his body, his heart & flesh being white.
At length the council concluded to trust to his professions, and to try him they
gave him one half of the medecine, without informing him however that he had
not the whole. Soon after, the Shawanese heard that there were other Indians
on the Island when they set out to go & see them. When they approached the
camp the new neighbours sent them a messenger to warn them not to come to
the village, but the Shawanese fearlessly approached disclosing to the Creeks
(for such were the new comers), their origin &c. When they came to the
description of the medecine the Creeks pretended to doubt the truth of the story,
whereupon the Shawanese, vexed, destroyed all the Creeks by virtue of the
medecine. The next day however they bro' some of them to life by the same
means and compromised with them, calling them thereafter their brothers.

This visit completed, the Shawanese returned to their own village, where
they had left the Māākoatshaa, and thence proceeded to the north.

After the old men had died & other nations had sprung up, the Indians began
to wage war against each other, and the Shawanese, Pickaways [Pekowitha], &
Kishpookoo [Kishpoko] tribes of the Shawnee nation went to war against the
Catauba's. In the first expedition they took 2 female prisoners near the camp of
the Catauba's. One of the possessors of these female chiefs was of the
Māākootshaa [Mekoche] family & an Indian finding him asleep & being
curious to know if he really had no blood as he had pretended, tomahawked &
scalped him.

When the murderer returned with his prisoner who was the same female
which Young Māākoatshaa had taken, he carried her to the father of the young

man, he desired him to accept the scalp & the prisoner as a present. The old man, supposing it to be the scalp of a Catauba, accepted the gift and called the female his grand daughter. The old man however continued to grieve for the loss of his son for two or three years, when the daughter having learned to speak Shawanoa told her grandfather all the circumstances of the murder. The old man returned to examine the scalp for a scar which was on the head of his son before death, & finding the scar there was convinced of the truth of the facts alledged by the daughter. He then called a council of his old friends & explained to them the facts which was proved by the production of the scalp. To avenge themselves for his death they put the scalp into an earthen pot, filled with blood, & sent it to the Chippeways & other surrounding nations as a challenge for war. The nations accepted the challenge & were severally beaten by the Shawanoas, which displeased the old men who had promoted the war so much that they sent the kettle to the 6 nations, in hopes that their strength & prowess would overpower their own nation and give them cause to exult in their downfall.

The 6 nations prepared for battle and came on, to the number of 7000 men. They attacked the Shawanoa village at break of day, and had well nigh killed the whole of their warriors, when the remaining few took the weapons & habiliments of those killed and putting them upon the women, the latter joined the party and by their numbers and appearance so much deceived the 6 nations that they supposed themselves attacked by a fresh force, and fled.

By this time the warriors & chief men found out the cause of the war and determined to take the medecine from the Māākootshaa. They accordingly watched their opportunity and taking from him the 1/2 of the medecine originally given they returned to Tshilikāūthee [Chalaakaatha, i.e. the village where this division of the Shawnees lived,] who was on the Mississippi, where it is kept at the present day. But as the Māākootshe [Mekoche] protested against the delivery of the medecine & claimed the right of keeping it on account of his family being very ancient, the Tshilikāūthee [*Chalaakaatha*, in this instance the chief of that division,] was obliged to convince him of his own power by shooting the Sun, which occasioned an eclipse & darkened the earth until they restored its light by the medecine. Māākootshee confessed the superior power of Tshilikāūthee & consented to relinquish his claim to the medecine on condition that he was not entirely deprived of character & standing in the nation, whereupon they appointed Māākootshee to be the counsellor for the whole nation, but this character they do not sustain at the present day as the nation is divided.

It is fortunate for us that the Prophet was willing to recount this legend and that Trowbridge recorded it, for today only fragments of it are retained by the Shawnees. The overseas origin of the Shawnees, or part of the tribe, that was mentioned in the Prophet's account also appears in John Johnston's *Account of the Present State of the Indian Tribes* (1820): "The people of this nation have a tradition that their ancestors crossed the sea. They are the only tribe with which I am acquainted who admit of a foreign origin. Until lately, they kept a yearly sacrifice for their safe arrival in this country. From whence they came, or at what period they arrived in America, they do not know." (Compare

Bluejacket's account in Spencer *The Shawnee Indians*: p. 303; and Spencer "Shawnee Folk-lore": pp. 319-20; and Black Hoof's account in Trowbridge *Shawnese Traditions*: pp. 61-2).

The similarity between the Shawnee and Kickapoo languages is a subject of frequent comment by the members of both tribes. Spencer (*The Shawnee Indians*: p. 394) records a tale that purports to explain how the Kickapoos separated from the Shawnees and hence explains the observed similarities (a common origin) and differences (changes that have developed since the separation): "A group of ten hunters had killed a bear and decided to roast and eat the feet. As it was roasting the men slept. Three of the men awakened and decided to eat some of the bear. The other seven later awoke and found only the hind feet. These seven drove off the other three, who became the Kickapoo" (cf. also Spencer "Shawnee Folk-lore": pp. 325-6). This same story is cited by E. W. Voegelin (E. W. Voegelin, C. Rafinesque, C. F. Voegelin, and E. Lilly *Walum Olum*: p. 70) and I secured the identical tale from Mary Spoon in 1971.

The long and close relationship of the Delawares and Shawnees is well known to historians. The two tribes were closely associated in Pennsylvania, and in the subsequent westward migrations. Usually the Shawnees paved the way and the Delawares followed. The Shawnees went first to the Allegheny and Ohio, and the Delawares joined them shortly thereafter. The Shawnees then moved to the Scioto in Ohio, and the Delawares followed them there. There then occurred a series of movements into Indiana, Missouri, and so forth, and it was the Shawnees who preceded the Delawares to Kansas Territory. The Shawnees were there when Isaac McCoy went out to survey the reserved lands for the Delawares. Before this, a group of Shawnees, and a splinter group of Delawares settled at Cape Girardeau, and again the Shawnees went first. These Delawares became the Absentee Delawares, who next went to Texas and joined the Caddoes, ending up at Anadarko, Oklahoma. As one would suspect, this Delaware-Shawnee relationship is strongly reflected in the traditions of both tribes.

In 1776 the Delaware chief White Eyes recalled this tradition of friendship, stating that the *combined Shawnee and Delaware tribes* had driven the Talligewi (Cherokees) south. He based the claim of the Shawnees and Delawares to the Ohio country upon this conquest (T. Walker et al *Council, Pittsburgh, Oct. 15, Nov. 6,*

1776: p. 35): "My Grandchildren the Shawnee and we who are joined together are heads over this river the [Ohio] and the lands there belong to us; the reason of my saying it belongs to us is we conquered the Nation Dallagae [Talligewi], we took them Prisoners, & gave them as Present to the Six Nations, but we did not give them the Lands we took from them when we conquered."

Another tradition linking Shawnees and Delawares is the "Grasshopper War" folktale (J. Witthoft "The 'Grasshopper War' in Lenape Land"). This story, now lost by both tribes, but preserved in rural white tradition, tells of how a great battle between two neighboring Indian communities developed over a trifling incident, a children's quarrel over the possession of a slain grasshopper. After the battle the two factions separated in revulsion and guilt and went in opposite directions to become the Delawares and Shawnees. Witthoft believes that the story is either Shawnee or Delaware in origin, and that it served to explain why the Delawares and Shawnees, who had come together from distant areas in the seventeenth century and spoke obviously related languages, had once been the same people who had separated and whose languages had changed. Its function for the tellers would thus have been the same as the Kickapoo-Shawnee "Roasted Bear Feet" tale cited above. James Mooney, however ("Shawnee": p. 534) was inclined to view the Grasshopper War as a factual incident, and dates it about 1755 or 1756.

The Shawnees also have traditional historical accounts of their first meetings with Europeans. Charles Bluejacket told two of these to Joab Spencer in the period 1858–59 (Spencer "Shawnee Folk-lore": p. 324). He called the first one "The Serpent Tradition." "Our old men (meaning the elders and wise men in the far remote past) used to tell our people that a great serpent would come from the seas and destroy our people. When the first European vessel came in sight, the Indians saw the pennant, with its forked end darting and moving like the forked tongue of the serpent. 'There,' said they, 'is the serpent our old men have been telling us about!' When the old men first tasted rum, tears ran down their cheeks. 'This,' they said, 'is what will destroy our young men.' " The second tale, which Spencer captioned "Legend of Greed" relates that: "the white man asked us for a small piece of land,—a piece that a string cut from a buffalo-hide would reach around. We told him, 'Certainly, we will gladly make you so small a grant as that!' whereat the white man began to cut a very small strip from the edge of the hide, cutting around it. This he kept doing, going round and round, until the hide was all converted into a very long string that surrounded a large piece of land." Variants of this tale, involving cords from the bottom of a chair, and a bull's hide, were told to Trowbridge by the Shawnee prophet (Trowbridge *Shawnese Traditions*: p. 10). This tale is of Old World origin, and is part of the traditional history of several tribes.

Present-day Shawnees continue to marvel at the similarity of their speech to that of other Algonkian speakers, such as the Ojibwas and Crees, whom they encounter at Indian gatherings or while traveling. I have frequently been asked by Shawnee friends if I have encountered a Shawnee band on my travels in Canada. This question is then followed by a story sounding like this: "We met a man once, at a fair (circus, football game, or whatever) who said he was from up there. He talked *just like us*! He disappeared into the crowd before we could find out what part of Canada he was from."

Another common item of Shawnee traditional history is that a large body of their tribe separated from the rest many years ago and made its way to Mexico. The late Ranny Carpenter once told me that these people lived "about a hundred miles from Mexico City" and that they possess a reservation with lush groves of tropical fruit trees and rich farmland. These "Mexican Shawnees," could they be located, would welcome their Oklahoma brethren and would provide them land upon which to establish themselves.

3

Traditional Economy

Shawnee tradition assigned to men the role of hunters and warriors, women the role of gardeners and housewives. This division of labor by sex, which was of prehistoric origin, remained little changed in the early historic period. Henry Harvey, who lived among the Shawnees in Ohio, described their annual cycle or "economic round" in the days before this part of the tribe removed to eastern Kansas (*History of the Shawnee Indians from the year 1681 to 1854 Inclusive*: p. 146-8):

> In the warm season the Shawnee remained around their villages near the Auglaize River. Here they raised considerable quantities of corn and beans. The women and children planted and tended it. They watched the ponies off as they had no fences. The men lounged about for the most part but now and then fished or hunted deer. By the time fall arrived their corn would be all used up, as they never saved for winter.
>
> In the fall all prepared for the winter's hunt. The entire family went on these hunts, together with dogs, cats, and ponies with as much camp gear as they can conveniently carry. Several brass or copper kettles, some wooden ladles, bowls, large spoons, a tomahawk, and each one a large butcher knife. Babies were carried on their mother's back, either on a cradleboard or wrapped in her blanket and held to her back. On the march the warrior went ahead.

Harvey's account neatly delineates the traditional male and female roles. In the spring and summer the activities of the women were preeminent, while in the fall and winter the men were the providers. This former pattern is still recognized in the ceremonial cycle of present-day Shawnees, where a ritual football game (dedicated to the Thunderbirds, and designed to bring rain) opens the ceremonial season. This is followed by the spring Bread Dance (actually a series of ritual acts and dances, not merely a single dance) which celebrates the women's role as food providers, and continues (at Whiteoak) with the Green Corn Dance, in which women again take the lead in the dancing. In the fall, this pattern is reversed, and in the fall Bread Dance the male role as hunters in the coming autumn and winter is more strongly emphasized, though men's and women's dances alternate just as in the spring performance. At Whiteoak, but not at the two Absentee dance grounds, a women's dance begins the spring Bread Dance, a men's dance begins at the fall Bread Dance.

In today's changed world, the Shawnee man can no longer hunt for a living, but must instead seek his provender in the economic world of the whites. Nonetheless hunting still has a strong appeal to most Shawnee men and boys. Wayne Longhorn, a traditional Shawnee of the Absentee band, once commented to me that his participation in the squirrel hunts that precede the two Bread Dances were the high points of his year.

Early nineteenth century Shawnee hunting practices are described by Harvey (*History of the Shawnee Indians*: p. 148) who tells of the men going out to hunt with rifles. The game they killed was hung up out of reach of wolves, and the hunters pushed on in quest for more. They continued to hunt for several days before returning to camp. Having secured a quantity in this way, the hunter returned to camp with what he could carry and stayed overnight with his family, feasting on what he had brought with him. When he had rested, and had supplied his family with food, he set off with his pony after what game he had secured. A Shawnee hunter never forgot the location of his hanging game and Harvey notes: "So honest are they, that no Indian will interrupt what he finds hanging which others have killed."

When the hunter returned with the game, the women and children skinned it, prepared the skins and furs, and sliced the best of the venison in long thin strips to dry, except for the hams, which they dried before the fire for trade. They boiled bony parts, which could not be cured to advantage, and the family feasted upon this nutritious meat broth. The hunter then resumed his work, and this pattern continued through the winter, or until the skins and furs became unfit for market, which generally happened toward the end of February. When the deer season closed, the trapping season began.

Most of the captivity accounts mention Shawnee war parties taking time out to hunt on their return from combat. Usually no details regarding hunting techniques are provided but Thomas Ridout, captured by the Shawnees in 1788, gives the following delightful account of a wild turkey hunt (M. Edgar *Ten Years of Upper Canada in Peace and War, 1805–1815*: p. 359): "The next day my friend the chief, accompanied by half a dozen more Indians and myself, all mounted horseback, rode to the village where the council was to be held. On our way thither, we put up a flock of wild turkeys. Having no fire-arms, we hunted them down, and having caught a very large one, weighing about twenty-five pounds, it was tied, alive, to my back as I rode, and thus we galloped to the village."

Like other Woodland Indians, the Shawnees were skilled in imitating the calls of various wild animals in order to lure them into arrow or rifle range. Turkeys, deer, and even panthers were attracted in this manner. Sometimes an animal call could be a bit too realistic. Thus we read "A Shawnee is said to have been seized by a panther which he attracted by his calls, but that animal was as frightened as he when it found out its mistake, and fled incontinently" (A. B. Skinner *Observations on the Ethnology of the Sauk Indians*, Part III: p. 142).

A strict etiquette of the hunt was observed by the Shawnees. Thus T. W. Alford (*Civilization*: p. 53) writes that when two Shawnee men went hunting together or happened to come together when hunting in the woods, the first game killed or trapped by either of them was graciously offered to the other, with the remark, "I enliven your spirit," or "I enliven you as a man." The game thus presented was always courteously received, accepted with the remark *"Niawe"* (I thank you). Thomas Ridout, even though he was a captive, was extended this courtesy of the hunt by one of his captors, the war chief Nenessica. This chief, when he killed any deer, always sent Ridout the tongue as a compliment. The one exception to this rule of giving the first game (or the best part of it) to a companion was when an otter was killed. An otter was always retained by the man who killed it, with congratulations from the other. If one presented an otter by mistake or overcourtesy, it was indignantly refused (Alford *Civilization*: p. 53).

The trapping season followed immediately after the winter hunt, and the families provisioned themselves and set out in the same way. The raccoon was the principal quarry, and the Shawnees took advantage of their knowledge of the habits of this

animal to catch them. As soon as the season arrived for the frogs
to come out, they knew that the raccoons would shortly come to
the ponds searching for them, walking on every log that lay in or
near the water in order to reach their prey. Accordingly the
Shawnee trapper would put a long pole across one of these logs
and another directly over it, with stakes at the sides so that the
upper pole would fall true. A trigger with a sinew noose was then
arranged so that the raccoon, in traversing the log, tripped the
trigger and caused the upper pole to fall on him (Harvey *History of
the Shawnee Indians*: p. 148).

The trapper made the rounds of his traps with his pony. The
game was skinned, and the skin was dried on sticks by the tent.
The flesh of the raccoon was eaten and the bones given to the dogs.
Again, if one Shawnee trapper found the trap of another, he would
not rob it but instead remove the game carefully, hang it on a bush
nearby, and reset the trap for his neighbor (Harvey *History of the
Shawnee Indians*: p. 148).

As was the case with many North American Indian tribes, the
Shawnees thought that a man's abilities as a hunter could be
substantially enhanced by the use of magical techniques. Most
Shawnee hunters carried a hunting "medicine" or charm to lure
game, and some could practice the esoteric technique known as
"medicine hunting," drawing game to a spot near the camp by
singing a magical song and employing other ritual procedures.
Present day Shawnees have lost this lore, but Richard Gibson told
me that his grandfather had told him of its use. Fortunately one of
these Shawnee "medicine hunt" songs that had diffused to the
Ojibwas is preserved in John Tanner's *Narrative* (*A Narrative of
the Captivity and Adventures of John Tanner*: pp. 350–60): "Song
for medicine hunting-rarely for Metai. O-shaw-wah-no nah-o-bah-
guh-he gun-nun-na, ho-kah-mih a-no-gweh, whe-he-ya! Neen-da-
bwa-wa set-to nah-na, whe-he! ha-ha! To a Shawnee, the four
sticks used in this song belonged. When struck together they were
heard all over the country." The pictograph shows a hunter
holding the four "nah-e-bah-e-gun-nun" or sticks. Though this is
an Ojibwa song, Tanner says that: "Authorship is claimed by a
Shawnee, from whom the Ojibbeways acknowledge to have
received it; and here, it is probable, the performance originally
concluded" (Tanner *Narrative*: pp. 359–60). The sticks mentioned
in the song, and shown in the pictograph, are tapping sticks
which were struck together by the man performing the "medicine

Fig. 1.   Pictograph of medicine hunting song (*Tanner 1956, p. 000*)

hunt" ritual as the magical hunting songs were sung. Among the Menominis, who practiced the "medicine hunt" in the same manner as the Ojibwas and Shawnees, the four sticks represented the legs of the deer (F. Densmore *Menominee Music*: 60-1). One of the sticks was called the "beater" and was pointed in the direction the hunter expected to take the next day. The sticks were called *paka'sikona'tig* in Menomini, and were nine inches or more in length. Densmore writes that a typical Menomini hunting bundle, probably much the same as those formerly used by the Shawnees, would contain the hunting medicine "revealed by the owl" and the four sticks representing the legs of the deer, also red and blue paint, various roots and medicines. The whole was wrapped in white buckskin. Such a bundle collected by Densmore was 24 inches in length and 9 inches in diameter (ibid.: p. 65).

In addition to the bow and arrow and warclub, which were later replaced by the rifle and tomahawk, some Shawnees used a variant of the bolas in their hunting and also in capturing wild horses. Alfred Switch described the manufacture and use of this interesting device, which I have not heard of among any other North American tribe. Switch said that old chief Little Axe, of the Absentee band, had shown him this implement. As described by Switch it consisted of a piece of wood about four feet in length. It was shaved down to a diameter of about one inch for most of its length, but at one end it was enlarged "to about the size of a bowling pin". The device was thrown at the forefeet of a running horse and became entangled in them, causing the horse to fall. It could then be easily captured. On another occasion Switch mentioned that another Shawnee, William Switch, also used this device for taking deer, rabbits, wolves, and other game.

Alfred himself still makes excellent hunting bows in the traditional Shawnee style. They average five feet in length, are of the "self-bow" type, and are flat both on the back and the belly except at the grip. One that I examined had a pull of about forty pounds. Switch's bows are very similar to the famous "Sudbury bow" in the Peabody Museum at Harvard (cf. T. M. Hamilton *Native American Bows*: p. 30-2).

In a 1937 interview preserved in the Indian Archives of Oklahoma Historical Society (Vol. 6: p. 479), Edward J. McClain, an Eastern Shawnee, describes the preservation of meat by Shawnee hunters: "After returning from a hunt, Shawnee hunters would cut the meat into strips and place it on the roofs of their log houses to dry. This was done at all seasons of the year, even summer. In the old days the only flies were green flies. This was done with both buffalo and deer meat."

Alford (*Civilization*: p. 40) describes old-style methods of cooking meat employed by the Absentee Shawnees: "I want to say that for fine cooking of meat the women of my boyhood time had the best of it over the modern methods. Meat broiled over an open bed of coals has a juicy tenderness that cannot be equaled in the finest kitchen. . . . A duck or squirrel wrapped in wet corn husks and baked or roasted in hot ashes, cannot be surpassed, according to my notion. Besides broiling and roasting over an open fire, meat was cooked in kettles, or baked in ovens when a rich gravy added to the pleasure of eating it. Beans and some corn dishes . . . were sometimes boiled with meat."

To boil meat, two stout sticks three feet long with forked ends were driven into the ground some six or seven feet apart; another pole was laid in the forks of the sticks and kettles were swung from it over the bed of coals. This was also the method used to roast meat, when a large piece was to be cooked. "Swung from the pole, turned frequently, and the red hot coals kept at an even heat, meat acquired a tenderness and flavor that cannot be described. Moreover, the odor that filled the air when the meat was being cooked this way stimulated one's appetite more than the most costly sauces of today," (Alford *Civilization*: p. 40).

Aboriginally the Shawnees practiced the type of horticulture known as slash and burn. An area of forest near the village would be selected as a garden. To prepare it for use the large trees would be chopped down or girdled so that they would die; then the underbrush would be chopped out, piled up, and, after it was dry, burned together with the fallen timber. This left wood ash to fertilize the soil. Next, using digging sticks, the women would plant their corn. When it was about a foot high, beans, squashes, and pumpkins would be inter-planted with the corn. The vines of the squashes and pumpkins often attached themselves to the dead trees and stumps still standing in the field. The corn was hoed from time to time by the women, using hoes of shell, stone, or elk shoulder blades fitted to wooden handles.

The Shawnees cultivated a variety of types of corn. A flint corn, with solid good sized kernels and opaque pearl-colored hull was used for hominy. A corn with a whitish hull, deep or narrow grain, a soft flour-like white kernel and a small cob was used for bread flour. A large medium-hard grain variety was used for corn meal. There was also a quick maturing small-eared corn for early roasting ears and succotash. All varieties were white. Galloway found all of these types still preserved by the Shawnees in 1927 (W. A. Galloway *Old Chillicothe*: p. 183). The seed of each kind was carefully preserved and kept separate from the others.

Like other tribes of the Eastern Woodlands, the Shawnees carefully preserved the best ears of corn for seed. Lacking corn cribs, the method generally employed was that of stripping back the husks without breaking them off, and braiding them together securely in long ropes with the ears dangling. These ropes were hung inside the bark lodges or cabins, high up against the roof, when the family had no other storehouse (Alford *Civilization*: p. 35; cf. also Alford in Galloway *Old Chillicothe*: p. 184).

Corn was undoubtedly the most important vegetal food of the Shawnees, and they had many ways of preserving, preparing, and cooking this staple. Edward McLain, the Eastern Shawnee informant whom I mentioned earlier, described one Shawnee method of preserving corn in a 1937 interview: "Corn was gathered, shucked, and placed over the coals in an upright position. A long iron rod running over the fire held the ears in place. They were cooked ten or fifteen minutes, being frequently turned. Next, a knife was run lengthwise of the cob between the rows of kernels. The kernels were then sun dried. Later they could be cooked with grease or boiled with meat. Sometimes black-eyed peas were added and a little salt and sugar for flavor. (Foreman

Collection, Indian Archives, Oklahoma State Historical Society
Vol. 6: p. 479).

Essentially the same procedure is described by Alford, who calls
the resultant product "*wes-ku-pi-mi*" (*Civilization* pp. 35–6; Alford
in Galloway *Old Chillicothe*: p. 184). He also describes another
method: "Another way of preserving fresh corn with its peculiar
delightful flavor was done by grating it from the cob, making a
soft, milky mush which was then poured into an iron oven or
baking kettle with a close fitting lid. It was baked very slowly and
carefully until it became a solid cake. This was called *ne-pan-wi
tak-u-wha* (Production bread). When it was eaten it was prepared
much as we prepare commercial cereals today" (Alford *Civilization*: p. 36; cf. also Alford in Galloway *Old Chillicothe*: p. 185).

Florine Ponkilla, Mary Spoon's sister, describes a variant of
this dish which she calls "Nee-Peeh-Dug-Wah" (F. L. Ponkilla
"Fresh Cornbread"): "Use twelve or as much as you wish fully
ripened roastners [roasting ears] and gritted. Cook in greased
skillet until done, take and crumble into pieces and dry in sun. To
prepare, put in boiling water as you would oatmeal. When cooked,
season with vegetable shortening and sweeten to taste."

A few Shawnee women still pound the corn used to make corn
bread in the aboriginal "hominy block" or wooden mortar. This is
a hollowed-out section of log set upright in the ground. The pestle
used with it is a slightly thinner section of log about four feet in
length. This is thinned and rounded at the lower end but left large,
to provide weight, at the top. In recent years, however, most
women have taken to grinding their corn in a commercially
secured hand mill, or even taking it to the local mill in town to
have it ground. Alford describes the various steps in making corn
bread, which is the basic Shawnee food, thus: "As for our daily
bread, our Indian women brayed ripe corn of the soft variety in a
mortar until it was very fine. It was then sifted through a sieve, the
coarser parts returned to the mortar and pounded again until a
fine meal or flour was obtained. This was made into a dough with
water (wheat flour was added when one had it), and baked in the
iron kettle or deep oven with fitted lid on which hot coals were laid.
Sometimes the cakes of dough were wrapped in several layers of
clean cornhusks which had been moistened, and buried in hot
ashes to bake until thoroughly done. The delightful taste of bread
baked in this way cannot be described" (*Civilization*: p. 38).
Sometimes pumpkin and beans are added to this basic dish,
providing an interesting nuance to the flavor.

Corn bread, or corn cake, was quick to be adopted by white settlers in eastern North America, who came to refer to it as "johnnycake." This name has usually been considered a corruption of "journey cake," but Lowdermilk (quoted in J. L. Kuethe "Johnnycake") suggests that it is a corruption of "Shawnee cakes," which is much more plausible to me. Though the "johnnycake" was prepared by many eastern tribes, only the Shawnees featured it in their two principal religious observances, the spring and fall Bread Dances, which could explain why their tribal name became attached to it.

The mortar and pestle was employed also in making "*tak-wha-ne-pi*" or "bread water", a slightly fermented corn drink which Alford believed the Shawnees had learned to make from the Creeks, since they often called it by the Muskogi name *sofki* (Alford *Civilization*: p. 37). The flinty variety of corn, which had been allowed to ripen and dry on the stalk, was brayed in the mortar until the skin covering the grain was broken and separated from the kernels. "It was then put into a broad, shallow, woven basket, called *law-as-qah-thi-ka* (wafter) and wafted in the open air until cleaned of all skins or chaff. It was then boiled in water until the kernels were thoroughly cooked and it became a heavy whitish mass; more water was added, and a small quantity of seeping fluid—made by letting water seep through clean wood ashes—was added to the corn mixture. All was then poured into a large wooden vessel, covered, and set away until it fermented. Then it was ready for use and would keep indefinitely. It has a most pleasing taste, something like a sweet pickle, and was kept on hand in hospitable Indian homes and offered to visitors" (Alford *Civilization*: p. 37).

A variant of this was called "*osah-saw-bo*" or viscid fluid (Alford in Galloway *Old Chillicothe*: pp. 185-6: Alford *Civilization*: p. 37). It was made in the same manner as *sofki* except that the seeping fluid was left out, and it was not allowed to ferment. Instead nut meats, such as walnuts, pecans, or hickory nuts, were pounded and added to the corn, and all cooked together. "It was a delicious food and one that we especially enjoyed—nothing was equal to it." (Alford *Civilization*: p. 37). I have tasted this dish, as prepared by Mary Spoon, and fully agree with Alford as to its merits.

Another delicious tribal speciality is hominy. The Shawnees prepare it from ripe grains of the soft, starchy, variety of corn. "The grains were boiled in water mixed with wood ashes until the skins would slip from the grains. Then the grains were washed in clear water until thoroughly free of skins. It was then cooked in a kettle, sometimes seasoned with meat, until the grains were tender and soft. This was called *suh-day-wal-di* (swelled grains)" (Alford *Civilization*: p. 37; see also Alford in Galloway *Old Chillicothe*: p. 185).

My personal favorite in the Shawnee cuisine is sour bread. Florine Ponkilla ("Shawnee Sour Bread") supplies the recipe for this delicacy: "Mix one level teaspoonful baking soda, two cupsful white cornmeal, one level teaspoonful sugar, two cupsful lukewarm water. Let stand two or three days. Stir it thoroughly and add one cupful flour. Stir again to make dough, pour into well-greased breadpan, and cook at 350 degrees until well browned."

Another famous Shawnee bread is blue bread, sometimes called blue biscuits. A small quantity of a peculiar kind of ashes, made by burning matured black-eyed pea hulls, is added to cornmeal or hominy grits. Water is added to make dough, which turns bluish in color although the black-eyed pea hulls ash was white. The dough is molded by hand into three-cornered biscuits which are then dropped into a kettle of boiling water. "When cooked they had a very pleasing flavor entirely their own, and were a deep blue color. They sometimes were dried and kept for future use, being reboiled when required" (Alford *Civilization*: pp. 38–9; Alford in Galloway *Old Chillicothe*: pp. 186–7; F. L. Ponkilla "Blue Bread").

Shawnee hunters and warriors, carried as their "emergency ration", a small bag of corn meal. It was an ideal food for travelers, because it was light, did not spoil, and was easily stored if it were kept perfectly dry. This type of corn meal was prepared in the same way as the meal used in making corn bread except that in this case the grains were thoroughly parched before being pounded into meal. A supply of this type of corn meal was kept on hand in every Shawnee home for use in an emergency, such as a sudden journey. A hunter or warrior would never set out without a supply of it. It was very much condensed and was carried in a small bag placed inside a larger bag of buckskin to keep it dry. A small quantity stirred into a cup of water made not only a good drink, but a nourishing meal by itself. In an emergency one might live on this provender alone when no other food could be obtained (Alford in Galloway *Old Chillicothe* p. 186; Alford *Civilization*: p. 38).

All of the above dishes employ corn or cornmeal as their

principal ingredient, and corn still reigns supreme in Shawnee cookery. At a very early date, however, the Shawnees learned to appreciate the white man's wheat, and adapted it to their own taste in a number of dishes. The captive Thomas Ridout (Edgar *Ten Years of Upper Canada*: p. 360) describes the preparation of wheat cakes by a party of Shawnees in 1788:

"The bread I speak of had been made a few days before, out of the remains of a little wheat in their possession. To make it into cakes, baked in the hot ashes, it went through the following process, in which I bore a part. In a wooden mortar made of the sassafras tree—a tough wood—about a quart of wheat was put at a time; then, being moistened with a little warm water, it was pounded with a wooden pestle till the husk separated; it was then sifted in a tolerable fine sieve, made of small split of wood; being kneaded with a little water, it was placed upon the hot hearth and covered with hot ashes until baked." Note that this wheat bread was prepared in essentially the same way as the aboriginal corn bread.

Today's Shawnee housewife uses wheat flour in baking bread, biscuits, and cake. One type of bread utilizing wheat flour is termed "Indian bread" and corresponds to the bannock of Canadian Indians. It employs salt instead of yeast to make the dough rise, and is usually baked in a dutch oven.

No account of Shawnee dishes would be complete without mention of the renowned "fry bread". At the present time it is featured at all secular gatherings of the Shawnees and neighboring tribes, as well as at the informal feasts held after the Bread Dance and other sacred ceremonies. Florine Ponkilla offers her recipe for this famous Indian dish as follows ("Fry Bread"): "Three cups sifted flour, One teaspoon salt, 2-1/2 cups lukewarm milk or water, 3 tablespoons baking powder, 1 tablespoon sugar. Mix all ingredients together thoroughly. Add lukewarm milk or wat [water] and knead until it forms a dough. Roll out on a floured board and cut square or round. Fry in deep vegetable shortening until brown."

In addition to corn, beans, squashes, and pumpkins, that were raised by the women in their gardens, wild plant foods had an important place in the diet of the Shawnees. Alford notes the great importance of berries and other wild plant foods to the tribe (*Civilization*: pp. 40-1). Berries and fruits were generally eaten uncooked but fruits that could be dried were valued highly. The persimmon, for instance, a fruit that is rich in sugar, was carefully cured. When freed from seed and a kind of fibrous core that imparts an astringent taste, it is very good. Alford writes, "From persimmons our mothers used to make a kind of cake that resembles a date cake of the present day, which was called *muc-hah-see-mi-ni tak-u-wha* (persimmon bread). To cure or dry persimmons they were first freed from seed and fibre. The remaining pulp was kneaded into oblong cakes of a uniform size, and then thoroughly dried in the sun. When needed for use it was freshened by steaming in hot water, or it was very palatable when eaten dry. Other fruits such as plums and berries were similarly prepared for drying, some being slightly baked before drying. (Alford *Civilization*: pp. 40-1; cf. also Alford in Galloway *Old Chillicothe*: p. 188).

Alford then goes on to describe a dish made with wild grapes that is still a favorite among the Shawnees (*Civilization*: p. 41): "Mother used to make a dish that was a favorite with us all, called *psg-ibhaw* (sour food, which was a misnomer), that was delightful to my taste . . . It is made of wild grapes that are slightly scalded so the thick, rich, juice may be pressed from the grapes. The juice is then heated, and while boiling, dumplings are dropped into it. Sugar was added to the juice—when we had it."

Ridout mentions the Shawnee group with which he was associated stopping to dig a wild root which they used for food (Edgar *Ten Years of Upper Canada*: p. 360): "We remained a day or two longer in this village than we otherwise would have done, had it not been for a root found here somewhat resembling a potato. To me, who had but once tasted bread for six weeks, this root was a luxury." This root may have been the tubers of the Jerusalem artichoke (*Helianthus tuberosus* L.), widely used as a food by North American Indians.

When they lived in the East, the Shawnees made syrup and sugar from the sugar maple each spring, but after moving further west they were forced to substitute soft maple, boxelder, and even hickory sap for the sugar maple sap, though the end product was not so good (Alford in Galloway *Old Chillicothe*: 188-9; Alford *Civilization*: p. 41). O. M. Spencer, during his captivity, participated in sugar making with the Shawnees, noting that during a remarkably fine season he and his Indian foster mother, in a period of several days, collected sap sufficient to make a hundred weight of sugar (*The Indian Captivity of O. M. Spencer*: pp.

125–6). Another source of sugar for the Shawnees was wild honey from a bee tree (Alford *Civilization*: p. 41).

Cody and Agnes Mack mentioned that the Shawnees made use of sumac berries in a sort of tea. "It was delicious," said Agnes, who recalled drinking it as a girl. She also remembered that she had once been told to make some of this beverage when she was very small and picked the "fuzzy leaved" sumac, which is poisonous, by mistake. This caused her entire family to become ill. During the same interview, her husband Cody commented that the Kickapoos were already digging wild onions (on 8 March 1972) and that soon the Shawnees would dig them as well. Cody said that his family used to travel all the way to Derby, Kansas, to dig this plant each year. Both Cody and Agnes mentioned that milkweed stems, when young and tender, were used as food by the Shawnees. Again, there are two kinds of milkweed and the wrong sort will bring on stomach cramps and vomiting.

Today's Shawnee housewife sets a table quite similar, in terms of the variety of dishes and their mode of preparation, to that of the surrounding non-Indian population. On special occasions, such as ceremonies, family gatherings, etc., the meals become veritable banquets, combining traditional Shawnee dishes with others borrowed from the Euro-American cuisine. Most Shawnee women are excellent cooks, and I have never been served a bad meal in a Shawnee home or camp. In the eighteenth and early nineteenth century, of course, fare was much simpler, though probably not very different, even then, from the menu of the white frontiersman.

The literature of Shawnee captives provides a number of accounts of Shawnee meals. These vary from rough and ready trail fare prepared by warriors on the march to elaborate feasts in the villages. O. M. Spencer describes one of the former types of meals (*The Indian Captivity of O. M. Spencer*: p. 47): "Here, while one Indian kindled a fire the other went in pursuit of game, and soon returned with a raccoon, which he had killed with his rifle, proceeded to dress it by singeing off the hair, then dividing it, broiled it on the fire. The Indians ate voraciously, but being exceedingly weary I could eat very little; besides I had just witnessed a most sickening scene, calculated for a time to destroy all relish for food." The "sickening scene" which spoiled young Spencer's appetite was a member of the war party cleaning and stretching a fresh scalp.

Later, at a Shawnee village on the Auglaize, Spencer was served a delicious three-course meal (op. cit.: p. 74): "An elderly, noble-looking Indian, whom I took to be the village chief, now led us to his cabin, where his wife, who appeared to be a very mild and humane woman, gave us first some boiled hominy and then a little corn cake and boiled venison. This to me, at that time more than half starved, was a most delicious repast." Further in his narrative, Spencer describes a meal served him at Blue Jacket's village (op. cit.: p. 89): "We were kindly received by Wawpawmaw-quaw, whose wife, a very pleasant and rather pretty woman of twenty-five, according to the custom set before us some refreshment consisting of some dried green corn boiled with beans and dried pumpkins, and making, as I thought, a very excellent dish." Spencer also comments on the cleanliness of the Indians in regard to their eating utensils (*The Indian Captivity of O. M. Spencer*: p. 122): "Cooh-coo-cheeh was remarkably nice in her cookery, requiring her kettles to be scoured often and her bowls and spoons to be washed daily, and nothing offended her quicker than the appearance of sluttishness . . ."

Other accounts of eighteenth century Shawnee meals are provided by Thomas Ridout. His descriptions indicate that even at this time (1788) the Shawnees had learned to appreciate many European foods. Sortly after his capture Ridout partook, together with his captors and fellow prisoners, of a breakfast consisting of: ". . . chocolate and some flour cakes baked in the ashes, being part of the plunder they had taken from us. (Edgar *Ten Years of Upper Canada*: p. 348)" Later, at the village of his captors, he was taken to the village council house: ". . . in the centre of which was a fire, and over it hung a kettle with venison and Indian corn boiling. We sat down by the fire and were for some time left to ourselves. At length, two or three women came into the house, and taking some meat and corn out of the kettle, put it into a bowl and gave us thereof to eat, with wooden spoons. Salt they had not, but in lieu of that gave each of us a piece of sugar made of the sap extracted from the maple tree, in the making of which the women were now occupied in the adjoining forests" (Edgar *Ten Years of Upper Canada*: p. 354).

Ridout's breakfast the following day was at the home of his captor and that man's wife:

> The woman, at length, began to prepare for breakfast. She cut some venison
> (deer, wild turkeys, and other game being in abundance in this part of the

country) into small pieces, and seasoning it with dry herbs, she put the whole
into a frying-pan with bears' oil; she also boiled some water in a small copper
kettle, with which she made some tea in a tea-pot, using cups and saucers of
yellow ware. She began and finished her breakfast without noticing me in the
least. When she had done she poured some tea in a saucer, which, with some
fried meat on a pewter plate, she gave me.

   This was a luxury I little expected to meet with, not only on account of the
distance it must have come from, but being a prisoner, I could hardly expect
such fare. The tea proved to be green tea, and was sweetened with maple sugar.
The meat, also was very savory and palatable. As soon as I breakfasted I
returned to my bed, for I could scarcely stand. In the course of the morning a
kettle was put on the fire and a quantity of venison put into it. When done, the
Indian brought in two or three of his friends to treat them, and I had my share.
My master or friend did not sit round the bowl with his guests, but behind them
on the ground, smoking his pipe, entertaining them with diverting stories,
which kept them in continual laughter. And this was his usual custom when he
gave a treat. (Edgar *Ten Years of Upper Canada*: pp. 355-6).

Other commentary on Shawnee fare is offered later in Ridout's
account: "I tasted bread made of Indian corn but once or twice
after leaving the village, but lived entirely on boiled or roasted
flesh, without salt, but sometimes with dried herbs. We also met
with a root which was found near the surface of the ground,
resembling ginger in appearance, and warm and pleasant in
taste. Dried venison with bear's oil was reckoned a great dainty,
and such I thought it" (Edgar *Ten Years of Upper Canada*: pp.
358-9).

   The Shawnees formerly grew their own native tobacco, but no
longer do so. Cody and Agnes Mack said that sumac leaves were
gathered in the fall, just after they had turned red, and were dried
and used as a smoking additive. Agnes recalled how pleasant the
smell of tobacco mixed with sumac leaves had been when she was
a small girl.

   The traditional craft of basketry disappeared among the
Shawnees about 1930. Pottery making had died out well before the
turn of the century (E. W. Voegelin and G. K. Neumann "Shawnee
Pots and Pottery Making": p. 4). Alford describes the Shawnee
method of making baskets and sieves: Raw material was secured
by cutting down a hackberry or elm of the correct size. A section of
trunk clear of knots was chosen and carefully barked the desired
length. The trunk selected then was pounded with the smooth flat
edge of an axe. Every fraction of the surface received its gentle
beating, until the layers of wood representing the annual growth
rings became loosened, and could be peeled from the trunk in
narrow uniform strips in thin but strong tough sheets. These

strips were then woven into baskets, leaving spaces between the strips as required for the purpose of the basket. "Some were woven so closely they would hold water, some were used as sifters for meal; others were used to grade grains of corn, letting all under a certain size pass through. Marvelous, the ingenuity of those women!" (Alford *Civilization*: p. 39). This same process of basket making was described by Mary Spoon and Ranny Carpenter. Ranny noted that his band, the Loyal Shawnees, commonly used the white oak to make their hominy sieves. A fine collection of Shawnee baskets can be found at the Museum of the American Indian, Heye Foundation, in New York City. These were collected by M. R. Harrington early in this century. I have seen no baskets in Shawnee hands.

Wooden bowls, ladles, and spoons were traditionally carved by Shawnee men. A few are still seen as family heirlooms, brought out at the Bread Dance, but they are now carved only rarely. Strangely enough those still produced today, among both Shawnees and Kickapoos, are being made by women. In 1978 Agnes Mack showed me a fine spoon that she was in the process of completing. It has a deep bowl and a short handle with a doughnut-shaped ring at its end. Similar spoons are carved by Dorothy Reed, a Kickapoo woman. Spoons of bison or cow horn were also made, and Mary Spoon showed me two spoons of this type, family heirlooms, one of which had belonged to her father. They were made by cutting out the top of the broad end of a cow's horn, leaving the small end as a handle.

Native spoons figure importantly in the Kickapoo and Shawnee religions. Among the Kickapoos even today and among the Shawnees until just a few years ago, it was considered imperative that each member of a family have a native-made wooden or horn spoon in his or her possession to take to feasts and ceremonies. Unless a person was so equipped, or could borrow a spoon of this type, they were not fed. This rule also extends to the afterworld, where a person who died lacking a personal spoon was condemned to spend eternity "eating foam" (i.e. being unable to secure satisfaction from eating).

Hide tanning was practiced until a few years ago by the Absentee Shawnees, and Alfred Switch still produces a few buckskins, though he admits his product is not as good as those of the "old timers". Mary Spoon said that formerly she tanned her own hides, but in the period of my field work, although she still smoked hides on occasion, she generally purchased her buckskins, already tanned, from Mexican or Oklahoma Kickapoo leatherworkers. Ranny Carpenter recalled that his grandmother used to tan hides as follows: First she would soak the hide in water, then throw it over a smooth log (bark removed) set in the ground at a 45 degree angle. She would then scrape off the hair, being careful to feel out thick spots in the hide and scrape them even. Then she would work a mixture of water and deer brains into the hide and leave it for a time. Next she would carefully wash out the hide and stretch it by lacing it on a circular hickory frame. While it was on this frame she would scrape it to an even thickness. Removing it she would work out any stiff places. Next she would smoke it over a smudge of corncobs and cedar leaves, which gave it a good color and a pleasant smell.

Mary Spoon smoked her hides by making a small fire of corncobs, then placing the hide, sewed into a conical shape, over this. Some Shawnees, she said, used other fuel when smoking hides, such as butternut wood. Smoking the hide in this manner gives the buckskin a rich brown hue, makes the moccasin or other garment made from it more water resistant, and keeps the garment from stiffening when it becomes wet.

W. A. Paxson (in Galloway *Old Chillicothe*: pp. 274-5) describes essentially the same process of tanning as given by Ranny Carpenter as it was employed by "Indian Joe", a Shawnee who remained in the vicinity of Old Chillicothe, Ohio, after the Shawnee removal. This man, who died in 1855, was well known for his tanned hides, which he sold to local whites:

> Joe used different materials and methods for tanning various hides, according to the purpose for which the skin was to be used. For making the "whang leather," he generally used the skin of the ground-hog, as it was so much tougher than any other. He always used the brains of the slain animal in this process. When the neighbors brought him a ground-hog skin to tan, he always had them bring, at least, the head of the animal, if not the whole carcass. Then I have seen him sit for hours at a time and manipulate this skin and brains over and over until the entire brain substance was completely absorbed into the skin, after which the leather remained pliable, and was not, apparently, affected by time or weather. He would also use an ooze made from oak bark and leaves, which he would pound up in an old iron kettle till well macerated. After soaking the hides in this ooze for a long time, he would then take them out and "man handle" them, that is, just rub and stretch them. He would use what was known as mesentery fat, which my grandfather would let him have when they butchered the hogs—sometimes as many as a dozen at a time—and any old tallow from the beeves that were killed from time to time.

Apparently the Shawnees manufactured bison hide trunks of

the type made by the Sauks, Foxes, and other Central Algonkian groups. So far as I know, none of these survive in Shawnee hands or in museums, but the Latorres report seeing one in the Mexican Kickapoo village: "We have seen only one bison-hide trunk, whose top had been lost. This trunk had once belonged to a Shawnee Indian" (F. A. Latorre and D. L. Latorre *The Mexican Kickapoo Indians*: p. 75).

Such was the traditional economy and material culture of the Shawnees, features of culture now rendered obsolete and replaced by elements from the white man's culture. Only the distinctive foods remain, diet being, next to religion, the area of culture most resistant to change.

4

Costume and Decorative Art

The aboriginal dress of the Shawnees was simple but elegant. Paintings of Shawnees such as those included in the *McKenney and Hall Portrait Gallery of American Indians* (J. D. Horan), J. L. Berlandier's *The Indians of Texas in 1830*, heirloom photographs in the possession of my informants and the ceremonial dress of present day Shawnees, all support the impression that Shawnees, even in their gala attire, favored understatement. Thus, when compared with Plains or Pueblo tribes, or even the Woodland Ojibwa, the Shawnees appear rather subdued. Berlandier, in fact, commenting upon the dress of the Cherokees and Shawnees in 1830, said that they "look like selectmen (i.e. conservatively dressed town officials of the White man's world) . . ." (*The Indians of Texas in 1830*: p. 52).

The basic costume for the Shawnee man in the nineteenth century, still retained by the Absentee band as ceremonial dress for the Bread Dance, consists of the following items: on the feet he wears a pair of soft-soled moccasins puckered to a single seam at the top, with large ankle flaps. These flaps, always worn turned down, are often covered with velveteen that is decorated with appliqué beadwork. Often a large part of the top of the moccasin is ornamented with beadwork as well. The beadwork on the moccasin tops may be either geometric or stylized floral in design, and it is applied in such a way as to completely cover and disguise the top seam. On his legs the man wears woolen broadcloth or buckskin leggings. At present these invariably have the seam at the side, but prior to 1850 an alternative style, with the seam in front and an extension at the bottom partly covering the moccasin top was sometimes worn (Berlandier *The Indians of Texas in 1830*: Plate 12). The seams of the cloth leggings end in large flaps that are often decorated with ribbonwork. In the buckskin leggings these flaps are cut into long fringes almost to the seam; and yarn pom-poms, spaced at intervals of five inches, are fastened along the seam itself. At the knee these leggings are bound with loom-beaded kneebands with long yarn ties. Less common are finger-woven yarn kneebands. A wide broadcloth breechcloth, generally blue or red in color, passes between the legs and hangs over the belt for about a foot both in front and in back. Sometimes the ends of the breechcloth are decorated with stylized floral designs in appliqué beadwork or ribbonwork. More commonly the selvage of the cloth provides the only decoration. The same belt that holds up the breechcloth also anchors the tops of the leggings, which are attached to it by a thong on either side. Sometimes a light blanket or a woman's fringed shawl is folded into a sort of kilt and wrapped around the man's waist over the breechcloth, the tops of the leggings, and the tail of his shirt.

The Shawnee man wears a cloth shirt. Though obviously copied from shirts worn by white settlers in the early nineteenth century, they are now considered a tribal badge by Woodland Indians who live in Oklahoma. Each tribe has its own distinctive style, and subtle differences in tailoring serve to indicate the tribal affiliation of the wearer. A Shawnee shirt, for example, has a wide pleated yoke in the front, (of about eight inches for an adult) with a buttoned opening in the center. This yoke is set off by a ribbon trim. Two or four ribbons likewise extend from the yoke to the shoulders in front, where a few inches are allowed to hang loose for decoration. Similar ribbons with loose ends are sewed across the back of the shirt. The arms of a Shawnee shirt are quite full, and are gathered at the wrists into pleats and ornamented at the cuffs with ribbons of the same colors as those at the shoulder and bordering the yoke. A collar is attached at the neck. Most Shawnee shirts are of a single color, such as black, dark blue, dark red, light blue, yellow, with ribbon trim of contrasting hues. Kickapoo shirts have a narrower yoke (of about six inches) many more buttons up the front, and shorter ruffled cuffs, in order to display the German-silver bracelets of which the Kickapoos are very fond.

Over the shirt, and around his waist, the Shawnee man wears a yarn sash. The better examples of these are done in the ancient finger-weaving technique, actually a form of braiding, and are up to five inches in width. They are long enough so that, when tied at the side, the long braided ends hang below the wearer's knee at the right side. At the present time the Shawnees no longer produce their own sashes, and most secure their "yarn belts" from the Creeks or Yuchis. These Creek and Yuchi sashes are usually made on a loom, not finger-woven, and have extra large yarn tassels (six or seven inches in length) at the ends. On his arms, if he owns them, the well dressed Shawnee man wears a pair of wide silver or German-silver armbands with engraved designs, and about his neck he ties a bright silk scarf of the same color as the trim on his shirt. Some also wear a choker necklace of bone and glass or metal beads and a bandolier or two of mescal beans, glass beads, or metal bead chain. If only one bandolier is worn it is invariably worn off the left shoulder so as to "cross over the heart," possibly indicating a former function as a talisman or medicine ornament. Mescal bean bandoliers were definitely considered a powerful "war medicine" by the Shawnees (W. La Barre *The Peyote Cult*: p. 109.) If he does not wear a bandolier, another option is a vest, usually black velveteen, decorated with commercially secured fringe at the bottom and sometimes with beadwork, sequinwork, or cloth appliqué designs on front and back. Campaign ribbons and other military insignia are often attached to such a vest by a veteran.

On his head the Shawnee man in native costume wears, and has worn for at least the past century, a wide-brimmed Western-style hat, often ornamented with a beaded hatband and an eagle feather slanting up from the band at the left side or dangling down from the top of the crown in back. Such hats, however, are still regarded as "White man's clothes" and dancers in the Bread Dance carefully remove them and place them on their seats before rising to join in the dance. Before they began wearing hats, cloth turbans, with a number of ostrich feathers in the back, were worn on the head (Berlandier *The Indians of Texas in 1830*: Plate 12). A "wearing" blanket completes the male costume. The late Absentee Shawnee chief Bill Johnson, Sr., was particularly proud of his blanket, made of two pieces of rainbow selvage woolen broadcloth, one red, the other blue, seamed up the center. Most younger Shawnee men today omit this item of dress.

The Shawnee man's ceremonial costume is seen today only at

the two Absentee ceremonial grounds, and there only on high
ceremonial occasions. Even there only a few men appear in
complete costume. At Whiteoak the tradition is weaker. Aside
from Lewis Dick, who appeared in full costume during the period
of my fieldwork, most of the male dancers wear no special garb,
though one or two may appear wearing the characteristic
Shawnee man's shirt or an approximation of it.

The Shawnee woman's costume consists of the following pieces:
On her feet the well dressed Shawnee woman or girl wears a pair
of moccasins of the same style as that worn by the men. She wears
a long skirt, generally of a single dark color, ornamented with
bands of ribbon a few inches above the hem. Usually these skirts
are ankle length. At the 1973 spring Bread Dance at the "Old
ground" near Little Axe one woman wore a slightly shorter skirt
and with it knee-length leggings with wide, ribbonwork decorated
flaps at the sides. One or two long petticoats are worn beneath the
skirt. Over it, sometimes, the woman or girl wears a long, wide,
apron. This is generally white or pastel-colored organdy or some
other light material. On her upper body the Shawnee woman or
girl wears a loose blouse with full length sleeves and an extremely
wide ruffled collar which opens at the front. These collars are of
the type known as the "Bertha collar" to dressmakers. The tails of
this blouse are worn outside the skirt, but the apron is tied over
them. If she can afford them, or has inherited a set, the collar of
her blouse will be ornamented, near the bottom or outer edge, just
above the ruffle, with numerous small brooches of German silver.
These brooches are of the "Scottish" type introduced into the
Indian trade in the eighteenth century. Larger brooches of the
same type are worn spaced around the middle of the collar. One,
two, or three still larger brooches of the same type may be worn at
the throat, as well as several necklaces, which are usually of jet
beads or shiny "basket" beads, more rarely of heirloom wampum,
or a wide net beadwork collar of "basket" beads. This wide beaded
collar, of a style that is shared with the Creek and Yuchi, is worn
over the collar of the blouse and opens at the front like the collar
itself. A few women and girls wear a finger-woven sash, of the
same type as that used by the men, around the waist.

The woman's hair, brushed until it shines, is parted in the
middle and gathered into a bun at the nape of the neck. In her hair,
at the back of the head, the well dressed Shawnee woman wears a
long, curved, German silver comb ornamented at the top with

elaborate cut-out and stamped work. She also wears an hourglass shaped "hair bow" or "head piece" made of rawhide or wood covered with black velveteen and ornamented with tiny silver brooches or studs, and with a silver band around the narrow part. It has a seed bead edging and small bunches of colored ribbons fastened at each of the four corners. The ornament is worn vertically, tied to the hair in back just above the bun. It is not perfectly symmetrical; one end is slightly narrower than the other, and this smaller end is worn uppermost. The hair bow has long ribbons, of graduated widths, suspended from its lower edge so that it will hang down the wearer's back, often past the hem of her long skirt. Large spangles or brooches are often attached to the uppermost of these ribbons. Bracelets and finger rings of native manufacture adorn the woman's wrists and hands, and silver earrings, often with designs that are symbolic of the Peyote religion, dangle from her ears. She also carries or wears a shawl with long decorative fringes. When worn, this shawl is arranged under the wide Bertha collar of the woman's blouse. When carried, it is folded over the left arm.

The woman's ceremonial costume, like that of the men, is worn only at ceremonial dances. Unlike the man's costume, which survives only among the Absentee Shawnees, the woman's gala dress can be seen at all three Shawnee ceremonial grounds, but at Whiteoak the hourglass shaped headpiece is not seen. Neither Shawnee men nor women wear their ceremonial costume when attending or participating in the ceremonies of other tribes as a rule, and the few who do are criticized for doing so. As one informant commented, "We don't want everyone, other tribes, seeing our ceremonial dress and copying it."

The present ceremonial costume of both men and women has apparently remained almost unchanged for more than a century. Before 1870, however, judging by heirloom photographs, old paintings and engravings, and museum specimens, there was considerably more variety in costuming, especially in the dress of the men. One favorite item of male apparel, which is now seen only at the ceremonial War Dance of the Kishpokotha division, was the roach headdress. This headdress consists of fringes of long porcupine back hair or turkey beards combined with shorter fringes of red deer hair, sewed to a base in the shape of an elongated teardrop so as to stand erect on the wearer's head. A hole in the base at the larger end serves to admit the braided scalplock of the wearer. A "spreader" which is a small piece of carved elk antler or bison scapula, also equipped with a hole at its front end, is threaded on the scalplock as well, so as to fit inside the inner fringes of the roach. A bone pin is then thrust through the scalplock just above the bone spreader on the crown of the wearer's head to anchor the front of the headdress there. Thongs, tied around the wearer's neck, hold the tail of the headdress in place. Mounted on the spreader inside the outer fringes of the roach is a socket made of turkey leg bone, and in this a single eagle tail feather is set so as to revolve with the wearer's every movement. Only one feather was worn with this headdress by the Shawnees. E. W. Voegelin writes: "Among the historic Shawnee, warriors wore only a single feather in their hair; informants denied that more than one feather was ever worn, as was the case among the Sauk, for example." (E. W. Voegelin, C. Rafinesque, C. F. Voegelin, and E. Lilly *Walum Olum*: p. 113) Voegelin's statement was confirmed by my informants John Ellis and Mary Spoon. Alfred Switch said that two or three roach headdresses of this type, made of turkey beards, were formerly included in the contents of the *Kishpokotha* war bundle, to be used by the dancers in the War Dance when the bundle was opened.

Another headdress that is no longer seen is an otterskin cap or turban. Examples of this can be seen in plates 16, 17 and 56. In each case it is worn with a single golden eagle tailfeather erect at the back. A Shawnee turban of wolfskin, with wolflike "ears" made of red horsehair at either side and a wolf tail fastened at the back, is in the collections of the Museum of the American Indian, Heye Foundation, New York City.

Yet another Shawnee man's headdress in the Museum of the American Indian was made on a framework of ash splints, like those used in baskets. One splint circles the wearer's head, and two more cross over it, one from front to back, the other from side to side. At the point where the two cross on top a number of stripped hawk feathers are attached in a radial pattern. Also attached at the top, so as to slant slightly backwards, is a bone socket with a single eagle tailfeather fixed in it so as to revolve, like the socket worn with the roach headdress. The wooden framework of the headdress is covered with woolen cloth, half red and half blue, and is circled at the bottom by a silver band with fancy cut-out work. This headdress is, of course, the same type as that called *gastoweh* by the Iroquois. In addition to the Shawnees and Iroquois tribes it was known to the Delawares, Hurons, Ojibwas, Miamis, and probably other Eastern tribes as well. Tom Sloan, an Absentee Shawnee, wore a headdress of this general type in the ceremonial War Dance of the Kishpokotha division in 1970, but it was made from the top of a Western-style straw hat, without the brim and pushed up round on top. On the front he had attached a strip of beadwork, and two eagle feathers were loosely attached at the top.

Another costume item recalled by my informants and represented in the Museum of the American Indian collections are "hair plates." These consist of a series of circular German silver plates attached to a long leather or cloth strip and worn hanging down the wearer's back from his neck to his heels. The plates are graduated in size from about three and a half inches at the top to tiny dime-sized discs at the bottom. When worn in the dance these hair plates drag gracefully behind the dancer as he bends near the earth. Their name derives from the fact that formerly such plates were actually worn attached to the hair, threaded on a braid at the back of the wearer's head. In commenting upon the reasons for binding a Shawnee baby to the cradle board, Alford (*Civilization*: p. 5) comments: "Then too, the little head was bound closely to the flat surface to make it grow flat, so that when he reached maturity there would be a flat spot on the back of his head where a plate would fit, to which could be attached an eagle feather, the desired headdress of a Shawnee brave."

Silver gorgets, produced by white silversmiths for the fur trade or by native Shawnee smiths, frequently appear in the nineteenth century Shawnee portraits (Horan *The McKenney-Hall Portrait Gallery*: p. 157). Silver nose rings and earrings were also popular (op. cit.: pp. 157, 161, 165). Often a Shawnee man would slit the helix of his ears away from the ear proper and wrap this with coils of silver wire. The weight of the metal would stretch the helixes into great pendant loops, which were highly admired. Other costume items from this same period were shirts with ruffles on either side of the neck opening in front, probably imitating the jabots worn by white gentlemen of that era, and a "hunting coat" made of calico or homespun, a version of the white gentleman's frock coat (Horan *The McKenney-Hall Portrait Gallery*: pp. 157, 161, 163). Turbans of cloth also appear in these early portraits (op. cit: pp. 161, 163).

Perhaps the most beautiful and elaborate item of Shawnee male costume, now so long obsolete that only a few examples survive in museums, was the shoulder bag. Identified Shawnee specimens seen in museum collections have a wide beaded shoulder strap done in either stylized floral or geometric designs. This strap terminates in three points at either end. From the strap is suspended a pouch, which has a long triangular flap covering the opening. Like the shoulder strap, the pouch is gorgeously beaded with the tiniest of seed beads. An earlier type of shoulder bag was made of black-dyed buckskin ornamented with porcupine quillwork embroidery. It lacks the triangular flap of the beaded shoulder bags, but has a fringe of deer hair-filled tin cones just below the opening at the top and also at the bottom, and a narrow shoulder strap. A particularly beautiful shoulder bag of this latter type is in the collections of the Linden Museum, Stuttgart, Germany (Plate 55). Another, which is also of black buckskin, is among the North American Indian items in the Rijksmuseem foor Volkenkunde, Leiden, Holland. Shoulder bags were used by many Indian tribes in eastern North America, and regional and even tribal styles are recognizable. According to Richard Gibson, the last Shawnee to wear this item of regalia was the late John Snake of Little Axe.

Our picture of Shawnee dress in the early historic period can be rounded out from the various accounts of captivity. Ridout, for example, describes the Shawnee costume he was given to wear during the time of his captivity (1788) thus: "My dress consisted of a calico shirt, made by an Indian woman, without a collar, which reached below the waist; a blanket over my shoulders, tied round the waist with the bark of a tree; a pair of good buckskin leggings, which covered almost the thighs, given me by the great war-chief; a pair of moccasins, in which I had pieces of blue cloth to make my step easier; a breech-cloth between my legs; a girdle around my waist; and a small round hat, in which the Indian placed a black ostrich feather by way of ornament (the smaller the hat the more fashionable)" (M. Edgar *Ten Years of Upper Canada in Peace and War, 1805–1815*: p. 358).

O. M. Spencer likewise describes the dress of the Shawnees with whom he lived (1792–93), including that of the old Indian "priestess" who had adopted him, a Mohawk who was living with the Shawnees and had become acculturated to Shawnee ways.

> Her dress like that of the old squaws in general was very plain and simple, consisting of a calico shirt extending about six inches below the waist and fastened at the bosom with a silver brooch; a stroud or petticoat, simply a yard

and a half of six quarter blue cloth with white selvedge, wrapped around her waist and confined with a girdle, and extending a little below the knee; a pair of leggings or Indian stockings of the same cloth, sewed so as to fit the leg, leaving a border of two inches projecting from the outside and extending to the instep, and a pair of plain moccasins. The form of the dress is the same among the Indian women of all ranks and ages, varying only in its quality and in the richness and variety with which it is adorned; its ornaments not being regulated by rank or station, but by the ability of the wearer. All the young and middle-aged among the women are passionately fond of finery, the young belles, particularly, having the tops of their moccasins curiously wrought with beads, ribbons, and porcupine quills; the borders of their leggings and the bottom and edges of their strouds tastily bound with ribbons, edges with beads of various colors; and frequently on their moccasins and leggings small tufts of deer's hair, dyed red and confined in small pieces of tin, rattling as they walked . . . Besides these ornaments, according to their ability they covered the bosom, shoulders, sides, and bottoms of their shirts (sometimes made of cross-barred silk handkerchiefs) with large and small silver brooches, and wore on their wrists and arms silver bracelets from one to four inches in width.

Nor is this fondness for show confined to the women; on the contrary it is even stronger in the men, who in addition to the ornaments worn by the women wear large silver medals and gorgets on the breast, silver rings in the nose, and heavy pieces of silver in the ears, the rims of which, being separated from the cartilage by cutting, are weighed down two or three inches from the head. (O. M. Spencer *The Indian Captivity of O. M. Spencer*: 87–8).

Spencer also describes his own winter costume as follows: "The weather had now become cold and my summer clothes, being not only too thin for the season but nearly worn out, were thrown aside; and a white shirt, blanket capote, blue leggings, and waist cloth supplied their place, so that I was dressed in full Indian costume" (ibid.: p. 117).

The Shawnees of this period were quite fond of wearing items of captured white man's dress, often modifying these to suit their own taste. Spencer tells how one of his captors cut off both rows of plated buttons from Spencer's blue silk vest, together with a strip of the cloth two inches wide, and later used these as kneebands (ibid.: pp. 88–89). He also records seeing a Shawnee brave wearing the dress coat of a field officer of infantry, with silver epaulets on his shoulders and a watch suspended from each ear. These items were a part of the spoils of St. Clair's defeat in 1791 (ibid.: p. 28).

At the present time, at all three Shawnee ceremonial grounds, it is customary for the principal functionaries to paint for the occasion of a ceremony. At Whiteoak the painting is done as a ritual act at the beginning of the ceremony. At the two Absentee grounds the painting is done privately at the same time the dancer dons his or her costume. At Whiteoak I have noticed two principal designs used by the men: either a short red line extending out from the outer corner of the eye for a couple of inches or two parallel

lines at the outer corner of the eye with three red dots in between.
At the Absentee grounds the first of these is seen, but not the second. Absentee men also use two or three red lines (three being
more common) radiating from the outer corner of the eye. All of
these are done in red paint. The only exception to this was at the
1971 spring Bread Dance when I observed Henry Johnson wearing a single line of green paint extending out from the corner of
each eye. He later told me that this indicated that the ceremony
was "wide open" and that all were free to wear whatever items of
costuming and whatever style of face painting they wished. At all
three Shawnee grounds the only design ever used by women and
girls is a simple, small, red spot on either cheek.

Formerly there were special "medicine paints" used only by
individuals and considered to be their personal property. These
were often given to a young person by an older one. Thus Cody
Mack told me that when he was a boy he had been given a special
paint to use in the Ride-in and War Dance at the Sand Hill dance
ground of the Thawikila division of the Absentees. This paint
consisted of two parallel red lines at the corner of each eye with
three blue dots in between. In addition Cody was instructed to
paint a blue handprint on the left side of his horse's rump and a
red one on the right side. The handprint is a widespread warrior's
symbol among eastern and prairie tribes.

At the two Absentee grounds the men and boys who are the
"hunters" for the Bread Dance paint their faces with three
horizontal lines of black paint across either cheek and vertical
black lines on forehead and chin. At Whiteoak the men and boys
participating in the Buffalo Dance wear the usual face paint. In
addition these dancers, who are stripped to the waist, have the
design of a bison's head painted on their chest in bluish-grey mud,
their nipples serving as the "eyes" in the buffalo head representation. Anthropologist Robert K. Thomas, who observed the dance
several years ago, reports seeing the impression of human hands
on the chests and shoulders of the dancers in the same bluish-grey
paint, but I have never observed this.

I once asked Ranny Carpenter, who was the drumkeeper at
Whiteoak, if the different face-painting designs used by the men in
the Bread Dance and Buffalo Dance had any special significance,
because some men seemed to prefer one way or the other. He
replied, "Some people are very particular about the way in which
they are painted, but the only way I know for Shawnee men is a

single red line going out from the corner of each eye. This is done so that the Creator will recognize the worshipper as an Indian, a Shawnee. They are painted the same way at death. With so many Shawnees mixed with whites now this is necessary. Take me, for example, I look like a white man." Ranny indicated that the "real Shawnee paint" was red and came from the inside of a certain kind of pebble. When the pebble is broken open a small amount of paint is found inside. He said the only place he knew where these stones could be found was a place near Medicine Park, Oklahoma. Ranny had a small pouch of this "real Shawnee paint" which he used for Bread Dance paint, but when it was nearly gone he was asked to save it and use it only for painting the dead.

Today face painting is limited to ceremonial occasions, but formerly face paint was worn as a part of everyday dress. Alford writes of painting his face with red, blue, and green paints as a small boy, and of being humiliated when his schoolteacher made fun of him (*Civilization*: pp. 78-9).

In the first half of the nineteenth century certain accessories were invariably carried by the Shawnee man. Henry Harvey (*History of the Shawnee Indians from the Year 1681 to 1854 Inclusive*: p. 147): writes: "The warrior went ahead of his family when they were on the march, his blanket drawn close around his body, a handkerchief curiously twisted to a knot on his head, with a gun on his shoulder and a gunstick in his hand, his tomahawk in his belt, which is so constructed that the poll is his pipe and the handle the stem, and he carries his tobacco in the skin of some little animal, often the polecat skin." A bit later Harvey adds (ibid.: p. 148): "There are a few things sure to be seen in an Indian's possession, unless very poor indeed; these are a poney, a gun, tomahawk, a dog, butcher knife, and blanket. These things are his outfit, and if thus furnished, he is not considered a poor man by his people."

Concerning the blanket, which had multiple functions, Harvey writes, (*History of the Shawnee Indians*: p. 148): "A Shawnee is seldom without a blanket. It is used as a cover at night and a wrapper by day. They use them while out hunting and as ceremonial dress. Blankets are cleaned before ceremonies if not spotless. The blanket is also used to wrap provisions."

Apparently the Shawnees had few items of dress or equipment which served to indicate a particular rank or status. The otterskin turban seems to have been vaguely associated with the chief or

"wise old man," but only vaguely; and today, at least, I have seen
younger men wearing this headpiece in the dance. Likewise, the
roach headdress, *gastoweh*, and hair plates with a single erect
eagle feather indicated warrior status—but again the association
was not sharply defined.

At present Shawnees, except when dressed for a dance or
ceremony, are attired much like other non-Indian Oklahomans.
Men and boys favor Western-style shirts, levis, broad-brimmed
hats, and cowboy boots, while women and girls wear the same
dresses, blouses, and slacks as their white and black sisters. Only
one qualification should be added—I can never recall seeing a
Shawnee woman or girl wearing a hat except for the express
purpose of shading herself from the hot rays of the sun. Women's
hats, those exotic bits of felt and feathered frippery so beloved in
the major culture apparently have no appeal for the Shawnee
woman or girl. Interestingly, this same observation was made by
Lewis H. Morgan more than a century ago. He noted (*The Indian
Journals, 1859-62*: p. 51) that all of the Shawnee women whom he
observed assembled for a treaty payment "wore the gown" (that is
they were dressed like white women of the period) but on their
heads they tied a silk scarf instead of wearing a hat. There were,
he says "no bonnets among them." Morgan also notes that the
Shawnees of that day slept in the nude (ibid.: p. 86). In this respect,
however, today's Shawnees have changed to approximate the
customs of the major society.

Formerly the Shawnees, like other tribes of eastern North
America, produced beautiful porcupine quillwork. An excellent
example of their decorative art in this medium can be seen in the
Shawnee "Schrotbeutel" ("shot pouch") illustrated in Benndorf
and Speyer's *Indianer Nordamerikas 1760-1860*: Plate 34). The
shot pouch is of buckskin and of a type that was worn folded over
the wearer's belt. One end is beautifully embroidered in stylized
double-curve floral designs and has a fringe of deer hair-filled
jingles of metal. The other end has a simple decoration of crossed
ribbons (which is still seen in Shawnee ribbonwork of the present
day) and is fringed at the end. This piece was supposedly collected
before 1840. It is now a part of the ethnological collections of the
National Museum of Canada, Ottawa. Another beautiful example
of Shawnee porcupine quillwork is a black buckskin shoulder bag
in the Linden Museum, Stuttgart, Germany, mentioned earlier
(Plate 55). This piece was collected from the Shawnee by Prince

Paul von Wuerttemberg in 1822. No quillwork is made, or even remembered, by today's Shawnees.

Most of the decorative art that is produced by present-day Shawnee craftspersons is lavished on items of ceremonial costume and on the gourd rattles, feathers, and other ritual items used in the Peyote religion. Beadwork and ribbonwork are the major artistic expressions of the women, while the men produce drumsticks, peyote gourds, staffs, and feathers. Much of the craftwork produced today is pan-Indian in nature—that is, the pieces and their designs are not characteristically Shawnee but instead mirror the inter-tribal "American Indian" culture which has developed in Oklahoma in the period since 1920 (cf. J. Howard "Pan Indian Culture of Oklahoma"). A few craftworkers, however, strive to produce characteristically Shawnee pieces with Shawnee designs. During the period of my fieldwork Mary Spoon and Lilly Ellis were two of the few remaining Shawnee moccasin makers. Both also made beaded hatbands, belts, buckskin and cloth leggings, ribbon shirts, women's blouses, and women's hair bows or head ornaments, all in distinctive Shawnee style. Mary also made apple-face dolls, dressed in miniature Shawnee women's costume. Some other women do creditable ribbonwork and beadwork.

Mary Spoon said that she inherited the beadwork designs of leaves which she sometimes used on the velveteen cuffs of her moccasins from her mother. Her mother, Mary said, used actual maple leaves, selected for their good shape, as patterns. Mary did not do this, relying instead upon her memory. Another motif used by Mary she called "fans":

Fig. 2. "Fans," a Shawnee beadwork design

This design is used by several of the tribes with whom the Shawnees were associated, such as the Iroquois, the Miamis, and the Delawares. I mentioned to Mary that the Iroquois interpret this design as the "world on the turtle's back" of their mythology. She had never heard the Shawnees interpret the design in this way, though she commented that the Shawnees have the same "world on the turtle's back" cosmological concept.

Most of the ribbonwork designs that are employed by Shawnee women, including Agnes Mack, Lilly Ellis, and the late Mary Spoon and her daughter the late Frances Gokey are stylized floral designs, though occasionally diamonds and rectangular motifs are used on legging flaps. Lilly Ellis proudly showed me a small drawstring handbag that had been made by her mother where hundreds of tiny ribbonwork diamonds were employed in a striking pattern. It was the equal of any fine ribbonwork I have ever seen.

One who has examined the beautiful examples of nineteenth century Shawnee costume pieces and decorative art preserved in the world's larger museums cannot avoid lamenting the loss of so much of this tradition by today's Shawnees. Still, much has been retained. I am always thrilled when the gorgeously dressed women and girls file into the ceremonial ground at the Bread Dance to place their offerings of cornbread in the center. I am also stirred when the man and boys, attired as warriors, parade in on horseback to start the "Man's Dance" at the Absentee "New ground". The effect of the open air setting at any Shawnee ceremonial, the blue sky above, the beaten brown earth below, with the surrounding oaks casting dappled shadows on the brightly costumed dancers is unequaled by any museum display. Surely Kokomthena, the Shawnee Creator, looking down upon her grandchildren from her heavenly abode, is pleased with their appearance.

5

Housing, Settlement, and Travel

Today's Shawnees live in houses that are in no way different from those of their white neighbors. In recent years an ambitious and efficient tribal housing program has produced many excellent homes. Partly as a result of this and partly because of their generally superior economic situation, as compared with other Oklahoma Indians, today's Shawnees are among the best housed of all Oklahoma Indian groups. The same could be said of the temporary quarters that they occupy when they attend ceremonies and powwows. Commercially secured tents, campers, and house trailers of excellent quality substitute for the ruder shelters of earlier days. Most younger Shawnees, in fact, have not the haziest notion of what sort of dwellings were used by their ancestors, and when Shawnee schoolchildren are asked by their teacher to draw an old-time village of their people, they often populate it with Plains Indian tipis.

To learn of aboriginal types of Shawnee housing, then, one must turn to historical sources and the testimony of older informants. It seems likely from these accounts, though unfortunately most are not explicit on the subject, that the early day Shawnees had two principal types of dwelling, one for summer and another for winter, a practice still followed by their ultra-conservative kinsmen and neighbors, the Kickapoos. Of the two types, the summer house survived longer among the Shawnees, and was still remembered by a few of my Absentee Shawnee informants. The winter house, however, had been largely replaced by the Scandinavian-derived log cabin by the end of the eighteenth century (see C. A. Weslager *The Log Cabin in America From Pioneer Days to the Present*: pp. 60-1). Today the log cabin has come to be thought of as the "old-time Indian" winter dwelling by older Shawnees, and Mary Spoon even described the celestial home of Kokomthena ("Grandmother"), the Shawnee female deity, as a log cabin.

Both summer and winter houses were built on a pole foundation. They differed from one another in both shape and size. The summer house had a rectangular or elongated oval floorplan, and had either a gabled or an arched roof. The winter house had a circular floorplan and a domed roof. It was also much smaller in size and hence easier to heat. Harvey is probably describing the winter dwelling when he writes (H. Harvey *History of the Shawnee Indians from the Year 1681 to 1854 Inclusive*: pp. 147-8): "The Shawnee tent is made of small poles. The large ends of the poles are stuck in the ground and the small ends lashed together at the top. It is covered with animal skins so that the upper ones lap over the under ones. The fire is built in the center of the floor and the smoke goes out the smoke hole left at the top . . . In the tent are spread their skins, on which they repose. All lie down together and cover themselves with their blankets, which each one always has if it is in their power."

In 1937 Sam Perry, a Loyal Shawnee, described Shawnee houses with circular floorplans, made by sticking the butts of poles that were ten to sixteen feet long in the ground in a circle ten feet or more in diameter. The ends were then tied together in a domed shape, after which the framework was covered with sheets of elm bark four or five feet in length. These sheets of bark were removed from the trees after the sap had risen and were flattened by putting them on the ground and weighting them. Skins, he says, were used as lodge covering when bark was not available, indicating the accuracy of Harvey's account (Indian Archives, Oklahoma State Historical Society Vol. 8: p. 185).

We have two descriptions of what I believe to be the Shawnee summer house from the late eighteenth century, Ridout's (1788) and O. M. Spencer's (1792-93). Ridout writes (M. Edgar *Ten Years of Upper Canada in Peace and War, 1805-1815*: pp. 354-5): "At length the old chief to whom I belonged, and whose name was Kakinathucca, appeared and led me to his own house. This was about twenty feet long and fourteen feet wide, with sides and roof made of small poles and covered with bark. The entrance was at the end, and an old blanket hung at the doorway." Ridout says little of the furnishings except for a platform bed (ibid.: p. 355): ". . . the Indian planted four forked sticks at the entrance, on the left side, and laying other sticks on them, laid bark and skins upon it, and then gave me a blanket to cover me." Presumably there were other platform beds of this type in the house as well.

O. M. Spencer's account is more ample, though unfortunately we cannot be certain that this dwelling is typically Shawnee, because it was occupied by a Mohawk woman resident among them (*The Indian Captivity of O. M. Spencer*: pp. 83-4):

> . . . a description of the bark cabin of Cooh-coo-cheeh may perhaps be worth reading. Covering an area of fourteen by twenty-eight feet, its frame was constructed of small poles, of which some, planted upright in the ground, served as posts and studs, supporting the ridge poles and eve bearers, while others firmly tied to these by thongs of hickory bark formed girders, braces, laths, and rafters. This frame was covered with large pieces of elm bark seven or eight feet long and three or four feet wide; which being pressed flat and well dried to prevent their curling, fastened to the poles by thongs of bark, formed the weather boarding and roof of the cabin. At its western end was a narrow doorway about six feet high, closed when necessary by a single piece of bark placed beside it, and fastened by a brace, set either within or on the outside as occasion required. Within, separated by a bark partition were two apartments, of which the inner one, seldom entered but by the old squaw, was occupied as a pantry, a spare bed room, and at times as a sanctuary, where she performed her incantations; the other, having on each side a low frame covered with bark and overspread with deerskins serving both for seats and bedsteads, was in common use by the family, both as a lodging, sitting, cooking, and eating room. On the ground in the center of this apartment was placed the fire; and over it, suspended from the ridge-pole in the middle of an aperture left for the passage of the smoke, was a wooden trammel for the convenience of cooking.

The furnishings of this house were simple but adequate (ibid.: pp. 86-7): "Her household furniture consisted of a large brass kettle for washing and sugar making; a deep close-covered, copper hominy kettle; a few knives, tin cups, pewter and horn spoons, sieves, wooden bowls, and baskets of various sizes; a hominy block, and four beds and bedding comprising each a few deerskins and two blankets; so that, altogether her circumstances were considered quite comfortable."

When leaving their houses for an extended period, the Shawnees of this period indicated their absence, and also protected the contents of their homes, by placing a log against the door. This provided: "abundant evidence of the right of possession in its owner; a right seldom if ever violated, even by the most worthless among them" (ibid.: pp. 68-9).

The best description of the building of a summer house is Alford's (T. W. Alford *Civilization*: pp. 15-7):

To build a we-gi-wa (which generally was made of the bark of an elm tree, though there were other trees from which the bark could be used), a tall, slender tree without low limbs was selected. The bark was severed all around the tree near the ground, with an ax or other sharp implement, then it was cut in the same way above, as high as could be reached; the bark was then cut through, straight down from the higher circle to the lower one. Into the opening thus made was inserted a flat wedge-shaped end of a hard stick prepared and seasoned for this purpose, with which the bark was pried off and open in a wide sheet. This was easily accomplished in spring and summer, when sap was in the trees. Then the bark was laid flat on level ground, with flesh side under, weighted down with small logs, and allowed to dry to a certain extent, but used while still soft and pliable. Then poles were cut of straight young trees and set into the ground at regular distances apart, outlining the size desired for the we-gi-was. All bark was peeled off the poles to keep worms from working in it. Two of these poles with a fork at the top of each were set at opposite ends and at half way the width of the we-gi-was. Upon these forks were laid the ends of a long pole, lengthwise with the we-gi-wa, and tied securely thereon with strips of rough bark. This formed the top comb of the roof, to which the rest of the poles were bent at a suitable height for the walls and firmly secured there with strips of bark. Then upon and across these were laid other poles at regular distances from the top comb, down the slope to the end of the roof, and on down the sides to form walls. Upon these cross poles were laid the sheets of bark to close the roof and walls, securely held in place by other poles laid on the outside of the bark and tied fast to the poles within. The work seems intricate and would be to a novice but to a dexterous Indian woman of sixty years ago, it was easily and quickly done.

Interior arrangements are thus described by Alford (*Civilization*: p. 17): "Some of our people made their beds in somewhat the same manner, by driving four forked sticks into the ground, in a square or oblong size [sic], and upon these were laid two strong long poles that were a support to other shorter poles laid crosswise and securely tied, making a firm, smooth support for bedding. Others, not so industrious, merely spread their bedding upon brush laid upon the ground floor of their we-gi-was. There were other contrivances made by the ingenious housekeeper, such as shelves, benches, and tables. Extra clothing and other supplies were hung from the poles that served as rafters . . ."

My own informant, Lilly Ellis, provided a similar description of a Shawnee summer house, one that was used by her mother when she was a child, and probably one of the last in existence. She fondly recalled how cool the structure was in summer. Lilly did not know of any type of Shawnee winter dwelling except the log cabin. One suspects that even after the log cabin came to be the preferred winter dwelling, an occasional winter house in the aboriginal style was built by a family when on the hunt, or travelling, hence the accounts of Henry Harvey and Sam Perry quoted above. The log cabin, however, seems to have been in general use as the Shawnee winter dwelling as early as 1761 (J. Kenny "Journal of James Kenny, 1761-1763:" p. 22).

A typical Shawnee "Indian Cabin of Yesterday" is pictured in Alford's *Civilization* (facing p. 64). It seems quite small, probably no more than ten feet wide and twenty feet long. It is built of horizontally laid logs, notched at the ends and has a gabled roof with shakes. A doorway is located in the center of one side and apparently a log fireplace with a chimney is on the opposite side, as a feature resembling a chimney appears above the roof in this location. At the right end is an open lean-to with a sun roof. A wooden corn mortar with its pestle appears at the front of the picture near the cabin and a work table and bucket at the rear, also near the house.

My informant Louis Warrior fondly recalled visiting his grandmother, who dwelt in such a cabin, when he was a boy. She lived alone in the woods and was a renowned herbalist. Her cabin, according to Louis, had a dirt floor and a chimney of logs plastered with clay on the side opposite the entrance. His grandmother swept the dirt floor daily with a splint broom, and every item in the cabin was in perfect order.

Log structures were also used as ceremonial lodges by the Shawnees, just as they were by the Delawares (the Big House) and the Iroquois (the Longhouse). When speaking English the Shawnees referred to their log ceremonial structures as "Council Houses". These log council houses undoubtedly account for the rectangular shape of the present-day Shawnee ceremonial grounds, which are their modern functional equivalent. It is doubtful that any log council houses were built by the Shawnees after they moved to the Indian Territory, today's Oklahoma. The Reverend Isaac McCoy, however, has left us an excellent description of one, perhaps the last of its kind, which stood, until 1840, on the Shawnee reservation in present day Johnson County, Kansas. We also have a photograph of a council house formerly located in Shawnee township, Allen County, Ohio, near the present city of Lima. This presumably dates from the late eighteenth century. The earliest description of a Shawnee council house known to me dates from 1761, and is in the journal of James Kenny. On 19 September 1761, Kenny went down the Ohio river from present Pittsburgh to Beaver Creek, where he visited a deserted Shawnee village. Kenny writes (loc. cit.) ". . . walking along a Path on high Land above ye River came to a Town (about a Mile below Gray Eyes) [he is referring here to the Delaware chief also known as White Eyes] where was near to 20 well made (but small) Stone Chimneys & several frame buildings, some of which had no Shingles or Clapboards on; ye Houses were mostly Burn'd or destroy'd that belong'd to ye Stone Chimneys. *There was like one or two Chaples with Images of faces cut on ye Posts, but marks of Tomhocks struck in ye sd faces & one had ye nose cut off.* I am informed that this town was where ye French had inticed ye Shawanes to come & settle, to be handy to go to war against ye English, etc." (Italics mine).

The reference by Kenny to "Chaples with Images of faces cut on ye Posts" indicates clearly that he was describing the same type of structure as McCoy did almost eighty years later. McCoy's account, heretofore overlooked by both historians and anthropologists, adds a fascinating new dimension to our knowledge of Shawnee religious architecture. Similarities to the Iroquois log Longhouse, and especially, in the carved posts, to the Delaware Big House, are most interesting. The account reads as follows (Rev. I. McCoy *History of Baptist Indian Missions*: p. 529):

> Most of the tribes have each a council-house. That of the Shawnees is a hewn-log building, erected by themselves, about thirty feet wide and eighty feet long, and one story high. It contains one apartment only, without either upper or under floor. There is a door in each end, but no window, excepting three small holes on each side, about as high as a man's head when seated, resembling the apertures for the use of small arms in a block-house. Openings in the roof allow the smoke of the fires on the earth, in the center, to escape. The roof is a kind of very ordinary shingling with boards. The only seat is a continuation of hewn logs laid along the walls. The sides of the building are kept in place by cross beams resting upon two rows of wooden pillars. On one side of one of the pillars nearest one of the doors is carved in relief the figure of a rattlesnake about five feet long, and on the other side the likeness of a snake without a rattle. On two opposite sides of one of the pillars nearest the other door are carved in relief also, uncouth resemblances of the human face somewhat larger than life, partially painted, and with a twist of tobacco tied to the pillar crossing immediately above each figure. On each of two opposite sides of a pillar in the interior is carved as above the figure of a turtle, colored so as to increase its resemblance to the living animal. Metal is inserted for eyes, from which on the late occasion, I discovered a person wiping the dust, and increasing their brilliancy by rubbing.

A reconstruction of this unique structure, prepared by George C. Knotts and myself, appears in Plate 1. The floorplan, with doors at either end, matches the layout of the Loyal Shawnee ceremonial ground at Whiteoak. The carvings of "uncouth resemblances of the human face" undoubtedly represented some Shawnee deity, perhaps "Our Grandmother," the Shawnee female deity. This is indicated by the mention of the twist of tobacco, undoubtedly an offering, tied to the pillar crossing immediately above. A Delaware Indian friend of mine, the late Reuben Wilson of Copan, Oklahoma, kept a carved wooden mask of Misingw, the Delaware deity, in his home with tobacco tied above in an identical manner.

In commenting upon other representations Joab Spencer (*The Shawnee Indians*: p. 383) notes that: "In their council houses they sometimes have representations of animals, cut in relief on posts of their houses, but they represent only certain divisions of the tribe, as that of the Turtle clan, etc." Spencer is probably correct in attributing clan (name-group) symbolism to the animal carvings, as both turtle and snake are found among the Shawnee clans or name-groups. Why only these two were selected for representation in the carvings I do not know.

It is clear that Spencer had never seen an intact Shawnee council house, for he mentions that on a visit to the farm of Charles Bluejacket, a Shawnee, he noted a piece of squared timber lying in the barn lot. This had a turtle carved in relief on each of two opposite sides. Spencer comments that "the work had been well done," and that when he asked Bluejacket for an explanation: "Bluejacket told me it was a post from an old council house of the Shawnees that had stood, as I gathered from him, on his land, where he was then living, in Johnson County, Kansas. This was the last council house, as such, ever erected by them. After 1840 they met for council in their log Methodist meeting house." (ibid.: p. 389) Curiously, Spencer never seems to have suspected that the council house had served a religious purpose in addition to its political one.

The subject of a photograph with the legend, "Old Indian Council House, Formerly Located Shawnee Twp., Allen Co., Ohio," that was given to me by Alfred Switch, is clearly different from the structure just described by Spencer in that it has a door in the middle of one side and no door at the end which appears in the photograph. If, however, there are doors in the two sides which do not show in the photograph the floorplan of this council house would correspond to the layout of the two Absentee Shawnee ceremonial grounds, which have entrances on two of the long sides and also at the east end.

A traditional Shawnee settlement had the council house, or later the ceremonial ground with its associated football field, at its center. Close by was the dwelling of the chief and the lodges of important religious functionaries such as the keepers of various sacred bundles. Small cabins, in which the bundles themselves were housed, were nearby. The dwellings of other tribesmen radiated out from this hub in all directions. Surrounding the village were the cultivated fields of the inhabitants. O. M. Spencer describes the appearance of these fields (ibid.: pp. 85–6):

> On the south side of the Maumee for some distance below the mouth and extending more than a mile up the Auglaize to an Indian village, the low rich bottom, about three-quarters of a mile in width, was one entire field covered with corn, which, being in tassel, presented a beautiful appearance. It is, perhaps, not generally known that formerly the Indian women inhabiting large villages wherever it was practicable cultivated portions of the same field, separated from each other only by spaces of a few feet, and varying in size according to the number and strength of their families; seldom raising corn as an article of commerce, but merely to furnish bread for their own subsistence. Around these large fields they made no inclosures; nor, indeed, having no cattle, hogs, nor sheep, were fences necessary. As for their few horses, they were either driven out into the woods or secured near their cabins, and having bells on, were easily prevented from trespassing by the boys, whose duty it was, by turns, while amusing themselves with their bows and arrows, to protect the fields.

In the early reservation era this eighteenth-century pattern was still followed in the layout of Shawnee villages, though the acquisition of livestock necessitated the construction of rail fences. At the present time it can still be seen to some extent in the residence pattern of older Shawnees, but the younger generation, like other Americans, are being pulled from their rural environment by the demands of urban employment. Even today, however, though they may live in Oklahoma City, Tulsa, Vinita, Shawnee, Norman, Moore, or Tecumseh most Shawnees still identify strongly with one or another of the three existing ceremonial grounds or, in the case of the White Turkey band, with a ground that is no longer functional, the Sand Hill ground northeast of Shawnee. If at all possible they will secure a few days of leave from their job to attend the ceremonies at "their" ground, and in beer-hall boasting extol the excellence of the "stomp" leaders there. M. E. Opler has discussed the importance of the "town" among the Creeks (*The Creek Indian Towns of Oklahoma in 1937*) and the Shawnees' feeling of identification with one or another ceremonial ground seems to be in all respects identical.

Alfred Switch said that the Shawnees, when they assemble at their ceremonial ground, camp around it according to the direction from the ground that their permanent homes are located. For example, a family living on a farm several miles east of the dance ground will, when they "camp in" for a ceremony, place their tent just east of the ceremonial rectangle. The ceremonial encampment thus becomes a concentrated version of the surrounding settled area. This is probably an ancient pattern.

At the ceremonial ground each family usually camps in the same spot each time. Thus a Shawnee can quickly ascertain, from past experience, whether a particular family is "camped in" on any particular occasion. Visiting tribes, such as the Kickapoos, also have their designated camping spots. Thus, at the Little River or "New ground" of the Absentee Shawnees, the Kickapoos will always be found camping at the southeast edge of the dance ground. At Whiteoak, before they stopped attending as a tribal group, the Quapaws always camped on the high ground north and east of the ceremonial area. A particular family will customarily "build up" its family camping spot by erecting a pole or two-by-four framework for its canvas or brush-covered cooking and dining arbor, and by bringing in picnic tables, old refrigerators (used as cupboards), et cetera. These remain permanently at the camping spot; and no well-bred Shawnee would think of appropriating another family's camping spot and fixtures without permission, even if that family were not camped in at that particular ceremony.

In the seventeenth, eighteenth, and nineteenth centuries the Shawnees were great travelers and had developed standard procedures to be followed when on the move. A description of Shawnees on the march is provided by O. M. Spencer, who writes (*The Indian Captivity of O. M. Spencer*: p. 75): "I have often seen families traveling, and while the poor squaw, bending under the weight of a heavy load, and the girls, carrying packs or the smaller children on their shoulders, were laboring along, the lazy Indian in front might be seen with nothing but his rifle and blanket, and the boys with only bow and arrows or a reed blowgun." What Spencer did not understand was that the warriors had to be ever on the alert for enemies, likewise to shoot and pursue any game which happened to cross their path. As military men have long known, troops struggling under the weight of full field packs are less ready to engage the enemy, and in 1792–93, the period in which Spencer made his observations, the Shawnees were on continual battle alert.

Alford (*Civilization* p. 15) describes Shawnee travel at a later period, in the days just prior to allotment: "Our homes, *we-gi-was* or cabins, could be built in a few days, and often were abandoned with little concern. We had little in the way of household effects: few clothes, a few buffalo robes, blankets, a few cooking vessels, and the crude and limited supply of utensils and implements used in carrying on the work about the camp. There were few wagons. The family effects generally were tied in bundles and strapped on the backs of horses—some were carried by the women. There was conversation and often merriment, as the groups tramped along through woods or prairie, over mountains or hills and boggy swamps. Streams were forded and when too deep or swift to wade, rafts were made to ferry across." Ridout also mentions the building of rafts by the Shawnees he was with, in order to cross the Miami river, a very rocky and rapid tributary of the Ohio (Edgar *Ten Years of Upper Canada*: p. 352).

Additional information on Shawnee travel is found in a 1937 interview with Edward J. McClain, an Eastern Shawnee (Oklahoma State Historical Society, Indian Archives Vol. 6: p. 481). He notes that while Shawnee men usually rode bareback, the women used a buckskin saddle with a horn; also that, when traveling, a man would occasionally dismount and run alongside his horse to rest him. The "drag," or travois, usually associated with Plains Indians, was employed by the Shawnees, and women and children sometimes rode in it. When a horse was pulling a travois it was not ridden simultaneously, but rather led. John Shawnego, a member of the White Turkey band of Absentee Shawnees, also provided information on the regulation of travel that same year (Oklahoma State Historical Society, Indian Archives Vol. 44: p. 282). He notes that when the Shawnees were on the march, the leader of the party always went ahead to scout the route for those who followed. To indicate the best route he would snap twigs of bushes and trees so as to point in the desired direction. When traveling over bare ground he would lay down sticks to indicate the trail.

Today's Shawnees, with their fast cars, pickup trucks, and campers, are a far cry from their eighteenth and nineteenth century ancestors on the march. Yet, strangely enough, the ambience at one of the present day Shawnee ceremonial grounds is probably not much different from that of a century or two ago, despite the vehicles which brought in the participants and the commercially secured tents or campers which shelter them. The cooking fires glowing at the family camps, the friendly invitation to "come and sit" or "drink some coffee with us" remains the same. After all, to Shawnees and other Native Americans, externals count for little. People, not their housing or transportation, are the important part of a gathering.

6

Kinship and Social Organization

As noted earlier, the Shawnees were originally separated into five great divisions: Chalaakaatha, Mekoche, Thawikila, Pekowi, and Kishpoko. Each was a descent group whose members inherited their affiliation patrilineally. A division conceptually formed a distinct territorial unit centering on a town that bore its name (T. W. Alford in W. A. Galloway *Old Chillicothe*: p. 21; C. A. Hanna *The Wilderness Trail*, I: p. 148; E. W. Voegelin "Mortuary Customs of the Shawnee and Other Eastern Tribes": pp. 256, 269). These traditional divisions are still remembered by today's Shawnees, but it is more common to identify a person in terms of membership in one of the three governmentally recognized bands. The Absentees, in addition, usually identify themselves as belonging to one of three ceremonial centers, the first of which is the White Turkey band, named after a former chief. This group was formerly concentrated in a settlement around their ceremonial ground, which is no longer functional, called the "Sand Hill" or "Horse-shoe bend" ground, located northeast of Shawnee, Oklahoma. The second is the Little Axe "Old Ground" group whose ceremonial ground is located between Tecumseh and Norman, Oklahoma. The third is the "Little River" or "New Ground" group, whose ground is also between Tecumseh and Norman. This last split off from the "Old Ground" membership group a few years ago.

Each of the traditional five divisions of the tribe, and each of the present bands and subgroups, are divided into *m'shoma* or "name groups." These name groups do not regulate marriage or descent, and one does not acquire membership in the name group until one is given his or her name at a ceremony held a few days after birth. It is the name, in fact, that determines one's name group or "clan" as these groups are termed in English by the Shawnees. Each name group has an appropriate stock of names, and a speaker of Shawnee can usually determine a person's name group by hearing that person's Indian name. Members of a particular name group are taught to feel a bond of affinity for others of the same name group, and a stylized form of joking, based upon physical and mental attributes of the creatures after which the groups are named, is a characteristic feature of Shawnee group interaction. Thus a member of the Horse name group might be chided for "always kicking", and a Turtle for being too slow.

Most authorities today believe that the Shawnee name groups are a modern derivative of patrilineal clans or gentes that were formerly present among the Shawnees (E. W. Voegelin, in footnote to C. C. Trowbridge *Shawnese Traditions*: p. 16; C. Callender *Social Organization of the Central Algonkian Indians*: p. 108). The particular cultural factors which have led to a change from clans to name groups among the Shawnees are not known. Callender (*Social Organization of the Central Algonkian Indians*) discovered that the same process has taken place in other Central Algonkian tribes such as the Sauks, Prairie Potawatomis, and Kickapoos. He suggests that when a declining population and related factors threatened the ceremonial organization, ritual functions of the former clans were preserved by making them nonunilineal, though still corporate units (ibid.: p. 98).

The earliest mention of Shawnee clans or name groups is found in the account of the interrogation of a Shawnee chief who had been taken prisoner near Charles Town, South Carolina, in 1753. This man, a town chief, told the Governor "We are distributed by different names, the Cow, the Bear, the Buffaloe. There are also Wolf Shavanahs and other Names given us" (W. L. McDowell ed. *Documents Relating to Indian Affairs, May 21, 1750–August 7, 1758*: p. 427). The next account is that of Trowbridge, written in 1824, who says (*Shawnese Traditions*: pp. 16–17): "Anciently this nation was divided into 34 tribes, viz: 1. Snake tribe—Snake man, 2. Turtle tribe, 3. Raccoon tribe, 4. Turkey, 5. Hawk, 6. Deer, 7. Bear, 8. Wolf, 9. Panther, 10. Elk, 11. Buffalo, 12. Tree, 13. Corn man—(Corn Tribe), 14. Wind, 15. Night, 16. Cloud, 17. Moon, 18. Water, 19. House, 20. Fish, 21. Stone, 22. Dirt, 23. Big fire, 24.

Skunk or Polecat, 25. Squirrel, 26. Rabbit, 27. Fox, 28. Otter, 29.
Beaver, 30. Swan, 31. Eagle, 32. Bald Eagle tribe, 33. Pigeon Hawk
tribe, 34. Black Bird tribe. [Trowbridge gives phonetic renderings
of the Shawnee versions of each name, omitted here]"

He then goes on to say (*Shawnese Traditions*: p. 17): "At this
day there are but 12 tribes, which are those first above mentioned.
They do not pretend that this division was originally made for the
purpose of government, but say that the several tribes were
originally single families, the heads of which bore the name by
which their descendants were afterwards distinguished. *The
children are always considered as belonging to the tribe of their
father*, in which respect they differ from the Wyandots, whose
children are of the same tribe with the mother. [Italics my own,
and for "families or clans" read "divisions" and for "tribes" read
"clans"] Trowbridge's statement is most interesting, in that it
definitely establishes that at that time the Shawnees possessed
patri-clans. His mention of the tradition that these groups were
originally single families, who took their names from the original
family head is also of interest, and seems to indicate that they had
once been patrilineages. Trowbridge notes (*Shawnese Traditions*:
p. 17) that each of the Shawnee divisions had the same number of
patri-clans and that these had the same names in each division.

There is good evidence that by the time of Lewis H. Morgan's
fieldwork among the Shawnees (1859-60) these patri-clans had
already changed to their present name group form. Morgan
(*Ancient Society*: pp. 172-3) lists thirteen clans for the Shawnees:
(1) Wolf, (2) Loon, (3) Bear, (4) Buzzard, (5) Panther, (6) Owl, (7)
Turkey, (8) Deer, (9) Raccoon, (10) Turtle, (11) Snake, (12) Horse,
and (13) Rabbit. The same thirteen appear in his *Indian Journals*
(*The Indian Journals, 1859-62*: p. 45) except that "Hare," which is
clearly a misprint, replaces "Horse," and the spellings of the
native names for some of the groups differ in the two works. There
is also a notation after the Loon clan to the effect that it is lost.
Note that the first nine of the twelve clans that are listed as still
extant by Trowbridge are also given by Morgan, including the
Rabbit, though this was supposedly defunct in 1824. The only new
group listed by Morgan is the Horse, which is probably an
addition resulting from white acculturation.

Regarding the structure of the clans, Morgan notes (*Ancient
Society*: p. 173) that: "Descent, inheritance, and the rule with
respect to marrying out of the gens are the same as among the

Miamis [that is descent is traced in the male line, gens exogamy is practiced, and the "office of sachem together with property were hereditary in the gens"] (Ancient Society: p. 172). Although he indicates that Shawnee "gentes" [clans] were unilateral, exogamous descent groups, he notes some exceptions to the pattern. These exceptions in fact, together with other material to be noted presently, indicate that by 1860 the Shawnee patri-clans already had changed to name groups. The first exception noted was that a person's name, and hence his clan, might be changed if that person were sickly (*Indian Journals*: p. 45), another was that if a chief had no son to succeed him in office the eldest son of his eldest sister might take his place. "This may be modified [because this individual, by the law of exogamy, would be of a different clan from his mother's brother] by naming the son into the father's [the son's mother's brother's] tribe [clan]" (ibid.: p. 77).

In *Ancient Society*, then, Morgan describes the Shawnees as having exogamic patri-clans, but also indicates that under certain circumstances a person's name, and with it his clan, could be changed. Another passage is even clearer on this point (*Ancient Society*: p. 173-4): "The Shawnees had a practice, common also to the Miamis and Sauks and Foxes, of naming children into the gens of the father or of the mother or any other gens, under certain restrictions, which deserves a moment's notice . . . Among the Shawnees these names carried with them the rights of the gens to which they belonged, so that the name determined the gens of the person." This last seems to indicate that by 1860 name groups, as described for the Shawnees by the Voegelins in 1935, were already present, a fact that is confirmed by T. W. Alford's account of his own naming, which took place in 1860 (*Civilization*: pp. 3-4).

After Morgan, our next listing of Shawnee "clans" (name groups) is in Connelly's "The Shawnees" (in J. Spencer *The Shawnee Indians*: p. 387): (1) Rabbit, (2) Raccoon, (3) Panther, (4) Turtle, (5) Wolf, (6) Deer, (7) Turkey, (8) Snake, (9) Bear, (10) Wildcat, (11) Eagle, and (12) Owl. This list was supplied by David de Shane, an Eastern Shawnee. Unfortunately there are no details concerning the structure of the groups. Of these, the first nine appear on both Trowbridge's and Morgan's lists. Eagle appears as number 31 on the Trowbridge list and Owl as number six on Morgan's. Only the Wildcat group is unique.

The Voegelins, in their excellent treatment of the subject (C. F.

Voegelin and E. W. Voegelin "Shawnee Name Groups" 617) list only six groups: (1) Turkey, (2) Turtle, (3) Rounded Foot, (4) Horse, (5) Raccoon, and (6) Rabbit. They explain, however, that all but the last group includes more than one creature. Thus the Turkey group represents all forms of bird life, and is the same as Chicken, Eagle, Chicken-Hawk, or Fowl. "The old name for this group is said to have been Eagle" (ibid.: p. 622). The Turtle name group likewise embraces all forms of aquatic life; the Rounded Foot all carnivorous animals, such as Dog, Wolf, and Panther, the Horse all herbivorous animals, such as Horse, Deer, Buffalo, and Elk, and Raccoon all animals which can scratch, like the Raccoon and Bear. Only the Rabbit group "always stands alone" (ibid.: p. 622).

Callender, on the basis of a review of Trowbridge's, Morgan's, and the Voegelins' data, suggests that the six groups given by the Voegelins are in fact phratries composed of formerly distinct clans. Thus the evolution would be from patrilineage to patri-clan, patri-clan to name group, and name group to name-group phratry. He views the grouping of once distinct name groups into phratries as a response to loss of population, a response insuring sufficient individuals of the proper groupings to fill ritual offices (Callender, *Social Organization of the Central Algonkian Indians*: p. 102). The hypothesis is tempting but the earlier data is too scanty, in my opinion, to accept it as conclusive. We do not know, for example, if certain clans were considered ritual equivalents in Trowbridge's or Morgan's day. Further, not all present-day Shawnees agree with the Voegelins' idealized six-group scheme. Mary Spoon, for example, included both Dog and Wolf in one name group, and likewise admitted that the Chicken group, also called Bird, was perhaps the same as Turkey. To Mary, however, Bear was definitely a separate entity from Raccoon, and Deer distinct from Horse. Her list, then, would include eight name groups: (1) Wolf or Dog, (2) Bear, (3) Horse, (4) Rabbit, (5) Chicken or Bird, perhaps the same as Turkey, (6) Turtle, (7) Raccoon, and (8) Deer.

The acquisition of his own Shawnee name and name group in 1860 is described by Alford (*Civilization*: 3–4):

> When I was ten days old I was given a name, in accordance with the custom of our people, by an old friend of the family. Therefore I belonged to the same social clan or Um-so-ma as the person who named me. The name given me was Gay-nwah-piak-si-ka (one of long following or file, as the leader of a drove of wild horses) which soon was shortened to Gay-nwah, for the same reason that Thomas is shortened to Tom. No surname was used among the Shawnees.

Had I been a girl my parents would have waited two days longer before I should have received my name, which in all probability would have been the same (the last syllable left off to denote gender), if the same Um-so-ma had been desired to be represented in the name. A child always is classed in the same social clan with the person who names him, is considered under the same kind providence or care. This clan division is the occasion of strong partisanship and much pleasant rivalry among the Shawnees. It is simply a social division and should not be confused with the real clanship of the tribe [Alford refers to the five traditional divisions], which determines the chieftainship and in fact the very existence of the tribal organization . . .

Alford (*Civilization* p. 39 footnote 1) states that there are "six branches of Um-so-ma" (name groups).

The Voegelins, in their study, note that name-givers at the present time have difficulty in finding appropriate names for boys (Voegelin and Voegelin "Shawnee Name Groups": p. 618) a fact confirmed in 1971 by Mary Spoon. They made a survey of Shawnee personal names and found that 20 percent of them were Rounded Feet names, 18 percent Turkey, 15 percent Turtle, 13 percent Horse, 2 percent Raccoon, and only 1 percent Rabbit. They present an informant's account of a typical naming ceremony, from which the following essential features emerge: (ibid.: pp. 622–26): From one to nine days after a child is born, while the mother is still in seclusion, the father asks two old men or two old women to come to his house on the evening of the ninth day after the birth of the baby. These two must have no record of having a number of their offspring die. They may be relatives or merely family friends. Both may belong to the same name group. When both have arrived the father instructs them, asking that they give careful consideration to the name-group animals and their attributes and suggesting that in their sleep they strive to dream about a suitable name. The two name givers then retire and "offer prayer during the night to the Creator, who owns the people, the names, and everything." Each prays extempore and privately. When a name occurs, the name giver must determine to which group it belongs. For example, if the name refers to feathers, it belongs to Turkey, if to water, to the Turtle. Because the name chosen will affect the future welfare of the recipient the name-givers take their job very seriously. The name should not be a duplicate of any name that has ever been used before, either for a deceased or a living person, even though the Shawnees have no taboo concerning reference to the dead by a personal name. Duplications, in fact, do occur, but only rarely.

According to the Voegelins' informant, James Clark, the child is commonly named into the name group of the name-giver if the parents do not specially request another name group. The parents usually request that the child be named into one of the parent's name groups unless one or both parents are sickly. Usually no particular name group is specified (ibid.: p. 624).

On the morning of the tenth day the female relatives of the child rise before dawn to prepare the morning breakfast. The mother bathes the child in the seclusion hut where the child was born. Paternal and maternal relatives are assembled here. Now the name-givers, if they are women, give the baby a sponge bath in lukewarm water. If the namers are men, the mother bathes the child (ibid.: p. 624).

Next the mother sits down, holding the child. The two name-givers stand while the relatives sit or stand nearby. Each name-giver, in turn, makes a speech telling the name that he has selected and goes on to tell of the habits of animals of the eponymic name group. Each offers a name from a different name group, having consulted privately before the ceremony to assure this outcome. The parents of the child being named now choose the name that sounds best to them. If the two disagree the mother's vote is decisive "because she gave birth to the child (ibid.: 624). The father then thanks the name-giver saying "I am glad a Turkey (or other) name was found; maybe it will take good care of the child; perhaps the child will grow up to be a man, then an old man, a grandfather. We choose this name_____" (ibid.: p. 624). The mother then gives her child to the name-giver while the father hands the name-giver a short string of white, finely cut beads to use in the naming of the child. The name-giver holds the child while he addresses the Creator and the assembled group, announcing the reasons for selecting the name, and praying for long life. (ibid.: p. 625) The name-giver then returns the child to its mother but continues his speech: ". . . Some day perhaps this boy will be a grown man . . . Then he will have food set out for his relatives, whenever they come to visit, just as we set food out here now . . . At that time, this name will have carried him a long way; he'll be a young boy, then a young man, then an old man some day and they will call him grandfather. It will carry him that far, a long way. Everybody will call him _____ (mentioning the personal name)." As he pronounces the name, the name-giver holds the string of beads in his extended hands. "That's what everybody will call him_____(mentioning the name again); from this morning on they will call him_____; everybody all the time will call him_____."

After having repeated the personal name four times, the name-giver ties the white beads around the baby's neck. They are worn by the child until the string breaks, after which they may be picked up and saved for the child by the mother. Some of the relatives smile and address the child, saying: "You have a good name_____. Well, well, we're going to eat with_____this morning; it's good." The parents tell the name-giver that they thank him for giving their child a good name. The assembled group then breakfasts together. A taste of each of the different foods is offered to the child, the mother touching her fingertip to each variety of food and letting the baby lick her finger. After breakfast the relatives give the child small gifts and say, "I brought this for you, _____ (mentioning the name). I heard you had come; I'm glad that you came, and I bring this to you." (ibid.: p. 626).

A few days after the ceremony, the mother may present the name-giver with a gift such as a shirt for a male name-giver, or a length of dress goods for a woman, or even a horse; but such a gift is not obligatory. Among the Loyal Shawnees, but not among the Absentees, the child is obliged to give its name-giver a dinner once a year for four successive years. The Loyal Shawnees, and formerly the Eastern Shawnees, but never the Absentees, sometimes name groups of children after the spring or fall Bread Dance as a variant procedure to the individual naming. The naming ceremony is sometimes held at Peyote meetings among the Absentees. After "morning water" has been drunk at sunrise, the child is named before breakfast with the same procedure as naming at home. Illegitimate children are named in the same fashion as legitimate offspring except that the father of the child is absent (ibid.: p. 626).

Name changing follows the same procedure as the original naming, but in an abbreviated form, and it introduces one significant new concept: the original name, because it is regarded as having been unsuccessful, must be symbolically discarded before the new name is given. Generally a name is thought to have been unsuccessful when the individual bearing that name is sickly. Either the parents or a shaman decide that the name is at fault (ibid.: p. 626). Accounts of name-changing presented by the Voegelins show that names were deemed unsuccessful because the parents had been negligent in the original naming or because the original name for some reason did not "agree" with the individual bearing it (ibid.: p. 626). In either case the evidence that the name was unsuccessful would be the child's tendency toward illness and frail health. Still another reason for changing a name would be the discovery that the original name was already possessed by another Shawnee, for a person bearing the name of another living person is likely to die when his or her namesake dies. (ibid.: p. 626) In 1971 I attended a Delaware name-changing ceremony that was being held for a teenage girl whose name was changed because her mother had discovered that the girl's original name had already been given to another woman in the tribe. On the other hand, such a discovery did not always lead to a name change. Mary Spoon informed me that one of her daughters was accidentally given the same Indian name as another Shawnee girl. Both kept their names in this instance. It is said that several of the names borne by members of the Loyal band of Shawnees are also in use among the Absentees.

In most name-changing ceremonies only one name-giver is asked to bestow the new name. The Voegelins (ibid.: p. 627) mention a name-changing ceremony in which the child was taken to a river and totally immersed, the name-giver praying to "Grandfather water" to "wash off his name". Following this rite the name-giver, a woman in this instance, took the child from the river back to his parents' home, explaining what she had done and how she had prayed, and then she bestowed the new name.

As noted above, the individual is thought to share in some degree the characteristics of the animal or bird connected with his name group. According to Jennie Cegar, one of the Voegelins' informants, the Shawnees have known for ages past: "Rounded-Feet man is of a bad disposition; Horse man is less so, though he kicks like a horse; the best disposed people are the Turtle people. Rabbit is the most docile and fine people grow out of Rabbit; it never bites" (ibid.: p. 628).

Totemism in the strict sense is not practiced by the Shawnees in regard to their eponymous animal, and an individual is free to hunt his name group creature and eat it. Nevertheless a definite emotional bond exists between members of a name group and the name-group fauna because "the animals of your name group know that you have a name connecting you with them." (ibid.: p. 628) Thus members of a name group are thought to have the same strengths and weaknesses as their name-group creatures, and it is thought that these creatures may give members of the name groups supernatural help on occasion. At any informal gathering of Shawnees, if there are two or more members of one name group present and only one of another, that single person is liable to be teased unmercifully by the others. He may have a hard time of it unless he has a ready wit or someone of the same name group happens by to enter the fray.

Name-group affiliation also enters into the consideration of a man or woman's eligibility to fill roles in social, religious, and political activities. Here, as in the teasing of one name group by another, the characteristics of the name-group animal are extended to the person belonging to the unit named from that creature. Thus, because raccoons customarily hunt in and near bodies of water, it was formerly the custom, in time of drought, for a council of the Shawnees to select a man from the Raccoon name group to bring rain. This man was given Indian tobacco by the chief and told to go to a spring and offer it to the water as a prayer to the thunderbirds. Likewise, whenever a traveling group of Shawnees came to a large body of water, all Raccoon men in the party were made to stay behind, for if they did not stay in the rear the water might rise and drown the people (ibid.: p. 630).

Members of the Turtle name group also have a sympathetic connection with water. The keeper of the Kishpokotha division's sacred bundle must be either a Turtle or a Turkey man; Turtle is preferable. When rain is needed "the old man in charge of the bundle takes it out in the woods, opens it, and offers a prayer, calling for rain . . . This old man has to be a Turtle man. Turtle lives in the water and so do the Thunderbirds; that's why it rains quickly when he takes it out." (ibid.: p. 630)

Name-group affiliation enters into the spring and fall Bread Dances as well. At these, two men and two women from each of the six name groups are chosen to comprise the twelve male hunters and twelve female cooks. The "Queen Bee" or leader of the cooks at the spring Bread Dance must be either a Turtle or a Turkey, as must her male opposite, the leader of the hunters. The reason for this is that the spring Bread Dance is a prayer for the crops, and general fertility and the female role is emphasized. Because the turtle and turkey both lay eggs, they are felt to be peculiarly fertile (the same symbolism is involved in the white man's Easter eggs, at the same season of the year). The fall Bread Dance, which emphasizes the male role as hunter, has Horse or Rounded-Feet leaders, since horses (as mounts for the hunters in times past), deer, buffalo, and elk, and also carnivorous animals (Rounded-Feet) play conspicuous roles at this season. In the spring men-against-women football games, whose purpose like the spring Bread Dance is to bring rain and promote fertility, a Turtle or a Turkey man and woman take active parts.

The ceremonial Ride-in and War Dance of the Kishpokotha division takes place in mid-August. It involves the opening of a sacred bundle that is in the keeping of a Turtle name-group man. The night before the dance this man: ". . . brings the bundle over to the dance ground and leaves it in the thickets far off. Early the next morning he takes a Turtle, a Turkey, a Horse, and a Rounded-Feet man with him and goes down to open the bundle and puts bunches of feathers contained in the bundle on these four men." (ibid.: p. 630).

Each of the five divisions of the Shawnees has, or once had, a sacred bundle of this general type, that, when moved from one place to another, must be transported slowly and reverently. Thus, because the turtle is a slow animal, a man of the Turtle name group is best qualified to carry it. The Voegelins cite a historic exception to this rule, and for a particular reason (ibid.: p. 631): "When the Absentee Shawnee moved from Oklahoma to Kansas during the Civil War, they knew they were in danger of being followed and attacked by their pro-southern neighbors, the Creek; accordingly, the head chief of the Absentee chose two men from the Turkey group to take charge of the Thawikila division's bundle on the trip north, 'because a turkey is ready to fly quickly' (Jennie Cegar)"

If it becomes necessary to move the Kishpokotha bundle, three Turtle or Turkey men are put in charge, never members of any other name groups: "A Rounded-Feet man can't touch the bundle, unwrap it or have anything to do with it; something would happen; the people who belonged to that bundle would be destroyed. At a pinch a Turkey man can substitute for a Turtle man and handle the bundle, but no matter how good a man is, if he isn't in either of these two name groups he can't take care of the bundle." (ibid.: p. 631).

The Shawnees conceived the office of chief as a distinctly peaceful station. Therefore, traditionally, a chief should be from the Rabbit name group. A chief's child was often given a Rabbit name so that he might succeed his father in office. This was not a hard-and-fast rule, however, and the chiefs sometimes belonged to other name groups. Likewise the Rabbit name group was in no way regarded as a pool of potential chiefs (ibid.).

In the name-group joking certain name groups were paired, such as Turtle and Turkey, and Horse and Rounded-Feet. Certain others were traditionally opposed: "Horse and Rounded-Feet men versus Turtle and Turkey men can help one another in joking together. Coon and Rabbit just stand alone, but Coon and Turtle joke each other all the time because when coon was running along the river he found turtle's eggs and ate them; this didn't suit turtle very well. That's why Coon men and Turtle men joke so much together." (ibid.: p. 631).

When a Shawnee dies, the man or woman in charge of the funeral and the two men or women gravediggers and corpse-handlers must belong to different name groups from that of the deceased. (Voegelin and Voegelin "Shawnee Name Groups": p. 619; E. W. Voegelin "Mortuary Customs of the Shawnee and Other Eastern Tribes": p. 244).

It is said that formerly members of a particular name group preferred to tell animal stories that selected its own animals as the actors or heroes of the stories (Voegelin and Voegelin "Shawnee Name Groups": p. 629). Spencer (*The Shawnee Indians*: p. 396) goes so far as to imply that the cycle of wildcat and rabbit tales of the Shawnees was told only by members of the Rabbit name group. If so, this rule has not pertained for many years.

In summary, the present-day Shawnee name groups seem to be derived from the exogamous patrilineal clans described by Trowbridge in 1824. These name groups still retain many features that are commonly associated with clans in other tribes, particularly in the ceremonial sphere. They definitely lack other "clan" attributes. As the Voegelins note ("Shawnee Name Groups": pp. 631–2): "All informants agree that inheritance of property is in no wise determined by name group membership, that competitive games are never played between members of different name groups acting as units, that a traveler did not necessarily stop for shelter or hospitality at the home of one of the same name group, that the name groups had no officials, no sacred bundles, and never foregathered as units, that individuals never decorated their persons or their personal possessions with representations of name group animals as such." Further, the name groups do not practice true totemism: "Descent from the name group animals is not claimed. An individual is free to kill the animal or animals affiliated with his own or any other name group." (ibid.: p. 632) Most importantly, they are not exogamous, although one of the Voegelins' informants stated (ibid.: p. 632 footnote 9) that they had formerly been so, perhaps reflecting the early nineteenth century situation when the name groups were true clans. The same informant (loc. cit., footnote 8) states that the Shawnees claim descent from the name group animal.

In 1859 Lewis H. Morgan secured a Shawnee kinship nomenclature from Mrs. Graham Rogers, wife of the elected Head Chief of the Shawnees (*Indian Journals*: p. 77) Diagrammed out from Morgan's verbal notes the system appears in figure 3.

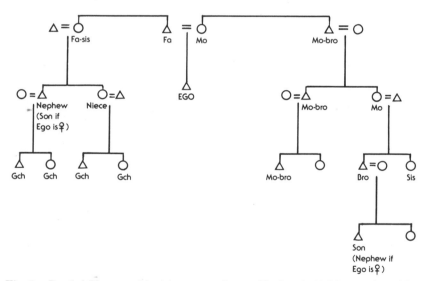

Fig. 3. Partial Shawnee kinship system. Secured by Lewis H. Morgan from Mrs. Graham Rogers, a Shawnee, in 1859.

Though incomplete, this system seems to be of the standard Omaha type. The present-day Shawnee system is of the Omaha type as well, as are the nomenclatures of the Kickapoos and Sauks, neighbors and close friends of the Shawnees for many years.

Goody (J. Goody "Cousin Terms") has demonstrated a strong correlation between cross-generation (Omaha and Crow) kinship nomenclatures and unilineal descent groups. White had com-

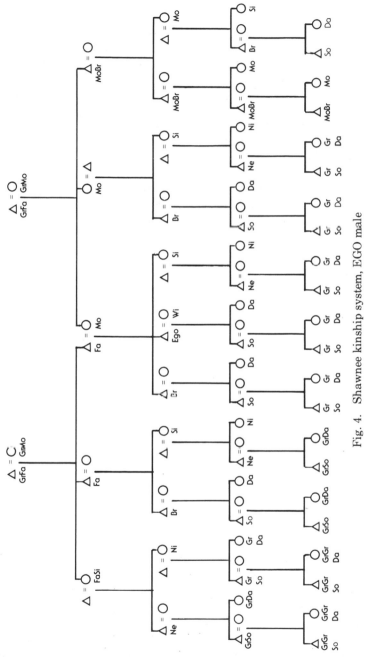

Fig. 4. Shawnee kinship system, EGO male

mented earlier upon this phenomenon in evolutionary terms (L. A. White "A Problem in Kinship Terminology": pp. 567–570): "As the clan system develops . . . and comes to exert its influence more and more upon the social life of the tribe, the Dakota-Iroquois terminology will be transformed into the Crow type in a matrilineal society and into the Omaha type in a patrilineal society."

The Omaha type kinship system, or nomenclature, I believe, came into use among the Shawnees at a time when they possessed strong, exogamous, patri-clans, that, as I have noted above, they retained until at least 1824. The "overriding of the generations" principle, that we see in EGO's addressing all of the members of his mother's clan as either mother or mother's brother indicates that clan affiliation looms more important than actual generation (Cf. White "A Problem in Kinship Terminology": pp. 566–573). The fact that descent was reckoned in the male line among the Shawnees, rather than the female, as among the Creeks, Cherokees, Choctaws, and other Southeastern groups, would indicate that hunting and male activities were more important economically, at least in the minds of the Shawnees, than gardening and other female economic pursuits. Thus the Shawnees, in spite of their designation as "Southerners" and extensive contacts with matrilineal, Crow-nomenclature, Southeastern horticulturalists, stand closer in terms of their kinship system to the Central Algonkian Sauks, Foxes, and Kickapoos. This finding is consonant with other aspects of Shawnee culture, such as their burial complex, which also shows very little Southeastern influence (E. W. Voegelin "Mortuary Customs of the Shawnee": pp. 334–5).

The persistence of the Omaha type of kinship nomenclature among the Shawnees long after they have lost the patri-clans that fostered this nomenclature poses another problem. Presumably we have here an example of cultural lag, which is the best suggestion I can offer at the moment. There are many factors which determine the social structure and kinship terminology of any particular group, and our knowledge of the complex interaction of these factors and their differential resistance to cultural change is as yet quite limited.

Morgan (*Indian Journals*: p. 77) indicates the former practice of the avunculate by the Shawnees in commenting that a Shawnee boy's most important relative was his mother's brother "more so than Ego's father". The avunculate, a special close relationship between a boy and his mother's brother, is often found in societies that possess strong patri-clans and employ an Omaha type of kinship nomenclature. The sororate, a custom that is also associated with clans, was also practiced by the Shawnees. Trowbridge (*Shawnese Traditions*: p. 31) writes: "It is thought to be the bounden duty of the husband to marry the sister or some other near relative of his wife after her death, and tho' they sometimes act contrary to this rule, they incur in such cases the displeasure of the surviving friends of the wife." The "other near relative" would of course be one of her parallel cousins and thus a member of the same patri-clan as the deceased. By marrying his deceased wife's sister or parallel cousin (both termed "sister" in the Shawnee nomenclature), Ego would preserve the bond between his patri-clan and that of his former wife. If he did not, this bond would be severed, hence the "displeasure of the surviving friends (clan members) of the wife" noted by Trowbridge.

Kinship terms were commonly used as terms of address, and Morgan comments (*Indian Journals*: p. 78) that two Shawnees never speak each other's names on meeting, using kin terms instead. Trowbridge however (*Shawnese Traditions*: p. 28) states that: "Brothers & Sisters call each other by those appellations and so they address their parents; but friends & more distant relatives address each other by their proper names." My own experience with contemporary Shawnees indicates no hard-and-fast rule in the matter. Some of my Shawnee friends are fond of addressing all relatives with kin terms, and even extend these to Shawnees to whom they are not related, members of other tribes, and even whites. Others invariably use first names even for members of their own family.

Morgan (*Indian Journals*: p. 78) mentions that two Shawnees commonly shook hands upon meeting in his day (1859) and that he believed it was "the old usage". My informants also regard hand-shaking as an old Indian custom.

Ordinal names (that is, special names indicating the order of birth in a family such as first born son, second born son) were not used by the Shawnees, who simply referred to "older and younger brother" (Morgan *Indian Journals*: p. 46).

At the present time the two sexes, among the Shawnees, stand equal to an amazing degree, and this appears to be a long-standing phenomenon. Perhaps only the matriarchal Iroquois, among all the peoples of North America, accord women so high a position in their social and religious systems. Thus E. W. Voegelin (E. W. Voegelin, C. Rafinesque, C. F. Voegelin, and E. Lilly *Walum Olum*: p. 20) comments that the Delawares: "*. . . like the Shawnee and other Central Algonquian groups*, accord women equal consideration with men in almost all matters, and maintain a balance of functions for both sexes in religious ceremonies as well as in daily life." (Italics my own) Today's Shawnees have no need for "women's lib", for the equal and complementary roles of the two sexes is incorporated unconsciously but thoroughly into the fabric of their daily life, and formally and explicitly into the tribe's ceremonialism. No Shawnee, male or female, would be shocked, as many non-Shawnee televiewers were, when singer Helen Reddy referred to God as "She", for their Creator has always been female! What they might find strange would be to learn that in certain societies women are regarded as the "property" of men, either guarded in harems or relegated to the society pages of newspapers because their public activities are regarded as frivolous and inconsequential.

Some inequality of the sexes did exist in Trowbridge's day. Polygyny, for example, was permissible, though not very common. Since Trowbridge notes that "anciently it was customary to have but one wife at a time . . ." it may be that the excessive warfare of the late eighteenth and early nineteenth centuries had produced a sexual imbalance, temporarily fostering this custom (Trowbridge *Shawnese Traditions*: p. 31).

A bit further on in the same source we read (*Shawnese Traditions*: p. 32): "It is not uncommon for a man to have for wives at the same time the mother & her daughter, but these are cases only where a young man marries a widow, who advances in age during the youth of the daughter, and then, finding herself in danger of being abandoned by her husband, she proposes to him a connection with her daughter, & thus the connection is preserved."

Polyandry, though known, was apparently rare (ibid.: p. 32): "It is not customary for one woman to have two husbands at the same time, nor has there been more than one instance of the kind within the narrator's recollection. This was the case of two brothers, who lived with one woman for some years, but the union was rather the result of chance, and their connection alternate."

As among the whites of that time, a double standard obtained in regard to adultery (ibid.: pp. 31–32), it was considered very criminal when committed by a woman, but was passed off with a shrug when the man was at fault. The Shawnee husband generally discarded his wife upon the first proof of her infidelity, and "nothing but repeated promises of better conduct can prevent him from proclaiming her to the world as a prostitute. Sometimes these promises and apparent abstinence from a gratification of her sinful desires for a long period of time, result at last in her return to the enjoyment of the affection of her husband" (ibid.).

Trowbridge also learned that a Shawnee husband could divorce his wife if she neglected her appearance or shirked her work in house and garden (ibid.: p. 32). "In some cases however, wives are so fortunate as to make interest with the female relatives of their husbands, who often prevent their entire dismissal, when the husband forms a new attachment. This is one of the reasons for a plurality of wives." (ibid.: p. 32) The Shawnee wife had the same right to divorce as her husband "But she seldom exercises it unless her husband be an indolent drunken fellow, whose habits were such as to throw all the labour of supporting the family upon herself." (ibid.: p. 32) In the event of a separation the immediate care of the children devolved upon the mother, but the father considered himself obligated to provide them with clothing from time to time. Sometimes, when the father did not have sufficient confidence in his ex-wife to entrust the children to her care, he provided for their maintenance in some family to which he was related. (ibid.: p. 32)

There was a customary division of labor by sex in Shawnee society, but it was, and still is to a great extent, merely one of custom and convenience. Thus, most of the older Shawnee women whom I interviewed had, in the course of their lives, hunted, fished, split firewood, roped and saddled draught and riding horses, and done most of the other heavy outdoor tasks of the ranch or farm. Most of the older men, likewise, had prepared meals, tended small children, cut and sewed their own garments, and done beadwork. In neither case was such activity regarded as demeaning or unusual.

Trowbridge describes the late eighteenth century pattern as follows (ibid.: pp. 33–34): "Until some thirty or forty years ago, it was the duty of the women, to perform all the labour properly belonging to the other sex among the whites. They planted & hoed the corn, gathered & dried it, dressed the meat, carried the game, constructed lodges, removed the encampments & replaced them when necessary, and in short, took from the husband every care attendant upon their situation, while he employed himself in the chase, or in the enjoyment of the society of his friends. But now a days, the husband assists his wife in all things necessary to their comfortable existence, with the exception of carrying wood for fires, which is considered the particular duty of women." Trowbridge's principal informants were Tenskwatawa (the Shawnee prophet) and Black Hoof. His information presumably refers mainly to the Ohio Shawnees, who were ancestors of the present Eastern and Loyal Shawnee bands. These Shawnees adopted white patterns (particularly in terms of men involving themselves in agricultural work) much earlier than the Absentee Shawnees. Alford, describing his mother's activities in the 1860s, describes the same pattern that had been abandoned by the Ohio Shawnees sixty or seventy years earlier (*Civilization*: p. 5):

> My mother was typical of the Indian women of that time: strong, vigorous, and self-reliant. Her patience and fortitude were unfailing, her courage undaunted and contagious. I believe too that she was intelligent, far beyond the average woman of her time. She took upon herself the burden of providing for her family, not only doing those housewifely tasks expected of the women of today, such as the preparation of food, the making of clothing for her children, and the general care of the home and family, but much more. In those days the Indian women planted and cultivated all crops. She plowed or dug the ground, planted the corn or other seed, cultivated it, then harvested it. She ground the corn into flour or meal with which she made bread for her family; she dressed the game that her husband brought home and tanned the hide—if it was fit to be used—and she cured the meat.
> My mother did all these things during those early years of my recollection, but I can remember that father gradually took upon himself more and more of this labor, as the family increased, and he no doubt saw the injustice of leaving so much of the hardest work for a woman to do.

A final word on the relations of the two sexes is provided by Trowbridge (*Shawnese Traditions*: p. 34): "It is quite common for the husband to strike his wife for slight causes, particularly if she be possessed of an ungovernable temper. And frequently the wife retaliates, by pulling his hair, or his testicles, the latter of which they most generally resort to." One of my female informants, E. D., recalled Shawnee women "twisting the balls" of their husbands in domestic arguments, a powerful technique for keeping male-chauvinist bullies in line!

Aside from the specializations engendered by considerations of age and sex, there were only two classes of individuals in traditional Shawnee society who could be termed occupational specialists in the sense of having rights and duties different from other men and women. These two were the chiefs and the priest-shamans. Even members of these two classes, when they were not busy exercising their chiefly or shamanistic prerogatives, had to support themselves and their families in the way that other men and women did. They were expected, moreover, to comport themselves differently from other persons. The behavior of a chief is described (E. W. Voegelin, C. Rafinesque, C. F. Voegelin, and E. Lilly *Walum Olum*: p. 202): "A chief, particularly, is always supposed to greet everyone. The modern Delaware, *like the Shawnee*, have a specific code of politeness as regards greetings, which includes formal handshaking." (Italics my own) My informant Mary Spoon expanded upon this: "A chief is supposed to conduct himself in such a way as to reflect honor upon his position. He should greet all visitors in a friendly way, shaking hands with them as soon as he notices their presence. He must never show impatience or anger when people don't show up promptly for their duties at the ceremonial ground but must always be smiling and patient. A chief shakes hands with visitors. This is an Indian custom known before the white man came."

At present-day Bread Dances and other ceremonies the chief is always alert to welcome visitors. Any strange automobile that drives into the camp surrounding the ceremonial ground will be approached by the chief within five or ten minutes, and its occupants will be greeted and welcomed (although they may be sometimes warned that picture taking or recording is prohibited). This greeting is generally followed by an invitation to supper. Although the chief and his family bear the principal burden of feeding visitors and usually proffer the first meal, other families in the camp are quick to extend their own invitations to subsequent meals, thus relieving the chief of the entire burden.

The behavior of the priest-shaman is ideally much the same as that of a chief. His comportment should be calm and dignified at all times. A common theme in accounts of a priest-shaman passing on his sacred bundle and/or supernatural power and lore to his son is the "worthiness" (or behavior) of this or that child. Commonly the eldest son was passed over if he did not demonstrate, even as a child, the stable, agreeable temperament that is considered to be a requisite for the role of a bundle keeper or curer.

7

Government, War, and Peace

When first contacted by Europeans, each of the five divisions of
the Shawnee tribe was governed by hereditary chiefs. This
pattern was undoubtedly of prehistoric origin and continued
through the eighteenth century and well into the nineteenth,
when it was gradually abandoned. Morgan, writing in 1859 notes:
"John Francis was the last hereditary chief of the [Ohio]
Shawnee. After his death the office became elective" (L. H.
Morgan *The Indian Journals, 1859-62*: p. 46 footnote 72). The
Absentee Shawnees, always more conservative, retained their
hereditary chiefs much longer. White Turkey, chief of the
Thawikila division of the Absentees, died in 1899 and was the last
hereditary chief of that group (T. W. Alford *Civilization*: p. 174).
Big Jim, chief of the allied Kishpokotha and Pekowitha divisions,
died in 1900. He was the last universally recognized hereditary
chief of those divisions. Even before the deaths of these men the
authority of the traditional chiefs had been so eroded that Alford
writes (*Civilization*: p. 174): "My friend John King was next in line
for chief [after White Turkey], but as the government no longer
recognized tribal laws, chieftainship was an empty honor and
John King would not accept it. He was a member of the Business
Committee and as such had some real authority." In addition to
the principal chief there was also a "second chief" for each
division (Alford *Civilization*: p. 51). This man apparently
functioned as a sort of vice president, governing in the absence of
the principal chief.

Today in all three Shawnee bands, the office of chief is largely honorific and ceremonial in nature. The chief has certain ritual functions but no authority. His position might be compared to that of the English monarch: he commands some respect, has a certain amount of influence, but functions mainly as a living symbol of the traditional Shawnee way of life. The actual business of the three federally recognized Shawnee bands is conducted by elected tribal councils headed by a business committee. The council meets annually; the business committee meets quarterly (M. H. Wright *A Guide to the Indian Tribes of Oklahoma*: p. 245).

The workings of the former system are described by Trowbridge (*Shawnese Traditions*: p. 11). He speaks of the chiefs as hereditary. When a chief died, if his son was of good character and was respected by the tribe, the surviving chiefs and principal men assembled and by their unanimous vote appointed him as the legal successor of his father. Hunters were sent out for game and a feast was prepared "for the whole nation, tribe, or village, as the case may be," where the adoption of the new chief was generally declared by the old men. If there were several sons the chief was chosen from them by those old men of the council without respect to the relative ages of the aspirants for the office. If there were no sons the chieftainship went to the most fit person, who would not necessarily be a relative of the deceased. "To the decisions of the chiefs & principal men in such cases, the nation at large cheerfully submit, and as the general interest & their own popularity are equally connected they seldom fail to choose aright." (ibid.: p. 11) He notes (ibid.: p. 13) that chiefs were seldom appointed before the age of thirty, and that although the sons of chiefs, as heirs apparent to the chieftainship, were treated with more respect than the common people, they had no authority until their appointment in regular council.

It is not clear from Trowbridge's account whether his informants were speaking of the Shawnee tribe as a whole when they spoke of the "whole nation" or merely the totality of each of the five divisions. In view of the fact that the Shawnees have been fragmented throughout their recorded history, it would seem that no chief ever spoke for more than a part of the entire tribe. Yet Alford (*Civilization*: pp. 44–45) clearly implies a *tribal* as well as individual chiefs when he writes:

> Originally there were five clans [divisions] composing the Shawnee tribe, including the two principal clans, Tha-we-gi-la and Cha-lah-kaw-tha, from one

of which came *the national or principal chief*. The remaining three Pec-u-we, the Kis-pu-go, and the May-ku-jay, each had its own chief *who was subordinate to the principal chief in national matters*, but independent in matters pertaining to the duties of his clan. Each clan [division] had a certain duty to perform for the whole tribe. For instance the Pec-u-we clan, or its chief, had charge of the maintenance of order and looked after the celebration of things pertaining to religion or faith; the Kis-pu-go clan had charge of matters pertaining to war and the preparation and training of warriors; the May-ku-jay clan had charge of things relating to health and medicine and food for the whole tribe. But the two powerful clans, the Tha-we-gi-la and the Cha-lah-kaw-tha, had charge of political affairs and all matters that affected the tribe as a whole. Indeed, the tribal government may be likened to the government of the United States, in which each state (clan), with its governor (chief), is sovereign in local matters, but subordinate to the president of the United States (principal chief) in national matters. [Italics my own]

Alford's statements are difficult to reconcile with reality. How, for example, could the Pekowitha division maintain order in other divisions living hundreds of miles distant? Or how could the Kishpokotha train the warriors or declare war on behalf of other Shawnee groups separated from it by such a distance? At best, Alford's scheme must be viewed as an ideal pattern, an ideal that was never approximated during the recorded history of the Shawnees. Instead, each of the five divisions or even segments of divisions (individual villages) seems to have operated as an autonomous political, religious, and military unit most of the time. Sometimes it joined forces with one or two other divisions of the Shawnees; fragments thereof; or even with other tribes, such as the Delawares or Mingo Iroquois.

Like most of their Algonkian neighbors, the Shawnees had both "peace" chiefs (village chiefs) and war chiefs. Trowbridge (*Shawnese Traditions*: pp. 11–12) states that the office of war chief was considered more important and honorable than the village chief and was given as a reward for great talents, exertion, and bravery. To become accepted as a war chief a man must have led at least four war parties into enemy territory and each time have taken at least one scalp. At the same time he must have brought back all of his followers unhurt to their villages. If he accomplished all this he could demand his appointment as a right, and a feast was accordingly prepared where the news of his acceptance was promulgated by the other chiefs and old men.

I believe that Trowbridge errs in placing the war chiefs above the peace chiefs in general consideration. If Trowbridge was told this by the Shawnee prophet it can probably be explained as a function of the almost chronic warfare of that period. The fact that the Prophet was the brother of Tecumseh, a great war chief, is probably also germane. In fact Trowbridge contradicts his earlier statement in the following paragraph (ibid.: p. 12): "In matters relating to the cession of lands or to the international affairs the war chiefs always render their assistance, *but in the councils they never precede the village chiefs either in their speeches or propositions for the adoption of any measure*" [Italics my own].

As one might expect from their generally high social status, the women of the Shawnees had a strong voice in tribal government. Trowbridge mentions "female chiefs" who seem to correspond to the "chief matrons" among the Iroquois (ibid.: pp. 12-23). As was the case with the men there were female war chiefs and female peace chiefs. Both groups were always mothers, sisters, or other close relatives of the male chiefs. Their duties were not numerous nor arduous. The principal job of the female peace chief or "peace woman" was: "by her entreaties & remonstrances to prevent the unnecessary effusion of blood," and if one of the male war chiefs were bent upon some war expedition not countenanced by the tribe, the council chiefs would ask the "peace woman" for her assistance. This woman would then go to the war chief in question "and setting before him the care and anxiety & pain which the women experience in their birth & education she appeals to his better feelings and implores him to spare the innocent & unoffending against whom his hand is raised. She seldom fails to dissuade him, and in consequence of her general influence & success in such cases, is made *dernier resort* by the village chiefs."

In addition to this duty the female peace chiefs had general charge of the female affairs of the village. They ordered and directed the planting of crops and the scheduling and cooking of feasts. In the latter duty they were joined by the female war chiefs, each group cooking at a separate fire. The female peace chiefs cooked the white corn and smaller vegetables and the female war chiefs the meats and coarser articles of food (ibid.: p. 13).

Beneath the chiefs in rank were the councilors. Trowbridge (ibid.: p. 13) delineates their functions: "There is no particular body of Counsellors or wise men, like the Lupwaaēēnoawuk of the Delawares. But in important councils, the aged men of the nation are invited. They sit behind the Chiefs and when necessary they explain the proceedings at any previous council referred to, and generally afford their advice & assistance in the proceedings; but these old men have no authority whatever, nor any influences, other than is common to their age & experience in the national affairs."

Alford writes of the councilors in much the same vein (*Civilization*: pp. 45–46): "Besides the chiefs of the clans, there was a group of men in the tribe who made up the Council, which was composed of members of all the clans. The men on the Council were intelligent and staunch, fully able to advise about the affairs that affected the tribe. They took upon themselves much of the responsibility of governing it. My father was a member of the Council, and his associates were men of intelligence and wisdom." Alford (ibid.: p. 45) also notes that each Shawnee chief appointed certain men, probably from the ranks of the council, as his subordinates "to distribute the work of his clan division." Such appointments were made for life but a man might be removed for bad conduct.

Both Harvey (H. Harvey *History of the Shawnee Indians from the Year 1681 to 1854 Inclusive*: p. 148) and Alford (*Civilization*: p. 45) indicate a high level of morality among the Shawnees. A Shawnee, when hunting, could leave a deer, wild turkey, or other game that he had killed hanging in a tree with a piece of clothing or other sign of ownership, and it was never molested. "So it was with a bee tree, which was considered one of the richest treasures a hunter could find. Any mark of ownership would hold such a find until the owner or finder could come to take the honey or to carry home his game." Alford goes on to relate the amusing story of a Shawnee named Billy Axe, one of the first in the Pekowitha division to learn to read and write in English. When Billy found a bee tree he took a card from his pocket and on it wrote in English "This is my bee tree" and signed his name. When he returned to take the highly prized delicacy he found the tree cut and his honey gone. Since no Indian could have read the card, he knew that a white man had taken it (Alford *Civilization*: p. 46).

Friendly counsel, followed by warnings, group pressure, and then physical punishment were the usual steps taken by the chiefs to secure conformity to the rules of good behavior. Alford cites a case in which a group of young men had formed the habit of riding off to the trading post and getting drunk, wasting their families' resources in the process. A council was held in which the young men were warned of the danger to their health, character, and the general peace by the chief of their division. This proved ineffective, so next a "council of all the chiefs was called by the principal chief, and they were instructed to talk to the young men." This too, was to no avail. Finally a general council (apparently including all of the Absentee Shawnees) was held. At this council the principal chief addressed the wrongdoers himself. After warning the young men he turned to the assembly of people and commanded them, each and every one, to take the matter into his own hands. Anyone who saw any of the young men in an intoxicated condition was ordered to *shoot him down as though he were an enemy*. This final, drastic order proved effective and the young men finally desisted (ibid.: pp. 47-8).

Although the Shawnees maintained no jails or law officers, the chiefs served as magistrates and appointed committees of adult men to punish persistent lawbreakers when the need arose. The punishment was always fitted to the offense, and punishments ranged from flogging to banishment from the tribe or death (ibid.: p. 49). The chiefs generally concerned themselves only with offenses of a criminal nature. Trowbridge writes that there was no mode of compelling the payment of a debt but the creditor was authorized, by custom, to take any property of the debtor whose value corresponded with the amount of the debt. The creditor did not receive either assistance or encouragement in retaking his property in such cases (Trowbridge *Shawnese Traditions*: p. 13).

Women of the tribe were punished equally with the men. Slander was the most heinous crime of which a woman could be convicted. Alford (*Civilization*: p. 49) tells of a woman named Betsy Squirrel who loved to tell defamatory stories about others, especially women. She was warned to desist, but continued in her malicious gossip. Finally the chief sent a committee of three men to thrash her with switches. Her husband, who objected to having his wife whipped, was restrained by two of the men until his wife's punishment was completed, after which he too was flogged.

An adulterous woman was punished by whipping, and the blows were inflicted "on the offending part of her body". After her punishment she was driven away by her husband. Incest was considered highly criminal, but there was no prescribed punishment for the offense. The tribe generally held the parties to an incestuous union in great contempt, and they were considered incapable of forming regular matrimonial connections afterwards. Rape was also lacking in a prescribed punishment, although it was considered a criminal act. The relatives of the woman, however, did not attempt to punish the offender "generally attributing the offence to his passions which have mastered his better judgement." (Trowbridge *Shawnese Traditions*: p. 15)

In case of theft, the chiefs reprimanded the offender severely each of the first three times that he was apprehended. If he stole a fourth time he was brought before the council at the command of the chiefs, condemned, then tied to a post and whipped with a hickory switch. For each succeeding offense after the fourth the flogging was repeated. If this treatment failed to correct the thief's behavior, the chiefs would abandon the thief to the mercy of those from whom he had stolen. One of these victims generally ambushed and shot the man. A death under these circumstances was not considered to be murder and was not avenged by the relatives of the victim (Trowbridge *Shawnese Traditions*: p. 15).

In the case of murder lacking in such extenuating circumstances the social position and popularity of the killer often affected his ultimate fate. If the murderer were a man of power and respectability in the tribe, the chiefs assembled immediately and attempted to procure wergild to pay for the life of the dead man. The customary payment was sixty fathoms (120 yards) of wampum, an amount that was almost impossible to collect in a short time. While trying to round up the wergild the chiefs visited the relatives of the slain man and informed them of their intention. Sometimes the relatives refused to accept wergild and in this case the murderer was warned to be on his guard. If the murderer were an unpopular man or had little influence, the chiefs would simply not intervene, and in fact might secure and deliver the murderer to the angry relatives. One of the relatives would then execute the murderer and the score was considered even. If, however, the death were avenged by a person unrelated to the murdered person, then the avenger would be subject to the same punishment himself. In the event that the relatives of the murdered man elected to accept wergild the murderer accompanied the chiefs when the wampum was delivered and stood in the presence of the mourning relatives during the entire proceedings of the council. If a woman were murdered it was considered a far greater crime than if a man were slain. In this case 150 fathoms (300 yards) of wampum was the required wergild. If a woman killed a man, she was never executed for the crime. Instead the matter was always settled by the payment of 120 yards of wampum to the relatives of the deceased (ibid.: pp. 13-4).

In respect to external relations the Shawnees, as their tangled history would suggest, have had formal and informal alliances with many groups. They have likewise battled with many tribes from Canada to Florida and from New Jersey to California. The following list of names used by the Shawnees in reference to other tribes, abstracted from C. F. Voegelin's *Shawnee Stems* (Shawnee Stems and the Jacob P. Dunn Miami Dictionary, Parts I-IV) indicates the vast geographical range of this remarkable tribe: Apaches, *Taashi*; Arapahos, *Laapaho*; Catawbas, *Kataapalenawe*; Cherokees, *Kato?hwa*; Cheyennes, *Shaayeeni*; Chickasaws, *Chikasha, Chiikashee, Achikasha*; Choctaws, *Cha?ta, Cha?tee*; Comanches, *Paato?ka, Kameechi*; Creeks, *Mashkwa, Mashkwakoki, Homashka, Homashkooki*; Delawares, *Lenaape, Wapanakia*; Foxes, *Mskwa?ki, Hothaaki* (the latter is probably an error, as it is the same as Sauks; Iowas, *Haayaw?howe*; Kansas, *Kaatha, Kaatheo*; Kaskaskias, *Kakkakkia* ("Katydid"), *Ka?kashki*; Kickapoos, *Kiikapo*; Kiowas, *Kaayowe*; Mahicans, *N?hikana*; Miamis, *Loowaani, Miamia*; Mohawks, *Ka?nawaakiki* (also said to refer to an old band of Delawares now absorbed into other Delaware bands); Munsees, *Homen?thi*; Ojibwas, *Achipwia, Hochipwe*; Ottawas, *Hotaawa*; Osages, *Hoshaashi*; Otos, *Matao?kala*; Peorias, *Peewaale*; Quapaws, *Hoka?pa*; Sauks, *Hothaaki*; Seminoles, *Shimanooli*; Senecas, *Naatowe*; Sioux (Dakotas), *Shaha*; Wichitas, *Wiichitaa*; and Wyandots, *Naatowe* (the same name that is used for the Senecas). In addition Voegelin gives the Shawnee word for "Indian" as *Lenawe* or *Hilenawe*, and the one for white man as *Teko?shiya*.

Often the alliances and traditional friendships of the Shawnees were expressed in kinship terms, as if each tribal group were an individual member of a large family. Thus Trowbridge writes (*Shawnese Traditions*: p. 55): "They call the Delawares Grandfather, Wyandots Elder brother, Senecas (the Six Nations) Elder brothers, Munsees Cousins, and other tribes younger brothers." Elsewhere in the same work, however, we read (ibid.: p. 9): "They term the Wyandots their elder brothers, the Delawares their grandfathers, the Miamis their younger brothers, the Ottawas younger brothers, Chippeways their *youngest* brothers, Pottawatomies youngest brothers, Kickapoos first brothers, Foxes second brother, Sacs younger brother & those more distant are known by the general appellation of brothers. The Six Nations of New York are called their cousins." Morgan (*The Indian Journals*: p. 51) confirms part of the above, stating that his informant Buraseau told him that the Ojibwas, Potawatomis, and Ottawas once formed an alliance with the Shawnees and after this the three tribes called the Shawnees "uncles". E. W. Voegelin (E. W. Voegelin, C. Rafinesque, C. F. Voegelin, and E. Lilly *Walum Olum*: p. 194) also notes that the Delawares referred to the Shawnees as "grandchildren" and were called, in turn "grandfather" by them, a fact confirmed by my informant Mary Spoon.

Alford comments at the beginning of the Civil War that the Absentee Shawnees had a close association with the Creeks of Tallahassee town, The Delawares, the Piankeshaws, and the Kickapoos (*Civilization*: p. 6) and Speck, writing of the Yuchis (F. G. Speck *Ethnology of the Yuchi Indians*: p. 11) notes: "A strong feeling of friendship is . . . manifested toward the Shawnee, which probably is a sentiment surviving from early affiliation with the southern branch of this people on the Savannah river." Witthoft and Hunter (J. Witthoft and W. A. Hunter "The Seventeenth Century Origin of the Shawnee": p. 52) also cite a close relationship between the Absentee Shawnees, particularly the Kishpokotha division, and the Creeks of Tuckabatchee town. This involved an arrangement whereby the Shawnees were to receive the sacred paraphernalia of the Creek Green Corn, including several sacred brass plates, at whatever time the people of Tuckabatchee neglected the rites.

At the present time, in their Oklahoma locale, the closest relationships of the Eastern and Loyal bands of Shawnees are with the Oklahoma Seneca-Cayugas, Oklahoma Delawares, and Quapaws. Those of the Absentee Shawnees are with the neighboring Kickapoos, Seminoles, Yuchis, Creeks, and Caddo-Delawares, and to a lesser degree with the Sauks. These observations are based upon the attendance of Shawnees in large numbers, and on a regular basis at the ceremonies of these tribes and vice-versa, as well as on genealogical information provided by my informants. In all three Shawnee bands the greatest amount of intermarriage, through the years, has been with the Delawares.

While still in the East the Shawnees warred, at different times, with the Catawbas, Choctaws, Chickasaws, Ojibwas, Ottawas, Potawatomis, Miamis, Cherokees, and the six tribes of the Iroquois Confederacy (Trowbridge *Shawnese Traditions*: p. 9). In the nineteenth century, after moving west, the Shawnees encountered and sometimes battled with Plains tribes. They were involved in the famous encounter with the Tonkawas in 1865, in which the latter tribe was almost exterminated (W. La Barre *The Peyote Cult*: p. 109). At this same period in their history small parties of Shawnee and Delaware "mountain men" traveled widely over the western Plains and even as far as California. On these hunting and trapping expeditions they often encountered and defended themselves against groups of western Indians. Gregg (J. Gregg *Commerce of the Prairies*, I: p. 302) describes a typical incident which occurred in 1837: "A small party of 5 or 6 Shawnees fell in with a large band of Yutas (Utes) near the eastern borders of the Rockies, south of the Arkansas. The Ute received them in a friendly manner but later tried to rob them. The Shawnee, to their surprise, defended their goods and killed several Utes, including a favorite chief. The Shawnee made their escape unhurt."

During the American Civil War many Shawnee men enlisted in the Union army, some as members of a mixed Delaware-Shawnee company (A. H. Abel *The American Indian as Participant in the Civil War*: p. 113) and others in Company M, 15th Kansas cavalry (Alford *Civilization*: p. 12). In the twentieth century Shawnees have served with honor in both world wars, the Korean conflict, and in Viet Nam. These modern warriors are still honored in the traditional manner by being selected for prominent roles in the War Dance that is held each August by the Absentee band at the Little River ceremonial ground. One frequently sees military insignia, such as campaign ribbons and shoulder patches, incorporated into the traditional Shawnee man's costume worn in this ceremony and in the Bread Dance.

In the eighteenth century and the early part of the nineteenth the Shawnees were renowned as warriors, feared by both Indian and white foes. Trowbridge (*Shawnese Traditions*: pp. 17–23) provides the best account of how the Shawnees conducted their military operations during this period, and I have paraphrased his remarks below. Many of these traditional features are still preserved in the procedures followed at the annual War Dance of the Absentees.

The decision to declare war on another tribe was determined in general council by the peace chiefs and war chiefs. Apparently war could not be declared unless the peace chiefs consented (ibid.: p. 17). Once the sentiment for war had been expressed by the peace chiefs, the principal war chief, who was a member of the Panther clan, rose and declared the necessity for going to war. Usually the reasons for declaring war were "individual murders, which have been so often repeated on both sides as to embroil the whole of the tribe [clan] & at length the nation en masse" (ibid.: p. 23). The principal war chief then called upon all of his own clan to join him in "raising the tomahawk." This was a signal for the tribe, or whatever part of it was there assembled, to go from a peacetime to a wartime footing, and from that time on the peace chiefs surrendered their control of the tribal government to the war chiefs, who immediately began the mobilization.

Friendly tribes were invited to join the proposed expedition by the sending of a tomahawk painted with red clay through the different villages. All of the warriors disposed to join the Shawnee war party assembled their weapons and set out for the village of the principal war chief of the Shawnees, where a grand council of war was held. Before war was declared, the peace chiefs may have demanded redress for the injuries inflicted upon the Shawnees by the opposite party. Once war had been declared, however, there were no further negotiations with the enemy, because the element of surprise was considered indispensable to the success of the war party.

A war dance, the same dance still performed as a religious ritual by the present-day Shawnees, always preceded the departure of the war party from the war chief's village. At this dance the leader announced his order of march and plan of attack. The party then set off at a trot, in single file, toward the enemy territory with "the chief at the head singing the War song to enliven the march" (ibid.: p. 18) Trowbridge does not indicate the exact type of song employed, but I suspect that the Shawnees, like the Iroquois, used the stirring antiphonal stomp or Lead dance songs. The Iroquois, who call these "standing-quiver" dance songs, say that the name derives from the fact that the warriors "warmed up" for their march toward the enemy country by dancing around their stacked arms before snatching them up and starting off on their mission of destruction (W. N. Fenton *Songs From the Iroquois Longhouse*: p. 31).

An important member of every large war party was a priest-shaman, who carried a sacred war bundle, which was usually the one belonging to one of the five divisions of the Shawnee tribe. This man's supernatural powers, and those of the various objects contained in the bundle that he carried, were considered nearly as important to the success of the expedition as the valor of the warriors. Sometimes a priest-shaman, before the party set out, would send out a hunter for a deer. When he returned with the venison the priest-shaman would slice off a number of pieces of meat corresponding to the number of men in the war party and put these into a kettle to cook. When it was cooked he would remove the meat and put it into a skin, reciting "diverse incantations" (Trowbridge *Shawnese Traditions*: p. 22). He would then open the skin and divide the meat among the warriors. Often, when he had finished parceling it out, it would be found that there were more pieces than had been put into the kettle. This was regarded as a good omen, as it meant that the war party would take a prisoner for every surplus piece. On the other hand, if any pieces were found wanting, it augured the loss of that many of the warriors.

There were also female priest-shamans who divined for war parties before they set out. O. M. Spencer records how such a priestess conjured for a Shawnee war party in 1792 (*The Indian Captivity of O. M. Spencer*: pp. 115-6):

> On their way to join the Miamies, who had encamped near the point, the two Loons and about fifty Shawnee warriors from Snake's town and Blue Jacket's village halted near our cabin and sent to consult Cooh-coo-cheeh about the success of their expedition. The old woman immediately entered her sanctuary, where she remained nearly an hour, during a part of which time, sitting under the shed, I could hear the noise as of a stick striking the sides of the cabin and the beds and particularly the kettles within it; and afterward a low humming sound of the voice, at which time I supposed she was uttering her incantations. Coming out soon after with a countenance unusually animated, though with a look of great wildness, she stretched out both arms and then gradually bringing the tips of her fingers together as if encircling something exclaimed, "Mechee! mechee! mechee!" which the Indians, instantly interpreting to be "Many scalps, many prisoners, and much plunder," reported to the party, who, flushed with the confident expectation of success, immediately proceeded to join the main body.

This war party returned victorious and gave the priestess who had predicted their success six blankets, several pounds of tobacco, and a small keg of whiskey in gratitude for the aid that she afforded them in achieving their victory (ibid.: p. 117).

Although Trowbridge does not mention the fact, the customary practice of other tribes and hints from my informants, as well as the practice in the present-day War Dance of the Absentee Shawnees, indicate that the priest-shaman who accompanied a war party would open his sacred war bundle when the party was near the enemy country and distribute certain items from it to members of the war party to wear as protective charms. I am convinced that the current custom of four selected warriors wearing bunches of stripped hawk feathers removed from the Kishpokotha war bundle while participating in the War Dance derives from this custom.

The priest-shaman also served as the surgeon of the war party. When a Shawnee warrior was wounded in battle he was immediately carried from the field by his comrades and delivered into the care of the priest-shaman: "who probes his wound with a feather of the turkey buzzard dipped into a decoction prepared for the purpose. Other medicines are administered internally and the recovery of the patient was speedy. They have the fullest confidence in the powers of these medicine men & believe that if a man was shot through the body without breaking any bones, his cure could always be effected, unless circumstances should prevent a speedy operation by the Doctor." (Trowbridge *Shawnese Traditions*: p. 22)

Galloway (W. A. Galloway, *Old Chillicothe*: pp. 276–283) records a romantic tale, ostensibly based on fact, regarding the accidental discovery of a Shawnee medicine, used to allay pain, by Rebecca Galloway. In the tale Rebecca shows the source of this medicine, a flowering tree, to her friend Tecumseh who is much alarmed but then explains to her (ibid.: pp. 279–280): "The red man takes the powder of the flowers and (p. 280) leaves, or of that other fruit that you held in your hand, into battle with him. If the bullet bites or the arrow pierces, the potion quiets the pain. If the warrior falls in battle, it eases him. What you had in your hand the fruit is the best. With it, the pain of the fire at the stake is little. If wounded, the warrior can be removed to a place of safety without pain. This powder is as powerful to quiet pain as your opium is, but does not do the harm it has done. No paleface knows its power. It is our secret." Unfortunately I can offer no clue as to the identity of this tree or shrub.

While on the march to the enemy territory, when they paused for the night, the War leader and the warriors of his clan encamped considerably in advance of the main army, serving as an advance guard and scouting party. The war party's encampment was set up in an oblong form, crosswise of the path being followed. A row of forked sticks was placed on either side of the fire and across these were placed "laying poles" against which the warriors reclined. Warriors on the march never stretched out horizontally on the ground to sleep, but rather lounged in a semi-erect position.

Each had his rifle, shot pouch, and powder horn at his head leaning against or hanging from the "laying pole".

War parties sometimes left a small quantity of tobacco at the side of a spring from which they drank upon the march, praying at the same time to the spirit of the spring for success on their journey and a safe return.

Once the party neared the enemy village, hunters were sent out to procure twelve deer. These were roasted at night and the following morning the party feasted on the venison. At this final feast the leader addressed his men, urging vigilance and courage: "My brothers!—the Enemy is at hand. We must fight. Retreat would be disgraceful. We shall conquer if we are brave. The water will wash them away, the wind will blow them down, darkness will come upon them, & the earth will cover them. Let us go forward together & we shall succeed" (Trowbridge *Shawnese Traditions*: p. 18). At the site of this same feast the warriors removed and hid most of their clothing, preferring to go into battle naked except for the breechcloth. They also hid their cooking kettles, wooden bowls and spoons, and blankets. In case of defeat this site was the rallying point from which they would return to the village.

The principal war chief arranged the plan of attack. Usually it was simple. The party employed cover and concealment on their approach toward the enemy village. When very near it the chief again exhorted them to be vigilant and brave, and to await a signal, generally a gun fired from one end of the line, before attacking. In battle, it was every man for himself. At the conclusion of the engagement, if they had been successful, the leader congratulated his troops and called up the chief warrior of the Wolf clan to lead the party on their return home.

The Panther clan, with any prisoners captured, marched at the rear. Trowbridge does not mention them, but most war parties carried special "prisoner ties" that they used to bind their prisoners for the march home. These were not only functional but also served as talismans or "medicines" for supernatural assistance in securing prisoners and were beautifully made and decorated. Sometimes such prisoner ties were worn as ornamental sashes by their owners. An early description of one of these prisoner ties is found in the account of the interrogation of a party of six Shawnees who were taken prisoner near Charles Town, South Carolina, in 1753. One of these men had such a prisoner tie made up of black buffalo wool. When Governor Glenn questioned the man about it he said, "This belt I had it made for myself, and bought it that if I took any Prisoners and tied him, I might put it round his neck." (W. L. McDowell ed. *Documents Relating to Indian Affairs, May 21, 1750-August 7, 1754*: p. 424). Though I know of no Shawnee specimens which have survived, Shawnee prisoner ties were undoubtedly similar to those used by the Sauk (Cf. M. R. Harrington *Sacred Bundles of the Sac and Fox Indians*: pp. 179, 193-94, 210, 204-205, plates XXVI m, XXXVI d and e) and other Midwestern tribes.

When the victorious war party neared the home village the leader dispatched a messenger to the principal peace chief, informing him of the return of the party. The peace chief in turn communicated this information to the principal female peace chief, who prepared a feast for the warriors. As the party reached the village they raised the war whoop, which brought out all the boys and young people, armed with sticks. This crowd attacked and beat any prisoners, which continued until the party reached the council house. Here the prisoners were bound to a post, and the principal female war chief stripped them and gave them a scrutinizing examination. She then addressed her "children" the warriors, thanking them for the "good meat" that they had brought her (Trowbridge *Shawnese Traditions*: p. 19).

Next, one of the peace chiefs entered the council house with, according to Trowbridge (ibid. p. 19) "a drum and a gourd" [I am inclined to doubt the use of a gourd in the War dance, both on the basis of present practice and the statements of informants, who insisted that gourds were employed only in ceremonies of a nonmartial nature]. This chief then spoke to the assembly, declaring that because it had always been the custom of their forefathers on such occasions, they should dance the War Dance. He then began to beat the drum and sing War Dance songs. The warriors soon joined the dance, most of them stripped naked except for the breechcloth and ornaments.

The War Dance always began in the morning and continued throughout the day until evening, a custom which is still followed today in the ceremonial War Dance of the Absentee Shawnees. From time to time the dance was interrupted by the warriors who, one by one, struck a post placed in the circle and recounted their feats of bravery in the battle just past or other earlier battles. When the dance ended the warriors remained in the council house.

The following morning they were addressed by the [principal (?)] chief who told them they must remain in the council house for a period of four more days, during which they must eat sparingly and drink strong decoctions of medicinal roots. At the end of this period they were free to return to their families. Trowbridge was told that (*Shawnese Traditions*: p. 20): "The reason assigned for this abstinence & use of medecine is, that during their absence they drink a great deal of a strong decoction of roots which infuse a spirit of energy & strength, and that if they enjoyed connection with their wives before counteracting the effect of this medecine by some other, the consequences would be fatal to them." I am inclined to doubt this, at least as the primary explanation for the four-day debriefing, and suggest instead that the main purpose of this detention was to symbolically and psychologically prepare the warriors to abandon the "red road" of war and to once again tread the "white road" of peace; in other words to prepare the soldiers for civilian life.

The literature of Shawnee captives offers a number of observer-participant accounts of the return of Shawnee war parties and the ceremony and high drama with which they were always invested. Ridout (M. Edgar *Ten Years of Upper Canada in Peace and War, 1805-1815*: pp. 353-54) relates:

> When we came within a quarter of a mile of the village I was ordered to dismount and myself and another prisoner named Baffington, were painted red, and narrow ribbons of various colors (part of the plunder) tied to our hair. The Indians began to fire their guns and to set up the war-whoop, and rattles being put into our hands, we were ordered to shake them and sing some words they repeated to us . . . The other prisoner and myself were then marched in triumph to the village, shaking the rattles in our hands on entering it. I had to cross a small rivulet, and in descending the bank an old woman came out of a wigwam or hut, and gave me a stroke on the neck with a small billet of wood. However, it did not hurt me. Immediately on entering the village we were conducted to the council-house, at the door whereof we were obliged to sing and shake the rattles for half an hour, and then entered the house (without suffering any ill-treatment).

He then describes being fed in the council house, in a passage we have quoted earlier (Edgar *Ten Years of Upper Canada*: p. 354). Ridout later describes his entry, still as a prisoner, into another village, and the war poles he observed there (ibid.: p. 362): "Having arrived within a half a mile from the village . . . he [Ridout's master] directed us to stop, and went himself to the village to prepare for me, as I afterwards learnt, a good reception. At the place we stopped, there were two poles, fifteen or twenty feet high, standing upright, the bark stripped off, the one painted red and the other black. They were called war poles, and indicated that prisoners had been brought to that village."

O. M. Spencer's account of the return of the party that had captured him differs in a few details. On their way back, fearing possible pursuit by the Americans, the Shawnees took care to cover their tracks by wading upstream: "Entering this stream, we waded up it about half a mile, the leading Indian directing me to step in his track while the other followed treading in mine." (*The Indian Captivity of O. M. Spencer*: p. 46). The arrival of the trio in the first Shawnee town is thus described (ibid. pp.: 72-74):

> Still traveling down the Auglaize, about three hours after sunrise on the morning of the twelfth of July we came in sight of an Indian village, when Wawpawmawquaw, cutting a long pole, tied the scalp to the end of it and elevating it over his head raised the the scalp-halloo, a shrill whoop, which both Indians repeated frequently until we entered the town. Here we found all its inhabitants assembled; more than fifty men, women and children collected in front of the nearest cabin, who, as soon as the first salutations by the principal men were ended, seated themselves, some on logs and some on the ground, listened with deep attention while Wawpawmawquaw with that gravity of manner and those intonations of voice peculiar to Indian chiefs and warriors again told the story of my captivity. He was proceeding at last to describe the act of tomahawking and scalping the unfortunate white man when a little old Indian, suddenly springing upon me and throwing me down with violence, gave a loud shout, accompanied with many extravagant and furious gesticulations, and vociferating (as I was afterwards told) that he had vanquished his enemy. Immediately all the women began to scream and the children, down to the small papoose, setting up a long shrill war-whoop, gathered around me. I clung to Wawpawmawquaw, but young as I was I should have been compelled to run the gauntlet through the women and infant warriors had I not, from great debility occasioned by dysentery, been scarcely able to move faster than a walk.
>
> About noon that day we arrived at another village on the Auglaize. Here also, the inhabitants flocked out to meet us, and in like manner were entertained with an account of the late expedition of the Indians and the story of my captivity; but although the women and children manifested a great deal of curiosity, examining my dress and scanning me from head to feet, none of them offered me any rudeness.

Young Spencer was not forced to run the gauntlet, but most prisoners of the Shawnees were, including his fellow captive William Moore. The account of Moore's run is a classic description of this famous Shawnee custom. (Spencer *The Indian Captivity of O. M. Spencer*: pp. 100-1):

> On his arrival at Blue Jacket's village, Moore, being only a private prisoner to one whose family had no manes to appease or blood to retribute, was not subjected to the disposal of a council; but custom immemorial requiring that as a man and a warror he should run the gauntlet, an early hour was fixed for the interesting exhibition. That day soon arrived; and men, women, and children,

invited from the neighboring villages, flocked to the capital of the Shawnees, anticipating as much pleasure as we would expect at the celebration of our nation's anniversary. Here, after gratifying their curiosity in examining the prisoner, armed with clubs, switches, and other instruments of punishment they arranged themselves facing each other in two rows about seven feet apart and numbering more than two hundred persons, each distant four or five feet from each other extending three hundred yards along the level space between the village and the Maumee River. The chiefs and principal warriors stood at the head of the lines within a few rods of the cabin selected as the goal, while the rest of the men with the women and youths, promiscuously occupied the other parts.

Moore was now led out and stripped to the waist, when the Indians, aware of his strength and activity, tied together his wrists, for the double purpose of hindering his speed and preventing him from retaliating on his tormentors, yet so as to afford him the means of protecting his face. Starting a short distance from the head of the lines, he soon bounded through them; and breathing a few moments, returning with the same speed, had reached the middle of his course when the Indians, fearing that from his fleetness he would run through with little injury (as most of their blows instead of falling on his back fell clattering on each others' sticks) half closing their ranks attempted to obstruct his progress. Appealing in vain to their sense of honor and justice, frequently crying (as he told me) "Honor bright!" and "Fair play!" and finding that he would probably be severely beaten, he undertook himself to redress his wrongs; and so effectually did he use his feet, head, and right wrist, kicking some, striking down others, and with his head overturning a number, that the rest readily made way, and opening for him an ample passage, amidst the shouts of the warriors he soon reached the goal. Having passed the ordinary trial he was now congratulated as a brave man and by some applauded for his late resistance, all but the sufferers being highly diverted at his successful expedient to rid himself of a severe beating.

The prisoners taken in battle, if they were successful in running the gauntlet, and if they were not consigned to be burned to death at the stake, were ultimately given by the chiefs to various persons in the village who had requested a slave. Often women and children were spared and adopted into families that had recently lost a son or daughter in death. Children of other tribes, and even whites, captured and adopted in this manner, had full Shawnee citizenship and grew up thinking of themselves as Shawnees. The male adoptees often became the leaders of the next generation of Shawnee warriors, sometimes leading Shawnee war parties against their own people. The famous chief Blue Jacket is an excellent case in point. Adult males were adopted less frequently, as they were liable to attempt escape and resist socialization as Shawnees. Some were adopted. One of them was the famous frontiersman Daniel Boone. Usually, however, adult male captives could expect to be tortured to death and even eaten in some instances, when they fell into Shawnee hands.

The Shawnees continued to burn adult male captives until at

least 1790. A prisoner destined to be burned at the stake was painted black and conducted to the village, where he was confined for one night. The following morning he was taken to the torture site. Here a white oak sapling was stuck into the ground and to the upper end, about twenty feet from the ground, a grape vine was attached. This vine came down far enough so that the prisoner's arms, when raised, could be tied to it. After a period of ominous silence, the prisoner was led to the sapling and his arms made fast to the vine. His tormentors then yelled, in unison, four times, and the torture began. Brands were seized from a large fire built nearby, and each in turn applied the burning end to the captive. When the pain compelled him to jump from his place, the elasticity of the pole would immediately swing him back to his original position, or a spot near it, where others stood ready with fresh torches to continue the torture. "Thus he was continued in the most excruciating pain, from sun rise until past noon, when he died. He was then skinned & quartered, and his limbs were boiled for a feast, and distributed among the spectators. A young man who is now here with the Prophet, says that he was at that time quite a boy, but he recollects very well that he ate a piece of the body for venison, and thought it good." (Trowbridge *Shawnese Traditions*: p. 21)

Ridout (Edgar *Ten Years of Upper Canada*: pp. 363-64) describes the torture of a white captive while he was a captive among the Shawnees. This man was first stripped naked, his face was painted black, and his ears cut off. The poor wretch was then driven ahead of the pursuing Indians through a valley and to the top of a hill where he was recaptured and tortured at the stake for about three hours until he died. Ridout writes: "The Indian did not return till the afternoon. At the approach of evening they fired their guns, and with large twigs beat their wigwams on the tops and sides, shouting. I inquired of the negro what that meant. He said that it was to drive away the spirit of the prisoner they had burnt. This ceremony continued for three succeeding nights." (Edgar *Ten Years of Upper Canada*: p. 364) Memories of torturing, cooking, and eating prisoners of war are still retained by both the Shawnees and the Kickapoos. One of my informants, a man who functions as one of the leading warriors in the War Dances of both tribes, told me of a dream he had experienced in which he, in his role of a warrior, stripped flesh from the chest of a captive, roasted it, and then ate it. Details of the torture procedure in this man's dream account were quite complete, and matched closely those in the Trowbridge account.

Trowbridge (*Shawnese Traditions*: p. 21) notes that the usual reason for torturing captives was to avenge the death of a Shawnee chief killed in battle. Prisoners who were painted black before entering a village, and hence marked for torture, never escaped death unless the party escorting the captive was met outside the village and he was claimed by the principal female peace chief. More likely the captive would be reached first by the four old hags who were the heads of the cannibal society, which was a group of men and women who considered it their sacred duty to roast or boil and then eat the body of every prisoner delivered to them by a war party. These four old women, whenever they heard the "prisoners yell" of a returning war party, painted their lips with red clay to simulate blood and hastened to meet the returning warriors. The peace women started from the village at the same time, and if they reached a prisoner in time to touch him before the others, the person was safe and the cannibal society did not attempt to touch him. But if any one of the four heads of the cannibals touched the prisoner first she immediately said to the warriors "Thank you my children, you bring me good broth" and the prisoner's fate was sealed (ibid.: pp. 53–54).

Trowbridge (ibid.: p. 54) notes that the members of the cannibal society came from the "Linewaa M'soamee" or "Indian" clan of the Pekowitha division, and that they had an annual feast at which the members collected and ate prisoners. Black Hoof's account (ibid.: p. 64) explains that the symbol of this society was a representation of the deceased body of a man, or the body in a recumbent posture. They ate their human flesh from bowls made of the skulls of former victims and prided themselves on the exhibition of great voracity when burning and eating prisoners.

Captives of the Shawnees who showed great patience and fortitude when subjected to torture were greatly admired. Catawba captives claimed their highest admiration in this respect.

Shawnee youths began to bear arms in war at the age of fifteen, and, according to the Shawnee Prophet, they ceased to do so "only in death" (Trowbridge *Shawnese Traditions*: p. 21). Defensive armor was not used by the Shawnees, at least in historic times. Instead they relied upon the "aid of their tutelar god to protect them" (ibid.) Various individual war medicines consisting of small bunches of herbs, animal and bird skins, were carried and special items of adornment were worn in battle, such as the hawk feather plumes contained in the Kishpokotha division's war bundle. Some of these fetishes were thought to make them invisible to their enemies or to give them the power to elude them. E. W. Voegelin mentions the use of mescal beans (*Sophora secundiflora*) as a war medicine among the Absentee Shawnees in 1865 (La Barre *The Peyote Cult*: p. 109). My informants Ranny Carpenter and Mary Spoon also mentioned mescal beans in this context.

Shawnee youths were continually trained by their elders in various skills that they would need in war. E. W. Voegelin writes, for example (E. W. Voegelin, C. Rafinesque, C. F. Voegelin, and E. Lilly *Walum Olum*: p. 121): "The Shawnee state that warriors all knew, of necessity, how to swim under water and how to hide themselves so completely in water for many hours that nothing save a small part of the nose was above the surface. This ability gained through training or by virtue of a blessing from supernatural beings, often saved a warrior's life by enabling him to escape detection when enemies were searching for him.

It is not surprising, in a society where war and the role of the warrior were so important, to find that there were many metaphorical expressions used in reference to warfare. Thus "to play" with another tribe meant to make war against it (ibid.: p. 201). Likewise to take the "red road" or "raise the red tomahawk" meant to go to war, while to follow the "white path" meant to pursue a peaceful course. I have noted above how the principal female war chief and the women of the cannibal society referred to the warriors as "my children" and thanked them for bringing "good meat" or "good broth" (captives). Some of these metaphors, learned by whites in the days of frontier diplomacy, have passed into common American English, such as "to bury the hatchet" and "the dark clouds (meaning war) are gathering".

Though not used extensively in the historic period, the Shawnees retained, in Trowbridge's day, the memory of building forts of logs covered with earth (Trowbridge *Shawnese Traditions*: pp. 57–58, 65). Inside these forts, which they tried to build around a spring to have water in case of a siege, they transplanted walnut, hickory, and beech trees to provide food. Trowbridge's informants told him that the Shawnees had built the first fort known to the Indians. Other tribes, defeated when they attempted to storm the Shawnee fort, profited from the example and later built their own fortifications. During their wars with the American in the late eighteenth century the Shawnees used their log council houses as forts when attacks caught them by surprise or when the residents of a town decided to fight rather than withdraw. In 1779 the Shawnees of Old Chillicothe who took refuge in their council house successfully stood off an American army of 265 men, although their own force included only 25 warriors and 15 boys, not all of whom had rifles (Alford in Galloway *Old Chillicothe*: pp. 60–5).

In regard to peacemaking, the Prophet told Trowbridge that the Shawnees never sued for peace themselves but rather received proposals of peace from their enemies (*Shawnese Traditions*: p. 23). To conclude a treaty of peace, messengers carrying calumets or peace pipes, each of which had a quarter circle of eagle feathers suspended from its underside, traveled to the village of the enemy tribe (the Shawnees). These messengers were by no means immune from attack, and hence proceeded cautiously. Arriving at the enemy village they entered it boldly, holding their calumets extended in front of them, and sought out the village or peace chiefs. "To the peace chiefs the messengers proposed the terms of negotiation: telling them that the loss of many of their young men and the desire to attend to the education of the survivors compels them to acknowledge the opposite party their superiors in prowess & arms, & to ask for peace" (ibid.: p. 23) The village chiefs then called a council, at which the emissaries repeated their request; and at length the conquerors (the Shawnees of course) granted their wish. Finally all of the warriors were called in, and the chiefs explained to them the wish of the ambassadors and their decision to grant it. The warriors then assented to the treaty and the pipe of peace was passed around. Although wampum was used in other contexts by the Shawnees, the tribe apparently did not use wampum belts to commemorate treaties of this sort.

In the historical literature, especially the accounts of captivity the Shawnees are invariably depicted as a warlike, predatory tribe, and tales of their bloodthirsty war parties and tortures at the stake affected the attitudes of generations of white Americans. Curiously, however, one of the earliest accounts of the Shawnees, that of Father Marquette in 1673, presents a very different picture: "They are not at all warlike, and are a nation whom the Iroquois go so far to seek and war against without any reason: and, because these poor people cannot defend themselves, they allow themselves to be captured and taken Like flocks of sheep; and, innocent though they are, they nevertheless sometimes experience The barbarity of the Iroquois, who cruelly burn Them" (E. Kenton *The Indians of North America*, II: p. 277) A similar impression of the pacifistic nature of the Shawnees would be gained by anyone visiting the neat and friendly homes of the twentieth century descendants of the tribe about whom Marquette was writing. How, then, do we reconcile the peaceful beginning and end of our story with the "warlike" Shawnees of the eighteenth and nineteenth centuries?

As an anthropologist I should like to issue a warning against viewing any tribe or nation as inherently "warlike" simply because it has been represented as such by several generations of writers. War is a cultural and historical phenomenon, not a matter of genetics or individual psychology. The Shawnees, like other Native Americans, fought bravely to defend themselves and their territory from other tribes and from whites. The ways in which they did this were culturally determined, and any atrocities they may have committed in the course of their struggles were fully matched by the deeds of their enemies. Their custom of burning captives at the stake was practised by most of the tribes of the East and Midwest, and was abandoned by the Shawnees at the instigation of their own leaders, such as Tecumseh. Their custom of scalping was also general and was, in fact, taken up by the white frontiersmen who fought the Shawnees, though it was unknown in Europe. Simply stated, then, the Shawnees were as warlike *as they had to be to survive* in their historical and cultural milieu. Let us hear no more then, of the "warlike and cruel Shawnees"!

The Cycle of Life

Shawnee parents usually desired sons more than daughters, and the firstborn son was given special attention (T. W. Alford *Civilization*: p. 4). Trowbridge notes, however, that boys and girls were treated with the same care and kindness (C. C. Trowbridge *Shawnese Traditions*: p. 29). A child was kept in its mother's arms until it was about a month old, at which time it was bound upon the cradle board. Children were kept on this cradle board most of the time during the day, until they were strong enough to sit alone, at which time they were allowed to creep about the house. From this time on the cradle board was used less frequently, unless the family was traveling (Trowbridge *Shawnese Traditions*: p. 29).

Alford recalls his own experiences in this respect, noting that the "tkith-o-way" or cradle board, was often elaborately carved and ornamented to indicate the pride and prosperity of the parents (*Civilization*: pp. 4-5). He gives the Shawnee rationale for the use of the device, which was primarily the safety of the child but also the convenience of the mother, who could go about her daily tasks with her child swung on her back. He also notes that by strapping the child on a cradle board its little back would grow straight and strong. The child's head was bound closely to the flat back of the board to make the soft little skull grow flat. When it reached maturity it would then have a flat spot at the back of the head. This was the place where the men wore the silver "hair plate" together with an eagle feather, which was the headdress of a Shawnee brave. (ibid.: pp. 4-5)

The cradle board though it is still recalled by my informants, most of whom had been bound in one when they were infants, is now obsolete among the Shawnees. Another device for holding a baby while the mother works is still in general use. This is the baby swing, a small hammock made from a blanket folded over two ropes. The ropes are tied at either end to eye bolts in the wall of a corner of the room. Every so often the mother, or any other member of the family who passes near, gives the swing a slight push, rocking the baby. In the traditional Shawnee bark house the ropes of the baby swing would have been tied to the pole framework about four feet above the floor.

Orphaned children were usually raised by couples who had few or no children of their own. These surrogate parents were usually relatives of one or the other of the orphan's parents, but if there were no relatives of the proper age, friends of the deceased parents took in the children. (Trowbridge *Shawnese Traditions*: p. 29) There was and is no difference in the treatment of legitimate and illegitimate children among the Shawnees, but Trowbridge notes that "the displeasure of its grand parents is generally shown in their conduct to the mother". In Trowbridge's day, and now as well, if an illegitimate child were to resemble the reputed father, the parents of the father would bring pressure upon their son to marry the mother. Should this eventuality not take place, the care of the child would devolve entirely upon the mother.

It was and is uncommon for Shawnee women to give birth to twins. The Shawnee Prophet, however, was one of either twins or triplets (cf. Drake p. 63) Trowbridge says that two of these triplets died shortly after birth (*Shawnese Traditions*: p. 30) but my informant Ranny Carpenter insisted that Tecumseh was one of the triplets and that the third triplet, who was deformed, died as a boy. Although the Shawnee laws (C. F. Voegelin, J. F. Yergerlehner, and F. M. Robinett "Shawnee Laws": p. 39) recommend twelve children as the ideal, the Prophet told Trowbridge that he had never known a woman to have more than ten children (*Shawnese Traditions*: p. 30). Certainly Shawnee families were large in the nineteenth century. Today their size is decreasing, just as it has in the major culture, a fact noted by several of my informants. Few Shawnee couples today have more than five children.

Shortly after a child was born the parents arranged its naming ceremony, a custom that is still followed by most Shawnees at the present time, even in the highly acculturated Eastern band.

Trowbridge writes that this event took place six months after the birth of the child (*Shawnese Traditions*: p. 26) but Alford notes that it occurred ten days afterwards in the case of a boy, twelve days afterwards for a girl (*Civilization*: p. 3). The Voegelins (C. F. Voegelin and E. W. Voegelin "Shawnee Name Groups": p. 622) indicate that the naming ceremony begins on the evening of the ninth day after birth, with the actual naming occurring on the morning of the tenth. This naming not only provides the child with a name but also places it in a name-group or "clan", as I have explained in chapter six. An individual's name may be changed if for some reason it is considered unfortunate, such as a case where another person is found to have the same name, the individual is sickly, or, in the case of an adult warrior, he has been frequently wounded. Present-day Shawnee practice in this respect appears to be identical with that described by Trowbridge (*Shawnese Traditions*: p. 27), Morgan (L. H. Morgan *The Indian Journals, 1859-62*: p. 45) and the Voegelins (Voegelin and Voegelin "Shawnee Name Groups": pp. 626-7). In Trowbridge's day individuals were generally unwilling to tell their own names, and it was necessary for a third person to supply this information (*Shawnese Traditions*: p. 27).

There was no system of formal education among the Shawnees. Instead, children "learned by doing." Each father, however, gave instruction to his sons, and each mother discharged the same duty in respect to her daughters. The close relationship between the father as teacher and the son as student is evident in Alford's account of his own childhood (*Civilization*). Trowbridge speaks of the strict discipline in Shawnee families of his day and notes that both boys and girls were punished for disobedience by whipping, the boys being punished by the father, the girls by the mother. If, after repeated whippings, a boy did not mend his behavior, the father sent him out of the house until he showed signs of penitence. (Trowbridge *Shawnese Traditions*: p. 28) Alford, however, indicates that whippings were rare, which perhaps indicates a change through time in Shawnee culture: "Indian parents gave few commands, because they were advocates of freedom of action and thought, but absolute obedience was exacted. Children seldom were punished, for a few words of praise from a parent or an elder was regarded as the highest prize that could be given for good conduct (*Civilization*: p. 21). Punishment was not unknown in Alford's day, however, and a bitter form was to tell a visitor or friend of the child's faults in his presence. The most severe punishment was to scratch the child's calves and thighs with a "*la-lah-so-waw-ka,*an implement kept for this purpose, made by piercing a block of soft wood with pins or hard thorns about one-eighth of an inch apart, with the thorns or pins protruding on the reverse side. The instrument itself was about one and one-half inches wide." (Alford *Civilization*: pp. 21-22) Alford says that for a parent to use a switch or a stick to beat their children was considered a disgrace to both the parent and the child (*Civilization*: p. 22).

Shawnee children of both sexes learned to conceal their feelings at an early age. Alford describes his experience when he was sent to mission school: "I was eager to learn all that was taught me. But I had been so drilled and instructed in the art of concealing my feelings that I, like the other Indian children, presented an appearance of utter indifference" (*Civilization*: p. 77).

A good idea of the dress and general appearance of Shawnee children in the mid-nineteenth century is provided by Alford (*Civilization*: p. 77).

> In warm weather the boys wore one garment, simply a long shirt usually made of calico that our fathers bought from the licensed traders. In winter we added leggings to this dress, and sometimes a hunting shirt was worn over the calico one. The hunting shirt was made of tanned buckskin, fringed all around the bottom, the collar, the sleeves, and the pocket. We wore shoes or boots when we could get them, but generally we went barefoot. We had not hats, but sometimes wore caps made of the skin of a wildcat, a coon, or a beaver, with bunches of feathers puffed or stripped from the stem to look like a fine plume, placed on the top of the cap. We boys wore our hair short, very much as the girls of today wear their hair bobbed. This is the way Shawnee men always have worn their hair. Never did they braid it, as some other tribes do.
>
> The girls however, wore their hair long and braided. Sometimes they wore a colored handkerchief tied about their heads; more often they went bareheaded. They wore long dresses of calico or linsey, a coarse half wool material, with skirts gathered full about the waist. After the school was established our good friends of the East sent us through our missionary some clothing like white children wore, usually discarded clothing their own children had worn.

The moral training of the young began early in Shawnee society: "Children were taught that good conduct would earn a reward and evil conduct would bring sorrow; from early childhood this principle was instilled into their minds. Standards of conduct were just as rigid as the laws of any other people, but force seldom was used to enforce good conduct. *Each person was his own judge.* Deceitfulness was a crime. We lived according to our own standards and principles, not for what others might think of us. Absolute honesty towards each other was the basis of character.

(Alford *Civilization*: p. 19) Among the Shawnees, moral principles were codified to a degree unusual for a Native American people. Alford, for example, gives the text of the Shawnee "golden rule," which is translated as follows (T. W. Alford in W. A. Galloway *Old Chillicothe*: p. 178; Alford *Civilization*: p. 20): "Do not kill or injure your neighbor, for it is not him that you injure, you injure yourself. But do good to him, therefore add to his days of happiness as you add to your own. Do not wrong or hate your neighbor, for it is not him you wrong, you wrong yourself. But love him, for Moneto loves him also as He loves you!"

The moral tone of Shawnee society was high, but nineteenth century Shawnee children were by no means "goody-goody" types. They were as fond of sports, games, and assorted pranks as any children. Thus Alford writes: "We had a game that we played with smooth, round stones, or we sometimes found peach seeds or stones which we whittled into balls that we used in a game like marbles as played by white boys. We played ball too, but our game was not like the baseball of today. All the games we played were calculated to develop strength, skill, and resourcefulness. The only toys we had were those we ourselves made. We wrestled and ran races and rode the ponies, fished and hunted, and set traps for birds and rabbits." (Alford in Galloway *Old Chillicothe*: p. 173; Alford *Civilization*: p. 23) The "game like marbles" described by Alford is probably the same one that the Shawnee Prophet described to Trowbridge (*Shawnese Traditions*: pp. 51-52): "Tetepauhalowaawaa—or The Rolling game, was formerly their principal amusement in this way. The ground was made perfectly level and smooth for a distance of forty or fifty feet and in width about 4 feet—in this form (Figure 5).

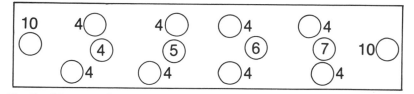

Fig. 5.   Diagram of a Shawnee rolling game ground (*Trowbridge 1939, p. 52*)

Each of these circles is intended to represent a hole & the figures within & near them denote the number to be counted for the ball which is rolled into it. The party is divided & stand at opposite ends of the place prepared. They are provided with an equal number of balls, (6 for each party—and they roll them towards the little holes. When either party gains to the number of 60, the game ends. They never roll at the hole nearest the end at which they stand."

The ball game mentioned by Alford, above, also mentioned by Trowbridge (*Shawnese Traditions*: p. 52) is somewhat of a puzzle to us. It may have been an all-male version of the Indian football game still played by today's Shawnees as a semireligious activity, with the men and boys pitted against the women and girls. Again, it may have been the Southeastern version of stickball or lacrosse. Culin (S. Culin *Games of the North American Indians*: p. 513) cites William Jones to the effect that the Shawnees played this game either men-against-men or men-against-women. In the latter version the men used the ballsticks and the women their hands, and the goals, described as "hoop wickets" were nearer together than when the men played alone. All of my informants, however, firmly denied that the Shawnees ever played the game among themselves, although Richard Gibson said that sometimes the Absentee Shawnee men took part in the "match" (Men-against-men) lacrosse games of the Seminoles on invitation from that tribe.

Another of the Shawnee boys' games described by Alford is a variant of the widespread hoop and pole game (Alford in Galloway *Old Chillicothe*: pp. 172–73; *Civilization*: p. 22). A hoop was made of wild grapevine bent around until the ends lapped a bit, then tied at the joint with strips of bark. It was filled with a netting of pliable bark. The boys would then choose sides and stand in two lines, facing each other about fifteen or twenty feet apart. A boy from one side would roll the hoop along the ground, and the boys on the opposite side would shoot at it with their bows and arrows as it passed. A boy whose arrow stuck in the netting of the hoop was a winner. When this happened the boys on the opposing side stuck their arrows into the ground and the winner tossed the hoop flatwise at the row of arrows. He could keep all those which he knocked down.

Except for the ceremonial football games played in the spring, boys and girls did not associate with one another in their play: "Indian girls never were allowed to play with the boys. In fact from the time a little Indian boy could walk he felt a sense of superiority to his sisters, and a boy who would have played with a girl was a subject for ridicule. Little girls played much as little girls do today, I suppose, mimicking their mothers' household tasks, making cakes, and molding vessels of mud or clay. No doubt they "kept house" and mothered the smaller children, even as I have seen my own little girls doing in recent years" (Alford in Galloway *Old Chillicothe*: p. 173; Alford *Civilization* p. 23).

When he was about nine a Shawnee boy began a special program of training for endurance and self-control. Alford tells how, when he was this age, in the fall of the year after the first frost, he was instructed by his father to take off his shirt and run down to the creek and plunge into the icy water: "It made me shiver to think of the cold plunge, but I never thought of disobeying him, for very well I knew that father had begun to train me to be a man, a brave—possibly a chief. Pride filled my heart! I did as father had told me, the other children looking on with admiration and respect. Every morning that winter I repeated that performance, breaking the ice when it was necessary." (*Civilization*: p. 24)

After several weeks Alford's father considered him to be ready to plunge into the creek four times instead of just once. On the fourth plunge he was told to grasp something in his hand as he came up out of the water: "It might be a leaf from a tree, a horse hair, a shell, or just any object—but whatever it was it would indicate my o-pah-wa-ka which would be a divine direction, for through that source I should receive some blessing from the Great Spirit, some power to perform worthy acts, that would guide me through life. I was not to open my hand after closing it under the water, until I stood before father. I did as I was instructed, but failed to get anything in my hand, which was interpreted to mean that I should earn my blessing in some way, by worthy actions" (Alford *Civilization*: pp. 24-5).

The practice of sending young boys out to break the ice and take a cold dip to strengthen them continued in some conservative families until at least the 1920s, for my informant Cody Mack said that his grandpa required him to do it, plunging in the sacred four times, when he was a small boy.

Although parents and other close relatives were the principal teachers of the children among the Shawnees, there were also certain old men and old women to whom all of the children of a village could go for advice and comfort. The boys would seek out the old men of this class, known as "grandpas," and the girls the old women, or "grandmas." Ranny Carpenter, a descendant of

Tecumseh, told a story involving the socialization of the young
Tecumseh and his brother who later became known as Tenskwatawa ("Open Door"), the Shawnee Prophet, in which one of
these grandpas figures.

> I heard a story that Tecumseh, his brother Open-door, and a third brother
> were triplets. The third brother was rather ugly. He had a long, narrow, head.
> One day the three brothers, all just little boys, stopped in their play to drink at a
> spring. The spring was a beautiful blue and reflected, from its still surface, like
> a mirror. As the boys knelt to drink they saw their faces reflected in the surface.
> The third brother, with the deformed head, saw his reflection and said "Is that
> ugly creature me?" His two brothers said that it was, and could not help from
> laughing at his discomfort at learning of his appearance. This so disheartened
> the third brother that he eventually became withdrawn, sickened, and died.
> Bothered by feelings of guilt after their brother's death, Tecumseh and Open-
> door went to see one of the village grandpas. There were a number of such men
> in every Shawnee village. They were old men to whom children could come with
> their problems, to secure advice and comfort. Tecumseh and Open-door told this
> grandpa what had happened, saying that they were sorry but that "we couldn't
> help laughing at our brother." The grandpa replied that he understood, but that
> the two were, nevertheless, responsible for their act and its result. "Brothers
> must always look after each other."
> As the two remaining brothers grew up, Tecumseh always felt responsible for
> Open-door. Open-door was a warrior, while Tecumseh was a holy man, a
> "saint" with clairvoyant powers [so said Ranny]. He constantly watched over
> his brother and got him out of situations in which his warlike activities had
> drawn him.

Regardless of the historical accuracy of this story, it clearly shows
the behavioral norms of brothers in Shawnee society and the
function of the grandpas in dispensing good advice. Apparently it
was one of the grandmas, rather than their own mother, who gave
Shawnee girls advice about their oncoming first menstruation (J.
Spencer *The Shawnee Indians*: p. 391). At this time women
customarily retired to a menstrual hut away from the family
dwelling.

At the age of puberty or slightly before (about twelve or thirteen
years of age), Shawnee boys were sent out into the woods to fast
and seek a spirit helper. This spirit helper was a supernatural
creature who usually appeared to the supplicant in the form of an
animal or a bird after the individual had fasted and prayed for a
sufficient period. The spirit helper would give the faster instruction in some area, which was usually healing, and also would
promise aid in future years if the faster would call upon it in the
proper manner. Often the spirit helper gave, or told the faster how
to procure for himself, a personal "medicine" or fetish symbolic of
their relationship to one another.

When being sent out on the vision quest boys had their faces blackened with charcoal so that all would know their errand and not speak to them or offer them food. Not all boys were successful. An account of a successful vision quest is contained in a 1937 interview with Sam Perry, a Loyal Shawnee (Indian Archives, Oklahoma State Historical Society 8: pp. 172–74). Perry tells how a Shawnee boy was sent out on the vision quest by his parents. He was reluctant at first but finally set out. While fasting alone in the woods he experienced a terrifying storm, which rended tall trees, but he showed no fear. Finally he was visited by a spirit who gave him instruction as to how to become a sweat-lodge doctor. The spirit told the boy how to construct the domed sweat lodge, covering it with skins. The patient is brought into the sweat lodge, but his head remains outside. Water is poured on the hot stones and the patient sweats for an hour or two. The spirit tells the boy: "The sweating will bring out the location of the misery. You will chew some wild tobacco, mixed with other herbs, and will blow on the affected part and the man will be restored to health." After giving these instructions to the boy, the spirit promised to come again and give further instructions. He gave the boy a lock of his hair to keep as a token of his vision.

My informant Mary Spoon told of her own son being blessed in this manner while on the vision quest. According to Mary he has never revealed his experiences while in the woods or told what herb medicines he is authorized to use, but he had effected at least three remarkable cures. One involved Mary herself. She experienced a tightening of the chest and a persistent cough. Her son, when told of her trouble, went out into the woods and secured some herbs, which he boiled up together with cornmeal and administered to his mother. Soon Mary was all right again. So far her son has limited his practice to members of the immediate family, perhaps because of a fear of interference on the part of White authorities for practicing medicine without a license.

Ranny Carpenter told of his own unsuccessful attempt at securing a "blessing" in this way.

> In the old days the Shawnees used to send their young people, especially boys, out on errands at night so that they might receive a blessing. When I was about thirteen years old I was not afraid of anything. I used to sleep on the porch of our house and I would listen to my father and my uncle, John White, talk about old Shawnee ways. One night my uncle John told how he had been blessed. "All you have to do is go out four nights to a certain place and something will come to you—sometimes the first night, sometimes the second or third, but always by the fourth. You have to stay awake and not be afraid." He told me how he went out alone, on horseback. He camped at this place and

turned his horse loose. It would never run off. After midnight he dozed off. He was awakened by a voice saying, "Your horse has strayed off." He awakened fully and saw a little man standing beside him. The man said, "I will help you get your horse back. He has wandered down to the stream for a drink" Uncle John went where the little man told him, and surely enough, there was his horse! He thanked the little man. The little man told him: "Since you were not afraid, I am going to give you a blessing. Whenever you need help, just burn a little tobacco and ask for help and I will hear." Uncle John did this for the rest of his life, and he always managed to have food on his table and keep his family well.

When I heard him tell this to my father, I determined to do the same as he. Surely I could stay out four nights as he had. I was afraid of nothing; and I knew every tree, bush, and stone in the place he mentioned. I had even built a log corral with a snubbing post in the center in that very place.

The next night I began. I sat on the corral all night but nothing happened. The second night, just before dawn, I heard a strange whistling noise. Now, I know every bird in the woods. All my life I have practiced identifying birdcalls with the birds that make them, but this one I didn't know. In spite of myself I got scared and ran back home.

The third night I determined to do better. I said to myself that nothing would keep me from staying out, and perhaps securing a blessing. Again, just before dawn, the whistling came. I looked at the place where it came from but I couldn't see a thing. I waited. Again it came, this time closer. The third time it was almost beside me. I was drawn, in spite of myself, off the top rail of the corral, and down to the ground. I seemed to be paralyzed. I couldn't move. Mustering all my strength, I got to my feet and began running toward the house. I felt that thing was right behind me. I didn't stop until I was home in bed. I never tried to get a blessing again.

Alford (*Civilization*: p. 25) describes what he terms a "test of endurance" that he underwent when he was "about ten years old." If not an actual vision quest, it would seem to be a related phenomenon. Alford was sent out, his face blackened with charcoal, to kill some small animal, such as a quail, squirrel, or rabbit, and he was given no food until he returned with game. "Sometimes it was found in a few minutes or a few hours. More often it took long hours of searching and wandering—just a matter of luck. It took me two days to kill the quail my father had sent me out to bring home. Quail was plentiful then, but I just could not kill one with my bow and arrow, it seemed. After wandering for hours without food, my aim was not steady, and there is something in feeling that so much depends on one's efforts—that a test is being made. But at last my arrow brought one down, and I retraced my steps homeward."

Although the object of this mission was ostensibly to train the boy as a hunter, one suspects that the boy's parents may have had an ulterior motive, because the boy's face was blackened. A Ponca informant, Peter Le Claire, once told me that his parents, though did not formally send him out to fast on the vision quest, were in the habit of sending him on long journeys to visit an aunt, which would cause him to be overtaken by darkness before he arrived. They told him later that it was their hope that he would encounter a spirit helper en route. I suspect that Alford's "test of endurance" may have been similarly designed.

Trowbridge tells us (*Shawnese Traditions*: p. 28) that young men became entitled to the privileges of adults at age sixteen, but that if they were not "well endowed" they usually waited until they were eighteen or nineteen before they availed themselves of these privileges. Between the age of sixteen and nineteen the older men of the tribe took the youths aside from time to time and gave them instruction in the traditions of their people. "These traditions are told to them at different times & by different persons, and by frequent repetition they become familiar to the young man, who in turn relates them to his children." (Trowbridge *Shawnese Traditions*: p. 28). It was expected that a young man would obtain his own support after the age of sixteen, or at the latest after eighteen. Trowbridge was told, however, of young men who stayed around their father's cabin until they were past twenty: "Such are generally cold & indifferent, & not susceptible to the charms of the opposite sex" (*Shawnese Traditions*: p. 29).

Although Trowbridge indicates sixteen as the recognized age of majority (*Shawnese Traditions*: p. 28) he contradicts himself elsewhere in the same work (p. 15) "When young men arrive at the age of eighteen they begin to earn something for themselves, but are considered, notwithstanding, under the control of their parents until the age of 20, when they are free & invested with all the powers & privileges of manhood. They seldom marry before arriving at this age." The "Shawnee Laws" (Voegelin, Yergerlehner, and Robinett: "Shawnee Laws": p. 37) indicate that Shawnee men customarily married at age twenty-five. Both this source and Trowbridge (*Shawnese Traditions*: p. 33) imply that Shawnee women married at a younger age, about sixteen.

Both Trowbridge and Alford indicate that there was no formal courtship procedure in the 19th century. Trowbridge writes (ibid.: p. 30): "There is no particular custom respecting the manner of courtship which is considered as binding," and "Kissing is not practiced by them (ibid: p. 46)," while Alford comments: "There were no courtships among our young people such as there are today (*Civilization*: p. 67)". Alford qualifies his remarks, however, by noting (ibid: p. 67): "Young people sometimes did arrange matters for themselves. For instance, should a maiden like the looks or the manner of a young brave she might seek a place behind him in the dance, . . . and give him her hand without a handkerchief. The giving of the naked hand always denoted a "willingness" to be regarded as a future mate. Then the young man could, if he desired, make further advances. This he did in a very dignified way. There were no gushing speeches, no promises, but a perfect understanding resulted from the few words quietly spoken, the glances of affection, and perhaps a handclasp."

Trowbridge notes that Shawnee marriages usually were arranged by the parents of the parties involved, and no contract of marriage could be entered into without their consent. When the parents of a young man had chosen a wife for him, they proceeded to collect a quantity of hides and other goods to make up a present for the family of the girl whom they had chosen. This was carried by the mother of the young man to the mother of the intended bride. The young man's mother indicated to the mother of the girl that her son wished to marry the latter's daughter and offered the bundle of goods in testimony of her good faith. The goods were left at the intended bride's lodge for a short time, during which the mother and father of the young woman conferred, finally deciding to either accept the goods in token of consent, or to reject them, which ended the matter.

If they accepted, the goods were divided among the female relatives of the young woman. These women, in turn, prepared and cooked a large quantity of vegetables for a feast and carried this food to the house or village of the parents of the young man. They were accompanied by the bride-to-be and her parents. The bride-to-be was left at the lodge of her destined husband, whose friends then invited his relatives to the feast that had been supplied. Here the groom's father told them of the impending marriage. The wedding feast followed "in great hilarity and humor" after which the guests left and the marriage was consummated (Trowbridge *Shawnese Traditions*: pp. 30-1).

Alford's description is much the same: "Usually marriages were arranged by the parents. The parents of a son seeing a maiden they thought would make a fit wife for their son, would approach her parents with a proposal for their son. Either of the young people might object, in which case there was no compulsion, but as parents were usually more particular than young people, their wishes were considered in the matter . . . Usually there was a period of feasting, each family contributing to the good cheer and all the intimate friends enjoying the occasion. There was no marriage ceremony, neither were there any divorce courts." (*Civilization*: pp. 67-8)

Once the two families had reached an agreement concerning the marriage of their children, it was expected that the prospective bride and groom would go along with the plan. If they did not, pressure was often exerted upon them by their siblings. "In case the young man refused to obey his father when advised to marry the object of his choice, appeal was made to the *sisters* of the disobedient, whose opinion, founded upon the state of their affection for the female in question, decided the point. If they were attached to her and desirous that the match should take place, their brother was obliged to yield. In like manner, if the female refused, her *brothers* decided between her parents & herself & she was compelled to submit to their will in the premises" (Trowbridge *Shawnese Traditions*: p. 31).

Further information on Shawnee marital arrangements in the early nineteenth century is found in Trowbridge (*Shawnese Traditions*: p. 33). He remarks that marriage with near relations was absolutely prohibited, but that at that time marriages with second cousins occasionally took place, though it was considered to be highly improper. Bride service, he says, was unknown to the Shawnees, but the custom of "paying for a wife" (bride payment) he was told, had been in force "a long time ago" and was always resorted to when the presents offered by the mother, as before described, were rejected. He notes that in his time it was common for a man and a woman to live together without benefit of marriage, and he adds "Every couple nowadays connect themselves & separate, as suits their convenience or inclination," (*Shawnese Traditions*: p. 33).

Trowbridge notes that a woman's reputation was not affected by having children, even if the father were not known, "for any intimacy is construed for the time into a state of matrimony & the reputed father seldom denies his offspring" (*Shawnese Traditions*: p. 33).

Trowbridge asserts that at least half of the married women were without children, and that this had been the case for the preceding forty or fifty years. He estimated that the average number of children in a family, including these childless women in his calculation, was about four, and that the average interval between births was two years. Shawnee women, he says, began to bear children at the age of sixteen, and few continued to do so after 35 or 40 (*Shawnese Traditions*: p. 33).

It should be kept in mind that Trowbridge secured his material at a time of great stress in Shawnee culture, and that his reportage may reflect a certain degree of social disorganization not unlike that experienced in Europe and even the United States in World War II. Such casual arrangements as those mentioned by Trowbridge were by no means uncommon even in Alford's time, however, for he writes that young people sometimes arranged matters for themselves and: "having arrived at such an understanding the two announced their intentions to their respective families, and took up their lives together, and built a we-gi-wa or cabin for their home" (*Civilization*: pp. 67–8).

Some additional bits of information on the Shawnee concept of married life is found in "Shawnee Laws" (Voegelin, Yergerlehner, and Robinett "Shawnee Laws"). This corpus of material was supposedly made up by the Creator for the use of man, providing him with a way to live. One portion of the law concerns the instruction of a new bridegroom, who is supposedly sexually naive. Therefore a sexual initiation with the wife takes place with the help of the husband's mother (ibid.: p. 37):

> Henceforth men teach one another everything, in order that they may respect their sisters. When a man is twenty-five years old, at the time he is customarily married off, he doesn't know a thing about the way to have intercourse with his wife. At the time they must marry, therefore, young men are given personal instruction in the way each one should try to act when having intercourse with his wife. It seems that once a woman helped her son learn the way he should try to act. 'You must pull over your clothes like this," she said to her daughter-in-law, 'and you must lie still,' she told her. She helped her son get an erection. When he had an erection, he got on top. 'Crawl off,' she told him. Properly she directed his penis to the woman's vaginal orifice. 'Now, if you get it to go in, say 'all right' to me, and I'll turn the two of you loose,' But people become frenzied when they do not follow exactly the way it was arranged for them, the way they ought to follow, the way it was intended for them.

Elsewhere in the "Laws" we learn that a wife separates from her husband for eight days each month (ibid.: p. 38), and that a husband is forbidden intercourse with his pregnant wife (ibid.: p. 39) Infrequent intercourse is considered conducive to the health of husband, wife, and children (ibid.: p. 39) and old men doctor overly virile young men (ibid.: p. 39). There is a law prohibiting intercourse for six months after the birth of a child (ibid.: p. 39) also a law prohibiting adultery of the husband, and specifying penalties (ibid.: p. 39). The ideal family size that is recommended is twelve children (op. cit.: p. 39) though this is probably just an instance of the Shawnee fondness for the symbolic numeral twelve.

Trowbridge says that a Shawnee couple rarely showed any evidence of affection in public. "On the contrary the Indian prides himself upon controlling his feelings and manifesting a perfect indifference to his wife, in the presence of others. (*Shawnese Traditions*: p. 34)" He hastens to add that they "entertain very strong affections, notwithstanding these appearances."

In the government of the children the father and mother divided the responsibility; the father usually correcting the boys, the mother the girls. Sometimes the father extended his corrections to the girls, but the wife seldom interfered with the conduct of her sons, instead referring their conduct to the father (ibid.: pp. 34-5).

Shrewish women, termed "scolds" by Trowbridge, were uncommon among the Shawnees, as community norms discouraged such behavior: "The husband generally interferes with his wife if she scolds, and if he cannot prevent her by persuasions, he often uses force. For these reasons it cannot be considered a prerogative of the sex" (ibid.: p. 35).

Women had complete charge of the household and its affairs and often assisted their husbands in trading. The husband, however, might suggest any alteration in domestic discipline that pleased him, and the wife must conform to it (ibid.: p. 35).

In regard to illness, Trowbridge tells us that in his day "ague & fever" (malaria), rheumatism, venereal diseases, headaches and toothaches were the most common complaints, with consumptions (or tuberculosis) and asthmas known but not frequent (ibid.: p. 35). Today malaria, venereal diseases, and tuberculosis have been largely eliminated and dental work is available to all who need it. Diabetes, high blood pressure, and heart disease are probably the greatest killers among present-day Shawnees.

The Shawnees, like other Native American peoples, combined the skillful use of herb remedies and simple therapeutic techniques with magic in their medical practice. Trowbridge notes that many roots and herbs (which his principal informant, the Prophet, refused to disclose) were used by the Shawnees of that period, particularly the priest-shamans (ibid.: 35). Some continue in use at the present, and their identity and application are closely guarded secrets. A knowledge of such herbs was often acquired, at least ostensibly, by an individual during the vision quest, as I have noted earlier.

Young O. M. Spencer records that he was treated by the old priestess Cooh-coo-cheeh, a Mohawk matron living among the Shawnees (O. M. Spencer *The Indian Captivity of O. M. Spencer*: p. 77): "Boiling a strong decoction of red oak and wild cherry bark and dewberry root, of which I drank frequently, and in which I occasionally soaked my feet for several days, she effected in a short time a perfect cure." Spencer was suffering from fatigue, hunger, dysentery, and swollen and blistered feet, which were the results of the long march to the Shawnee villages subsequent to his capture. Of Cooh-coo-cheeh Spencer then writes (ibid.: p. 78): "Cooh-coo-cheeh was . . . esteemed a very great medicine woman, eminently skillful in the preparation of specifics believed to be of great efficacy, but whose extraordinary virtues were more particularly attributed to her powerful incantations and her influence with the good spirits, with whom she professed to hold daily intercourse."

The Shawnees could set broken limbs skillfully. Alford tells how his mother, who seems to have been somewhat of a curer, set his broken arm (Alford in Galloway *Old Chillicothe*: p. 176):

> At one time I was thrown from a wild pony I was riding. My arm was broken! I felt no pain at first, but as I took hold of it with my other hand, it began to pain me, and I was scared frantic. I made the woods ring with my howls, as I hurried home to mother. She shamed me for making such a noise, appealed to my manhood to endure the pain quietly, while she was hurriedly examining my arm. Then she made me as comfortable as she could, while she hastened to prepare a bandage, for which she was known to be very skillful. Going to a creek near the house, she took a limb about the size of my arm from an elm-tree. Then she very dexterously slipped the bark from the limb, and placed it about my broken arm. She pulled the bone into place, adjusted it carefully, and bound the bark comfortably loose about it, with a dexterity that is seldom used except by skilled surgeons. I was kept quiet, given plenty of cold water until the fever had passed, and in due time my arm was perfectly healed.

Surgery, except for the removal of bullets from wounds, was avoided: "They never perform surgical operations, nor would they amputate a limb if it were broken to pieces, but with simples they would prevent mortification, & if the diseased never recovered the use of the limb, it would at least be healed" (Trowbridge *Shawnese Traditions*: p. 35).

Bleeding, a crude form of counter-irritation, was sometimes employed by Shawnee doctors. Trowbridge tells us (ibid.: p. 35):

"They bleed for the rheumatism and for a general lassitude in the system, which is considered a forerunner of disease, and is thus timely prevented, but bleeding is not often resorted to." Harvey (H. Harvey *A History of the Shawnee Indians from the Year 1681 to 1854 Inclusive*: pp. 169–179) also reports the use of the bleeding method by the Shawnee Prophet on a man who was suspected of having been "witched" (he was actually dying of tuberculosis). Neither Trowbridge nor Harvey describe the precise method employed by the Shawnees in the bleeding treatment. I would imagine that it involved the doctor making small incisions in the patient's body with a flint knife and then, using a sucking horn made from the tip of a bison or cow horn, sucking a quantity of blood from the wound. This technique was used until quite recently by several Oklahoma Indian tribes.

Trowbridge comments that the Shawnees of his day were familiar with the technique of feeling the pulse, and that they depended upon its state for a knowledge of the advance or height of fevers (*Shawnese Traditions*: p. 35).

Priest-shamans were not numerous among the Shawnees. Trowbridge says that there were generally two in each village (ibid.: p. 36).

Often illness was attributed to the machinations of witches, and there is still a residue of this feeling among present-day Shawnees. A typical instance is the one mentioned by Harvey to which I have referred above. This occurred among the Shawnees at Wapaughkonetta in 1819. As noted, the man was treated by the bleeding method. Later the suspected witch, a woman named Polly Butler and her daughter, were hidden by the Quaker missionary, who offered to die himself in the woman's stead. This saved her life.

The Shawnee theory of illness by witchcraft is neatly illustrated in a series of four paintings by the Absentee Shawnee artist Earnest Spybuck. These paintings are now in the collections of the Museum of the American Indian, Heye Foundation, and they are reproduced in this study with their permission. In the first painting (Plate 30) we see the witch at the bedside of his victim, shooting "witches arrows" into the victim's body by blowing with his mouth toward the victim's chest. He has entered the victim's home in the shape of an owl, a favorite vehicle for witches because of the silent wings of this night flyer, and he still carries his owl costume on his left arm. The witch is otherwise naked except for a breechcloth. The dark rings around his eyes indicate his evil nature. All three occupants of the house, the victim and two other members of his family, have been put into a deep narcoticlike sleep by the witch while he performs his nefarious work.

In the second painting of the series (Plate 31) we see that the victim has awakened, and that he is terribly ill. He is being treated with the contents of the family medicine cabinet by a woman and a man, who may certainly be close relatives and are perhaps his sister and her husband, but to no avail. Outside the door we see the witch, who has again assumed his owl shape (except for human feet) grinning evilly. The family watchdog, under the effects of the same sleep as the humans in the first scene, is unaware of the witch's presence.

In the third scene (Plate 32) the victim has been moved out of the family cabin to a tent in the yard, where he can breathe easier (according to Mary Spoon, John and Lilly Ellis). The women of the household are brewing native herb medicines over an outside fire. A child wanders disconsolately from tent to cabin and the family dog bays morosely at the moon, sensing the evil lurking in the atmosphere. The witch, now in the form of a black dog with a human face, prowls the premises, gleefully watching his victim's worsening condition.

In the fourth and last scene (Plate 33) a sweat doctor has been called in a final desperate attempt to effect a recovery. This doctor has erected a sweat lodge near the cabin and he (the seated man wearing only a breechcloth) and the victim (reclining figure) are about to enter the sudatory. The witch, however, at some distance from the scene in the woods, is attempting to counter this therapy by evil magic, involving what appears to be a small effigy of the victim, which he manipulates over a small fire.

Trowbridge (*Shawnese Traditions*: p. 36) mentions a society of magicians formerly present in the tribe (a hundred years or more earlier) but says that the priest-shamans who practiced the curing arts were entirely distinct from this group. This society of sorcerors was reputedly able to kill, dismember, and feed the body of a boy initiate to their dogs; then, by magically dancing around the remains, they were able to bring the boy back to life again, intact. This society would seem to correspond to the I'dus of the Iroquois, and to be more distantly related to the Midéwiwin or grand medicine society of the Ojibwas, Potawatomis, Menominis, Sauks, Foxes, and other Woodland and Prairie tribes. Though data are lacking, one can suppose that members of this society of magicians were suspected of secretly practicing witchcraft.

In regard to the mortuary customs of the Shawnees, we have an excellent corpus of material, extending in time from Joutel's account of 1687 to my own data secured from 1971-1976. These accounts of actual Shawnee funerals are supplemented by several informants' accounts of the burial customs of the five Shawnee divisions in the period from 1890 to 1938, as well as a description of the older Mekoche division rites secured by E. W. Voegelin in the 1930s. Voegelin's extensive data is contained in her excellent monograph *Mortuary Customs of the Shawnee and other Eastern Tribes* (1944). Because Voegelin's material is much too lengthy to present here, even in abridged form, I will merely present her summary of the 1890-1938 practices for the Shawnees as a whole, continue with a few historical accounts, and end with descriptions of two Shawnee funerals which I attended in the 1970's. Voegelin writes (E. W. Voegelin *Mortuary Customs of the Shawnee*: pp. 143-7):

> An analysis of field data shows that the present-day burial customs of the five Shawnee divisions, Thawikila, Kishpoko, Pekowi, Chalakaatha, and Mekoche, conform to one well-defined tribal pattern. This pattern, which is representative of the period 1838 to 1890 at least, varies among the divisions only in certain details. Omitting any discussion of such details for the present, Shawnee burial rites as practiced today by all five divisions may be summarized as follows:
>
> The body of the deceased is kept covered inside the dwelling house for about half a day after death, then prepared for burial. It is bathed and the extremities are tied if need be. It is then dressed in new clothes, including the man's or woman's shirt, either of buckskin or cloth, plain, handsewn, and lacking buttons. These garments are provided by the blood kin of the dead. Moccasins are used as footgear for both men and women. The hair is combed, and before burial the face is painted, a man's being painted variously or not at all, and a woman's having a round red spot painted on each cheek. After the body is dressed, it is laid supine, with the arms crossed over the chest, and is covered with a robe. It is then removed, feet first, from the house or tent where it was prepared and wrapped. Removal is through the regular doorway. The "tracks" of the corpse are "erased" by sweeping the ground or throwing out ashes when the body is removed from the house or later. Outside, the corpse is laid south or southeast of the dwelling house, either on the ground or on a plank. The body lies supine, head west, feet east. Some of the possessions of the deceased are set beside the body.
>
> The blood kin of the dead person are responsible for the funeral. They are called at once when death occurs and, without stopping to change whatever clothes they may have on, go immediately to the house of the deceased. The kin of the surviving spouse also attend, as do friends, but play an inactive role during the interment ceremonies. Young children should not attend funerals, or at least should not be present at the actual interment of the body.
>
> The close kin of the dead choose a funeral leader or director; in case a man

dies, the leader must be a man. This official, who comes to the house of death as soon as he is summoned, may also serve as a speaker during the burial rites, or the latter duty may be delegated to some other elderly man. Two or three corpse handlers who also serve as gravediggers are selected, a woman always being among these. None of the gravediggers should be related to the deceased, and all must belong to a different name group (gens) than that of the deceased. A necklace is put around each gravedigger's neck.

Women cooks are also hired for the ceremony. The grave attendants and cooks are paid from the bundled possessions of the deceased; remuneration of the director is optional.

The funeral rites last four days. A vigil, either inside or outside the dwelling, is held beside the corpse during the first night. Disposal of the body may be on the first day after death; interment in the ground with head west, feet east, is the customary form of burial. The gravediggers prepare the grave after a plot has been measured off with a thong or stick; the open grave is "closed" temporarily by laying a shovel or stick across it after it has been dug. A speech is made to the corpse as it lies outside in the yard. The body is then carried to the grave. The shovel used to close the grave is removed and the body is laid on its back in an extended position in the grave, head west, feet east, with a pillow under the head. Some divisions deposit a small amount of grave goods in the grave, others deposit none. The blood relatives of the dead walk in single file slowly around the grave, each person receiving from the director a small amount of native tobacco which he or she casts into the grave. Upon leaving the grave to return to the house, each person must look straight ahead and not glance backward over his shoulder toward the grave, as this would be an insult to the dead.

A burial address is delivered at the grave by the director or speaker. The gravediggers close the grave, assisted by the woman gravedigger and by any volunteers who care to help. A grave house is built over the grave.

All mourners wash themselves with a plant decoction for purification. Gravediggers and corpse handlers wash themselves also, and are subject to special purificatory rites. A large feast is served to the funeral guests after interment. The gravediggers do not share in this but are fed separately. Following the feast, most of the guests leave. A few close kin of the dead remain with the surviving spouse, one kinsman staying to light a fire at the grave each night until the fourth-day ceremonies. This fire lights the spirit on its journey. The sticks for the fire are laid in an east-west line.

On the third night after the death of either an adult or a child, the mourners reassemble at the home of the deceased for an all-night vigil. A meal is prepared for the deceased and served to the dead and his blood kin, prior to or during this vigil. Eating this food is referred to as "eating the last meal with the dead." The watch is held outside if the weather permits. Old men and women narrate myths and tales during the night. The vigil ends near dawn on the morning of the fourth day, at which time the spirit of the dead leaves this earth and goes above. After dawn all the mourners undergo purification rites and have their heads washed. Mourners who cannot be present wash their heads at their homes. The headwashing, which is done with unmedicated warm water, takes place outside near the dwelling of the deceased. After having his (or her) head washed, each mourner combs his hair. The dwelling and surrounding premises are also purified; the yard around the house is swept and new fires kindled. Distribution of the property which was laid beside the corpse prior to interment is made to the funeral attendants. A breakfast is served, the food for the meal having been provided by the blood kin of the dead.

If the deceased was a married person, a condolence ceremony is held for the surviving spouse, usually coinciding with the third-night vigil and fourth-day head washing. The disposal of the spouse is a matter which is decided upon by the blood kin of the deceased who discuss it before the third-night watch. Replacement of the mate by the levirate or sororate is possible, but the bereaved spouse is more often entirely released from all obligations and connections with the dead person's kin group.

At the condolence ceremony the bereaved spouse sits near or between the watch fires, in the midst of the assembled mourners. An affinal relative sits close beside him (her). The spouse and the attendant must remain awake the entire night; a pan of plant tea is set near them and at intervals the spouse's face is freshened with the tea to help him keep awake. At dawn the spouse's hair is washed and his face painted. New clothes are provided by the close blood kin of the deceased. A condolence speech is delivered in which the spouse is enjoined to lead a cheerful life. The extended mourning taboos are reviewed, and the spouse is then returned to his blood kin. This ceremony marks the end of the four-day period of more-or-less intensive taboos for the surviving spouse. At the breakfast which is served after the ceremony all present partake, including the spouse.

A series of taboos is imposed on all mourners during the four-day funeral rites. They must not change their clothes, wash their hair, or paint during this period. Gravediggers and corpse handlers are under special taboos; they must eat by themselves and should not touch young children for four days. If the deceased was a married person, the surviving spouse must not touch the corpse and must sit quietly within the dwelling house facing east throughout the four-day period. The spouse must also wear old clothes and should not paint or wash his face or perform his ordinary labor for four days.

Graves are dug about four feet deep, and have an east-west orientation. The interior of the grave is lined on the ends, sides, and bottom with wood or bark, and a piece of bark or wood is set over the body. Among the Absentee (and perhaps also among the Cherokee Shawnee) poles are laid across the top of the grave flush with the ground, bark is laid over the poles, and the earth taken from the cavity is piled over this bark covering. The upper half of the grave cavity is consequently empty. All earth taken from the grave must be replaced. A grave house, built of logs four or five inches in diameter, is erected over the grave. There are no regular cemeteries among the Absentee Shawnee today, their graves being dug northeast of the dwelling houses. Among the Cherokee Shawnee cemeteries are of recent introduction, their graves, also, having been dug near the dwelling until toward the close of the last century.

At the death of a chief all the families of his division are notified immediately, and the funeral rites differ somewhat from those accorded an ordinary person.

Some negative features of all present-day Shawnee interments are: lack of metal, shell, or stone ornaments or buttons on grave clothes; lack of stone, pottery or metal objects (such as weapons and dishes) in the grave as grave goods; lack of food in the grave (?); lack of stones for lining the grave or as headstones; lack of painted wooden grave posts; lack of any singing or dancing at funerals; lack of gambling with dice at funeral wakes or afterward at the grave. Cremation, reburial, scaffold burial, or burial under the floor of the house are not practiced. Property is not destroyed after a death; a spirit bundle is not kept; the surviving spouse does not cut or gash his body and is not subject to taboos against eating any special kinds of food. The living house is not abandoned after death.

These mortuary traits are shared in common by all five Shawnee divisions. There are other traits common to one, two, or three divisions, but not to all five. The following historical accounts of Shawnee funerals will serve to indicate some of these differences as well as changes through time.

Our earliest account of Shawnee obsequies is that of Joutel, dated October 1687. Joutel is describing the customs of the Shawnees living at Fort St. Louis on the Illinois river, who were presumably of the *Mekoche* division (see Voegelin *Mortuary Customs of the Shawnee*: p. 273). Joutel writes (H. Joutel *A Journal of the Last Voyage Perform'd by Monsr. de La Sale*: pp. 174-5):

> They pay a Respect to their Dead, as appears by their special Care of burying them, and even putting into lofty Coffins the Bodies of such as are considerable among them, as their Chiefs and others, which is also practiced among the *Accancea's* [Quapaws] but they differ in this Particular, that the *Accancea's* weep and make their Complaints for some days, whereas the *Chahouanous* [Shawnees] and other People of the *Illinois* Nation do just the Contrary; for when any of them die, they wrap them up in Skins, and then put them into Coffins made of the Barks of Trees, then sing and dance about them for twenty four Hours. Those Dancers take Care to tie Calabashes, or Gourds about their Bodies, with some *Indian* Wheat [grains of corn] in them, to rattle and make a Noise, and some of them have a Drum, made of a great Earthen pot, on which they extend a wild Goat's Skin, and beat thereon with one Stick, like our Tabors.
>
> During that Rejoicing, they throw their Presents on the Coffin, as Bracelets, Pendants, or Pieces of Earthen Ware, and Strings of Beads, encouraging the Singers to perform their Duty well. If any Friend happens to come thither at that Time, he immediately throws down his Present and falls a singing and dancing like the rest. When that Ceremony is over, they bury the Body, with Part of the Presents, making choice of such as may be most proper for it. They also bury with it, some Store of *Indian* Wheat, with a Pot to boil it in, for fear the dead Person should be hungry on his long Journey; and they repeat the same Ceremony at the Year's End.
>
> A good number of Presents still remaining, they divide them into several Lots, and play at a Game, call'd of the Stick, to give them to the Winner. That Game is play'd, taking a short Stick, very smooth and greas'd, that it may be the Harder to hold it fast. One of the Elders throws that Stick as far as he can, the young Men run after it, snatch it from each other, and at last, he who remains possess'd of it, has the first Lot. The Stick is then thrown again, he who keeps it then has the second Lot, and so on to the End. The Women, whose Husbands have been slain in War, often perform the same Ceremony, and treat the Singers and Dancers whom they have before invited.

Our second account, entitled "Death and Its Incidents" is found in Trowbridge (*Shawnese Traditions*: pp. 24-25) and describes the burial customs of the Shawnees around 1824. Presumably this material relates to the Kishpokotha division, the Prophet's division of the tribe.

> When life leaves the body, the friends of the deceased assemble around the corpse and there remain some time weeping. Then some friends, of a different tribe [clan] from that of the deceased, dress the body in new clothes & paint the

face. In this manner the corpse is kept two days, when it is carried to the grave by the same attendants who dressed & laid it out. The grave is dug in the earth about four feet deep, and to supply the place of a coffin it is lined with rough planks of wood, split with a tomahawk. All the relatives of the deceased, old & young, great & small, follow the corpse, and when arrived at the grave & the body is deposited, each of the friends, moving around towards the west, sprinkles over the body a small quantity of tobacco, repeating the entreaties which have been mentioned among the Delawares, that the deceased would not look back to earth, or think about the friends which remain behind, but rather pursue the course pointed out for the dead & trouble none whose lot it is to survive him. Nothing but the tobacco is put into the grave with the deceased. When the mourners & friends return to the village they find a mourning feast prepared for them, of which they partake, and at the close one of the aged men addresses the mourners, exhorting them to forget the loss of their friend & reminding them that such must be the lot of all. Then the property of the deceased, if he be a man, is distributed by the friends among those who performed the services of washing the corpse, digging the grave &c—and the party return to their respective homes. These services are performed by men if the deceased is of that sex, but in the case of the death of a female an equal number of each is employed.

The relatives mourn for a period of 12 days, at the end of which time a feast is prepared and after partaking of this they wash themselves and again participate in the customary amusements & employments. In case of the loss of a husband or wife, the period of mourning is extended to 12 moons, during which time the survivor abstains from all amusements or other connexion with society except such as is absolutely necessary, wearing the same suit of clothes, tho' they be reduced to rags, avoiding paint and ornaments & never washing the face or hands. At the end of this time the survivor, if he be a husband, is dressed in new clothes & ornaments, prepared by the family of his wife's parents; he is washed, and having joined a great feast prepared for the purpose he is discharged from the obligation to mourn longer. The same ceremonies are practiced by the parents of the husband towards his wife, if she be the survivor.

They seldom visit the graves of deceased persons—never, unless to remove the weeds. They never take up the bones for re-interment.

It has never been customary to burn the bodies of deceased persons.

They generally take leave of their friends before death, exhorting them to forget their loss, & to submit to the will of the great spirit who ordains that all shall die.

They believe that some of those who die will be restored again to life in the other world—but this will not be the case with all.

Elsewhere in the same work Trowbridge comments (*Shawnese Traditions*: p. 48): "It has been stated that the goods of deceased persons were divided among the attendants upon the funeral & friends around, but this practice does not extend to the household stuff, horses, guns & other property of that description. The latter is distributed to the children or placed in the hands of their guardians, and the former is construed to mean only trifling articles of merchandise, skins &c"

In his list of games, dances, and amusements Trowbridge mentions what was apparently a memorial dance for the dead (*Shawnese Traditions*: p. 51).

Kaukeewaakāūwaa—The turning dance. This is commenced at noon, the dancers, men and women intermixed, moving a short time in one direction and then turn directly about. This is esteemed a great dance and is in use only after the death of some distinguished personage. It is danced one year after his death. The relatives and friends collect a large quantity of goods, and then invite the villagers to a feast. They feast and dance for 4 days, at the end of which the goods are placed in a pile, and a person is appointed to divide them. Another is appointed who prepares a small string of buckskin and greases it. This is wound around his finger and he goes about, offering it to those who stand by. A small piece of the end is left sticking out and every one pulls at it. If one is so fortunate as to get the string, the others immediately try to take it from him, and no one is entitled to a present, but he who brings the string to the pile. Sometimes the competition is so great that whole day is taken up in winning and distributing the goods.

This description of the Turning Dance indicates the general validity of Joutel's 1687 account of Shawnee funeral rites. This ceremonial was not remembered by any of my informants.

Our next account is Harvey's description of the funeral of Chief Blackhoof in 1830 (Harvey *A History of the Shawnee Indians*: pp. 186-88, 253). Blackhoof (Catahecassa) was probably of Thawikila descent.

At the death of Blackhoof in 1830, the corpse was wrapped in a clean new blanket and a large quantity of fine new goods such as calico, belts, and ribbons were laid around and about the corpse, also his gun, tomahawk, & knife. The corpse was laid on a new, clean slab.

All Indians present had their clothing and hair hanging about them in the loosest manner. Many of them had their faces painted. All of the men were smoking. The spoil of a two day hunt of deer and turkey by young men selected for that purpose were in the yard in front of the cabin, also a large quantity of bread. All was stacked in one pile and carefully guarded by some boys. The pallbearers took four large straps, placed them under the body, and carried it to the grave. No small children were allowed to accompany the procession, lest they cry out. The children of the deceased followed the corpse then the head chief, then other chiefs, then Whites, then the whole company. The grave was 3-1/2 feet deep. Split puncheons about 10 inches wide were set on the edge at each side. The clothing of the deceased (which he last wore in health) was laid on his body but his old moccasins were cut in pieces and placed with the rest. No weapons were placed in the grave. Then another puncheon was laid over him.

John Perry, the new head chief, then took some small seeds [tobacco] from a cloth, and commencing at the head of the grave, walked carefully around it, sprinkling them all over it as he went. He then walked directly to the house, followed by all the company except for 3 grave diggers. After this was finished the men went to the creek and purified themselves by "puking" and washing their bodies. The group could now commence conversation and smoked all around, then devoured the feast.

Elsewhere Harvey notes that John Perry distributed seeds (which was undoubtedly native tobacco) from a cloth to all present. He also mentions that the same custom of loosening the hair and clothing and taking the "seed" in the mouth and chewing it was followed when the Shawnee chiefs said goodbye to him at the end of his missionary service in 1842 (Harvey *A History of the Shawnee Indians*: p. 253). This probably indicates that this parting was, to them, much like a funeral and that they did not expect to see him again in this life. The ceremonial hunt and the stacking of the venison, turkey, and bread in the yard mentioned by Harvey at Blackhoof's funeral is strikingly reminiscent of the procedure followed in the Shawnee Bread dance, to be described in a later chapter.

Alford's description of his mother's funeral in 1869 follows (*Civilization*: pp. 63-4).

I was nine years old when my mother died. She had been ailing for several days, and we children knew that there was something unusually wrong with her, but we were not allowed to go into the cabin where she lay. Father told us she was *ah-qui-lo-ky* (ill). Some of the neighbor women were with her, and a medicine man from Little River came to see her. A great sadness seemed to hover over the earth. It was only a few days, probably four or five, when I passed the door and saw that she was carefully covered with a white cloth, and all the women were silently weeping. Father came to where we children were sitting, gloomy and sad, and told us that our mother was *ah-san-wah* (vanished, or disappeared), an expression that always is applied to the death of a person by the Shawnees. A great many people came to the house. Everything was done in an orderly way and very quietly. There were no noisy protestations of grief, though sorrow was in every heart, for my mother was much loved by her people.

Just a little way from the house a grave was dug, and at the appointed time four men carried the body to the grave, by straps placed beneath it, and lowered it into the grave. Then a silent procession formed at the house, with my father at the head, we children next, then relatives and friends.

Between the house and the grave an elderly man stood with a small buckskin bag held open in his hand; it contained sacred tobacco, which always was used on such occasion. As the procession passed him, each person dipped his thumb and forefinger into the bag, taking a small bit of the tobacco, holding it thus, as he passed around the grave, from the foot to the head; there he would stoop slightly as he dropped the tobacco into the grave.

The procession continued until all had passed by the open grave, and returned to the house. Last came the elderly man who held the tobacco; he knelt at the head of the grave, and holding a bit of the sacred tobacco over the grave he made remarks. He called the deceased by name, and implored her not to allow the sorrow of her husband and children and other relatives to hinder her on her journey into that happy world beyond, but to go serenely and happily as was intended by *Kuh-koom-they-nah* (our Grandmother, or Great Spirit). Then after dropping a bit of tobacco into the grave, he said it was true that her husband and children, her relatives and friends were full of sorrow, for that was *wa-chi-tah* (natural, or intended), but their sorrow soon would be wiped out by the goodness of Kuh-koom-they-nah. The love they had for her here should make her happier in the land to which she had gone, and still happier would be their meeting when they joined her in the next world. The man then finished dropping the tobacco into the grave, which was covered by the men who had carried the body.

Although outwardly we were calm, our hearts were torn with grief as deep and sincere as ever children felt for their parent. Some of our neighbors remained to cheer us. The women cleaned the cabin thoroughly, and swept the yard. These good friends stayed with us until the fourth day, when everyone bathed, even to our hair, and changed into fresh, clean clothes. Then a ceremony of cheer was held for father and for us, in which we were advised to lay aside our grief and be happy, for so our departed loved one would wish us to do.

Alford's account is probably typical of the practices of both Kiskpoko and Pekowitha divisions at that time. He notes that the "rite of cheer" (condolence ceremony) that followed four days after all Shawnee funerals was varied slightly in the case of a widow who was left with children by the death of her husband (*Civilization*: p. 65).

> For the first day after the burial of her husband a widow was allowed to give way to her grief; then she was advised to choose a man to take the place of the departed one, for the sake of her children. She should then rest herself with sleep, and take food for the ordeal before her. Then on the third day her friends gathered about her in the evening, and a cheerful night was passed. The men and women all assumed a lively manner, and told stories of the bravery of the men, interesting legends, and even jokes, to keep her interested. A preparation of herbs and cold water was wiped over her face at intervals, to keep her fresh and awake. As the sun began to rise, an elderly man, some relative or intimate friend, took a position at the back of the widow's seat and addresses her in this manner: "My daughter, your husband has vanished, and has left you alone with your little children. He was a good man [there follows a list of his good qualities], but he is gone. It is not right that you should grieve for him; he would not have it so. It is right that you should select some man to take his place and be a father to your little children."
>
> He then called upon her to select the man whom she would like to take the place of her departed husband [the levirate]. If she selected one, the friends departed and left them alone together. This little ceremony of cheer was regarded as a marriage ceremony. If the widow did not select her mate, the usual order of selection was used, which simply was the desire expressed by two people to take up the duties of life together. No ceremony was then necessary.

Joab Spencer gives only a few details regarding funeral customs in his *The Shawnee Indians* (p. 391), but they cover aspects that are not touched upon by others. Spencer's material relates to the Kansas (now the Loyal) band of Shawnees, a group composed largely of members of the Mekoche and Chalakaatha divisions: "A fire is kept burning for three nights at the head of the grave of one just dead. A small opening was made from the mouth of the dead to the surface by inserting a long rod through the newly filled grave, then withdrawing it. Provisions were also kept at the head of the grave for 3 nights. They explained this custom by saying it took 3 days and nights for the spirit to reach the spirit land . . . The dead were feasted periodically lest they return and inflict illness on friends and kinfolk. Provisions were set out for them."

In a 1937 interview John H. Bennett, a white man who was familiar with Shawnee customs, described Shawnee graves (Indian Archives, Oklahoma Historical Society Vol. 14: pp. 367-68): "Shawnee graves were dug about three feet deep. The body was put in and covered with a layer of bark. Stout poles were then driven in the four corners of the grave and then a layer of other poles were "notched" to these so as to completely cover the corpse. Then a layer of 8 to 12 inches of dirt was thrown into the grave. Personal possessions of the deceased were put into the grave above this and a small grave house of poles covered with clapboards was built over the grave. One time when a young woman died, for some reason she was put up on a scaffold 8 or 10 feet high, made of poles, and was left there overnight before being buried."

On 11 and 12 June, 1971, I attended the funeral of Mrs. John Pershing Gokey (née Frances Spoon), that was held at the home of her mother, Mary Spoon, two miles north of Tecumseh, Oklahoma. With the consent of Mr. Gokey, Mary Spoon, and others in the family, I offer an account of the proceedings as a record of present-day Absentee Shawnee (Thawikila division) practices. I arrived at the home of Mrs. Spoon, for the purpose of paying a social call, at about 2:00 P.M. Friday afternoon. I noticed a number of cars parked in front and a tent pitched in the backyard, but I thought that it might be a birthday of one of the family members, a family reunion, or something of the sort, because Mary's home was often the site of such gatherings. Several members of the Spoon family and guests were eating at large joined tables in the kitchen. I was told that I was "just in time" and was asked to join the meal. Still not aware of what was happening, I did so. The behavior of the diners was seemingly lighthearted and many jokes were exchanged. They also chatted about the Delaware powwow at Copan, Oklahoma, that several of those present had attended the previous weekend.

Still in the dark as to the reason for the gathering I got up from the table and went into the living room, where I saw that all portraits of family members that I had noticed on previous visits to the house were missing from the walls. There were also two guest registers and a pen on a small table near the front door. "General" John Pershing Gokey, Mary's son-in-law, was seated in the living room so I asked him the reason for the gathering. He then told me that his wife, and my dear friend, Frances Gokey, had succumbed to a heart attack at 2:30 A.M. Thursday morning. I expressed my shock and dismay at this news. He invited me to stay for the wake and burial, which I did.

General informed me that his wife's body could be viewed at a funeral parlor in Tecumseh but would be brought to the Spoon house later that afternoon. I left the house shortly after this and joined others who had gathered, seated on chairs and benches, in the backyard. At about 4:00 p.m. a hearse from the funeral home arrived with the corpse. As it approached the Spoon house, Mr. Gokey was asked to absent himself and retire to the woods west of the house, because he was not supposed to see his wife's body at this time. Friends of the family continued to arrive throughout the afternoon, many of them bringing dishes of food.

Because he had no transportation of his own, I volunteered to fetch Lewis Cuppahe, a priest-shaman of half-Sauk, half Kickapoo background who had been selected to be the religious functionary at the funeral rites. I was asked to remind him to bring his flint, steel, and punk with him so that he might kindle the "pure" fire.

Shortly after I brought Mr. Cuppahe to the Spoon home he proceeded to make this sacred funeral fire. There already were two other cooking fires burning in the Spoon backyard. Cuppahe and Albert Spoon, the brother of the deceased, laid and kindled the funeral fire on the north side of one of the outbuildings west of the house. The fire was laid oriented to the east and west between two large back logs. I was told that it would burn this way the rest of that day, through the next night, and most of the following day. It would then be raked clean and rebuilt, this time oriented north and south, to burn for two more days. The purpose was to "light the spirit of the dead to the afterworld." The Shawnees like many other Algonkian tribes, believe that this journey takes four days. Unlike the Sauks and Kickapoos, however, they believe that the spirit starts on this journey immediately after death. The Sauks and Kickapoos also maintain a fire for four days, but it is kindled *after* the interment.

At about 6:30 P.M. all were invited to come into the kitchen and secure a plate of food to be eaten in the yard. Men ate first, then women and children. After this feast people visited the corpse, which was resting in its casket in the northwest corner of the living room. Mrs. Gokey, who had been an active dancer and craftswoman in life, was attired in full Shawnee woman's costume and surrounded by flowers. Sometime during this interval two of the deceased's brothers filed a small hole in the metal casket to allow the spirit of the dead egress (a custom that is also followed by the Oklahoma Seneca-Cayugas).

People remained around the yard all night. Some stayed only an hour or two, others all night. New arrivals took the place of those who left. The time was spent visiting and joking, and drinking coffee to keep awake. Women discussed their children and gardens, men told of their exploits on various jobs, or in the service. The coffin was closed at midnight. A poker game was gotten up by the family in the Spoon house, using pennies for poker chips. Coffee and tobacco for smoking and chewing were distributed throughout the night to those present. The poker game lasted until 4:00 A.M. when everyone was called to wash hands and faces and eat breakfast. The meal was eaten at the long table inside the kitchen, just off the living room of the house. Eggs, bacon, fried potatoes, and cold breakfast food and milk were featured. Shortly after this a small "ghost feast" was cooked at the sacred "Indian" fire out in the yard for the deceased. I did not observe how it was disposed of. After this a man (not a member of the Spoon family) took a shotgun and two shells from which the buckshot had been removed and went several yards west of the house and fired a salute. I heard only one report, though two shells were mentioned.

About 9:00 A.M. the brothers and sisters of the deceased were given tobacco by Lewis Cuppahe and were ushered into the house to "get rid of it" (that is, to sprinkle it on the inside of the casket). Shortly afterwards Mr. Gokey was called to do the same thing and to observe his wife for the last time. At twenty minutes to ten the hearse and "family car" provided by the funeral home arrived and the six pallbearers, brothers and brothers-in-law of the deceased, were chosen. Members of the Spoon family entered the family car, others used their own vehicles or rode with friends and followed the hearse to the Shawnee (Shawnee, Oklahoma) cemetery. Most of those still present at the Spoon home at this time went to the cemetery, but not the members of the Kickapoo tribe, who avoid visiting cemeteries whenever possible.

At the cemetery, the group assembled at the graveside and the casket was positioned on the mechanical device used to lower it

into the grave, with the head of the deceased to the west. Now
Lewis Cuppahe, the speaker, tobacco bag in hand, stepped
forward. From a position a few feet east of the casket he delivered
a short oration in either the Kickapoo or the Sauk language. Then
Albert Spoon called for the women and girls, beginning with the
immediate family, to come and sprinkle tobacco on the casket.
Each came to where Mr. Cuppahe was standing, took a small
quantity of tobacco in the *left* hand and then circled the casket
and open grave in a counterclockwise direction, sprinkling
tobacco during the first half of the circuit. When all of the females
had done this, the men and boys did the same. The casket was
then lowered and the cover put on the wooden box that surrounded
it. At this point speaker Cuppahe said, in English, "That's all, you
can go now."

Most of those present returned to the Spoon house, where they
washed their arms, hands, faces, and hair in a concoction of a
minty-smelling herb and water. The herbs had been gathered
earlier that morning and boiled in a tub of water on the sacred
funeral fire. The women and children washed first, then the men.
Next, a noonday meal was served. The men were served first, for
the most part, though the rule was not strictly observed on this
occasion. At this point I left (about 1:00 P.M. Saturday). I was told
that there would be a final feast Sunday evening. I also believe
that either late Saturday or on Sunday a giveaway of the personal
possessions of the deceased took place, as I observed Mary Spoon
carrying a large bundle of material, blankets, et cetera, from the
house to one of the outbuildings for temporary storage.

In an interview several weeks after the funeral, Mary Spoon
commented upon it and the funeral customs of her people in
general. She said that the Shawnees still have the custom, noted
by Harvey (*A History of the Shawnee Indians*: p. 186) of loosening
the hair and clothing at funerals [I did not notice this custom at
her daughter's funeral, though I was looking for it]. The
Shawnees have the same custom as the Kickapoos in forbidding
the burial of metal objects with the dead. The reason Mary gave
for this is that metal objects will "turn red hot" and burn the
deceased in the afterworld. The grave diggers must not eat until
the grave is completed and the dead laid to rest. At old-time
Shawnee funerals the dead were not allowed to be viewed after
being placed in the coffin.

Prior to filling the grave each of the burial party is given a small pinch of tobacco that they sprinkle around the grave. According to Mary this is an offering to the spirits of the dead. I asked Mary about the custom of firing a shotgun during a funeral. She did not know if it had any symbolic meaning. She considered it merely an old Shawnee funeral custom and she attributed it to the influence of early white military funerals that the Shawnees had seen. Mary had never heard of the Shawnees playing the moccasin game at wakes. The men sometimes play cards, she said, and the women sometimes play the bowl dice game to keep awake.

Members of the "Little River bunch" (the ultraconservative portion of the Absentees, composed of the Pekowitha and Kishpokotha divisions) still bury their dead, she believes, without coffins. They simply place boards in the bottom of the grave, then the body, then more boards above it. This gets away from the danger of *metal nails* near the corpse. Sometimes, she said, the Little River people are so conservative in their view of funeral procedures that they refuse to attend funerals of Shawnees who are not buried in the traditional fashion. This occurred when her late husband was interred and his own brother refused to attend on these grounds.

The two chief grave diggers are marked by ribbons around their necks. The old custom, still followed at Little River, is for these two to take a bath in a river or lake after they have dug the grave. The Kickapoos, Mary said, put all of the clothing of the deceased in the grave above the corpse, but not the Shawnees. Many Shawnees, even today, place a small wooden house over graves instead of tombstones or other markers. The grave house is a small gable roofed structure made the same length and width as the grave and about two-and-a-half feet high. A notch is always cut in the back to allow the spirit of the deceased to leave. For the same reason that they cut a notch in the back of the grave house, Mary said, the Shawnees always file a hole in the coffin. This custom has some antiquity for Morgan (*The Indian Journals, 1859-62*: p. 83) writes: "Friend Harvey says the Shawnees after they commenced burying in coffins have always had a three cornered hole cut in the coffin at the end near the head. This was to enable the spirit to enter and revisit the body." As I have noted, this custom was followed at Mrs. Gokey's funeral.

My final account is of the funeral of another good friend and informant, Esther (Secondine) Dixon, in October 1973. Mrs. Dixon's funeral; illustrates the mixture of aboriginal and white customs that are now seen in the funerals of the Eastern and Loyal bands of Shawnees. In this instance some of Esther's children favored a completely non-Indian service; but her husband, though white, insisted upon certain traditional features, following her last wishes. The result was a mixture of the two.

I was informed of Esther's death on Friday and drove to her hometown, Nowata, Oklahoma, the place of the funeral, on the following morning. The body was on view at the local funeral home prior to the funeral service, which was held at the same place. The casket was oriented with the head to the west, and Esther was attired in full Indian woman's costume. She clasped a single eagle feather, a symbol of her membership in the Peyote religion, in her right hand, which was positioned over her breast.

The service in the funeral home began at 1:30 P.M. It was in no way different from those of white Oklahomans, and was delivered by a local white minister. Following the service the body was transported in a hearse to the old Secondine family cemetery several miles to the east, followed by a procession of the cars of the mourners.

At the grave, once the casket had been positioned, there was another short sermon in English by the white minister. This was followed by a traditional Shawnee graveside prayer by Bert Ellis, an Absentee Shawnee who lives in Wann, Oklahoma. Mr. Ellis had been called in because of the unavailability of Bill Shawnee, who generally speaks at the funerals of the Eastern and Loyal bands. Mr. Ellis committed Esther's spirit to the care of Our Grandmother, the Creator, and sprinkled a few bits of native tobacco on the casket. He then called Edmund Dixon, husband of the deceased, to do the same, making the traditional counterclockwise circuit of the grave as he did so. Only these two participated in the tobacco-sprinkling service, though Ellis later told me that all of the funeral party would have done so "in the old days." Following graveside condolences the funeral party returned to Nowata, where a funeral supper, provided by relatives and friends of the deceased, was served in the guild hall of a local church. This ended the observances for most of the party.

The husband of the deceased and some of her Indian and white friends, however, were invited to the home of Mrs. Ranny (Emmaline) Carpenter, near the Whiteoak dance ground, to observe a wake for the dead. I attended this wake in the company of Nora Thompson Dean (a Delaware) and her family. When we arrived at the Carpenter house, Mrs. Dean immediately asked for, and was granted, permission to burn cedar at an outside fire and "fan off" the members of our party. This simple rite is performed by the Delawares and Loyal Shawnees on numerous occasions to dispel bad influences, in this case the spirits of the dead. Mrs. Dean expressed great relief once this ritual had been completed.

Following the fanning with cedar incense we reentered the Carpenter home, where relatives and friends of the deceased had begun to gather. At about 10:00 P.M. a late supper was served and those present then settled down for the night of "sitting up", passing the time visiting, telling stories, and watching television. I was unable to remain the entire night but was told that the following morning the group would wash themselves in the customary "tea" or medicine used on such occasions, which would end the observance.

I have noted, in chapter Six, that the man or woman in charge of the funeral and the two men or women grave diggers and corpse-handlers must belong to different name groups from that of the deceased (C. F. Voegelin and E. W. Voegelin "Shawnee Name Groups": p. 629). The Voegelins, citing their informant Jennie Cegar, add that formerly among the Absentee Shawnees, the man who delivered the speech at the grave was not the same man in charge of the funeral. They also state that it made no difference whether the speaker and the deceased belonged to the same name group. The prime consideration was that the speaker knew the formularized speech letter perfect (ibid.: p. 629).

9

Religion and Cosmology

In spite of nearly three hundred years of white acculturation, the religious concepts of the Shawnees and the ceremonials in which these are expressed show little evidence of this long period of alien contact. In viewing Shawnee religion and cosmology we find, as one might expect, that most of the basic concepts are shared with other North American Indian groups, and particularly with other Algonkian groups of eastern North America and the Midwest. Yet, though there are few elements that are the exclusive property of the Shawnees, the total configuration (with greater emphasis upon certain elements and concepts, less upon others) is distinctively their own. Individual Shawnees differ greatly in the degree to which they can conceptualize and describe the various figures in the Shawnee pantheon, yet in all but the highly acculturated Eastern band most adults retain the greater part of what I believe to be the aboriginal pattern and can list and give the attributes of the aboriginal deities. Following the order given by my informants and that of C. F. Voegelin (*The Shawnee Female Deity*) I will list and give the attributes of these deities, and having done so, I will then attempt to indicate how they function in the Shawnee religious system.

SUPREME BEING

At the head of the Shawnee pantheon, according to C. C. Trowbridge (*Shawnese Traditions*: p. 40) is the Supreme being: "They believe in one Supreme being who has a moral superintendence over the affairs of the world. He is called

Müyaataalemeelārkwau [Muyetelemilakwau], or the Finisher, and is served by two subordinate deities, one to take charge of the Indians, and the other of the Whites. "Morgan is undoubtedly referring to this same overall Supreme being when he lists, as the first three names of Shawnee gods and spirits, the following (L. H. Morgan *The Indian Journals, 1859–62*: p. 77): "1. Great Spirit, Ma-ya-ta-la-ta-ga, the Creator, 2. Great Spirit, Ta-pa-la-ma-la-kwa, the Master, 3. Great Spirit, O-a-si-man-a-too, the good or powerful being." The first two names listed by Morgan are clearly related to the term given by Trowbridge. The Great Spirit is mentioned, as such, in the Shawnee origin legend that was told to Joab Spencer by Charles Bluejacket in the period from 1858 to 1860. According to Bluejacket the Great Spirit had made the first man, before the Flood, but Our Grandmother was responsible for the second creation ("Shawnee Folk-lore": p. 319). Alford (T. W. Alford *Civilization*: p. 18) also mentions the Supreme being: "We believed in the existence of a Supreme Being whom we designated as Mo-ne-to, who ruled the universe, dispensing blessings and favors to those who earned His good will, and whose disfavor brought unspeakable sorrow to those whose conduct merited His ill will . . ." Alford's term "mo-ne-to" is clearly related to the third term given by L. H. Morgan (*The Indian Journals, 1859–62*: p. 77) and is the same term that has come into English as "Manitou," the Great Spirit of the North American Indians.

In a myth given by James Clark, an Absentee Shawnee of the Kishpokotha division, to E. W. Voegelin, the *idea* of creation emanates from the Great Spirit (Supreme Being), but the actual task is accomplished by Our Grandmother (C. F. Voegelin and E. W. Voegelin "The Shawnee Female Deity in Historical Perspective,": p. 371).

> In the beginning there was the Great Spirit, formed of wind, invisible, but in the shape of a man. He lives above the sun. There was just space; no earth, no water. The Great Spirit said, "Let there be a woman" and as soon as he spoke there was a being formed like a woman. Then to this woman the Great Spirit gave the work of creating this earth, light (the sun), water, people, animals. She is the one the people saw and knew. Before the flood she and the devil and her grandson and the great giants were all on this earth which she made, and the people talked to them. In this first creation people lived a long time and died four times, but not so today. The Great Spirit must have made the sky, or again it might mean that the Great Spirit was the sky. The female creator is under the Great Spirit. Afterward the female creator did her creating and made the rules which are to be fulfilled.

At the present time the Supreme Being or Great Spirit, though acknowledged as such by many Shawnees, remains only vaguely conceptualized. He seems to be addressed rarely in prayers and ceremonial speeches except where, as in the Peyote religion, He has become identified with the God of Christianity.

OUR GRANDMOTHER, THE CREATOR

Much more important in Shawnee worship today, and more clearly conceptualized, is the Shawnee female deity, commonly called Our Grandmother (*Kokomthena*) or the Creator. In fact, it would appear that between 1824 and the 1930s the emphasis on the Supreme Being or Great Spirit, a male deity, shifted to Our Grandmother, a female, which is a most interesting phenomenon. The earliest mention of the Shawnee female deity is found in Trowbridge (*Shawnee Traditions*: p. 41). He calls her Waupoathee and says, "This old woman seems also to have charge of the affairs of Indians, and is allowed to be nearer the residence of the Great Spirit than her grand child, whose location is immediately above the Indians and so near as to enable him to distinguish them & supply their wants." Morgan (*Indian Journals*: p. 47) has little to say about the Creator: "The Supreme Being of the Shawnee is a woman. Her name is Go-gome-tha-na meaning Grandmother." Later in the same work (Morgan *Indian Journals*: p. 49) he records that Tooly, a Shawnee, told him that the "Great Spirit" of the Shawnees was a woman.

Joab Spencer (*The Shawnee Indians*: p. 383) provides a Shawnee origin legend collected from Charles Bluejacket in the period between 1858 and 1860. It shows obvious European influence, but provides our first account of Our Grandmother's role in the Creation.

> Our traditions of the creation and the antediluvian period agree in all essential points with the Mosaic record. The first real divergence is in connection with the flood. The tradition gives an account of the white man's great canoe and of the saving of a white family, just as the Bible has it, but in addition it states that an old Indian woman was also saved. After the flood she lived in a valley, with a hill intervening between her and her white brother and his family, over which she could see the smoke rise from the white man's wigwam. When the sense of her loneliness and destitution came over her she began to weep very bitterly. There then appeared a heavenly messenger and asked her why she was so sorrowful. She told him that the Great Spirit had left her white brother his family but she was just a poor old woman alone, and that there was to be an end of her people. Then said the visitor, 'Remember how the first man was made,' and then left her. From this she knew that a new Creation was meant, so she made small images of children from the earth as directed, as the Great Spirit had made the first man. But when she saw that they had no life she again wept. Again her messenger appeared and inquired the cause of her

grief. She said she had made children from clay, but that they were only dirt. Then said the visitor, 'Remember how the Great Spirit did when the first man was made. At once she understood, and breathed into their nostrils and they became alive. This was the beginning of the red men. The Shawnees to this day venerate the memory of the one they call their Grand Mother as the origin of their race (Cf. also J. Spencer "Shawnee Folklore": p. 319).

Alford (*Civilization*: p. 19) distinguished between "Mo-ne-to", the Supreme Being, and the Great Spirit, or ruler of destinies, and speaks of the latter saying that she: "was believed to be a Grandmother who was constantly weaving an immense net which was called Ske-mo-tah, and it was the Shawnee belief that when the great net was finished it would be lowered to the earth, and all would be gathered into its folds who had proven themselves by their actions to be worthy of the better world, the happy hunting ground. The world would then come to an end, and some horrible fate awaited those who were left."

The best account of the Shawnee female deity is that of C. F. Voegelin *The Shawnee Female Deity*, based upon fieldwork done by himself and E. W. Voegelin and also on the field notes of Truman Michelson. He notes that in the Shawnee pantheon Our Grandmother (Kokomthena) reigns supreme, and that the three bands of Shawnees are remarkably consistent in their attitude towards her (*The Shawnee Female Deity*: p. 3), an observation that has been confirmed by my own field work: "To a greater or less extent, she establishes, observes, or participates in every aspect of Shawnee religion upon which information was secured . . . She enjoys only nominal association in parts of Shawnee religion which concern the individual *qua* individual; quest for guardian spirit and witchcraft, for example; she is firmly integrated in those parts of religion which are communal in expression or interest, as for example with the future of the group, i.e. prophecy, and with ceremonial dances."

Our Grandmother is described as an anthropomorphic female being with gray hair (sometimes one of the hairs from her head is found on newly born babies). At times she is conceived of as a giant who can pick up adult men and hide them in cracks in the lodgepole of her house. Other descriptions, however, depict her as being small. That she wears short skirts may be seen when her shadow is reflected in the full moon. In one folktale she is painted with the traditional Shawnee woman's face paint, a round red spot on either cheek, and she has her hair parted down the middle. Her personal name is most frequently given as Papoothkwe,

"Cloud-woman," but also Shikalapikshi and Lithikapo'shi, which are both untranslateable except for their feminine endings. (ibid.: p. 4)

The Creator is thought to speak her own special non-Shawnee language in addition to Shawnee and other Indian tongues. This special language is thought to be intelligible to children under four years of age but is unlearned as soon as they begin to speak Shawnee. Formerly certain Shawnee priest-shamans, those who attended the ills of children, could speak this infant-language, but when these doctors died, opportunities to secure specimens of the dialect were lost. (ibid.: p. 4).

Our Grandmother lives in a spacious lodge in heaven, described as a typical Shawnee bark house in one tale (ibid.: p. 5), and as a log cabin by my informant Mary Spoon. Now and then prophets and visionaries, and persons close to death, have visited Our Grandmother's celestial abode and returned to tell of it. As described in the Orpheus tale cited by C. F. Voegelin (ibid. p. 5) the lodge has the typical sleeping and lounging platform at one side. The four mortal visitors find the Creator sitting upon this platform weaving a special basket (*shkimota*), undoubtedly the same item as the "net" in Alford's description. Other features of her house are the typical furnishings of an aboriginal Shawnee dwelling: a central fire, pottery vessels, bark platters and plates, and carved wooden spoons; but she prepares her food in a little "inexhaustible food supply" pot. Her visitors are surprised when they find that they cannot consume all of the food contained in the little pot, which is emptied only after she has eaten (ibid.: p. 5).

The locale of Our Grandmother's house is variously described. In one tale several men travel west until they come to "a lot of water at the end of the earth" ("the edge of the ocean" or "the end of the earth") which they must cross to reach the abode of the Creator (E. W. Voegelin, C. Rafinesque, C. F. Voegelin and E. Lilly *Walum Olum*: p. 9). In an Eastern Shawnee variant of the Orpheus tale an ocean is crossed and much land is also traversed because several pairs of moccasins were worn out on the journey (Voegelin *The Shawnee Female Deity*: p. 5). In an Absentee Shawnee variant the visitors go to a western region beyond the end of the earth, crossing four oceans, with the passage over the last one being possible only as the rhythmically rising and falling sky rises and leaves a gap. The journey seems to have been over flat terrain, but upon arriving the visitors find themselves high above the earth and Our Grandmother shows them a "sky window" through which she observes her earthly children to determine whether they are obedient. On their return journey the visitors take a short cut, being lowered from the "sky window" in a basket and passing through a region between heaven and earth where birds and others live. (ibid.: p. 5) This suggests various "levels of heaven," and in this sense Our Grandmother does not live in the highest level, but on the next lower one, as the Supreme Being is presumably higher than she (Trowbridge *Shawnese Traditions*: p. 40); likewise the sun, the same sun that passes over the earth, passes over the land to which the Shawnee dead go, the place where the Creator stays and lives (Voegelin *The Shawnee Female Deity*: p. 5). Edward J. McClain, an Eastern Shawnee, makes this explicit in a 1937 interview (Indian Archives, Oklahoma Historical Society 6: p. 483) stating that there are "three heavens, one on the bottom of the sea, one on the surface of the earth, and one in the air. My own informant Esther Dixon mentioned that the Milky Way is the road traveled by the dead on their way to heaven, adding that people who on this earth are always kicking and abusing dogs will be set upon by a pack of vicious dogs as they traverse this route, and the dogs will prevent them from entering heaven.

Trowbridge describes this heavenly abode, shared by Our Grandmother and her household and the spirits of the dead (*Shawnese Traditions*: p. 41): "They entertain a confused idea of a future state of punishment & rewards, which seems to originate in a mixture of their own opinions and creed with those taught by the whites. Agreeably to their notion of such things the Great Spirit inhabits a rich, fertile country, abounding in game, fish, pleasant hunting grounds and fine corn fields. Four days after death the soul of the deceased takes her departure for this place, where they remain, pursuing the same course of life which characterized them here. They plant, they hunt, play at their usual games & in all things are unchanged. The soul inhabits a similar tenement of clay. This is the fate of the *good*."

My informants described the other world, the home of Our Grandmother, as resembling this earth in every way except that it is lacking the influences of white civilization. Mary Spoon said that the Shawnee heaven was "open country" or a "bare place" in the sense that there were no highways or towns. Each family lives in its own dwelling, a log cabin according to Mary. There are no doors or locks there. The people live by hunting deer and other game "like the way Indians lived years ago." This heaven is located in the west, in the heavens. For this reason the Shawnees are still buried today in an east-west orientation, with the head to the west. E. W. Voegelin (Voegelin, Rafinesque, Voegelin and Lilly *Walum Olum*: p. 86) secured a similar interpretation for the orientation of Shawnee graves from her informants.

Those who arrive safely in the afterworld find the Creator weaving her *shkimota* ("basket" or "net"). During the night her little dog (with the aid of her grandson, in a Loyal Shawnee account) unravels the weaving of the previous day and thus prevents Our Grandmother from completing it. Some day, however, she will finish it and this will signal the end of the world. The virtuous living will be gathered into the *shkimota*, but those who are evil will be destroyed. Those in the basket or net will be used to populate the new world (Voegelin *The Shawnee Female Deity*: p. 21).

Conservative Shawnees believe that the growing neglect of the Creator's rules means that the impending catastrophe will occur before long. This belief leads to the punctilious performance of the yearly cycle of ceremonies on the part of traditionalist Shawnees, lest they be omitted from Our Grandmother's *shkimota* when doomsday dawns. The dead, and the living when they participate in ceremonies, should always be painted and dressed in Shawnee costume so that Our Grandmother will not mistake them for whites. Formerly the Eastern and Loyal bands of Shawnees burned round scars on the forearms of boys and girls to further mark them off. These scars were said to act as lamps on the way to the Creator (ibid.: p. 19).

C. F. Voegelin (ibid.: p. 10) notes that even though Our Grandmother does not take sweat baths herself, she maintains a sweat lodge for doctoring her visitors. The souls of the virtuous dead are segregated by tribes and further subdivided into kin groups. An especially attractive portion of Our Grandmother's domain is reserved for the souls of warrior men and women, who spend their time in constant dancing and feasting. From this heaven, a soul travels to earth and jumps through the mother's vagina and into the body of the child through the fontanelle just before birth. A variant concept from the Eastern Shawnees has it that babies live rather on the little stars of the Milky Way before birth. Heavenly bodies are thought of as "suburbs" of Our

Grandmother's residence. The moon, apparently, is considered close enough to her home to be her reflector or shade, through which her image is seen, and so ceremonies are held at full moon when she can be observed bending over a pot cooking. Permanent associates of the Creator are her Grandson, her little dog, her "Silly Boys," and sometimes a bantam rooster. The Devil and Cyclone Person are also sometimes present (ibid.: p. 6).

After the Creator retired to her present abode, following her re-creation of the Indian race, she continued to dispense benefits to the Shawnees, supplementing her creations in the postdiluvian period. The origins of most specific items of nature and culture are generally attributed to Our Grandmother. She habitually gives visitors to her lodge useful knowledge to take back with them when they return to earth. These bits of knowledge range from herbal remedies through sacred ways of making fire to important additions to tribal ceremonies. All accounts stress her omniscience; she can read the thoughts of her visitors before they speak.

The Shawnee laws, a very important part of the knowledge and instruction received from Our Grandmother, number twelve (C. F. Voegelin, J. F. Yergerlehner, and F. M. Robinett "Shawnee Laws"). The first law sets forth their origin and purpose, describing their benefits and the consequences of failing to observe them. It also outlines modes of sexual conduct involving intercourse and such states as menstruation and pregnancy. The second is also general in scope. Each of the remaining ten laws centers on a particular animal such as deer, dog, bear, bird, wolf, buffalo, raccoon, turtle, turkey, and crow, spelling out the service it performs for humans and the manner in which it should be treated.

All of the major Shawnee ceremonies except for the Buffalo Dance of the Loyal Shawnees and the Peyote ritual were supposedly originated by Our Grandmother, and sometimes she descends to earth to observe their performance. Even if a ceremony is not primarily devoted to her she will punish its neglect. To this day when the women sing with the men during the *Kokeki* or Women's Cluster Dance, a part of the Bread Dance, an extra female voice, the voice of Our Grandmother, is sometimes heard above the brush arbor.

A number of writers have noted and some have suggested possible reasons for the shift in emphasis from the male Supreme

Being to Our Grandmother, the female deity. This shift occurred
sometimes between 1824 and the time of the Voegelins' work in
1933–35. The Shawnees appear to be unique among all Eastern
Woodlands Algonkian-speakers in possessing a female supreme
deity and creator, hence the subject is of considerable theoretical
interest (Cf. Voegelin and Voegelin "The Shawnee Female Deity
in Historical Perspective"). This shift from a male to a female
supreme deity is difficult to trace to any great change in Shawnee
economic or social structure. Inter-tribal acculturation is a
possibility, and the Voegelins suggest Iroquoian influences as the
most likely one. They point out that there runs through Iroquoian
mythology references to a female deity, Ataentsic, and her son
Iouskaha. This Iroquoian female deity is credited with the
creation of heaven, earth, and mankind, and both she and her son
superintend the world after the creation (ibid.: p. 374). They also
suggest possible Yuchi or Christian (i.e., the Virgin Mary)
influences as less likely possibilities (ibid.: pp. 374–75). In a recent
article Jay Miller has suggested that the Shawnees may have
changed from a male to a female deity because they wished to
differentiate themselves from the Delawares, who believe in an
all-powerful male creator (J. Miller "The Delaware as Women: A
Symbolic Solution": p. 513). I find this last suggestion to be totally
absurd.

    If the shift in emphasis from a male Supreme Being to Our
Grandmother is due to outside influence, I would agree with the
Voegelins that an Iroquoian model is the most likely source. In
this case the close association of the Eastern and Loyal Shawnees
(and their ancestors) with the Oklahoma Seneca-Cayugas (and
their ancestors, the Mingo Iroquois) would have provided ample
opportunity for such borrowing. More likely no outside influence
need be sought. Perhaps the shift merely represents an evolution
in Shawnee belief, a movement away from a male Supreme Being
who is too remote from human affairs to be of any great religious
concern and toward a more immediate and approachable female
deity by the harassed nineteenth century Shawnees.

OUR GRANDMOTHER'S GRANDSON

    Though distinctly subordinate to Our Grandmother, the
Creator, in the minds of present-day Shawnees "Waupoãthee
Skeelauwaathēēthar [*Wapothi Skilawethitha*] or "The boy of
Waupoathee", the grandson of Our Grandmother, was apparently

considered one of the two principal subordinate deities by the Shawnees in Trowbridge's day, the one who was in charge of the welfare of Indians (Trowbridge *Shawnese Traditions*: p. 40). The other subordinate deity, whose business it was to take charge of the Whites "has so little connection with the Indians that they do not pretend even to know his name" (ibid.).

When he was demoted from his high position and replaced by his grandmother we do not know, but present-day Shawnees assign only a minor role to Our Grandmother's Grandson. His personal name is Rounded-Side (Haapochkilaweetha), according to the Absentee Shawnees and Cloudy-boy (*Peputhichkila-weetha*) to the Loyal band (Voegelin *The Shawnee Female Deity*: p. 6). In some Shawnee folktales Our Grandmother's Grandson originates evil creatures and happenings but at the present time he is no longer the source of catastrophes. Instead, he innocently plays with cumulus cloud formations, fashioning them into ephemeral animals for the amusement of people on earth (ibid.: pp. 6, 9). In some variants there are two grandsons, Rounded-Side and his evil brother, who represent a dualism that is common to the stories of other Algonkian-speaking groups. Whether good or evil, Our Grandmother's Grandson is the protagonist in some important tales, such as the one in which he precipitates a great flood by piercing either a giant with a huge belly or a transparent fish monster that has stored up all the waters of the earth in its body (ibid.: p. 9). With the Shawnees this tale is a preliminary to the flood and Earth-diver myth.

OUR GRANDMOTHER'S SILLY BOYS

Sharing Our Grandmother's celestial abode are two "Silly Boys," who are giants whose feet make tracks that are five feet in length (ibid.: p. 6). In the Orpheus tale these Silly Boys have somewhat the same character as the giant in the European tale of Jack and the Beanstalk. Thus, when Our Grandmother has hidden four mortal visitors to her home: "Her Silly Boys enter and criticize her housekeeping, remarking that they detect a very evil smell, an allusion to their pretense at being cannibals. They are of course aware of the visitors whom they attempt to frighten. When Our Grandmother tires of her Silly Boys, she picks up a poker and hits them on their legs" (ibid.: p. 3). Thus Our Grandmother tolerates the nonsense of her Silly Boys, but manages to control them when they threaten the peace of her home.

THE EVIL SPIRIT OR DEVIL

In his present-day conception the evil spirit shows definite European or white influence. Nevertheless I am inclined to believe that he is pre-contact in origin in view of the fact that he is sometimes syncretized with Our Grandmother's Grandson or identified as the brother of that member of the Creator's household. At other times he is identified with the Giant Horned Snake, another aboriginal conception. Trowbridge writes (*Shawnese Traditions*: p. 41): "They believe in the existence of one evil spirit, whom they call sometimes Motshee Monitoo—or Bad Spirit, at others Meearleethēēna [*Mialithina*] which signifies (mean, or mean creature). They suppose that this evil being is alone in all his works, but that he has power to transfer his own spirit into animals & men, whenever he has criminal designs against any one. They do not ascribe to him power equal with the Great Spirit, but believe that he is suffered to punish men & to perplex them in a limited degree, and that even this power could be taken from him at any time."

Trowbridge's account places the Evil Spirit in charge of an Indian hell that was probably copied from that of whites.

> The wicked set out after death, upon the same road [the road to the Shawnee heaven], and when they have traveled until they are in sight of the abode of the good, they find that the road forks, and they are compelled to turn off and direct their course to the country inhabited by Motshee Monitoo. There they are led into a house where they find a large fire prepared for them. If the sufferer have led a very wicked life, he is burned entirely to ashes, but if his crimes have been small he is only maimed. In either case he is made to resume his former appearance and sense of feeling and then is compelled to travel on until he finds another house, where he undergoes the same kind of torment. This is repeated a number of times, according to his deserts, and finally the prisoner is released & suffered to go to the residence of the Great Spirit, where he is permitted to enjoy in a small degree the happiness allotted to his companions (*Shawnese Traditions*: pp. 41-2).

It is interesting to note that in this Indian hell, unlike that of the white man, there is an end to the torments after a suitable period of punishment, not *eternal* tortures. The punishment is fitted to the crime and has the goal of reincorporating the individual into society, in the afterworld as in this one. Nothing could be more Indian.

Sometimes, according to Trowbridge, Shawnee warriors prayed to the Evil Spirit (ibid.: p. 42): "In time of war & particularly on the eve of a battle which is expected to be severely contested they address their prayers to Motshee Monitoo, and when they can muster faith to rely upon him, they say that fear is entirely banished from them and that no man could be induced to fly, but would sell his life dearly, dealing death & destruction to all whom he met." Obvious postcontact influence is present in the Shawnee concept of the Evil Spirit being a white man, or a "cloven-hoofed Hebrew" (Voegelin *The Shawnee Female Deity*: p. 6) Mosquitoes and rats are sometimes said to be the consumed bones of witches' dust blown upon by the Devil (p. 12).

CYCLONE PERSON

C. F. Voegelin identifies Cyclone Person as a man, noting that he is sometimes mentioned as living with Our Grandmother in her heavenly household, sometimes with his colleague, West Wind (p. 6). My informants, however, insisted that Cyclone Person was female, noting that White news commentators were quite correct in giving hurricanes and destructive storms female names. Cyclone Person is a creation of Our Grandmother and hence is regarded as not distinctly evil, though certainly not a desired visitor. She commands respect, not because of any capacity for good she possesses, but because she often withholds disasters that she could inflict. In a now lost Spybuck painting she is pictured as a giant flying human head with long twisting locks of hair. When a cyclone or tornado uproots trees and tears the roofs from buildings, it is Cyclone Person's long hair that has become entangled with these objects and pulls them. Indians who follow the Shawnee religion strictly believe that they have nothing to fear from cyclones or tornadoes. Mary Spoon pointed out that when a tornado struck Shawnee, Oklahoma, some years ago it caused widespread destruction to homes and business establishments of whites, even to structures of brick and stone, but not a single Indian home was touched. Even the cattail mat houses of the Kickapoos were unscathed. Today's Shawnees maintain the same fatalistic attitude in regard to tornadoes and cyclones as that described by Oliver Spencer (*The Indian Captivity of O. M. Spencer*: p. 56). During a tornado that lay bare a wide swath in a nearby forest, and terrified young Spencer: "the Indians were perfectly calm . . . gazing with a delighted sort of wonder and frequently expressing their admiration at more vivid bolts or heavier peals, with the customary exclamation, wawaugh! waugh!" Mary Spoon commented that she liked to sit out on her porch during storms watching the wind bend the trees and the lightning flashing. Her home, she pointed out to me, and those of other Shawnees, lacks the cyclone cellar that one so commonly sees near White farm homes in Oklahoma.

THE FOUR WINDS

The spirits of the four cardinal directions are often addressed in prayers. They may be mentioned collectively or singly in terms of their specific attributes, that is, the north wind is associated with cold and winter, the south wind with heat and summer (Voegelin *The Shawnee Female Deity*: p. 14). The Four Winds may also function as Truth Bearers or Witnesses, intermediaries between Shawnees who are praying for assistance and the ultimate source of all assistance, the Creator (ibid.: p. 7).

When our Grandmother re-created the earth after the flood she gave specific instructions to the personified forces of nature. She told the Four Winds that they must treat Indian women as though they were their own sisters, and not stare at them when they were naked; she also told the women that they must respect the winds. Shawnee women, however, sometimes take unfair advantage of their knowledge of Our Grandmother's instructions and pull their skirts up to their waists when it is cloudy, thus frightening the windborne clouds back in embarrassment (ibid.: p. 7).

CORN WOMAN, PUMPKIN WOMAN, AND THE TREE MEN

Corn and Pumpkin are both conceived as female deities by the Shawnees, apparently because, like women, their function is to feed mankind. Trees, however, are conceived as male because their function is to protect and serve mankind with wooden implements rather than to feed him.

Corn Woman is mentioned in the ceremonial public prayers following the spring and fall Bread Dances at all three Shawnee ceremonial grounds, and she is granted special attention by the Loyal band at their midsummer Green Corn Ceremony. Pumpkin Woman is likewise addressed at the same time since she lives with Corn Woman and her flesh is mixed with that of Corn Woman in a certain amount of the bread prepared by the women for the Bread Dance. Likewise the last daytime or ceremonial dance at the Bread Dance, known as the Pumpkin Dance, is addressed to her.

The feminine nature of corn in the Shawnee mind is epitomized in the folktale about the rescue of Corn Person that was told to the Voegelins by their informant Mary Williams (ibid.: p. 7).

A long time ago two old women were being lived with by one man. Once when it was day time he alone, the man, stayed home. Finally it was late in the afternoon but still those with whom he was staying had not come, so he thought to cook for himself; after waiting awhile he went to find and gather roasting ears of corn.

When he came over there, he would begin to take roasting ears off the stalk. Perhaps he was lucky he came, for in that place corn is growing which is of curious shape. The thing which he found looked like a woman's vagina. Now he said that he heard about her; the man always heard, he said, "There is a saying that the Corn Person, our mother, is a woman; if it is really true that she is called this name, she will be embarrassed now when I have intercourse with her." Then he pulled out his penis; he stuck that in the place where the corn was cracked.

After he had intercourse with her, then from there he went back to the house. Now the Corn Person went away along through the night. Now the old woman who stays there arose early in the morning; right now she went to the corn crib when she arose. When she arrived there, there wasn't any corn.

Corn Woman, of course, had fled to Our Grandmother, the Creator, because of the man's action. An account follows telling how the rescuer had to cross four oceans to come to Our Grandmother's abode. Corn Woman was persuaded to return to earth only when the rescuer argued that it was Our Grandmother's intention that she should benefit the Shawnees on earth.

The Tree Men, though less important, are mentioned in the Bread dance speech given by C. F. Voegelin (ibid.: p. 74). Frank Daugherty, a Loyal Shawnee, told the Voegelins a story that illustrates the animistic nature of Shawnee belief in regard to trees: a little boy is scolded when he cuts a tree. It is explained to him that Our Grandmother created our grandfathers, the trees, to be made use of by Indians, not to be wantonly harmed. The tree, he is told, has feelings that may be hurt even as we here. The boy promises never to hurt a tree again (ibid.: p. 20).

THUNDERBIRDS

The Shawnees, like many other North American Indian groups, conceive of thunder as being caused by the beating of the wings of giant heavenly birds, sometimes described as having human faces. The flashing of the eyes of these birds produces lightning. Though they may cause destruction, the power of the Thunderbirds is generally considered to be a good and purifying force. The Thunderbirds are considered the gatekeepers of heaven by the Shawnees. Their high position in the Shawnee pantheon is indicated by the fact that they occupy a position directly below the houselike representation of heaven on the "sacred slabs" or prayer sticks which were made and distributed by Tenskwatawa, the Shawnee Prophet, in connection with his revitalization movement in the early nineteenth century (W. A. Galloway "A Sacred Slab of the Shawnee Prophet": p. 7). The Thunderbirds are the patrons of war and hence are honored in the War Dance of the Kishpoko division. The mirrors formerly carried by some of the dancers in this dance simulated lightning by catching and flashing back the rays of the sun and emphasized the connection between the Thunderbirds and war.

The Thunderbirds are thought to frequent certain deep pools of water. They carry on a never-ceasing warfare with the Giant Horned Snakes, Horseheaded snakes, and other water dwelling creatures and snakes in general, an idea that like the concept of the Thunderbirds itself, is widespread in North America. Great storms are interpreted as the result of battles between these opposing cosmic forces, the one representing good, the other evil.

GIANT HORNED SNAKES AND HORSE-HEADED SNAKES

Constantly at war with the Thunderbirds are the "Powers Below," whose chiefs are the Giant Horned Snakes. These creatures, who lurk in particularly deep spots in streams and lakes, often seize and drown unwary bathers and fishermen. They are thought to be able to travel below the earth as well as in the water. Their head chief is sometimes envisaged as a great snake with one red and one green horn, and some identify him as the evil grandson of Our Grandmother, the Creator, and the brother of her other grandson, Rounded-Side or Cloudy-Boy (Voegelin, Rafinesque, Voegelin, and Lilly *Walum Olum* pp. 22, 29, 35). In a tale accounting for the origins of witchcraft he is described as having the body of a snake and the head, horns, and neck of a large buck (Trowbridge *Shawnese Traditions*: p. 45). The Giant Horned Snakes are generally considered to be the embodiment of evil, and to be spirit helpers of wicked shamans. Nevertheless a piece of the horn or flesh of one of these creatures constitutes a powerful charm, of itself neutral in character, which can be used for either good or evil purposes. Both the Loyal and Absentee Shawnee bands still possess such fetishes or medicines at the present time. In both groups those owning such medicines must be careful not to "think bad thoughts" about others lest the evil wished for will happen to the wishers themselves as a result of their possessing this powerful substance. The Shawnees, partly because they are known to possess such bundles, are considered to be powerful shamans by neighboring tribes.

Tales of Giant Horned Snakes are widespread in North America, extending to such distant northern tribes as the Micmacs, and the concept is universal in the southeast. Usually the Giant Horned Snakes are the chiefs of all the snakes and water creatures in these tribes just as with the Shawnees. Mooney (J. Mooney *Myths of the Cherokee*: pp. 298–300) records a Cherokee myth in which a captured Shawnee shaman slays an Uktcni (Giant Horned Snake) and secures a magical jewel from its forehead. The Giant Horned Snakes are by no means mythical creatures to conservative Shawnees, however, and Mary Spoon reported that such a creature had been seen as recently as 1970 by a Shawnee at Little River.

Two young Shawnee men, with whom I had lunch at the spring Bread Dance at Little River, were apparently too much a part of the white man's world and educational system to believe that such a creature as the Giant Horned Snake could in fact exist. One of them, however, told of a "giant octopus" that had seized and drowned a Shawnee youth a few years previously. This creature, he said, could walk on land using its tentacles as legs. He went on to relate that the previous spring a pair of Shawnee youths, hunters seeking squirrels for the Bread Dance, who were hot and sweaty from their hunting, came to the bank of a stream that was sparkling and cool. Though custom prohibits such action for hunters on the ceremonial hunt, one of the boys decided to take a refreshing dip. He had stripped off his clothing, but just as he was about to plunge in, a dark cloud passed above, shading him and the waters before him. This was interpreted as a warning (from the Thunderbirds), and he immediately gave up his plan. *Tout ça change, tout le même chose!*

Lesser members of this class of evil creatures are the Horse-headed Snakes. According to Mary Spoon these are snakes with heads like horses. They whinny like a horse, and when they fly they produce a noise like horses' hoofbeats do. They commonly frequent hollow tree stumps (where water has collected). Mary recounted that once her late husband and two of their sons were out berry picking in the woods. A Horse-headed Snake was luring the two little boys to its tree stump lair when her husband heard the characteristic noise of hoofbeats. Knowing that there were no horses nearby he thought to himself, "I had better save those boys from that thing!" He hurried off in their direction and arrived just in time to see a bolt of lightning (the Thunderbird's arrow) hit the stump and kill the snake. The Creeks and Seminoles also speak of Horse-headed Snakes.

According to Trowbridge, the Shawnees of his day sometimes prayed, though in secret, to the Giant Horned Snakes (*Shawnese Traditions* p. 42): "They pray to four serpents who occupy the four cardinal points—to these their supplications are secretly made, accompanied by an offering of tobacco, thrown into the fire." The seemingly inconsistent attitude of the Shawnees toward the Giant Horned Snakes and other Powers Below has been noted in many other North American Indian tribes. My Ojibwa and Santee Dakota informants, in fact, sometimes described the Underwater Panthers (a concept that is closely related to the Giant Horned Snakes) as somewhat benevolent deities, because they are believed to have taught the use of herbal medicines to the Indians. The Shawnee attitude is not far from this. One might say that the notion is that because evil exists in this world it is best to come to terms with it, to control it (as in the sacred bundles) when possible, and to placate it with tobacco offerings when one cannot.

In line with this attitude, we are not surprised to learn that all of the members of the "snake tribe," including their chiefs, the Giant Horned Snakes, are thought to be creations of Our Grandmother, though she is opposed to evil as much as the Shawnees are opposed to it. The inconsistency is explained by relating that when the snakes were created, Our Grandmother told them to hold a council every year and explain her rules to their young and not to bother mankind, but that subsequently the snakes became disobedient (Voegelin *The Shawnee Female Deity*: p. 12).

SUN, MOON, STARS, AND EARTH

The Sun, Moon, Stars, and Earth are all considered to be deities by the Shawnees. Trowbridge writes (*Shawnese Traditions*: p. 37):

> They have no definite idea of the formation of the sun or moon, but suppose them to be a man & a woman of immense power & size—and that they were given to the Shawanoas, when the great spirit created all things, and that when the Shawanoas cease to exist the sun & moon will cease to be, and the world will have an end.
>
> They do not pretend to account for the cause of eclipses, but they believe them to be certain precursors of war. Eclipses are called Mukūtaa wee thee, Keesōhtoa [*Makate withi kisato*]—or Black Sun . . .
>
> Like the Sun & Moon, the Stars are supposed to be animate beings, and it is believed that the meteors, called shooting stars, are beings fleeing from the wrath of some adversary, or from some anticipated danger.

A meteor is also conceptualized by the Shawnees as a great crouching panther, hence the name of the great nineteenth century chief Tecumseh (Tekamthe), referring to this concept, is sometimes translated as "Crouching Panther," and sometimes "Shooting Star" (J. Mooney "Tecumseh": p. 714).

While the Sun and Moon are sometimes mentioned in prayers by the Shawnees, the Stars are thought to have special powers and are spoken of as Our Grandmother's partners. Like the Thunderbirds, who may be directly appealed to for rain, the Stars may also be so addressed. C. F. Voegelin (*The Shawnee Female Deity*: p. 8) notes the special relationship that the Shawnees feel to the stars: "Each of the forty-eight stars in the American flag has a Shawnee name. The Indians accepted the stars as witnesses to their treaty of peace with the whites. Subsequently, when the whites were going to fight, the stars came down to advise the Indians."

The Earth, like the heavenly bodies, is often personified by the Shawnees. In the reproduction of the 1933 fall Bread Dance prayer given by C. F. Voegelin, "Earth Person" is told that the Creator made her to "be still and hold us on your lap for eternity," and that she must "grow out well and settle down with a green head." (ibid.: p. 14). "Earth Person" is also mentioned in *Shawnee Laws* (Voegelin, Yergerlehner, and Robinett "Shawnee Laws": p. 39). An excellent description of the Shawnee conception of the earth is contained in Trowbridge (*Shawnese Traditions*: p. 37)

> They believe that we live upon an island, which is a plane of earth, extending to great length from east to west, & of comparatively small width, that underneath this island is a vast body of water, and that the earth is supported by a great Turtle, swimming in it, and placed there for that purpose by the Great Spirit.
>
> They suppose that to the south, on the opposite side of the sea, there is another island, inhabited by the whites, and on the extreme opposite edge of that island the sky touches the earth. That if it were possible to penetrate the sky at that point, the traveller would find on the convex side of it another earth, peopled throughout like this, and that he might travel upward through it until he reached the point in the heavens exactly over our heads. But as the sky is constantly moving up & down at the edge of that island it would be impossible for a man to get through.

A similar concept is indicated by C. F. Voegelin (*The Shawnee Female Deity*: p. 6) and I secured substantially the same description from my informants.

THE TRUTH-BEARERS OR WITNESSES

In order that her Shawnee grandchildren might communicate

with her, Our Grandmother created a number of intermediaries, known as Tipwiwe, "Truth Bearers" or "Witnesses." These Tipwiwe carry the words of prayer to the Creator and likewise attest to the sincerity of the supplicant. For the Shawnees Tobacco is the leader of the Truth Bearers. Fire, Water, and Eagle are also of first importance. Other Truth Bearers, such as Sky, the Thunderbirds, the sacred bundles, the Four Winds, the Stars, and medicinal herbs are subsidiary. (p. 7) Cedar is an important Truth-Bearer for those Shawnees who participate in the Peyote religion, as is the substance Peyote itself. Although C. F. Voegelin (ibid.: pp. 7–8) states that Dog might be considered a Witness for the Shawnees, this was vehemently denied by my informants, though they knew of the use of the dog (in the form of dog sacrifices at feasts) as Truth Bearers among the Sauks.

Tobacco, the principal Truth Bearer, functions as a witness in two ways. On minor occasions a pinch of tobacco is put on the ground. For major events such as the Bread Dance, a prayer for rain, or preparations for a war party or hunting trip, tobacco is burned. The Shawnees, my informants say, are not "pipe Indians" like the Dakotas, in the sense that they do not consume their prayer tobacco in pipes. Instead they place it directly in the flames or on the coals of the sacred fire built for that purpose. Enough tobacco to cover the center of the supplicant's palm, is placed in the sacred fire all at once, not a little bit at a time as is the custom among the Sauks. The smoke from the burning tobacco carries the words of the prayer aloft to the Creator and at the same time serves as a witness to the sincerity of the wish. Ideally, the tobacco used should be native tobacco (*Nicotiana quadrivalvis*). Because the Shawnees no longer raise their own native tobacco, they must purchase it at an exorbitant price from the neighboring Sauks.

Present-day procedures of praying with tobacco have not changed in the past 184 years, for the description of a Shawnee tobacco offering in 1792 is the same as that seen today (Spencer *The Indian Captivity of O. M. Spencer*: pp. 54–5):

> After supper, taking a small piece of tobacco and cutting it fine by passing the edge of his knife between his forefinger and thumb, receiving it as thus prepared into the palm of his left hand, the White Loon with great solemnity and apparent devotion sprinkled a few grains of it on the coals, an offering, as I afterwards understood, to the Great Spirit, moving his lips as if uttering some petition; then, mingling the residue with some dried sumach leaves which he drew from his bullet pouch and filling the bowl of his tomahawk, serving as a pipe, first smoked a few whiffs, then handed the pipe to his companion, who

also smoking a few minutes returned it; the Indians thus alternately puffing until the tobacco was consumed, frequently filling their mouths with smoke and forcing it through their nostrils, closing their brief use of the pipe with a peculiar suck of the breath and a slight grinding of the teeth.

The pipe smoking that followed the tobacco offering in this instance was apparently for enjoyment only.

The smoke from the sacred fire, sometimes called Fire Person, likewise serves to transmit people's prayer to Our Grandmother. An important additional function of Fire is to remind Cyclone Person that Indians are living near the fire. According to a Shawnee legend related by Mary Spoon, Cyclone Person is a Shawnee who, in a period of four days, gradually changed into his present form. His Shawnee friends fed him while he was undergoing this metamorphosis and he informed them on the last day that they should not return but rather let him know their future whereabouts, through Fire, so that he might avoid their dwellings and only visit those of the whites. When thus advised and reminded through the smoke of the sacred fire, Cyclone Person keeps his promise to the present day.

The Shawnees formerly kept an eternal flame or fire continually burning in a special lodge set aside for this purpose. Trowbridge writes (*Shawnese Traditions*: pp. 56-57):

In all these travels [from overseas to the Savannah river, and thence to the Mad river and on to the Mississippi] they took with them the sacred fire, and now that they see the settlements of the whites progressing so rapidly that [they] look forward to a time when it will be necessary for them to endeavour to retransmit the fire to Shawnee river. Twelve men will be deputed to carry this fire, who, when they have arrived at Shawnee river, will open the fire and put to the test the power of the whites. If it be foreordained that every thing is to belong to the whites, in four years the fire will become visible to all the world. Then the Indians grown desperate by a consciousness that their end is approaching will suffer the fire to burn and to destroy the whites, upon whom they will call, tauntingly, to quench it. The same persons who have now the care of the fire at the Mississippi will be the bearers of it to Shawnee river. Twelve days (years) after the destruction of the world by this fire the Great Spirit will cause it to be reformed & repeopled, but they don't know what description of persons will inhabit it.

The care of this fire is committed to two men, one of the Tshalakarthar [Chalaakaatha] and the other of the Kishpookoo [Kishpoko] family. Upon the death of either of these men another from the same tribe or family is appointed in his stead. This charge however formerly belonged to the Maakoatshee [Mekoche] family, but after a battle between the Six Nations & Shawnees it was taken from them. The keepers of this fire are members of the Panther and Turtle tribes [clans or name groups] of the families just named, and are chosen by their respective tribes. The office continues until death. The keepers are permitted to marry, but they never go to war, nor is the fire taken with the war party. One of these keepers lives in a lodge, one apartment of which is set apart for the fire, which is there kept in a small hollow rock, brought by Tshalakarthar [Chalaakaatha, the legendary Shawnee hero of that name] through the sea, on his back, to Shawnee river. The other keeper lives close at hand. This stone (it is so called, but is not really stone) is about ten inches long & five broad, and is suspended by a string from the roof of the lodge. It requires no wood, but is everlasting. Visitors are not permitted to enter this lodge unless on important business, and women are not allowed to enter at all. The office is not confined to Chiefs, but common people are commonly appointed. The stone containing this fire is rolled in a dressed deer skin, which is again wrapped in a dressed Buffaloe skin. The Prophet's father told him when he was a boy that these skins had been worn out and renewed three times since it was brought across the sea. The keepers visit the apartment containing the fire once or twice a week.

Today, apparently, this eternal flame is no longer perpetuated, though the Shawnees are very particular that the fires used in ceremonies be "pure" Indian fires, made with selected woods and ignited with flint, steel, and punk. Both Tobacco and Fire are considered especially suited as Truth Bearers for men, while Water is felt to be particularly suitable as a woman's witness (Voegelin *The Shawnee Female Deity*: p. 8)

Eagle feathers are used as Truth Bearers at ceremonial dances. Because the eagle does not breed with any other kind of bird, but remains faithful to its own species, accordingly his feathers serve as a faithful intermediary between man and the Creator (ibid. p. 8)

The other Truth Bearers are subsidiary and apparently there is no hard and fast rule as to which minor deity or natural phenomenon may or may not serve as such. It would seem that anything deemed suitable by the one offering a prayer is ipso facto a Truth Bearer (ibid.: p. 7). Most of the minor deities, except those thought of as being evil or destructive, may serve as Truth Bearers.

SHAWNEE COSMOLOGY

From an external, analytic, point of view, Shawnee myths dealing with the creation can be conveniently divided, in terms of their subject matter, into four periods. The first period concerns the time before Our Grandmother and her household were created by the Supreme Being. During this first period the Supreme Being descends from the void above and creates the basis of the earth, a gigantic turtle, and upon its back places the earth, which he then peoples with animals and men, including Our Grandmother, her grandsons, and her little dog. The second period concerns the period after this first creation and before the flood. During this second period Our Grandmother permits her grandson, or grandsons, unwholesome license. This period ends with a great flood. The third period concerns the time after the flood. Our Grandmother, alone and yearning for companionship, is permitted to re-create and repopulate the earth. The fourth period, which extends to the present, has Our Grandmother in her heavenly abode above the earth. No longer actively engaged in creation, she occasionally dispenses bits of knowledge to prophets and others of her grandchildren who have made the long and dangerous trip to the other world. From her heavenly abode she looks down upon the earth and occasionally descends to observe and even join in the ceremonies of the Shawnees.

The first period in Shawnee mythology is known today only from an origin legend supplied to Trowbridge by the Shawnee Prophet in 1824 (Trowbridge *Shawnese Traditions* 1–8) and from a single exceptional account by James Clark, one of the Voegelins' informants (Voegelin *The Shawnee Female Deity*. p. 8; "The Shawnee Female Deity in Historical Perspective" Voegelin and Voegelin: p. 371). We have already quoted the Prophet's account in chapter two. All of the events noted in it took place presumably before the great flood and during the period after the Supreme Being had turned over the supervision of the Shawnees to Our Grandmother, the Creator. The Black Hoof account (Trowbridge *Shawnese Traditions*: pp. 60–63) puts the creation of the various divisions of the Shawnees after the flood, not yet mentioned by the Prophet in his origin legend. The accounts of the battles with the Ojibwas, Catawbas, and the Six Nations of the Iroquois are of course semihistorical in nature.

The great flood, which ends the second period of Shawnee mythology, is precipitated by Rounded-Side, the Creator's grandson, in an Eastern Shawnee variant told to the Voegelins by Nancy Sky (Voegelin and Voegelin "The Shawnee Female Deity in Historical Perspective": p. 371).

> Long ago there were people right here, the one who created us, our Grandmother, and the little-boy, Rounded-Side, her grandson. "Don't do this, you must always go this way," she told him but that little boy would think, "What's that tabu for, I wonder." (In an Absentee Shawnee variant, the prohibition is specifically against going west.)
>
> Now that boy runs off. Now he goes this way. Finally he found him. He went in the house. There he is inside, a big man having a big stomach.
>
> Now that boy is there. Finally late in the evening he went home. Now he goes back again. He mocks the hoot owl.
>
> Now he moves fast. He runs. He moves fast. Now he has a knife in his hand. Now he sticks him, he sticks him in his stomach. (The boy cuts a transparent fish monster in the Absentee Shawnee variant.)
>
> Now that water is spilling out. Now the boy runs outside and he is being

chased by that water. Now he runs home. He moves fast. He comes running up
there to his grandmother.
Now they run away from the water. They climb on a tree. (In the Absentee
variant they escape in a boat.) All the people are drowned.
Now that one, Our Grandmother, is worrying. Finally she calls that crawfish.
Finally he comes. He brings earth in his hand. (In the Absentee variant, Turtle
and Water Lizard dive unsuccessfully before Crawfish dives and brings up
mud.) Now Our Grandmother takes the earth. He brings earth again, and a
little bit more again, Now she calls that buzzard. Now he comes. He, the
buzzard, comes. The buzzard rubs it on his wings. "You must dry the earth," she
tells him. Now that buzzard goes away, He goes and dries it. He goes and flys.
Oh, now the earth is dry all over. Now when it got dry, then the water goes
below. However, the old folks are all dead. (In a Cherokee Shawnee variant, the
Creator deliberately instigates a flood to destroy the people whom she made in
the first creation because they are too large, too strong, too destructive.)

This tale of a creature impounding the waters of the earth in its
body has a wide distribution is eastern North America. In a
Micmac version the creature is a giant frog. Gluskap, the culture
hero, saves the world, which is perishing from drought, by
piercing the creature's body and releasing the cooling waters.

There are several published variants of the postdiluvian
creation, the third period in Shawnee mythology. I have already
quoted a portion of one variant collected by Joab Spencer from the
Rev. Charles Bluejacket in the period 1858-60 (Spencer *The
Shawnee Indians* p. 383). This version continues: "According to
Bluejacket's tradition, the Indians in coming to this continent
crossed a narrow part of the ocean far to the north, being carried
across the water on the back of a turtle. They wandered in a
southerly direction until they reached the southern part of what is
now the United States, and from there the tradition is that they
were to go north, continuing their wanderings till they should
reach the point where they first landed, then all would become
extinct, or, as he expressed it, 'All be gone' ".

In a footnote Spencer gives an alternate version of how the
Shawnees crossed the "narrow part of the ocean far to the north"
(ibid.: p. 383, ft. 5): "Another version of the tradition is that a being
whom they knew not asked them to get in a small boat he was in,
and that he would take them to a good and happy country. But it
was so small that all were afraid to get into it. Finally one got in
and the boat grew larger. Then others, the boat growing larger as
each individual embarked. Finally, when no more would get in,
the strange visitor brought the occupants to the other shore—
America."

Black Hoof's version of the postdiluvian period, which was collected by Trowbridge, reads as follows (Trowbridge *Shawnese Traditions*: 60-4):

When the waters of the deluge had entirely overspread the earth, all its inhabitants were destroyed but an aged woman, who ascended to the clouds, where she gave way to grief at the loss of her grandchildren, and lamented that there appeared no probability of her having any more connexions to gladden her heart. The great spirit witnessed her affliction and bid her cease to mourn.

Sometime after this event the great spirit, in order to purify himself, and to resuscitate the powers of thought and invention, which had long been dormant, collected twelve different kinds of roots which he prepared for a *medecine*. With a decoction of these he washed his body, and soon became very pure and white. He then commenced a series of meditations, which resulted in a determination to renew and repeople the earth. He accordingly sent a craw fish below the surface of the waters, with directions to bring up a small quantity of the earth from this island which we inhabit. This order was obeyed, and from the earth contained in the paws of this little animal the great spirit reformed the earth. When he had accomplished the formation of this island he made some very large animals and placed them upon it, at the four cardinal points of the compass, to keep it steady. The Indians he next formed. They were placed in the centre, and all the lesser animals were distributed promiscuously throughout the island. The Shawnees were sat down in the centre of the island, and they found none about them who spoke their own language. They were taught, in common with their neighbours, to avoid every thing evil, and to pursue one great road, which led to their father, the great spirit.

Each nation of Indians was made by the great spirit, in the skies, and when they were finished he brought them down and gave them a place upon the earth. While he was descending he sang four songs, which were adopted by the Indians. This accounts for the great difference in the manner of singing, among different nations, each set of songs being appropriated to the party at whose descent they were sung. To the Shawnees he was more favorable than to any others. He gave them a piece of his own heart. None but males were created above. After they descended the great spirit formed a female and gave it to one of the males, with a view to their increase. Much difficulty was at first experienced, in producing a union of the sexes, but the object was at length accomplished. After the great spirit had given corn to the Indians, he extended personal instruction to them about their planting and hunting, as well as about their domestic affairs generally [the Shawnee "Laws"].

The Maakoatshääkee [Mekoche] (the last syllable indicates the plural) were put upon this island on the borders of Shawnee river. They had not been there long when they discovered the Pikewaakkee [Pekowitha] who told them that they came from Waaskoomisar [*Weskumisa*], a man in the south. The two nations soon became incorporated with each other. The Tsilikauthee's [Chalaakaatha], at present one the divisions of the nation, lived on the opposite side of the sea. They sent out a Maumeesemaukäätar (mishinewaa) to explore the country. He reached the sea coast, and discovered *the island*, of which he informed his chiefs. They resolved unanimously to go to the island in search of the people who might inhabit it, and accordingly marched down to the sea shore. Many leaders were appointed to conduct them across the sea, but every one refused, until one of the Turtle tribe accepted the appointment and led on. The whole party followed him and reached the shore of the island in safety, having marched all the way upon the bottom of the sea. When they arrived an encampment was immediately formed, and a fire was enkindled, the smoke of which ascended to the clouds. The Maakoatshääkee, whose residence was not very distant, discovered this smoke and dispatched a Maumeesemaukēātar to ascertain its cause. He returned and reported that a great body of people were encamped at the fire. The Chiefs directed him to go back and salute them as cousins, in the name of the whole nation. They rejected this offer, and many others which were made, and at length consented to be called *grandfathers*. They soon after came to live with their new relatives. The Kishpookookee [Kishpokoki, the plural form of *Kishpoko*] were found near the Pikewaa's [Pekowitha] and were incorporated with the Māākoatshaa's [Mekoche] in the same manner, and the Shāūwonoa's, who had previously constituted a separate band or tribe, also joined the confederacy. Its force was further augmented by the addition of the Thauwēēkeelau's [Thawikila] who came across the sea, but in what manner, they do not now recollect. They do not know why the confederated tribes adopted the name of one of the divisions, but they suppose that it was because the Shawnees were most numerous. The tribes all spoke the same language, which greatly facilitated their union. At this day there are none of the original Shawnees in existence, nor are there any Thauwēēkeelau's living [an error] but a few of the other tribes remain, and are easily distinguished as members of the respective parent stocks, although the usual division into tribes (as is found among other nations and described by the Prophet) is common to all of them.

When these tribes had confederated they formed twelve large villages. Some time afterwards, they resolved to travel *en masse* and by a circuitous route, to the north. They took up their march accordingly, encountered every nation with whom they met, and literally fought their way to the banks of the Mississippi, from whence they proceeded eastward, crossed the mountains and reached the Delaware a short time before the landing of the Quakers. But they did not remain there long. They recommenced their peregrinations and did not form any permanent settlement until they reached the mouth of the Scioto (a Shawnee name, pronounced Thiiōātoa). From this place they removed to the prairies near Chilicothe which place was named for one of their divisions, the Tshilikauthe's [Chalaakaatha], who lived there. A few afterwards joined the Creeks, but they have long since left them. Others went beyond the Mississippi. At this latter place, they number about three hundred, and at Wapaghkonetta there are, including all ages, about four hundred. These two parties, with that of the Prophet, near Malden, constitute the remains of the nation.

Black Hoof's account continues with an account of the first treaty with the whites. Note that in this version the Supreme Being ("Great spirit") is responsible for the re-creation of the earth after the flood. More recent accounts attribute the second creation to Our Grandmother, the Creator.

Another excellent version of this third period in Shawnee mythology was paraphrased by C. F. Voegelin from the account offered by Mary Williams, a young Absentee Shawnee woman, in 1933–34 (*The Shawnee Female Deity*: pp. 10–11):

Curiously enough, Our Grandmother did not create the Shawnee first, but began with the Delaware. When she completed a Delaware man and woman, she put them on the east side of a fire which she had kindled. Then she created one Shawnee division, in the form of an old man and an old woman. After this she created a young couple who were expected to have children who would constitute three of the Shawnee divisions. Here, apparently her interest in creating people ceased. On the way home her grandson, Rounded-Side, aroused her suspicions when he wanted to hunt deer. She warned him not to return to tease the couple she had created and left to "play together" (copulate). Her grandson immediately returned to the couple, created the pekowi and kishpoko divisions, and insulted the young woman whom Our Grandmother had created. The young couple were unable to have intercourse for two years because Our Grandmother misplaced their genitals when creating them. (The Creator's blundering, in an Eastern Shawnee variant, consisted in misplacing arms and backbone.) During the first year they fashioned dolls out of black mud and later threw the dolls away across the ocean. From these playthings of the young couple negroes originated. To the negroes Our Grandmother gave a language and a way to live. She seems to have had no objection to others creating people. Indeed, it was in her presence that her grandson created all the remaining Indian tribes so that the kishpoko division would never become lonesome, i.e. have plenty of enemies to fight. Once people were created, by herself and others, she was deeply concerned for their future welfare. She repaired the blundering she was guilty of in creating her first young couple, and they had twin boys from whom the remaining political divisions are derived.

In some such way, Shawnee people are accounted for, but the problem of providing a plan of living for these people still remained. The Creator asks her grandson, "What are you going to give pekowi to make a living from and keep healthy on? What will kishpoko have to make a living from?" and seems to regard this task as both more difficult and more interesting than that of creating the people. She accomplishes this task in the main single-handed, and while her grandson gives to the pekowi division "wheat and other kinds of herbs" and to the kishpoko alien tribes to fight, it is apparent that in doing so he is merely understudying the Creator's role.

Our Grandmother gave a sacred bundle to the first political division which she created; this bundle was then given into the custody of other divisions and was finally divided among the divisions. Opinion also has it that each division was originally given a separate bundle. Other members of the Creator's pantheon involved are the Thunderbirds and her grandson. The latter gave the kishpoko division its bundle which originally contained feathers from the Thunderbirds. Perhaps the small wooden figure of a boy in the bundle of the Thawikila division is a representation of Our Grandmother's grandson.

During the post-flood creations, Our Grandmother brought all the divisions together on this side of the ocean. It would seem that some or most of the divisions were originally created on this side, but at least mekoche and chalakaatha (in one variant only the latter) had to be brought over. Perhaps because the political divisions were then assembled together, other benefits which the Creator dispensed in the post-flood period are generally spoken of as lessons for the Shawnee as a whole. She taught them how to take care of themselves, how to live, to conduct ceremonial dances, how to raise corn and hunt, what kind of houses to build, and their laws. The Shawnee laws (kweteletiiwena) are noteworthy for their extreme length and comprehensiveness of subject matter. The laws for men are taught to boys, the laws for women to girls. A text has been secured of the former which is largely given in the first person, as though Our Grandmother herself were talking.

Mary Williams' account continues, taking us into the fourth and final mythological period (ibid.: p. 11):

After the Creator retired to her present residence—how and when are not vouchsafed to us—she continued to dispence benefits to the Shawnee, supplementing her creations in the post-flood period. She habitually gives visitors to her home instructions to take with them when they return to earth.

To the visitors in the Orpheus tale she brings plants which were also growing on earth and gives instructions in the use of these plants in doctoring so that their remedial effects may be taken advantage of on earth. At the same time she teaches her visitors the sacred ways of making fire. She also arouses in the minds of her visitors a healthy respect for her own powers by constantly answering their thoughts before they are expressed. One visitor thinks to himself that Our Grandmother is unaware of their presence at her door; again, he suspects that she knows what he is thinking about. To these thoughts Our Grandmother replies in a way which frightens her visitors.

"You don't have to tell me that you are here; I know that you are. I knew when you started on your journey; I knew when you thought of coming here before you held your council . . . Yes, I always know what you're thinking."

She replies to the surprise which her visitors express at her ability to finish all the food in the "inexhaustible food-supply" receptacle with a statement which is still believed. "Well, I'm the Creator, and I can do anything; that's why I can eat all the food. You are only children."

A separate creation legend, yet one tied to the wanderings of Chalaakaatha and his people in the first mythologic period, tells of the origin of the powerful Great Horned Snake medicine. It is entitled "Wausaloageethēē skēē (Witches) [*Wasalokithiski*] the account reads (Trowbridge *Shawnee Traditions*: pp. 43-4):

When Tshilikauthee had arrived with his warriors on this side of the ocean, they were one day traversing the borders of the sea, and they found a large animal (supposed to be a crocodile, of which they may have heard) lying dead upon the shore. They immediately cut him open and took out his heart which, with a piece of his flesh they deposited carefully in a bag and carried it with them in their journey. Upon their arrival at Shauwanoa, wee, Theepee, (Shawnee River) they began to encounter difficulties. Opposition was made to their progress by those who inhabited the adjacent country, and they were compelled to send out scouting parties & war parties, in order to maintain their possessions. One of these parties consisting of seven warriors and their waiting man or cook, after travelling a long time arrived at the banks of a small lake, where they found an immense turtle resting on the shore. The leader proposed that the party should get upon the turtle's back to see if he could bear their weight. Accordingly he sat the example and his warriors followed him. The increasing weight made the Turtle move, and the servant objected to following his companions. They ordered, insisted & entreated, but all in vain. In the mean time the turtle moved to the water. The warriors finding that they could not prevail upon the servant to follow them, concluded to abandon the turtle, but they found themselves sticking fast to his back. Supposing that their moccasins caused this adhesion, they cut them loose from their feet, but all their exertions availed them nothing. The turtle waded into deep water, and at length sank, carrying his load along with him. The servant remained upon the Shore of the Lake a long time, expecting their return, but at length his patience became exhausted, and he shaped his course for the village. When he arrived there he related the circumstances of the excursion and the fate of his companions. The old men assembled and listened with astonishment to his narration. They were much perplexed to know what course to take, but finally resolved to trust in their great medicine for relief, and to visit for the purpose of rescuing their friends, the spot where they had disappeared. Accordingly eight of them, accompanied by the waiter, sat out for the lake, carrying with them their medecine bag & the heart & flesh which they had taken from the animal on the borders of the sea. The servant led them to the spot, and after having made an encampment at some distance from the shore, they erected a forked stick about 2 feet high at the edge of the water and another at the spot where the warriors had got upon the back of the turtle. Upon them they laid a pole or beam, and in the middle of the space between the sticks they kindled a small fire. Then they returned to their encampment where they commenced singing a song to their Grandfather, the Turtle, imploring him to come & expose himself at the fire. They continued this song all night, and about midnight they heard a noise at the fire. In the morning they sent the servant to see if anything was there. He returned, telling them that their Grandfather lay by the side of the fire, dead, and that blood was running from his nose. The old men went down and found the turtle as the man had described him. They took some of the blood from his nose & mixed it with a small quantity of their medecine, by using which compound they restored him to life. They then told him to be gone, that they did not want him there, and that his proper place was the water. The turtle took their advice & left them, when they immediately returned to their encampment & recommenced their song. In *this* song they did not solicit the visit of the Turtle, but of their other Grandfather, the serpent, who inhabited and had charge of the lake. They continued the song without cessation all the day & the succeeding night, and they heard at midnight a similar noise at the fire. In the morning the servant was despatched as usual to ascertain if anything was there. He found a large serpent, but not the one who had charge of the lake, lying also dead, by the side of the fire. Upon acquainting the old men with the fact, they went down to the fire and by dint of the compound of medecine & blood before used they resuscitated him too. They told him that it was not himself but his master whom they wanted, that they might ascertain the cause of the evil treatment which had been given by one of his subjects (the turtle) to their companions.

The serpent accordingly fled to the water and the old men returned to their camp, where they recommenced their songs. They fasted, and did not cease to sing for some days & nights. At length about midnight a terrible noise was heard in the water & afterwards at the fire. In the morning the servant was sent as usual, to see what was to be seen, and he found the king of the serpents lying there dead, the blood streaming from his nose to the ground. The old men went down in great eagerness, but they did not restore him to life, fearing his power & despairing of the recovery of their brothers. On the contrary they proceeded to cut up the carcase. His body was like that of a snake & he had the head, horns, & neck of a large buck. His body was cut into small pieces and every thing connected with it, even to the excrement, was carefully preserved. The head, horns, flesh &c, was mixed with the heart & flesh of the animal found upon the sea shore, and forms the medecine which the witches use. It is still preserved and the flesh, tho' many thousand years old, is as fresh as if it had just been killed.

By means of this medecine they can take a piece of stick, of dirt, a hair or any thing else, & transform it into a worm, which they depute & send to any distance to accomplish their designs against the victims of their power.

The conclusion of Trowbridge's account leaves the impression that only witches possess and employ the medicine derived from the monster crocodile, giant turtle, lesser Giant Horned Snake, and king of the Giant Horned Snakes. To the present-day Shawnees, however, portions of the flesh of the Giant Horned Snake are thought to be contained in all of the surviving divisional bundles. Interestingly, the Delawares have a similar belief and legend. The Delaware legend, as related by Nora Thompson Dean, a Delaware of Dewey, Oklahoma, tells of the Giant Horned Snake causing many of the Delawares to drown. All efforts to defeat the monster fail. Finally two pure young men are sent to the heavenly abode of Our Brother the Sun to secure hot ashes from him. They reach the Sun's lodge by climbing sunbeams. The hot solar ashes that they bring back are put in the lake where the Giant Horned Snake lives, causing the water to boil. Weakened and desperate, the monster crawls out on the beach where it is finished off by two powerful Delaware shamans. As it expires, however, the Giant Horned Snake warns the Indians that there are many more like him still alive (in other words, there will always be evil in the world). The Indians then cut up the body of the Giant Horned Snake and divide its flesh among the tribes. In this way both the Delawares and the Shawnees secured the principal substance in their sacred bundles. The bundle containing the Delawares' portion of the Giant Horned Snake, Nora says, was collected several years ago by an anthropologist and is now in the American Museum of Natural History in New York City, but the Shawnees still have theirs.

The epic myths of the Shawnees provide the rationale for the belief system and ceremonialism of the tribe, the framework upon which every ritual act, private or public, is built. In addition to their epic myths, which I have quoted verbatim, paraphrased, or alluded to above, the Shawnees have many minor tales explaining how this or that animal or bird acquired certain characteristics, or how certain useful things were discovered. Our Grandmother, the Creator, or her grandson figure in some of these, in others they do not. All are charming, some are fascinating in their plot development. Unfortunately their length prevents me from adding even a representative sample to a chapter already much too long.

10

Magicians, Prophets, and Sacred Bundles

In his well-known essay, Malinowski distinguishes magic from religion by defining magic as "a practical art consisting of acts which are only means to a definite end expected to follow later on; religion as a body of self-contained acts being themselves the fulfillment of their purpose" (B. Malinowski *Magic, Science and Religion and Other Essays*: p. 88). Magic has its limited, circumscribed technique and has a definite end, while religion is more complex in its aspects and purposes and has no such simple technique. Although Malinowski's distinction is useful in understanding Shawnee ceremonialism, certain ceremonies contain elements of both. One also notes a trend away from magical rites in recent years, undoubtedly because Shawnee children now attend the white man's schools with their emphasis upon scientific explanations of natural phenomena. Although it would be incorrect to say that a belief in magic has disappeared among the Shawnees, one notes that all of the great magicians and prophets, including Tecumseh and his brother the Shawnee Prophet, flourished in the early nineteenth century. Even the lesser performers of wondrous acts mentioned by my informants lived in the early years of the twentieth century. Today a few older men are known to possess "magical" personal bundles and to know the associated techniques, but they are reluctant to employ them. Thus, though the great public religious ceremonies continue, the minor rites, many of which involved sympathetic magic, seem to have withered away.

MAGICIANS

Shawnee myths are replete with accounts of the magic worked by individuals with "power," and even today the Shawnee tribe as a whole is regarded as a nation of wonder-workers by the Creeks, Seminoles, Alabamas, Koasatis, Cherokees, and other Southeastern groups. The "Juggling Society" mentioned by Trowbridge, like its Iroquois counterpart the I'dus, apparently made great use of magic to impress initiates and nonmembers. This organization, already long obsolete in Trowbridge's day, admitted only young boys "about eight years old" as new members:

> The proceedings were kept very secret, and an admission was considered a mark of confidence & a great honour. When they were about to receive a young member, they assembled in some retired spot with the applicant & their house dogs. The boy was knocked down with a club, and his head & limbs were severed from his body. The head was preserved & the dogs were called to devour the mangled limbs. After they had done so they were driven away and then a bed of leaves was prepared in the middle of the lodge, a song was sung by the old men, the head deposited upon the leaves & the dogs called back. These animals being overcharged with food which they had eaten were kept near the head, where they vomited and discharged all they had eaten. This mass was covered with leaves, the society danced around the bed to the right four times in quick succession, during which the oldest men sung very violently, and at the end of the dance they seated themselves; and the boy, having exactly the appearance which he had before being killed, arose and took his place among the members. (C.C. Trowbridge *Shawnese Traditions*: p. 36)

Magic, or attempts at magic, also entered into curing ceremonies, as attested by the following account from Jacob Jameson, a young Seneca:

> In the year 1818, a cousin of mine was at the point of death, afflicted with a consumptive disease, and his brother had also been subject to a violent pain in his breast. During the illness of the first named, while the Physicians in the neighbourhood were making every effort to restore him to life without success, a negro who had been raised among the Shawnese Indians, and a Shawnese Indian, arrived. The Negro professed to be one of their medicine men & to possess the knowledge of all diseases & the modes of cure. My cousin was not superstitious, but anxious to make effort to save his brother's life he sent for this negro, & told him that he himself had long been afflicted with a disease & requested him to examine him & tell him the nature & seat of it. The Negro ordered him to strip himself & having examined his body by passing his hand over it exclaimed when he felt his breast, "Here it is. Here it is." This surprised the young man, who supposed that the negro must have heard of his illness; but on enquiry having learned that he had had no opportunity to learn it, he concluded to take him to Buffalo to see his brother. On their arrival at Buffalo, the negro visited the young man who was ill of the consumption & having examined him, said that his illness was caused by eating a hair, given to him in his food by his wife; & that if this could be removed from the place of its location which was near the heart, he would undoubtedly recover. But he declined undertaking the task alledging as a reason the weakness of the young man & his inability to endure the pain of the operation. Being solicited however to

make the effort to remove the cause of the disease he prepared a small house or wigwam of mats, making it perfectly tight & dark, into which he removed the patient, stripped of all his clothes. When there he commenced a singular noise with his voice, a gourd & other instruments, & after some time, he made a small incision in the flesh of the breast of his patient to which he applied a hollow tube of horn & commenced sucking. After drawing from the incision a quantity of blood &c he took the horn from it, & holding it up to those around, pointed to something on the End which had the appearance of hair, & said, Here you see the cause of this man's sickness. He will now recover. As little faith was put in the Doctor, a byestander caught the horn from his hand, & examining the end, found a piece of the silk of corn (this being in corn time) attached to a split in the End, & thus Ended the doctor's practice with us. (W.N. Fenton "Answers to Governor Cass's Questions by Jacob Jameson (ca. 1821-1825)": p. 127)

The Jameson account is a rather typical example of the performance of a sucking shaman, a type of practitioner who was known in many Native American societies. The use of sleight of hand by doctors in sessions of this sort probably served in many instances to induce the patient to believe that the source of his malady had been removed, and thus it aided in his recovery. In my opinion, to brand all curers who employed sleight of hand as utter charlatans, interested only in their own prestige, and fees, is a mistake, for convincing the patient that he *can* recover is often half the battle. Many present day physicians, I might add, occasionally administer placebos for the same purpose.

Great warriors among the Shawnees were thought to have magical power as well, power that they could use to best their enemies. Again, the question of belief is paramount, for if such magical ability was attributed to a war chief by his enemies, or his own followers, it might have an important effect upon the outcome of the contest. E. W. Voegelin writes of this type of magic.

The Shawnee of the present day tell of instance after instance when their enemies were overcome by warriors gifted with many sorts of supernatural power or supernatural knowledge. Such gifted warriors might "poison" the enemy from a distance, or magically encircle him with a woven halter; many warriors could take the form of small insects and thus be immune to harm from the enemy. In connection with the latter practice, it is interesting to note that the Shawnee claim the Delaware warriors could only transform themselves into large animals (from whom they had received supernatural blessings) and that, therefore, on more than one occasion the Delaware were in danger of being defeated by their foes and were compelled to call upon the Shawnee for aid. (E.W. Voegelin, C. Rafinesque, C. F. Voegelin, and E. Lilly *Walum Olum*: p. 89)

Persons skilled in legerdemain used this ability in various gambling games. Like their neighbors, the Shawnees were fond of playing the Moccasin Game (See Plate 29). J.H.B. Nowland, an Indiana pioneer, describes the game as played among the Shawnees, Miamis, and Potawatomis at an Indian village at the mouth of the Mississinewa River in 1832 (Culin *Games of the North American Indians*: p. 344): "The player, seated on the ground with six moccasins arranged in two rows before him and a little painted stick in his hand would sing an incantation to divert attention from his action, and, thrusting his hand under the various moccasins, secretely and skillfully deposit the stick. The spectators then bet on the moccasin." Samuel Perry, a member of the Loyal band of Shawnees, also describes the Moccasin Game in a 1937 interview (Indian Archives, Oklahoma Historical Society 8: p. 181). A bullet was hidden under one of three moccasins placed on the ground before the "hider". A member of the opposing side had to guess which of the three concealed the bullet. Perry says he was good at this game because he learned to watch for a small movement at the back of the hand caused when the bullet was released.

In the Moccasin Game magical power was attributed not only to the hider himself but also to the accompanying songs used to distract the guesser. Certain Shawnee men were thought to be able to magically move the bullet from one moccasin to another after the hider had raised his hands following the concealment of the bullet. At present the Shawnees no longer play the Moccasin Game but occasionally join with the Sauks and various Plains tribes in playing the Hand Game. This game is similar to the Moccasin Game except that the counters are hidden in the hands of the "hiders," two at a time, rather than under moccasins. At such a Hand Game sponsored by the Little River powwow club in 1972 some of the players jokingly claimed that they had "power"; likewise certain of the accompanying songs were identified as "medicine" (or magically potent) songs.

Sympathetic magic was incorporated into many Shawnee rituals that were employed to control the weather. In chapter six I have noted, in a different context, how the keeper of the Kishpoko division's sacred bundle, who is generally a member of the Turtle name group, opens that bundle when rain is needed (C.F. Voegelin and E.W. Voegelin "Shawnee Name Groups": p. 630): "The old man in charge of the bundle takes it out in the woods, opens it, and offers a prayer, calling for rain . . . This old man has to be a Turtle man. Turtle lives in the water and so do the Thunderbirds; that's why it rains quickly when he takes it out." The idea here is the magical connection between the bundle (connected with the

Thunderbirds), opened by a Turtle name-group man (Turtle having a sympathetic connection with water) and the desired rain.

Other examples of weather-controlling magic are cited by C.F. Voegelin (*The Shawnee Female Deity*: p. 17). An intricate string figure or cat's cradle, symbolically "tieing up a star," is talked to and untied in order to secure cool weather. A buffalo tail is carried to a spring by a calm man, and shaken very gently in order to secure rain. The tail is shaken gently, and by a calm man, so that the subsequent rain will be gentle and calm. The words accompanying these overt acts, which are magical in Malinowski's sense, are a prayer addressed to "Grandfather Water": "Our Grandmother put this water for people to use on this earth as they are on earth. This water was created a grandfather to take care of the people. Everybody will be glad to see it rain. And Our Grandmother created this water for all kinds of animals, big and little. But now it doesn't rain. People are dissatisfied and talk to you, Grandfather, to come and make it rain all over so that people may drink" (ibid. p. 18).

Charlie Webber, a Delaware, told anthropologist Frank Speck that the Shawnees practiced rainmaking at a public ceremony using a weasel skin that was in the custody of an old man "who has the exclusive right to handle it and to the place where it is concealed, and a dance accompanies the prayer." (F.G. Speck *Oklahoma Delaware Ceremonies, Feasts, and Dances*: pp. 70–71) The Delawares had a similar rite but it was private. In it the rainmaker proceeded to a running stream, dipped the skin into the water and lifted it upward, while saying a prayer addressed to the Thunder and his messenger the weasel as the sources from which relief is hoped to come. My informant Ranny Carpenter knew of the Shawnee weasel-skin rainmaking bundle. He said that the keeper of this bundle was approached in the drought days of the 1930s and asked to use his bundle to bring rain, but he refused on the grounds that the Shawnees of that day had too little faith, and the ceremony would probably bring a torrential flood.

Another sector of Shawnee life where magical techniques were employed was hunting. C.F. Voegelin (*The Shawnee Female Deity*: p. 77) mentions deer hunting magic where: "Other overt acts, accompanied by the proper words, cause a deer to stop so that he may conveniently be shot, make a deer more than normally

visible, make a hunter shoot straight, and so on." I have already
mentioned, in chapter 3, the type of "medicine hunting" involving
four tapping sticks formerly practiced by the Shawnees, from
whom it was acquired by the Ojibwas, and perhaps the
Menominis as well.

Except for the impressive illusions of Trowbridge's "Juggling
Society," the magical performance requiring the greatest skill on
the part of the shaman was the Shaking Tent ceremony. The
Shawnee version of this ceremony, which has a wide distribution
in northern North America, is described in the notes of James R.
Carselowey (Indian Archives, Oklahoma Historical Society 88:
pp. 160-61). To prepare for this ceremony, the shaman builds a
cylindrical structure some twelve feet in height, using four stout
poles as the uprights. The lodge, or at least its upper portion, is
covered with hides. The diviner enters his tent and sings a
magical song, whereupon the lodge begins to shake and sway
rapidly back and forth, as in a heavy gale. Next the voices of spirit
animals are heard in the lodge, apparently come to confer with the
shaman. From these spirit animals the diviner learns the cure for
diseases, whereabouts of missing persons or lost articles, et cetera. The Shawnee Shaking Tent ceremony, if we can believe
Carselowey's account, appears to be a classic form of this
circumpolar complex, and identical with that of the Ojibwas,
Ottawas, Menominis, and other northern Algonkian-speaking
groups.

PROPHETS

Prophets, or gifted persons who can foretell future events, have
long been recognized among the Shawnees, Delawares, Kickapoos, and other Algonkian tribes, as well as their Iroquois neighbors. The eighteenth and nineteenth centuries, a time of military
defeats, forced removals, and constant unrest for all of these
groups was also marked by the rise of great prophets in each of
them. For the Delawares there was the famous Delaware prophet
of Pontiac's conspiracy, in 1762; for the Kickapoos, Kenekuk, the
Kickapoo reformer, who began to preach about 1815 and whose
prophetic religion still flourishes among the Kansas band of his
tribe (J.H. Howard *The Kenakuk Religion*). For the Iroquois it was
the Seneca, Handsome Lake, who preached the "Good Message"
and revitalized the culture of not only his own tribe, the Senecas,
and other Iroquois tribes, but influenced non-Iroquois groups as

well. Handsome Lake, in fact, was approached by a delegation of "Shawanoes and others (probably Wyandots) in 1807. This delegation asked the great Iroquois prophet to "return directly with them" and tell of his vision, but he refused (J.S. Schenk *History of Warren County, Pennsylvania*: pp. 149-150). Handsome Lake's refusal may have been predicated on his unfamiliarity with the Shawnee language.

The failure of Handsome Lake to visit the Shawnees was a matter of little moment, however, for at that same time in their history the Shawnees produced two remarkable prophetic leaders of their own, Tecumseh (Tekamthe) and his twin brother Tenskwatawa, or Open-door, better known as the Shawnee Prophet. Together these two developed a revitalization movement that had both political and religious dimensions. The movement is extremely interesting in that it was not limited to the Shawnees but transcended tribal boundaries in both secular and religious aspects. Thus, while the brilliant Tecumseh sought to weld the diverse tribes of eastern North America into a great military and political alliance that would halt the westward expansion of the United States, his equally eloquent and charismatic brother preached an intertribal religion which provided a spiritual base for this resistance.

Tecumseh's dream of a Pan-Indian state that could stand against the land-hungry Whites was of course doomed from the start. Even if he had been able somehow to make the numerous rival tribes forget their ancient antagonisms and jealousies, Euro-American technology and military discipline would have prevailed in the end. Following their defeat at Tippecanoe by Harrison's forces, on 7 November, 1811, the Ohio Shawnees, under the leadership of Tecumseh and the Prophet, joined the British in the War of 1812. After some successes, the combined Indian and British forces were defeated in the Battle of the Thames, near what is now Chatham, Ontario. Tecumseh lost his life in this battle. His brother now assumed political as well as spiritual leadership of this group of Shawnees, but the movement was broken. The artist Catlin, who painted and interviewed Tenskwatawa in 1832, writes of him as follows:

> This, no doubt, has been a very shrewd and influential man, but circumstances have destroyed him, as they have many other great men before him, and he now lives respected, but silent and melancholy, in his tribe. I conversed with him a great deal about his brother Tecumseh, of whom he spoke frankly and seemingly with great pleasure; but of himself and his own great

schemes he would say nothing. He told me that Tecumseh's plans were to embody all the Indian tribes in a grand confederacy, from the province of Mexico to the Great Lakes, to unite their forces in an army that would be able to meet and drive back the white people, who were continually advancing on the Indian tribes and forcing them from their lands toward the Rocky mountains; that Tecumseh was a great general, and that nothing but his premature death defeated his grand plan (J. Mooney *The Ghost Dance Religion and the Sioux Outbreak of 1890*: p. 691).

Today's Shawnees have elevated Tecumseh to the level of a demigod. My informant Ranny Carpenter spoke of him as a "saint." Tecumseh's portrait graced the walls of many Shawnee homes which I visited in the course of my research. On the other hand, his brother, the Prophet, though apparently highly respected and honored by both Whites and Indians during his later years, has come to be thought of in a negative manner by many Shawnees, much like Our Grandmother's evil grandson as contrasted with her good one. This reputation would appear to be undeserved. Certainly the assertion that he was noted for his stupidity in his earlier years (J. Mooney "Tenskwatawa": p. 729) is belied by his later success in promulgating his religion. That he knew his Shawnee people and their culture intimately is attested by his excellent service as Trowbridge's principal informant. The Trowbridge account likewise reveals the Prophet's lively sense of humor: "One of the songs of the Prophet is said to have been sung by a young man in love, who, in some of his amorous encounters with the fair one found cause to suspect her of being pregnant . . . 'I guess you'll have a child . . . No (or none) navel' " (Trowbridge *Shawnese Traditions*: pp. 39-40).

Tecumseh and his twin brother were born in 1768 at the Shawnee village of Piqua, on Mad river, about six miles southwest of the present Springfield, Ohio. My informant Ranny Carpenter asserted that there were three brothers, triplets, the third brother having a narrow, deformed head, an assertion supported by Radin's Winnebago informant (P. Radin *The Winnebago Tribe*: p. 71). Some accounts indicate that their mother was a Creek Indian but Mooney doubts this (J. Mooney *Handbook of American Indians* II: p. 714). Their father, a Shawnee chief, was killed at the battle of Point Pleasant in Lord Dunmore's War, in 1774. On his death the two boys were placed under the care of an elder brother, who in turn was killed in battle with the Whites on the Tennessee frontier in 1788 or 1789 (Mooney *Handbook*: p. 714).

As a young man Tecumseh distinguished himself as a warrior,

but he was also noted for his humane character, evinced by persuading his tribe to discontinue the practice of torturing prisoners. His brother Tenskwatawa, then called *Lalawethika* ("Rattle"), had a bad reputation as a bully, drunkard, and womanizer when a youth. According to Forsyth (T. Forsyth *Letter of Thomas Forsyth to General William Clark*: p. 274): " . . . when a boy he was a perfect vagabond and as he grew up he w^d not hunt and became a great drunkard."

There are varied accounts of the circumstances surrounding Tenskwatawa's visitation by the Creator, which was shortly followed by his abandonment of debauchery and his preaching the new religion. Mooney ("Tenskwatawa": p. 729) writes:

> . . . one day, while lighting his pipe in his cabin, he fell back apparently lifeless and remained in that condition until his friends had assembled for the funeral, when he revived from his trance, quieted their alarm, and announced that he had been conducted to the spirit world. In Nov. 1805, when hardly more than 30 years of age, he called around him his tribesmen and their allies at their ancient capital of Wapakoneta, within the present limits of Ohio, and announced himself as the bearer of a new revelation from the Master of Life. He declared that he had been taken up the spirit world and had been permitted to lift the veil of the past and future—had seen the misery of evil doers and learned the happiness that awaited those who followed the precepts of the Indian god. He then began an ernest exhortation, denouncing the witchcraft and medicine juggleries of the tribe, and solemnly warning his hearers that none who had part in such things would ever taste of the future happiness.

Radin's Winnebago informant, paraphrasing an account that the Prophet presented to a delegation of eleven Winnebagos who had come to hear him speak, tells of Tenskwatawa's dissolute youth, his vision, and subsequent reform. This account, allowing for the fact that the Prophet probably paints his early life blacker than it really was in order to make his subsequent reform more favorable by contrast (a common technique of revivalists to this day), has a ring of authenticity to it. It also indicates that Tecumseh, initially, was not impressed by his brother's pretensions but was converted as a result of the Prophet's magic:

> At that time they (the other tribes) were having their night dances, so the Winnebago moved over to them. There they heard the prophet speak, He said that he had been sent by the Creator because the Indians were wandering away from their old customs. For that reason the Creator had sent him to tell them of it. He at first forgot all about it, for the devil misrepresented things to him and he believed him. The devil had told him that he would go to heaven and that he could not be killed. He had told him that he had given him a holy belt. He was a bad person. Whenever he got angry he would throw his belt down on the ground and it would change into a yellow rattlesnake and rattle. When he did this the rest of the people were afraid of him. He was very mean when drunk. They were

afraid of him, not only on account of his belt, which he could turn into a yellow rattlesnake, but also because of the fact that he was very strong. If, when he was drunk, a number of people jumped on him, afterwards he would find out about it and hit them. If they would resist he would kill them.

It was utterly impossible for him to be killed. He was unkind to the women. They would go with him not because they liked him but because they were afraid of him. It was a dangerous thing to say anything about him. Whenever he wished to drink he would take some person's valuables and buy drink with it. These are the things he did. The Creator had sent him on a mission to the earth, but the devil had misled him.

On one occasion (when he was drunk) quite a number of people jumped on him and nearly killed him. When he awoke the next morning he asked his wife who had done it and she told him. "Well, they will hear of me soon. However, I want to go and take a bath first and cool off and then take my revenge, when I get back." When he was in bathing a man [probably Our Grandmother's grandson,] came to him and said, "They have told me to come after you, so let us go." Then he went back with him and he took him to the place from which he had originally started [the other world, Our Grandmother's home]. Then the Creator said, "How are you getting on with the work which you were to do?" Then he remembered what he had been doing. Then the Creator said, "Is it for this that I created you?" Then he took his mouth and showed it to him and he saw that it was crooked and sticking out in all directions. Then he took his understanding (and showing it to him) he said, "Did I create you thus?" Then he looked into his ears and they were crooked and ragged. Thus he made him see all his bad characteristics and his evil mind. Then he took out his heart and showed it to him. It was all furrowed up and bad to look upon. "Did I create you thus?" said the Creator.

"Now, then, you will do better the next time," and he sent him back. This time, however, he (the prophet) did not come here to get revenge. He came to tell of the mysteries, but no one would believe him. "He is just getting crazier all the time," they said of him. Then he told all to gather in one place and he promised to say nothing but the truth. Then he made a small flat war club [the "rabbit leg" or "rifle stock" type], cleared a piece of ground and laid it there. Then he said to those assembled, "If anyone can lift this, then I will not say it (i.e. talk about my mission)."

Now he (the prophet) was one of triplets. The third one was teased a good deal and one day he said, "I am getting tired of this teasing and am going home." Then he died. They had been teasing him about his head, which was very narrow. There were thus two left. The brother who was left [Tecumseh] was a powerful man. Bullets could not penetrate him, and indeed it was impossible to kill him in any way. It was this brother who had told him not to talk (about his mission). Then the prophet said to him, "Well, if you can lift this war club I will not speak about it any more.: Then he [Tecumseh] tried to lift the little war club and failed. After that the brother made no more remarks about it.

Then he had them make a long lodge and they were told to go after a number of bears. As many as he told them to get, that many they sould bring home with them. Thus they knew that he was telling the truth. All the people in the country listened to him and what he prophesied came true, so they believed him holy. (Radin *The Winnebago Tribe*: pp. 70-2)

The religion formulated by Tenskwatawa and carried to the various tribes by Tecumseh and himself, was highly nativistic in regard to both content and personnel. Its general features are indicated by H.R. Schoolcraft (*Information Respecting the*

History, Condition and Prospects of the Indian Tribes, VI: p. 354) as follows: "He told the Indians that their pristine state, antecedent to the arrival of the Europeans, was most agreeable to the Great Spirit, and that they had adopted too many of the manners and customs of the whites. He counselled them to return to their primeval simple condition; to throw away their flints and steels, and resort to their original mode of obtaining fire by percussion. He denounced the woolen stuffs as not equal to skins for clothing; he commended the use of the bow and arrow . . . "

Thomas Forsyth, an a letter to General William Clark dated 23 December, 1812, gives as many of the "laws and regulations" of the Prophet's religion as he could then recall, admitting that he had forgotten many of them. (E. H. Blair pp. 274-8): *Tribes of the Upper Mississippi Valley Region and Region of the Great Lakes*, II:

1st Spirituous liquor was not to be tasted by any Indians on any account whatever.

2nd No Indian was to take more than one wife in the future, but those who now had two three or more wives might keep them, but it would please the Great Spirit if they had only one wife.

3rd No Indian was to be running after the women; if a man was single let him take a wife.

4th If any married woman was to behave ill by not paying proper attention to her work, etc., the husband had a right to punish her with a rod, and as soon as the punishment was over, both husband and wife, was to look each other in the face and laugh, and to bear no ill will to each other for what had passed.

5th All Indian women who were living with whitemen was to be brought home to their friends and relations, and their children to be left with their fathers, so that the nations might become genuine Indians.

6th All medicine bags, and all kinds of medicine dances and songs were to exist no more; the medicine bags were to be destroyed in *presens* of the whole of the people collected for that purpose, and at the destroying of such medicine, etc., every one was to make open confession to the Great Spirit in a loud voice of all the bad deeds that he or she had committed during their lifetime, and beg for forgiveness as the Great Spirit was too good to refuse.

7th No Indian was to sell any of their provision to any white people, they might give a little as a present, as they were sure of getting in return the full value in something else.

8th No Indian was to eat any victuals that was cooked by a white person, or eat any provisions raised by white people, as bread, beef, pork, fowls, etc.

9th No Indian must offer skins or furs or any thing else for sale, but ask to exchange them for such articles that they may want.

10th Every Indian was to consider the French, English, and Spaniards, as their fathers or friends, and to give them their hand, but they were not to know the Americans on any account, but to keep them at a distance.

11th All kind of white people's dress, such as hats, coats, etc., were to be given to the first whiteman they met as also all dogs not of their own breed, and all cats were to be given back to white people.

12th The Indians were to endeavour to do without buying any merchandise as much as possible, by which means the game would become plenty, and then by means of bows and arrows, they could hunt and kill game as in former days, and live independent of all white people.

13th All Indians who refused to follow these regulations were to be considered as bad people and not worthy to live, and must be put to death. (A Kickapoo Indian was actually burned in the spring of the year 1809 at the old Kickapoo town for refusing to give up his medicine bag, and another old man and old woman was very near sharing the same fate at the same time and place).

14th The Indians in their prayers prayed to the earth, to be fruitful, also to the fish to be plenty, to the fire and sun, etc., and a certain dance was introduced simply for amusement, those prayers were repeated morning and evening, and they were taught that a deviation from these duties would offend the Great Spirit. There were many more regulations but I have now forgot them, but those above mentioned are the principal ones.

Both of these accounts indicate the highly nativistic tone of the Prophet's teachings, likewise its strong anti-American quality. The "laws or regulations" listed by Forsyth have a great similarity to the doctrines of today's American Indian Movement militants. That the Prophet had a keen insight into the frailties of his Indian people is indicated by his ninth law. Tenskwatawa realized that when hides or furs were sold for cash, the cash was usually spent for liquor. If, on the other hand, the hides and furs were traded for useful articles, this pitfall was avoided. The tenth law is of course a bow to political expediency. Under the old colonial regimes of the French, English, and Spanish, the land base of the Shawnees had not been threatened as it was by the land-hungry Yankees of the post-Revolutionary era.

The prohibition against medicine bags, medicine dances, and songs, all features of "traditional" Indian culture, is of course something more than advocacy of a return to the good old days. Such changes as this are, however, quite characteristic of revitalization movements (Cf. A.F.C. Wallace "Revitalization Movements"). Like the Seneca, Handsome Lake, Tenskwatawa was selective in his reformulation of Indian life and saw this aspect of his people's culture as evil. His reasons for doing so are quite obvious. When cultures are undergoing extreme stress, as Shawnee culture was in the early nineteenth century, witchcraft tends to burgeon, and witchcraft has always been but a hair removed from ordinary Indian medicines and its practitioners, and therefore difficult to detect. For this reason the Prophet was compelled to proscribe *all* medicine bags and medicine rites. He encountered strong opposition on this point from many who otherwise might have supported him and was forced to resort to strong counter measures. In addition to the Kickapoo who was burned to death for refusing to give up his medicine bag, there were other executions of persons who refused to do so and hence were branded as witches. Leatherlips, the Wyandot sachem, was one (Schoolcraft *Information*, VI: p. 353), likewise several Delawares (B. Drake *Life of Tecumseh*, quoted in Mooney *The Ghost Dance Religion*: pp. 673-74).

Another innovative feature that caused many to turn against the Prophet was his proscription of dogs (J. Tanner *A Narrative of the Captivity and Adventures of John Tanner*: p. 144). Apparently this law was not consistently promulgated, for E. A. Kendall (*Travels* II: pp. 292, 296) indicates that the rule was "to keep but one dog in a family".

Tenskwatawa taught that if his followers listened to his words, at the end of four years the Creator would bring on two days of darkness, during which the Creator would travel invisibly throughout the land, and cause the animals that had been created to come forth again out of the earth. They were also promised that their dead friends would be restored to them. Both of these prophecies are amazingly similar to the promises offered by Jack Wilson, the Paiute, in connection with the Ghost Dance religion many years later. Among the Cherokee and Creek followers of the Prophet, it was thought that there would be a terrible hailstorm that would overwhelm both whites and Indian unbelievers, while the followers of the Prophet would be warned in time to save themselves by fleeing to high mountain tops (Kendall *Travels* II: p. 287).

The actual form of the religion preached by Tenskwatawa and Tecumseh is nowhere fully described. W.W. Warren (*History of the Ojibways*: pp. 321-24), Kendall (*Travels* II: p. 292) and Mooney (*The Ghost Dance Religion*: p. 677) indicate that there was an elaborate ritual. Kendall indicates that one ceremonial observance involved the men dancing naked, with their bodies painted, and with warclubs in their hands, a description that fits the "Man's Dance" or ceremonial War Dance that is still performed by the Absentee Shawnees today. This is probably the same as "*Tecumsehs* new war songs and dances" mentioned in the Stiggins Narrative (T.A. Nunez "Creek Nativism and the Creek War of 1813-14" Pt. 2: pp. 146, 147) and the "Dance of the Lakes" mentioned by R.S. Cotterill (*The Southern Indians*: p. 174). It may even be the same as the "certain dance" introduced "simply for amusement" mentioned in the Forsyth letter quoted earlier, though I believe that I can suggest a better candidate for this last item, and will do so later.

Certain pieces of the paraphernalia of the Prophet's religion are mentioned by Catlin and Tanner. Catlin speaks of a sort of mummy employed by the Prophet in his rituals: "He carried with him into every wigwam that he visited, the image of a dead person of the size of life; which was made ingeniously of some light material, and always kept concealed under bandages of thin white muslin cloths and not to be opened; of this he made great mystery, and got his recruits to swear by touching a sacred string of white beans which he had attached to its neck or some other way secreted about it. In this way, by his extra-ordinary cunning, he had carried terror into the country as far as he went . . . " (G. Catlin *Letters and Notes*: pp. 117-8) This grisly item is undoubtedly the same object which Tanner witnessed." (Tanner *Narrative*: p. 146).

Both writers also mention strings of beans which figured in the Prophet's ritual. Catlin, as noted above, says that these were attached to the neck of the "mummy" or otherwise secreted about it. Catlin painted Tenskwatawa holding his "sacred string of beans" in his left hand and his "medicine fire" in the right. (Plate 7) He gives no details concerning the latter object. From his painting it appears to be an item about a foot long with feather ornaments and bead dangles attached. Whatever its actual form, its name would indicate a relationship to the eternal flame or fire mentioned by Trowbridge (*Shawnese Traditions*: pp. 56-57). The "eternal flame" seems to have been an important concept in the Prophet's religion, and is undoubtedly the basis for his rule that his followers must never extinguish the fires in their lodges (Tanner *Narrative*: pp. 144, 147).

It is also possible that the item pictured by Catlin is one of the pictographic boards that Tenskwatawa manufactured and distributed among his followers. These boards or "sacred slabs" epitomized his doctrine. One of these slabs, collected in 1922 from Oliver Le Mere, a Winnebago, by Milford G. Chandler, is in the collections of the Cranbrook Institute of Science. It has been described by W.A. Galloway ("A Sacred Slab of the Shawnee Prophet") and is reproduced here as Fig. 6. According to Le Mere, "The story sticks were made and given to war bundle owners by the Shawnee Prophet. He only gave it to those who were sincere about life. It is said that he told those to whom he gave the sticks that at a time when the creation of things represented on the story stick would be ignored and not be kept sacred that the end of the world would come to pass, that is to say when the creation of the Great Spirit would lose the respect of the people." (Galloway "A Sacred Slab of the Shawnee Prophet": p. 6) Galloway comments that the slab is a representation of the universe and that " . . . it seems quite probable that its acceptance by the Indians signified the acceptance of the new religion" (ibid.: p. 7).

The characters on the slab were interpreted by Oliver Le Mere, the man from whom Chandler collected the piece. Le Mere knew the significance of all but one of the fourteen pictographs, and there is no reason to doubt his interpretations. From top to bottom these are:

> 1—a house-like representation, "Heaven;" 2—a row of four figures, apparently heads and shoulders of some beings, "Thunderers or Gate Keepers of Heaven;" 3—a horizontal line with four pendant notches, "Blue Sky;" 4—a circle bisected by a straight, horizontal line, "Sun;" 5—three fine, branching lines, resembling pine needles, "All Plant Life;" 6—unknown; 7—a horizontal line above which is a crude bird with outstretched wings and below which is a deer's (?) neck and head facing downward, "Fowls and Animals of Earth and Air;" 8—a horizontal line from which runs a short line, "Corn;" 9—a cross having at the end of each arm an enlarged pit, "Four Corners of the Earth;" 10—a horizontal feather element, "Trees;" 11—a wavy line splitting into a fork at the end, "Lightning;" 12—a straight, horizontal line, "Water;" 13—a representation similar to 4, "Earth;" 14—two horizontal lines running completely across the slab above which is a third running about three quarters of the way across, "Family" (ibid. p. 7).

The concepts selected for pictographic representation on this sacred slab are obviously the deities to be addressed in prayers by the faithful, the Truth Bearers or Witnesses of these prayers, and for the final pictograph, the intended recipients of divine favor. Forsyth, in the fourteenth of the "laws" or "regulations" of the Prophet's religion listed by him (Blair *Tribes of the Upper Mississippi Valley Region* II: p. 278) notes that: "The Indians in their prayers prayed to the earth, to be fruitful, also to the fish to be plenty, to the fire and sun, etc. . . ." Eleven of the fourteen pictographs on the sacred slab represent, or are closely associated with deities or Truth Bearers still mentioned, by name, by present-day Shawnees in Bread Dance speeches and other religious observances. These are: (1) Our Grandmother, the Creator (whose heavenly abode is the top pictograph on the slab), (2) Thunderbirds, (3) Sky (a Truth Bearer or Witness), (4) Sun, (5) Plant Life (Truth Bearers), (8) Corn Woman, (9) Four Winds, (10) Tree Men, (11) Lightning (a manifestation of the Thunderbirds and perhaps, secondarily, of Cyclone Person), (12) Water (an important Truth Bearer), and (13) Earth.

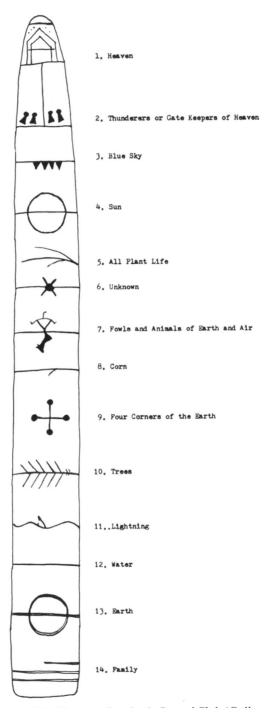

1. Heaven

2. Thunderers or Gate Keepers of Heaven

3. Blue Sky

4. Sun

5. All Plant Life

6. Unknown

7. Fowls and Animals of Earth and Air

8. Corn

9. Four Corners of the Earth

10. Trees

11. .Lightning

12. Water

13. Earth

14. Family

Fig. 6.   Diagram of the Shawnee Prophet's Sacred Slab (*Galloway 1943, pp. 6-7*)

This congruity of the core of the Prophet's doctrine, as epitomized on his sacred pictographic record slabs, with the core of traditional Shawnee religion, is most interesting. It indicates that Tenskwatawa, like the Seneca, Handsome Lake, did not preach any great alteration in his tribe's basic religion. A few items of attention-getting paraphernalia were added (the "mummy" and the strings of beans); certain elements of the traditional religion were emphasized (the sacred fire); and some traditional items were prohibited (medicine bags and medicines dances and in the secular sphere, dogs). Basically, however, the Shawnee Prophet, like his Iroquois counterpart, was operating well within the range of his tribe's traditional beliefs and practices, which he sought to perpetuate and restore to their former vitality.

One of the best contemporary accounts of the advent of the Prophet's doctrines among the northern tribes is that of John Tanner, a white captive who had been socialized among the Ottawas and Ojibwas (Tanner *Narrative*: 144–47):

It was while I was living here at Great Wood River that news came of a great man among the Shawneese, who had been favoured by a revelation of the mind and will of the Great Spirit. I was hunting in the prairie, at a great distance from my lodge, when I saw a stranger approaching. At first I was apprehensive of an enemy, but, as he drew nearer, his dress showed him to be an Ojibbeway, but when he came up there was something very strange and peculiar in his manner. He signified to me that I must go home, but gave no explanation of the cause. He refused to look at me, or enter into any kind of conversation. I thought he must be crazy, but nevertheless accompanied him to my lodge. When we had smoked, he remained a long time silent, but at last began to tell me he had come with a message from the prophet of the Shawneese. "Henceforth," said he, "the fire must never be suffered to go out in your lodge. Summer and winter, day and night, in the storm, or when it is calm, you must remember that the life in your body, and the fire in your lodge, are the same, and of the same date. If you suffer your fire to be extinguished, at that moment your life will be at its end. You must not suffer a dog to live. You must never strike either a man, a woman, a child, or a dog. The prophet himself is coming to shake hands with you, but I have come before, that you may know what is the will of the Great Spirit, communicated to us by him, and to inform you that the preservation of your life, for a single moment, depends on your entire obedience. From this time forward, we are neither to be drunk, to steal, to lie, or to go against our enemies. While we yield an entire obedience to these commands of the Great Spirit, the Sioux, even if they come to our country, will not be able to see us: we shall be protected and made happy." I listened to all he had to say, but told him, in answer, that I could not believe we should all die in case our fire went out. In many instances, also, it would be difficult to avoid punishing our children; our dogs were useful in aiding us to hunt and take animals, so that I could not believe the Great Spirit had any wish to take them from us. He continued talking to us until late at night, then he lay down to sleep in my lodge. I happened to wake first in the morning, and perceiving the fire had gone out, I called him to get up, and see how many of us were living, and how many dead. He was prepared for the ridicule I attempted to throw upon his doctrine, and told me that I had not yet shaken hands with the prophet. His visit had been to prepare me for this important event, and to make me aware of the obligations and risks I should incur by entering into the engagement implied in taking in my hand the message of the prophet. I did not rest entirely easy in my unbelief. The Indians generally received the doctrine of this man with great humility and fear. Distress and anxiety was visible in every countenance. Many killed their dogs, and endeavored to practice obedience to all the commands of this new preacher, who still remained among us. But, as was usual with me in any emergency of this kind, I went to the traders, firmly believing that if the Diety had any communications to make to men, they would be given, in the first instance, to white men. The traders ridiculed and despised the idea of a new revelation of the Divine will, and the thought that it should be given to a poor Shawnee. Thus was I confirmed in my infidelity. Nevertheless, I did not openly avow my unbelief to the Indians, only I refused to kill my dogs, and showed no great degree of anxiety to comply with his other requirements. As long as I remained among the Indians, I made it my business to conform, as far as appeared consistent with my immediate convenience and comfort, with all their customs. Many of their ideas I have adopted, but I always found among them opinions which I could not hold. The Ojibbeway whom I have mentioned, remained some time among the Indians in my neighbourhood, and gained the attention of the principal men so effectually, that a time was appointed, and a lodge prepared for the solemn and public espousing of the doctrines of the prophet. When the people, and I among them, were brought into the long lodge prepared for this solemnity, we saw something carefully concealed under a blanket, in figure and dimensions bearing some resemblance to the form of a man. This was accompanied by two young men, who, it was understood, attended constantly upon it, made its bed at night, as for a man, and slept near it. But while we remained, no one went near it, or raised the blanket which was spread over its unknown contents. Four strings of mouldy and discoloured beans were all the remaining visible insignia of this important mission. After a long harrangue, in which the prominent features of the new revelation were stated and urged upon the attention of all, the four strings of beans, which we were told were made of the flesh itself of the prophet, were carried with much solemnity to each man in the lodge, and he was expected to take hold of each string at the top, and draw them gently through his hand. This was called shaking hands with the prophet, and was considered as solemnly engaging to obey his injunctions, and accept his mission as from the Supreme. All the Indians who touched the beans had previously killed their dogs. They gave up their medicine bags, and showed a disposition to comply with all that should be required of them.

We had now been for some time assembled in considerable numbers. Much agitation and terror had prevailed among us, and now famine began to be felt. The faces of men wore an aspect of unusual gloominess, the active became indolent, and the spirits of the bravest seemed to be subdued. I started to hunt with my dogs, which I had constantly refused to kill, or suffer to be killed. By their assistance, I found and killed a bear. On returning home, I said to some of the Indians, "Has not the Great Spirit given us our dogs to aid us in procuring what is needful for the support of our life, and can you believe he wishes now to deprive us of their services? The prophet, we are told, has forbid us to suffer our fire to be extinguished in our lodges, and when we travel or hunt, he will not allow us to use a flint and steel, and we are told he requires that no man should give fire to another. Can it please the Great Spirit that we should lie in our hunting camps without fire, or is it more agreeable to him that we should make fire by rubbing together two sticks than with a flint and a piece of steel?" But they would not listen to me, and the serious enthusiasm which prevailed among them so far affected me that I threw away my flint and steel, laid aside my medicine bag, and, in many particulars, complied with the new doctrines. But I would not kill my dogs. I soon learned to kindle a fire by rubbing some dry cedar, which I was careful to carry always about me, but the discontinuance of the use of flint and steel subjected many of the Indians to much inconvenience and suffering. The influence of the Shawnee prophet was very sensibly and painfully felt by the remotest Ojibbeways of whom I had any knowledge, but it was not the common impression among them that his doctrines had any tendency to unite them in the accomplishment of any human purpose. For two or three years drunkenness was much less frequent than formerly, was less thought of, and the entire aspect of affairs among them was somewhat changed by the influence of one man. But gradually the impression was obliterated, medicine bags, flints, and steels, were resumed, dogs were raised, women and children were beaten as before, and the Shawnee prophet was despised. At this day he is looked upon by the Indians as an imposter and a bad man.

The ultimate rejection of the Prophet and his doctrines by the Ojibwas and Ottawas mentioned in Tanner's closing sentence was not his fate in all of the tribes that were influenced by his teachings. His memory was cherished by Radin's Winnebago informants who, in the years from 1908 to 1913, still repeated some of his prophecies (Radin *The Winnebago Tribe*: p. 73):

> Now, it is four generations since the Shawnee prophet prophesied, and from that time there have been many prophets among us, as he is said to have told the people. Many have prophesied, but none have told anything that seemed reasonable. The Shawnee prophet was good, but those who have come after him have prophesied so that people might praise them, or just for the sake of talking.
>
> It is said that the Shawnee prophet said that there would come a time when a woman would prophesy and that she should be immediately killed. The end of the world would be near then. Then he is said to have said that a little boy would prophesy and that one was to give ear to what he said.
>
> The Peyote people claim that their ceremony is the fulfillment of this prophesy and that it is true. The Shawnee prophet has said that there would be springs of water in front of the people's lodges and it is so at the present time, for the water is at our very doors. His prophesy was correct and he told the truth. Then he said that trees would travel and this is happening to-day, for trees are loaded into trains and are carried all around the country. He told the truth and he knew what was going to happen. He said that one day we would be able to write in our own language and we are doing that to-day, for we have a Bible in Winnebago and we are able to write to one another in our own language. All these things he was able to foretell four generations ago.

The most famous of Tenskwatawa's prophecies was his accurate announcement of a forthcoming eclipse (Mooney *The Ghost Dance Religion*: p. 674):

> By some means he had learned that an eclipse of the sun was to take place in the summer of 1806. As the time drew near, he called about him the scoffers and boldly announced that on a certain day he would prove to them his supernatural authority by causing the sun to become dark. When the day and hour arrived and the earth at mid-day was enveloped in the gloom of twilight, Tenskwatawa, standing in the midst of the terrified Indians, pointed to the sky

and cried, "Did I not speak the truth? See, the sun is dark!" There were no more doubters now. All proclaimed him a true prophet and the messenger of the Master of Life. His fame spread abroad and apostles began to carry his revelations to the remotest tribes.

The Prophet's twin brother also prophesied on occasion with telling effect. Tecumseh's most famous prophecy, still remembered today by Shawnees who know little else concerning the career of their most famous chief, occurred on the occasion of his visit to the Creeks in 1811. The prophecy was made at Tuckabatchee Town, near the present site of Montgomery, Alabama. The story was told to McKenney and Hall by a Tuckabatchee Creek a few years later (T.L. McKenney and J. Hall *History of the Indian Tribes of North America*, I: pp. 64-5):

> He made his way to the lodge of the chief called Big Warrior. He explained his object, delivered his war talk, presented a bundle of sticks, gave a piece of wampum and a war hatchet—all which the Big Warrior took—when Tecumthé, reading the spirit and intentions of the Big Warrior, looked him in the eye, and, pointing his finger toward his face, said: "Your blood is white. You have taken my talk, and the sticks, and the wampum, and the hatchet, but you do not mean to fight. I know the reason. You do not believe the Great Spirit has sent me. You shall know. I leave Tuckabatchee directly, and shall go straight to Detroit. When I arrive there, I will stamp on the ground with my foot and shake down every house in Tuckabatchee." So saying, he turned and left the Big Warrior in utter amazement at both his manner and his threat, and pursued his journey. The Indians were struck no less with his conduct than was the Big Warrior, and began to dread the arrival of the day when the threatened calamity would befall them. They met often and talked over this matter, and counted the days carefully to know the day when Tecumthé would reach Detroit. The morning they had fixed upon as the day of his arrival at last came. A mighty rumbling was heard—the Indians all ran out of their houses—the earth began to shake; when at last, sure enough, every house in Tuckabatchee was shaken down. The exclamation was in every mouth "Tecumthé has got to Detroit!" The effect was electric. The message he had delivered to the Big Warrior was believed, and many of the Indians took their rifles and prepared for the war. The reader will not be surprised to learn that an earthquake had produced all this; but he will be, doubtless, that it should happen on the very day on which Tecumthé arrived at Detroit, and in exact fulfillment of his threat. It was the famous earthquake of New Madrid on the Mississippi.

Tecumseh's last prophecy was the prediction of his own death. This occurred just prior to the Battle of the Thames, in 1813. The occasion of this prophecy, the subject of a well-known painting by W. Langdon Kihn (M.W. Stirling "America's First Settlers": Pl. 25) is described by Drake (*Life of Tecumseh*: p. 193) in these words: "When he had posted his men, he called his chiefs about him and calmly said, 'Brother warriors, we are now about to enter into an engagement from which I shall never come out—my body will remain on the field of battle.' He then unbuckled his sword, and placing it in the hands of one of them, said, 'When my son becomes a noted warrior and able to wield a sword, give this to him.' He then laid aside his British military dress and took his place in the line, clothed only in an ordinary deerskin hunting shirt." When the battle began, Tecumseh's voice was heard encouraging his men until he fell under the cavalry charge of the Americans, who had already broken the ranks of the British regulars. Deprived of their leader and deserted by their white allies, the Indians gave up the contest and surrendered. Tecumseh died in his forty-fourth year (Mooney *The Ghost Dance Religion*: p. 691). His brother, the Prophet, survived him by twenty-four years, and is buried in what is now the Argentine district of Kansas City, Kansas.

Tenskwatawa and Tecumseh are remembered as the greatest prophets among the Shawnees, but they were by no means the last. Theoretically it is possible for any Shawnee who has received the help of a spirit helper while on the vision quest to make the journey to the Creator's home while in a prophetic trance and receive communications from Our Grandmother. Usually such individuals do not learn about their own personal future (Tecumseh's last prophecy being an exception) but the future of all Shawnees. The following occurrence, reported by E.B. Townsend in 1883, is typical:

> About a year ago an old Shawnee woman while in a cataleptic state received a revelation from the Great Spirit to the effect that the Shawnees were adopting unwisely and in too great measure the ways and habits of the white man; that unless they changed their course, abandoned the following and teaching of the whites, and returned to the ways of their fathers and the traditions of their forefathers, they would dwindle away and be lost; but if on the other hand they abandoned their evil course and returned to the old Indian way; adhered to their own traditions and the teachings of their fathers all would yet be well with them; they would yet be prosperous and happy; would be re-united (the Eastern Shawnees, the Black Bob Shawnees, the Absentee and Upper Shawnees) and become a mighty people, dominant upon the face of the earth and powerful among all the races thereof not excepting the Latter Day Saints. Strange and weird as this story sounds it was received by the Shawnees as a work of inspiration, as much so as Christian whites accept the Inspired Word, and so strong was the influence it exerted that it threatened to bring about serious results. Children were taken out of school; many of the Indians (for a time) abandoned their civilized dress and pursuits and large numbers gave themselves up to feasting and dancing with a religious abandon which promised well for the woman's prophecies (Letter of E.B. Townsend, Special Agent at Shawneetown, Indian Territory, to Hon. W. Price, Commissioner of Indian Affairs, 6 April 1883, quoted in C.F. Voegelin *The Shawnee Female Deity*: p. 17).

A person who approaches Our Grandmother in a prophetic trance of this sort cannot repeat his or her visit, because only one prophetic trance is granted in a lifetime.

According to C.F. Voegelin (ibid.: p. 16) a distinction is sometimes made between those who flit to the Creator's home in a short time while in a prophetic trance and those who make the long journey travelling by the well-established but dangerous path that the visitors take in the Orpheus folktale. Only those individuals who have received the unequivocal help of a powerful guardian spirit are thought to be able to take the latter approach. Sweat lodge doctors or others who have been given a "doctoring way" on the vision quest are considered to be particularly well equipped for this. Any of the Four Winds, Sun, Moon, and perhaps the Truth Bearer Water are spirit helpers specified as especially helpful in overcoming the tremendous obstacles in the way. However, individuals who are guided to the other world by their guardian spirits may, in the name of prophecy, relate what their spirit helper rather than the creator said; in this case the guardian spirit acts as the intermediary between the Creator and the individual (ibid.: p. 16).

Sometimes prophetic insight was given to individuals who had not visited Our Grandmother at all during their lifetimes. Warriors, both men and women, defined as people who had had various misfortunes in war that were in a sense compensated for by a gift of prophecy from the Creator, attended councils and advised the chief and his councilors as to the future. A warrior woman, it is said, would not be reluctant, as an ordinary woman might, to get up and speak in council (ibid.: p. 17).

Less frequently an individual was born with a complete or partial knowledge of the future gained from the Creator during his residence with her as an unborn soul. The Prophet, Tenskwatawa, is said by some to have been such an individual (ibid.: p. 17) though the accounts of his cataleptic trance while lighting his pipe (Mooney "Tenskwatawa": p. 729) and Radin's account of his visions (*The Winnebago Tribe*: p. 70-72) would indicate the more usual visit to Heaven as an adult. C.F. Voegelin (*The Shawnee Female Deity*: p. 17) mentions an old Loyal Shawnee man who was able to predict the advent of automobiles before they had been invented because he was created with this foreknowledge.

SACRED BUNDLES

Like the Trojans with their statue of Pallas, the Hebrews with their Ark of the Covenant, and like most North American Indians, the Shawnees possessed a number of tribal palladia or sacred bundles. The Shawnee name for sacred bundle, *mishaami*, together with the terms for associated ritual concepts, is shared with the Sauks, Foxes, and Kickapoos and reflects prehistoric relationships with these tribes as well as considerable antiquity of the bundle complex itself (Voegelin *The Shawnee Female Deity*: p. 7–8). There apparently were separate bundles for each of the five great divisions of the tribe at one time: Chalaakaatha, Mekoche, Thawikila, Pekowi, and Kishpoko. At present two, and possibly three, of the divisional bundles survive. One is kept by the Loyal Shawnees, and is probably the divisional bundle of the *Chalaakaatha* because this was the leading division of the "Ohio" Shawnees and because Shawnee tradition says that the Mekoche division has lost its bundle (Alford in Galloway *Old Chillicothe*: p. 41). A second bundle is, or was until a few years ago, kept by the White Turkey band, the old Thawikila division. A third, the Kishpoko divisional bundle, is kept by the Pekowi and Kishpoko Absentee Shawnees of Little River.

Information concerning these bundles and their contents and functions is difficult to come by. In a very real sense today's Shawnees still believe that the welfare of their band, their tribe, and in fact, the entire universe, is bound up in these buckskin-wrapped packages. To even speak of the bundles and their contents is to run the risk of desecrating them; hence it is best to remain silent. Apparently, aside from their custodians, most Shawnees have only a hazy notion of the specific nature and contents of their group's bundle, and even the best informed among them are most reluctant to discuss the bundle. This section of my monograph, then, is inevitably a pastiche of odd remarks by my informants and fragmentary references from the literature set in a framework constructed from my general knowledge of the composition and function of such bundles among the Shawnees and related groups, particularly the Kickapoos and Sauks, whose bundles and practices are similar to those of the Shawnees.

Traditionally all of the principal bundles were given to the Shawnees by Our Grandmother (or, in Trowbridge's account, by the Supreme Being). To these original bundles items have been added from time to time since the creation of the Shawnees, such as the heart and flesh of the dead crocodile discovered by Chalaakaatha, the culture hero, and his followers on the sea shore, and the head, horns, flesh, and excrement of the Giant Horned Snake that they subsequently overcame (Trowbridge *Shawnese Traditions*: p. 43-44). Our Grandmother's Grandson and the Thunderbirds are also involved. The former is thought to have given the Kishpoko division at least part of its bundle, which originally contained feathers from the Thunderbirds (Voegelin *The Shawnee Female Deity*: p. 10-11). Some of my informants think that the trefoil-shaped tomahawk in the same bundle was added by Tecumseh.

Our Grandmother, in addition to her creation of the bundles, maintains a potential control over them. Whenever she wishes, she may inform the Shawnees of desired changes in either the contents of the bundles or in the ritual observances associated with them. This is done through communication with prophets who visit her in her heavenly abode. The prophets then announce the changes to the people. C.F. Voegelin, in an insightful paragraph, summarizes the Shawnee attitude toward their sacred bundles (ibid. p. 18)

> To describe the relationship between the Creator and the sacred bundles abstracted as one element of Shawnee religion falsely minimizes the extreme sacredness of the bundles. Their sphere of influence is all embracing rather than specific; they overshadow the Creator herself, and in many ways the attitude of the Shawnee towards the bundles contrasts sharply with their attitude to the Creator. The latter is known intimately to every child; the bundles are shrouded in mystery even to their custodians, their history and origin varies with each political division, and totemic name groups have various duties in respect to them. One senses that at the ceremonial dances the Shawnee talk about Our Grandmother but think about their bundles. If a study of the Creator is the prolegomenon to Shawnee religion, then the ultimate insight into this religion must rest on a study of the sacred bundles.

Each of the sacred bundles is assigned to the care of a designated custodian, who is always a man, and a person of high moral character. The bundle itself is kept near the keeper's home in a separate structure, that was formerly made of poles and bark (Voegelin, Rafinesque, Voegelin, and Lilly *Walum Olum*: p. 36) now a small clapboard structure that somewhat resembles a doghouse. The precincts of this little shelter are taboo to children (lest they be inadvertently harmed by the "power" of the medicine, which one of my informants compared to radioactivity) and to menstruating women and their husbands (menstrual blood has a contaminating effect upon any holy substance or proceeding). The ground around the hut should be kept free of grass and regularly swept clean.

The bundles are regarded and treated much as human beings, and it is believed that they may become cramped from resting too long in one position. Thus Paige Daugherty, now a prominent Peyote leader among the Loyal Shawnees, recounted that as a child he was given once a month the task of going to the little house where the Loyal Shawnee principal bundle was stored, together with other sacred bundles (probably personal bundles) and shifting their positions on the storage shelves slightly to prevent their becoming uncomfortable.

The custodian of the bundle was (and is) an important figure in the social hierarchy and was consulted whenever the chief and council were considering a migration: "Among the Shawnee a resolution on the part of one political subdivision to migrate elsewhere would be mentioned first of all to the custodian of that group's sacred bundle. The custodian might or might not be a political figure. In any major movement the Shawnee are concerned first of all with the transportation of their sacred bundle, since they feel that the welfare of each group is inextricably bound up with the proper care and respect of the group's sacred bundle (ibid.: p. 61).

The bundles provide the most sacred approach to Our Grandmother as well as a vehicle through which she delivers extremely holy, sometimes esoteric communications to her Shawnee grandchildren. At Whiteoak, and perhaps at Little River as well, the "Queen Bee" or head woman of the dance ground approaches the sacred bundle's little house before each major ceremony to learn from this oracle the proper date for scheduling the performance. Formerly bundles were opened and their contents manipulated in order to learn the course of future events, such as the outcome of a battle with an enemy tribe (Voegelin *The Shawnee Female Deity*: p. 18). The bundles are a holy mystery that attracts the inarticulate interest of the entire tribe. Immediately preceding the end of the world, it is thought, Our Grandmother will recall the bundles (ibid.).

Concerning the contents of the Loyal Shawnee sacred bundle I can say very little in addition to what has already been mentioned in the tribal origin legends and Trowbridge's description. From the nature of its contents the Loyal Shawnee sacred bundle would appear to derive much of its power from the "Powers Below", such as the Giant Horned Snake and other underwater and/or subterranean creatures. Its custodian during the period of my fieldwork was Frank Bob, a blind ritualist who also delivered the public prayers at the Whiteoak Bread dances. So far as I am aware this bundle is never opened in connection with any public ceremony.

The sacred bundles of the Kishpoko and Thawikila divisions are clearly associated with the Thunderbirds or "Powers Above." Because of their Thunderbird associations both are associated with war and are analogous to the "War bags" or war bundles of the Potawatomis, Sauks, and Kickapoos. Their keepers must be members of either the Turtle or Turkey name groups, and the Turtle group is preferred because "Turtle lives in water and so do the Thunderbirds" (Voegelin and Voegelin "Shawnee Name Groups": p. 630). If it should become necessary to move either bundle three Turtle or Turkey men are put in charge of the operation, never members of any other name groups.

The contents of the Kishpoko bundle include (1) an ancient trefoil-shaped steel tomahawk (Plates 22, and 23, Fig. 7). This tomahawk is precisely of the type that has been recovered archeologically at Indian sites that had been occupied by the French allies during the French and Indian Wars, and was considered a badge of the French allies at that time. The handle is roughly carved of wood, with a wavy line extending from the blade to the base of the handle. The blade is approximately nine inches in length; the handle about fourteen inches. Some Absentee Shawnees maintain that this tomahawk was the one added to the bundle by Tecumseh. Warclubs or tomahawks are a universal feature of war bundles among the Shawnees, Kickapoos, Sauks, Foxes, Iowas, Otos, Ojibwas, and other Woodland and Prairie tribes. (2) Four "plumes," each consisting of a bunch of stripped hawk tail feathers or complete downy eagle plumes. Three are largely composed of stripped hawk tail feathers (red-tailed hawk, marsh hawk, and Cooper's hawk) and one is composed of downy plumes from beneath the tail of an eagle. The hawk tail plumes have been made by stripping the web from either side of the quill of about ten tail feathers. The larger end of these pieces of stripped web has then been bent over a buckskin thong and half-hitched in place with sinew, as is done when manufacturing the hair fringes for the roach headdress, or securing the top of a cattail house mat. Then the fringe of stripped feathers, about twenty separate webs to each fringe, has been rolled into a bunch and tied about three-quarters of an inch from the top, leaving enough extra buckskin thong at either end to attach the ornament to the hair of the wearer. Though such ornaments are now confined to sacred bundles, they were apparently quite common items of male adornment in the nineteenth century, for Alford (*Civilization*: p. 77) mentions wearing a "plume" of this sort attached to the top of his cap when he was a boy. The original versions of these four plumes are said to have been feathers from the Thunderbirds (Voegelin *The Shawnee Female Deity*: p. 11). Such plumes have formed a part of the contents of Shawnee war bundles for at least a century; they are mentioned by Nancy Chouteau, one of Joab Spencer's informants, in a tale collected in the period from 1858 to 1860 (J. Spencer *The Shawnee Indians*: p. 393; "Shawnee Folk-lore: p. 322-3). (3) A small wooden image of a boy or man in full Shawnee costume, equipped with a tiny bow and arrows. Such images occur in Prairie Potawatomi (A. Skinner *The Mascoutens or Prairie Potawatomi Indians, Pt. I*: Plates V, VI), Sauk (M.R. Harrington *Sacred Bundles of the Sac and Fox Indians*: Plate 38), Fox (Harrington op. cit.: Plates 39–40), Ottawa, Ojibwa, and Eastern and Middle Dakota bundles. They are variously identified as clan ancestors (Potawatomi), warriors (Fox), and the Woods-Elf or Little-Tree-Dweller (Potawatomi, Ottawa, Ojibwa, Eastern and Middle Dakota). (4) Some informants hinted that this bundle, like that of the Loyal Shawnees, contained a portion of the flesh, bones, et cetera of the Giant Horned Snake. (5) According to Alfred Switch, two beautiful roach headdresses, made of the "beards" or stiff neck hairs of wild turkey cocks, together with dyed deer hair, formerly accompanied this bundle but are now missing, apparently stolen or sold. Perhaps these items were not considered elements of the bundle in the strict sense but had merely been placed with it for use by the warriors in the War Dance when the bundle was opened.

The custodian of the Kishpoko bundle during my fieldwork was a man named Little Charlie. The bundle is opened once each year, in August, on the occasion of the Ride-in and ceremonial War Dance of the Absentee Shawnees, held at the Little River dance ground. The bundle is opened at a place in the woods about one hundred yards south of the dance arbor and certain articles are removed from it to be worn or carried by the warrior dancers (Cf. Plate 22). The trefoil-shaped tomahawk is carried by the war chief (a position filled by George Whitewater, a man of Kansas

Kickapoo and Shawnee descent, in 1970; by Sam Creek, an Absentee Shawnee, in 1973 and 1975). The four "plumes" from the bundle are sported by four leading warriors; they are either attached directly to the hair on the crown of the head or tied to the spreader of the roach headdress. The wooden doll was formerly displayed during the Ride-in or ceremonial horseback parade around the dance arbor that precedes the dance, but I did not see it at the performances that I witnessed in 1970, 1973, and 1975. Anthropologist Carol Rachlin reports that she observed the doll, carried in a small basket by the venerable chief Little Jim, at a performance several years ago. Mary Spoon confirmed that the doll was formerly displayed during the parade, but said that it was carried in the hand of the War chief.

The sacred bundle of the Thawikila division was apparently a near-duplicate of the Kishpoko bundle. It definitely contained a wooden doll, for C.F. Voegelin (*The Shawnee Female Deity*: p. 18) writes: "Before the war with the Tonkawa, the bundle of the *Thawikila* division was opened and four ceremonial songs were sung. At the end of the fourth song, the small wooden figure of the little boy in the bundle became animate. He took up his bow and arrow, and then the Shawnee asked him to tell the Creator what they wanted. Then the child shot four arrows, showing that there were four big Tonkawa warriors. He shot one big warrior twice, annihilating him. Then he took up his blanket and became dormant again. The Shawnee concluded they would be victorious, went forth to war, and shot four of the big Tonkawa warriors." Mary Williams, the Voegelins' informant, suggested that the small wooden figure in the bundle is a representation of Our Grandmother's Grandson (ibid.: p. 11). The doll was provided with new garments from time to time. Mary Spoon recalled that when she was a very small girl an old lady came to visit her mother. This old woman announced that the moccasins on the bundle doll were badly worn, and inquired if it would be proper to replace them. Mary's mother replied in the affirmative, and Mary believed that the two of them then proceeded to make substitutes.

The present whereabouts of the Thawikila division's sacred bundle are unknown. Mary Spoon stated that following the abandonment of the old Sand Hill ceremonial ground, where this bundle functioned, its contents were combined with those of the Kishpoko bundle. It has been said, she added, that the contents of the two war bundles do not "get along together" and may have to be separated out again lest some calamity befall the Absentee Shawnees. The release of the contents of the Thawikila bundle to the Kishpoko bundle's custodian Mary attributed to her cousin _____ _____. This man, however, when I questioned him about the matter, vigorously denied that such a combination had been, or could be, effected. A third story regarding the fate of this bundle, and in my opinion probably the correct one, is that its contents were sold to a large eastern museum by the last custodian, who was an alcoholic, some years after the Sand Hill ceremonial ground became inactive. This fact was not discovered for some time. The discovery was made a few years ago when a dissident group of Pekowi and Kishpoko Shawnees, including the custodian of the Kishpoko bundle, "seceded" from the Absentee "Old ground" south of the Little Axe store and established their own dance ground a few miles to the north.

The departure of this group left the remaining "Old ground" membership without a sacred bundle. Because the Thawikila division had abandoned their ceremonies the Old ground organization sent a delegation to the home of the Thawikila bundle custodian, who had died by that time, to borrow the bundle for use at their ceremonial ground. His family was agreeable to this arrangement, but when the bundle was removed from the wall of the upstairs room where it had been stored, it proved to consist of only the outer wrappings. The doll, medicines, and other contents were missing. Chagrined, the delegation was forced to return empty-handed, and the ceremonies at the Absentee "Old ground" have had to continue without the sanction of a sacred bundle ever since.

Still another class of sacred objects to which the Shawnees claim partial ownership are the famous copper and brass plates of the Tuckabatchee Creeks. The brass plates are circular in form; the copper ones are shaped something like the head of a battle axe. Woodward (T.S. Woodward *Woodward's Reminiscences of the Creek, or Muscogee Indians*: pp. 14, 23) states that the plates were captured by the Creeks from De Soto and his men at a battle that took place at Thleawalla (Cuwally), a Creek town in Alabama: "The Indians say they were there and fought him [De Soto,]: and from the number of copper shields, with a small brass swivel (that an old man by the name of Tooley worked up into bells), would go to show and to prove that the Indians were correct. I have often seen the copper plates or shields, and a piece of the swivel, and from the cuttings or carvings on it, it was evidently of Spanish make." (ibid.: pp. 23-24) I have assembled most of the other published material concerning these plates elsewhere (J. Howard *The Southeastern Ceremonial Complex and Its Interpretation* pp. 65-74). It is probably to these plates that John Shawnego, a member of the White Turkey band of Shawnees, was referring in a 1937 interview (Indian Archives, Oklahoma Historical Society 44: pp. 281-82): "The Shawnee Indians have their own busk grounds. They observe and hold tribal ceremonial dances, yet they do not have the tribal medicine. It has been told that it was during a war with the Creeks or Muskogees in the old country that the Shawnees lost their medicine, and then the Tuckibutchee [Tuckabatchee] Town became the owner of the medicine." In 1975 I was told by Barney Leader, a Creek who is chief of Cedar River Tulsa square ground, that the famous Tuckabatchee plates had been stolen from the little house at the dance ground where they were stored. He said that the Creeks believed that the thieves were white men, as no Indian would touch sacred objects of this sort for fear of divine retribution.

Another sacred bundle of putative Shawnee origin is in the hands of the Forest band of Potawatomis in Wisconsin. This bundle, according to Potawatomi tradition, originated with the great Shawnee Tecumseh, who is remembered with admiration and respect by the Forest Potawatomis. Anthropologist Robert Salzer, who has been adopted into the Eagle clan of the Potawatomis, has responsibility for the "Tecumseh bundle." In a letter to me, Dr. Salzer provides information regarding this bundle:

> When Earl Buckman died (he had been adopted into the Potawatomi), his white wife insisted that I be adopted in his place. This met with approval from Potawatomi friends and, especially, the head of the Eagle clan at that time, Frank Thunder. When I was adopted, I took over responsibility for the "Tecumseh Bundle", which had been in Buckman's possession (he received it when he was adopted). On receiving it (with no ceremony), I asked what I should do with it—the procedures for renewing it, etc. However, no one could tell me anything about such matters. Some people said that all the power of the bundle had gone out because no one knew how to keep it powerful.
>
> I tried to find out more information on the history of the bundle and I found out that "old Mrs. Tecumseh" had some other things which were supposed to have belonged to Tecumseh. Through a translator, I was told that she (Mrs. Tecumseh) had a peace medal. I was permitted to look at it. It is one of the clasped hands type and is dated 1784. It felt like pewter and was hollow. Other people know more about such things, but it is my impression that this medal was made some time after 1784. Also there were supposed to be some papers. I was told that the papers had been taken to Washington D.C. many years ago to

support a Potawatomi land claim. They were in a paper bag. The Indian who was carrying them was kicked off the train and the papers were left on the train and lost.

I asked how the material had come to be in Wisconsin. I was told that Tecumseh had tried to bring the Potawatomi into his "confederacy" and had had some problems. In order to firm up his shakey Potawatomi support, he is said to have taken a Potawatomi wife. He had some children by her. After Tecumseh was killed, his Potawatomi wife feared for the safety of her children, since in addition to the White menace, there was also intrigue in Tecumseh's camp concerning who should take over. In any event, she took the children, the bundle, the medal, and "some papers", and went home to Wisconsin. The Tecumseh "line" has apparently been recognized since that time, although it is my understanding that the bundle became a tribal bundle.

The bundle is a large one and contains a number of mini-bundles and items which are of unknown significance to me. Its contents, however, conform with what I have heard called the "war bundle" type (a large steel spear head, a braided "prisoner" rope, paint pouches, cane whistles, several hawkskins, etc.) I think it was Dick Conn who said that there was British officer uniform cloth in one of the mini-bundles. Bob Voelker pointed out that most of the animal skins are prairie dwellers, including the Swainson's hawk skin. The cane whistles suggest a central Mississippi valley or more southern provenience. However such items were certainly traded around and need not be indicative of the provenience of the bundle.

Another bundle, apparently no longer in existence, was associated with the now-obsolete Eagle Dance of the Loyal Shawnee. A list of the contents of this bundle was secured by Erminie Voegelin for William Fenton (W.N. Fenton *The Iroquois Eagle Dance*: p. 203): "The bundle contained 12 feather coats for the dancers, which recall costumes still used in the Pueblo area, besides tobacco, 4 tail feathers, a raven wing—the doctor's emblem as in the Southeast—a drum hide and stick, and 1 gourd rattle." A description of the dance in which this bundle was employed is included in chapter fifteen.

In addition to these tribal or divisional palladia, certain sacred bundles were individual in nature. The weather-controlling and hunting bundles mentioned earlier in this chapter were such. The bundles used by Shawnee witches or "night flyers" mentioned in chapter eight were also strictly individual in nature. The principal ingredient in these was a bit of the flesh of the Giant Horned Snake. Their ownership was carefully concealed, yet every Shawnee seems to know that the snake flesh contained in them, though hundreds of years old, still appears fresh and oozing blood. A person possessing such a bundle is thought to be able to change himself or herself into the form of an animal or bird and thus travel great distances to work evil magic on a victim. The owl was a favorite vehicle for such shape-shifting, because it flies on silent wings. The witch pictured by Shawnee artist Earnest Spybuck is shown in such an owl costume. Because of this, Shawnee Peyotists who carry owl feathers into a Peyote meeting are immediately suspect as potential witches. A counter to such witches is a single eagle tail feather. As a symbol of the Thunderbirds and the Powers Above the eagle feather can divert the magic arrows thrown by witches and protect the carrier.

11

The Living Faith: Present-Day Shawnee Ceremonialism

In their ceremonialism the Shawnees dramatize not only their concepts of the cosmos, but also the sexual dualism that is so evident in their aboriginal social and economic patterns. The complementary roles of the male as hunter and the female as gardener are singled out again and again for special emphasis. The dualism of man-woman, and flesh-vegetable food, is apparent in each separate ceremony and also in the ceremonial cycle when viewed as a whole. Fortunately, in tracing these themes, we have an unusually complete body of information. Unlike most tribes now resident in Oklahoma, the Shawnees have managed to preserve to the present day their complete cycle of ceremonial dances and other religious observances. Comparing these modern rituals with the often sketchy accounts from the late eighteenth and early nineteenth century, it would appear that changes in the overall Shawnee ceremonial pattern have been slight. Hence, with the Shawnees, one sees forms preserved that probably characterized many related Algonkian-speaking groups that have since lost their ceremonialism because of White acculturation. This is certainly true in respect to the Delawares, Miamis, Weas, Piankeshaws, and the tribes of the Illinois Confederacy.

Presently one ceremonial ground, near Whiteoak, serves the Loyal or Cherokee band of Shawnees, while two more, which are both located between Tecumseh and Norman, serve the faithful among the Absentees. Only one organized Shawnee group, the Eastern band, located in and southeast of Miami, Oklahoma, has lost its ceremonial. The Eastern Shawnee ceremonial cycle, judging from scattered references, was quite similar to that of the Loyal band and in fact, since the abandonment of their dance ground, around 1880, conservative members of the Eastern band have joined in the ceremonies of the Loyal Shawnees.

Formerly most ceremonial activities took place in a large wooden structure known in English as the council house, which I have described in chapter five. Buildings of this type, judging from descriptions, were very similar in their interior arrangements to the longhouses of the Iroquis and the ceremonial "Big House" structures of the Delawares. Mentions of human faces, turtles, and snakes carved on the upright posts of the Council House are especially reminiscent of the Delaware houses of worship. One of the best descriptions of such a structure, which I have quoted in chapter five, is provided by Rev. Isaac McCoy (*History of Baptist Indian Missions*: p. 529). The ruins of this same Council House were later noted by Spencer (*The Shawnee Indians*: p. 389) who commented that such structures had gone out of use by 1840. Today's ceremonies are held at outdoor grounds of carefully scraped earth surrounded by log benches. At the two Absentee grounds these are provided with a brush arbor at the west end to shelter the singers and elders who sit there. Both Loyal and Absentee dance grounds still preserve, in their ground plans, the form of the log Council Houses of the past.

Ceremonials basic to all three grounds are the spring and fall Bread Dances, in which thanks is given to the Creator for the products of the hunt and for agricultural produce and prayers are offered for continuing bounty and good health. Indian corn bread, provided by the women, is ceremonially displayed in the center of the dance ground and distributed to the men at the conclusion of the ceremony, while roasted squirrels, supplied by the efforts of twelve male hunters, are similarly displayed and then distributed to the women. The Bread Dance, in addition to its function as a tribal prayer service, thus serves to dramatize the complementary roles of men and women in the Shawnee economic pattern and in this way reinforces group mores.

Likewise common to all three Shawnee ceremonial grounds is a series of men-against-women Indian football games. These are thought to bring rain and to promote the fertility of the crops. The last football game of the season is played near the end of June, and at its conclusion the deerhair-stuffed ball is ritually destroyed (Loyal Shawnees) or put away for the year (Absentee Shawnees).

Between the spring and fall Bread Dances the Loyal band celebrates, in addition, a Green Corn Dance. The Green Corn of the Loyal Shawnees seems to be essentially a junior version of the Bread Dance. Agricultural produce, rather than corn bread, is displayed in the center of the dance ground and is distributed at the conclusion of the dance. The Green Corn ceremony is clearly of some antiquity among the Shawnees, for O.M. Spencer describes a Green Corn which he attended in 1792 (*The Indian Captivity of O.M. Spencer*: p. 102–113). The Green Corn of the Loyal band is always followed by a Buffalo Dance, a ceremony attributed by some to the great war chief Tecumseh and by others to a mixed-blood Shawnee peace or civil chief named Daugherty. The Buffalo Dance is somewhat of a mystery. It is clearly intrusive into the Loyal Shawnee ceremonial cycle and is, in fact, performed outside the sacred precincts of the dance ground used for other rites. It involves buffalo mime by the male dancers, who are stripped to the waist and have bison heads painted on their chests and partake of a feast of mush, which is supposedly a favorite food of the buffalo.

The Green Corn and Buffalo Dances are not observed at either of the two Absentee Shawnee dance grounds. Instead, at about the same time (the third week in August) an impressive ceremonial Ride-in or horseback parade and ritual War Dance is held at the Little River dance ground. This event, in which members of the Kickapoo tribe join with the Shawnees, centers around the opening of the sacred bundle of the Kishpoko division and the display of split-feather head plumes and an ancient trefoil tomahawk by selected warriors. This is an antique Woodland Indian ceremonial and should not be confused with the ubiquitous "War Dance" of Prairie-Plains tribes. Its closest relatives are the Kickapoo ceremonial War Dance, which both Kickapoos and Shawnees say the Kickapoos received from the Shawnees, the now-obsolete Delaware Ilawkan or Man's Dance (Stewart "Oklahoma Delaware Women's Dance Clothes" p. 21), and the Sun or War Dance of the Oklahoma Seneca-Cayugas at Turkeyford, Oklahoma (J. Howard "Cultural Persistence and Cultural Change as Reflected in Oklahoma Seneca-Cayuga Ceremonialism").

An annual Death Feast is also held at each of the three

grounds during the summer as well as an unspecified number of all-night "stomp" dances of a largely secular nature. The fall Bread Dance, held on the first or second weekend in October, closes the Shawnee ceremonial year. It emphasizes primarily the male role of hunter, just as the spring Bread Dance emphasizes the female role of planter and cultivator of corn and other vegetables. At the fall Bread Dance, at the Loyal Shawnee dance ground, it is the men who begin the dancing, while in the spring it is the women. At both spring and fall performances, however, the sexes alternate in leading dances.

Today's Shawnees still take great pride in their ceremonial activities. Nevertheless present-day performances of the dances, though every effort is made to maintain them in their traditional form, show varying degrees of erosion due to White acculturation and the changing socioeconomic situation of the Shawnees. Ritual singers are in short supply at all three grounds, especially among the Loyal Shawnees at Whiteoak. Likewise, at Whiteoak the men and boys no longer wear native dress for the Bread Dance as ritually prescribed, though a few women and girls attempt to do so. Another innovation indicating the weakening of the old ways, and begun only twelve years ago, was the addition of a sermon in English, complete with reading from the Bible, following the traditional Bread Dance prayer in Shawnee. This was omitted at the 1971, 1972, 1973, and 1975 Bread Dances because of the violent objections of a few tribal elders, but it will probably creep back in with their passing. The Loyal Shawnee ground also shows a drift from traditional ways in that it is equipped with electric lights and that tape recordings and photographs have been permitted in the past few years, which is not true for the two Absentee dance grounds.

The ceremonials at the two Absentee dance grounds are much stronger. The costuming of the dancers is still very good, with both sexes assuming a good approximation of nineteenth-century Shawnee Indian dress, and there are still sufficient singers and dancers. Even at these two grounds, however, it is a fairly small group of conservative families who undertake the arduous preparations and assume the major responsibility for carrying out the daytime dances year after year. A factional dispute, which has divided what was until a few years ago a single strong organization into two bickering groups, has also weakened the performances. This would seem to be a recurrent phenomenon in Shawnee history, however, and not an effect of acculturation.

At all three grounds, though participation in the religious daytime dances may be weak, the crowd swells enormously after the evening meal when the largely secular nighttime or "Stomp" Dances begin. These Stomp Dances which are actually a whole series of separately named dances, follow all Shawnee ceremonies except funerals and death feasts. They consist of various women's dances and other social dances (mostly with animal references) in which the two sexes are mixed. These are interspersed with generous segments of the "Leading" or "Ordinary Stomp" Dance. They conclude, if the dancing has lasted through the night, with the "Drunken" Dance the following morning. The Leading or Stomp Dance is a great favorite of teenaged youth among the Shawnees and other Woodland tribes in Oklahoma, and is comparable in popularity and clientele to the Forty-Nine Dance among Prairie and High Plains groups. It is clear that this largely secularized and undemanding aspect of the gatherings has the most appeal for younger Shawnees, certainly in part as a symbol of "Indianess."

In the Absentee band another phenomenon has appeared that, in future years, may contribute to the decline of traditional ceremonialism. This began with the formation, in 1970, of a junior War Dance club sponsored by some of the leading families of Little Axe. This club, composed of about twenty boys between twelve and sixteen years of age, has taken up the Prairie-Plains style of "fancy" war dancing as seen at powwows throughout the country. Their initial performances, in 1970, exhibited a rather tacky cubscout type costuming and clumsy footwork. By midsummer of 1971, however, the boys had developed considerable style and the parents of several had provided their sons with good-quality roach headdresses and hackle bustle sets. Only their broad-yoked, Shawnee-style shirts distinguished them from the young fancy dancers of other tribes. That year two members of this club managed to place in the junior division fancy War Dance contest at the large pan-Indian powwow sponsored by the neighboring Sauk tribe. This enthusiasm for the Prairie-Plains style of war dancing has spread to one family of Loyal Shawnees as well, and in 1971 it caused this family to miss the Whiteoak Buffalo Dance when it was found to conflict with a pan-Indian powwow in which their son wished to participate. Two members of the Loyal band have also begun to participate in the Prairie-Plains Gourd Dance, which is another pan-Indian expression, and one has become a powwow singer in the Prairie-Plains tradition.

The Peyote religion, which has adherents in all three Shawnee bands, does not seem to militate against traditional Shawnee ceremonialism in any way. The leaders at all three dance grounds, in fact, are also Peyotists and attend Peyote meetings regularly during the late fall, winter, and early spring when the traditional Shawnee ceremonial cycle is dormant. Peyote religion regalia (such as beaded bolo ties, silver scarf slides and tie pins in Peyote motifs like the waterbird, sunburst, and tipi), and red and blue blankets double as ritual dress at the Bread Dance and the Absentee Shawnee War Dance. Such regalia seems to be regarded simply as "good Indian clothes."

Having thus briefly summarized, by way of introduction, present-day Shawnee ceremonialism, I will now consider its various component aspects in some detail. Because I will be covering ground that has not been previously explored in any depth by previous writers on the Shawnees, I will present a number of descriptive accounts of various ceremonies. I shall also introduce, wherever possible, historical references and comparative material from other tribes that sheds light on contemporary Shawnee practices.

SHAWNEE DANCE GROUNDS

As I have noted above, there are three functioning Shawnee ceremonial dance grounds at the present time. These are the Whiteoak ground, the Little Axe "Old ground," and the "Little River" or "New ground."

The Whiteoak ground, located approximately one mile south and five miles west of the village of Whiteoak, Oklahoma, serves the Loyal or Cherokee band of Shawnees and also those members of the Eastern band who still practice their native religion. In terms of the traditional divisions of the tribe, this ground's adherents are largely members of the Chalaakaatha and Mekoche groups. According to Ranny Carpenter, who was drumkeeper at this ground until his death in 1973, the ground has been located on its present site since 1905. Before that it was located "further up the creek."

The dancing ground itself is a rectangular, cleared area about sixty yards long and forty yards wide, the longer axis being east and west. It is marked off by log seats with "doorways" or openings at both the east and west ends. The singers customarily seat themselves in a central position on the north side. During all ceremonies except the Buffalo Dance the kettle is hung on a crane situated at the northwest corner of the dance ground, a few feet outside the log benches. The dance ground is in a central position in a pleasant glade below a low hill that lies to the north. An access road approaches from the northeast. The associated football field is located about fifty yards northwest of the dance ground. When ceremonial activities are in preparation or taking place, camps are set up in a row north and west of the dance ground, south of it, and directly east of it. These consist of tents, cook shelters with tables and iceboxes, and campfires with iron grills.

The Little Axe "Old ground", which is also called the "Delaware ground," is located one mile west and a half mile south of the Little Axe Store, on highway nine between Tecumseh and Norman, Oklahoma. This ground serves a part of the Absentee Shawnees, (mostly Pekowitha and Kishpoko in terms of the traditional divisions), but also persons of the White Turkey band (Thawikila division) whose ceremonial ground is no longer functioning.

The dance area itself is rectangular, about twenty yards wide and thirty yards long, with the long axis being the east-west one. The ground is equipped with log seats. These are "doorways" or openings at the center of the east end and on the north and south sides about one-third of the way from the west end. A covered arbor, located centrally at the west end, shades the singers. It is about ten yards long (north and south) and eight yards deep, with forked posts about ten feet high supporting stringers on which leafy branches are piled to provide shade. During ceremonies the cooking kettles are hung on a fire crane located about thirty yards east of the dance ground. The adjacent ball field is located northwest of the dance area and is oriented southeast to northwest.

The "Little River" or "New ground", sometimes called "Gibson's ground," is located about one mile west and three miles north of the Little Axe Store, on highway nine between Tecumseh and Norman, Oklahoma. This ground serves a part of the Absentee Shawnees who split away from the Little Axe "Old ground" a few years ago. Some members of the White Turkey band of Absentee Shawnees attend as well. A number of Oklahoma Kickapoos also regularly attend and participate in the Shawnee ceremonials at this ground and have their assigned camping area.

The dance area is rectangular in shape, about thirty-five yards long (east and west) and twenty-seven yards wide. Its various features are oriented in the same way as at the Little Axe "Old ground," that is, there is a covered bower at the west end where the singers sit, a doorway on the east end, and other openings on the north and south sides. Cooking kettles are slung on a crane located northeast of the ground, and the associated ball field is located to the north. A circular track, used by the riders in the horseback parade that precedes the War Dance each August, encircles the ground and is also outside those camps immediately adjacent to the ground on the north, east, and south. Other camps are situated outside this track.

In addition to these active ceremonial grounds, the following grounds, now wholly or partially abandoned, were remembered by my informants. The Sand Hill or Horseshoe Bend ground, located three miles north and three miles east of the Starlite outdoor theater in Shawnee, Oklahoma. This ground was still active from 1933 to 1935 when the Voegelins were doing their fieldwork among the Shawnees, but its ceremonial dances were apparently discontinued shortly thereafter. It is still the site of men-against-women Indian football games in the spring, so it cannot be said to be completely inactive. Adherents of this ground were mostly members of the White Turkey band of Absentee Shawnees, which is coterminous with the traditional Thawikila division of the tribe. Alfred Switch, who belonged to this ground when it was active, said that the ceremonial dances at the Sand Hill ground were abandoned because "the young men drank too much."

Several informants, both Loyal and Absentee Shawnees, remembered the Spybuck ground, located on Bird Creek near Sperry, Oklahoma. Eli Ellis, in a 1937 interview (Indian Archives, Oklahoma Historical Society 3: p. 370) stated that he was at that time "the last of the old men" in the Spybuck settlement, which centered around this dance ground. He was, he reported, the drumkeeper and held the tribal drum and "rattling gourd" used in their ceremonies. That same year Henry Spybuck (Indian Archives, Oklahoma Historical Society 2: p. 65) reported that the Spybuck dance ground had been moved because of an incident that occurred there. Two white men quarreled and killed each other about 100 feet from the dance ground. Because this defiled the ground, it was then moved 300 yards to the west of its earlier location. In 1913 a new ground was announced "on the George Spybuck place, near Spybuck bridge". The Spybuck ground was apparently abandoned in 1938 or 1939, and the Spybuck family moved to Little Axe. There are still a few Shawnee families living in the vicinity of Sperry and Skiatook at the present time, however, and my informant Bill Tyner once referred to them as the "Bird Creek bunch." A Delaware informant, Nora Thompson Dean, vividly recalls attending a "Ride-in" and ceremonial War Dance held at the Spybuck ground when she was a small girl, (apparently around 1912). An automobile "graveyard" now occupies the site.

Mr. and Mrs. John Ellis, Absentee Shawnees, both mentioned the Charles Starr dance ground. It was located on the land of a man by that name "two miles east and a half a mile north of the Chat and Nibble restaurant [a roadside eatery] in Shawnee." This would place it on the south side of town, in the vicinity of the old Shawnee mission and present clinic. This ground was active in the 1920s but its activities were discontinued even before Mr. Starr's death when a woman died at the ground. In this case the ground was not merely moved to a new location, like the Spybuck ground, but completely abandoned.

The precise location of the former Eastern Shawnee ceremonial ground was not learned. In a 1937 interview (Indian Archives, Oklahoma State Historical Society 6: p. 483) Edward J. McClain, an Eastern Shawnee, recalled that he had attended a "religious worship" at this ground when he was about four years old. McClain was born in 1873, so this would be around 1877. McClain recalled little except that he and his mother sat on "log seats" and there was "preaching" [probably the Bread Dance prayer]. The ground was probably abandoned shortly after this, as there is no other mention of it in the literature and it was not recalled by any of my informants. The late Little Joe Blalock, an Eastern Shawnee, told me in 1969 that the Eastern Shawnees had maintained their own Stomp Dances (the secular Leading Dance and other social dances) until 1930, when they joined with the Quapaws, Ottawas, and other remnant groups in intertribal celebrations at the Devil's Promenade dance ground near Miami, Oklahoma.

I have noted in chapter five how the Shawnee ceremonial grounds were, and to a great extent still are, the nuclei of Shawnee settlements. Today, although the institution of chieftainship has waned in importance, the officials of the various ceremonial grounds still have great prestige. Each active ground has two principal functionaries, a drumkeeper (who is male) and a chief matron or "Queen Bee" (who is female). These two assume the chief responsibility for seeing that the ground and surrounding area is properly maintained. They also, after conferring with the ground council, set the dates for the various ceremonial activities. The following commentary by Ranny Carpenter, who was drumkeeper of the Loyal Shawnees until the time of his death, indicates the Shawnee concept of this official's role:

> I am the drumkeeper of the Shawnees here [at Whiteoak, JH]. This is a great honor among my people and I try to live up to it. The old people try to get someone to fill this job who thinks of the people. It is hard to find suitable people for all the ceremonial seats, and some of them are vacant. When I was asked to be drumkeeper I felt good, and said that I would do my best.
>
> The Eastern Shawnees, for as long as I can remember, have joined in with us [the Loyal Shawnees] in our ceremonies. I have heard that they lost their ceremonies because they ran out of good people to fill the offices. They had to turn to men who owned bad bundles [i.e., witches] and this spoiled their ritual, so they gave it up.
>
> We are training a young man, you know him, _____ _____, to be a leader. He is windy, but he asked to be allowed to take part and he is doing quite well.
>
> We no longer hunt before the Bread dance. There is no game around here and the White farmers south of here object to our Indian boys hunting over their land; so we discontinued hunting several years ago. We appoint the twelve "hunters" at the time of the dance, one from each name group. Sometimes we have to give someone an Indian name so that they can function. We did this for Eddie Dixon and Charlie Dean [both white men married to Indian women] and now they can function as "hunters" in the Bread dance. The "hunters" are called up, one at a time, before the drumkeeper and other officials. They are asked if they will serve and their responsibilities are explained to them.

Though he does not mention it in this account, Ranny's wife Emmaline has served as chief matron or "Queen Bee" at the Whiteoak ground for many years, and her activities are as numerous and demanding as those of her husband.

The accompanying schedule (Figure 7) gives the dates of Shawnee ceremonials that I observed or that were reported to me in 1969, 1970, 1971, 1972, and 1973. Though incomplete, it serves to indicate the customary sequence of ceremonial activities at the various ceremonial grounds.

FIGURE 7

Figure 7

Shawnee Ceremonial Calendar

Year	Event	Loyal Shawnee	Absentee "Old" Ground	Absentee "New" Ground
1969	Spring Bread Dance	10 May	Unknown	Unknown
1970	" " "	2 May	9 May	9 May
1971	" " "	8 May	15 May	8 May
1972	" " "	6 May	6 May	6 May
1973	" " "	5 May	12 May	19 May
1969	Last Football Game	21 June	Unknown	Unknown
1973	" " "	23 June	None Held (Death at Ground)	7 July
1969	Green Corn Dance	2 August	——	——
1971	" " "	17 July	——	——
1973	" " "	25 August	——	——
1970	Ride-In and War Dance	——	——	22 August
1971	" " "	——	——	Not Held (Death at Ground)
1972	" " "	——	——	19 August
1973	" " "	——	——	18 August
1969	Death Feast	9 August	Not Known	Unknown
1971	" "	31 July	Not Known	Unknown
1969	Buffalo Dance	6 September	——	——
1971	" "	28 August	——	——
1969	Fall Bread Dance	4 October	Not Known	Unknown
1970	" " "	10 October	24 October	24 October
1971	" " "	9 October	9 October	9 October
1972	" " "	7 October	7 October	7 October

NOTE: These ceremonials during the period 1969 through 1973 were observed by me or reported to me. This table indicates the customary sequence of activities at the various Shawnee ceremonial grounds. Major ceremonial activities are scheduled for Saturdays so that working people may attend.

Figure 7. Dates of Shawnee ceremonials observed by the author or reported to him in the period 1969-1973. Though incomplete, the chart serves to indicate the customary sequence of activities at the various ceremonial grounds. Major ceremonial activities are scheduled to fall on Saturdays so that working people may attend.

MUSICAL INSTRUMENTS

To accompany their ceremonial dances, the Shawnees emphasize singing rather than instrumental music. E.W. Voegelin quotes an elderly Absentee Shawnee woman who said: "The Shawnee would rather sing. The artificial means for making music are all right, but it's better to use the natural one; it's better to sing." ("Shawnee Musical Instruments": p. 463) Thus, when referring to the singer-drummer who functions at ceremonial dances the Shawnees invariably allude to him as "the singer," not "the drummer." Likewise the men who sit one either side of him with coconut shell or cowhorn rattles are always referred to as "second men" or "helpers," never as "rattle men."

Despite their high evaluation of the human voice, the Shawnees nevertheless employ various musical instruments of native manufacture. Still others are mentioned in the literature or were mentioned by informants. Most of these are designed to provide rhythmic accompaniment to music or dance, the courting flute or flageolet being the only solo instrument. The best discussion of the manufacture and use of these instruments is found in E.W. Voegelin's "Shawnee Musical Instruments". She lists the following: Tapping sticks, used only in the now-obsolete False-face and Husk-face dances of the Loyal Shawnees; deer hoof, buffalo hoof, and sleigh bell leg rattles or garters, worn by male dancers; deer hoof tinklers on men's shirt and legging fringes; deer dewclaw tinklers on men's moccasins; sleigh bell belts, worn by male dancers; metal jingles or cylinders and pellet (hawk) bells used on men's leggings and women's shawls, and also at the bottom of the characteristic women's head ornament; gourd, coconut, pumpkin[?], and cowhorn rattles used by male singers for ceremonial and social dances; tortoise shell hand rattles used to accompany the magical songs of shamans, which are used also by False-face impersonators among the Loyal Shawnees; turtle (terrapin) shell and tin-can leg rattles or shackles used by women in the Lead Dance; small gourd rattles in the Peyote ceremony; cypress knee, wooden keg, metal kettle, and tin lard pail water drums; "tambourine" types of dry drums used in intertribal friendship dances; eagle-bone whistles; and flageolets or courting flutes, presumably of wood or river cane. She also lists buzzers and two types of bullroarers, used only as toys, and deer calls; turkey-call whistles, and cowhorn hunting horns used only by hunters (ibid.: pp. 463–75).

Of these, today's Shawnees employ only the following: sleigh bell leg rattles, used by male dancers in the Absentee War Dance; Pellet or hawk bells, attached to the bottom of some women's headpieces; Coconut shell hand rattles, used by the second men or assistant singers in the Absentee Bread Dance and by the leader in some social dances, such as the Bean Dance; Cowhorn hand rattles, used by second men in Loyal Shawnee dances; terrapin shell and tin-can leg rattles or shackles, used by women and girl "shell shakers" in the Lead Dance at all Shawnee dance grounds; wooden keg (at the two Absentee grounds) and metal kettle (sometimes at Whiteoak) water drums, to accompany ceremonial and social dance songs; small gourd rattles and metal kettle drums, used in the Peyote Ceremony; eagle bone whistles, used in the Absentee War Dance and the Peyote Ceremony; and cowhorn hunting horn, used by Eastern and Loyal Shawnee hunters. In addition to the instruments listed by Voegelin we could now add the earthenware crock water drum, which is commonly employed at Loyal Shawnee dances, and the single sleigh bell shaken in the hand by the second men at the Absentee War Dance. To the list of obsolete instruments we can add musical rasps. Morgan (L.H. Morgan *The Indian Journals, 1859-62*: p. 77) writes: "They notch a stick and for music scrape a stick along over the notches. This they put over a wood bowl to increase the noise." Musical rasps of bone, and turkey skull rattles have been found at Fort Ancient culture sites, which were presumably inhabited by ancestral Shawnees. We can also add the tapping sticks used in hunting magic (J. Tanner *A Narrative of the Captivity and Adventures of John Tanner*: pp. 359-60) and I likewise learned of the former use of conch shell trumpets as hunting horns and signal devices.

The drums used by the Shawnees for their ceremonial dances and most of their social dances are of the type known as "wet" or water drums. This type of drum takes its name from the fact that the head of the drum, which is a piece of tanned hide, is kept continually wet while the drum is in use, and the drum kettle itself is partly filled with water. The characteristic drumstick employed with this type of drum by the Shawnees and neighboring tribes is a straight shaft of black walnut or other heavy wood with an enlarged ball carved at either end. The ball at the end of the drumstick held by the singer prevents the sometimes wet and slippery drumstick from slipping out of his hand.

Bill Shawnee, who generally ties the drum for the Loyal

Shawnee dances, prefers a small earthenware crock, the type
formerly used as a pickle crock, as his drum kettle. This he fills
about one-third full with water and also places a piece of charcoal
inside to "hold the water." E.W. Voegelin indicates ("Shawnee
Musical Instruments" p. 471) a religious symbolism for the
charcoal, which is also placed in Absentee Shawnee drums.
Charcoal, because it is derived from and symbolic of the sacred
fire, "lights up everything" and the Creator and lesser deities can
see it. The juxtaposition of charcoal and water is also important.
Both Fire and Water, as I have noted in chapter nine, are
important Truth Bearers or Witnesses; hence drums with these
substances in them will better serve to carry prayers to the
Creator.

Once the water and charcoal have been placed in the drum
kettle, a carefully soaked and wrung-out buckskin is placed over
the top of the crock, the buckskin being large enough to overlap
the mouth of the crock for about eight centimeters all around.
Next Bill inserts, one at a time, seven round stones or glass
marbles under the edge of the buckskin next to the outer wall of
the crock. Using a length of clothesline rope or similar material,
he loops it around each of these stones and the buckskin drum
hide above them, and he ties the rope when he has completely
circled the top of the drum. He still has, however, several feet of
loose rope in his right hand. The stones serve to hold the buckskin
in place without tearing it. Next he brings the free end of the rope
down and under the bottom of the crock and up the opposite side,
and passes it under the rope at the top of the drum between two of
the stone bosses. The rope is then brought down obliquely under
the drum again, and up to catch the rope at the top of the drum on
the other side, but a bit farther on. He continues in this manner
until the head has been tightened all around. Each time the rope
passes under the drum it may be pulled down by placing the tyer's
foot on it and pressing down parallel to the wall of the crock. This
serves to tighten the drumhead. When the drumhead has been
tightened all around in this manner the loose end of the rope is tied
off and the drum is ready for use. Its tone may be enriched by
wetting the head from time to time, either by sloshing some of the
water inside the kettle on the head or pouring a cup of water on the
top of the drum and rubbing it about. Should the drum lose air and
"go dead," the singer may apply his lips to the drumhead at the
edge and blow air into it. When finished, if it has been properly

tied, the rope of a water drum forms a neat design of inverted "V's" all around the side of the drum.

The method of tying a water drum described above is essentially the same as that employed in tying the drum used in the Peyote Ceremony, except that the Peyote drum is tied over a small (no. 6 or no. 7) iron or brass kettle from which the bailing ears have been removed. Such kettles have three small legs on the bottom. On one occasion (1971) a drum tied on such a kettle was used at the Shawnee Bread Dance at Whiteoak. The only difficulty in using an earthenware crock as a drum kettle is that there is a tendency for the rope to slip to one side as it passes under the bottom of the crock. Because of this, Bill Shawnee sometimes files grooves at the foot of the crock. The Absentee Shawnees generally tie their drums over a cut-down nail keg, but the method employed in tying it is essentially the same as that given above. The finished drum in this case is a bit larger in size and hence is deeper in tone.

The Loyal Shawnees, but not the Absentees, paint the head of their drum symbolically before using it. At the Bread Dance this painting is done at the same time that the men and women dancers are painting their faces. The design is always done in red paint. According to Bill Shawnee this painting must be done in one continuous line without raising the finger. It is done this way: the singer, seated facing south with the drum upright between his knees (1) starts at the top (south) and traces a complete counterclockwise circle around the edge of the top of the drum. (2) His finger then continues in another quarter circle until it is at the east. He then draws a line across the drumhead from east to west. (3) His finger then continues in another quarter circle from west to south and (4) crosses the drumhead from south to north. The finished design symbolizes the sun and the four directions. This design is widespread in North America and is generally assigned the same symbolism as that given by Bill Shawnee. It is the most prominent design of the Southeastern Ceremonial Complex of the Mississippian archeological culture (Cf. J. Howard *The Southeastern Ceremonial Complex and Its Interpretation*: pp. 19-26, Fig. 1).

At both of the Absentee grounds, and sometimes at Whiteoak, the second men or assistant singers employ rattles made from the shell of a coconut. This type of rattle, which the Shawnees share with the Creeks, Seminoles, Yuchis, Alabamas, Koasatis, Quapaws, and perhaps other groups of Southeastern Indians, is the modern descendant of the aboriginal gourd rattle, that was still in general use among the Shawnees in the 1930s according to E. W. Voegelin ("Shawnee Musical Instruments": pp. 465–66). To prepare the coconut a small hole (about one centimeter in diameter) is drilled from the eye and the milk drained off. A somewhat larger (three centimeter) hole is then cut from the opposite end and the meat is carefully and thoroughly scraped from the inside with a crooked knife. After this the outside is then scraped, sanded, rubbed, and polished. Sometimes simple geometric designs filled with white paint, are added. The handle is a hardwood stick about thirty centimeters long. It is about five centimeters in diameter at its base, 3.5 centimeters at the grip, and then it widens to about 4.5 centimeters at the point of articulation with the bottom of the coconut shell. From this point it is whittled quite thin, just large enough to pass through the hole at the eye end. Carefully selected round pebbles, about twenty in number, are placed inside the shell before the handle is put on.

Alfred Switch, a singer of the White Turkey band, manufactures a variant type of coconut-shell rattle. Instead of the projecting wooden tip at the top of the rattle, Switch employs a round-ended metal screw and washer. The screw penetrates the handle inside the rattle and can be tightened from time to time when it becomes loose. In Switch's rattles the shell itself is filled about one quarter full with buckshot, producing a softer sound than the usual coconut rattle.

When I first attended Loyal Shawnee ceremonies in 1969 their second men were using coconut-shell rattles like those of the Absentees. Ranny Carpenter, however, admired a New York Seneca cowhorn rattle that I had in my possession and I gave it to him. Later, visiting at his home, I noticed a broken cowhorn rattle of the same type that Ranny said had been given to him by Stewart Jameson, an Oklahoma Seneca-Cayuga. I repaired it for Ranny and ever since these two cowhorn rattles have been served at all Loyal Shawnee dances. The use of the Iroquois type of cowhorn rattle by the Loyal band, however, should not be credited to me, for E.W. Voegelin writes: "A cowhorn trimmed at the base and sawed off 4 inches from the tip is now [1933–35] being employed by the White Oak sub-group of the Cherokee Shawnee in place of gourd rattles at religious dances. A piece of wood is fitted into the top hole of the horn, small pebbles are inserted as rattling substances, and another piece of wood is fitted into the bottom and as a handle. The Absentee Shawnee make no use of horns for rattles and say that it is 'against the rules' to do so" ("Shawnee Musical Instruments": p. 468). I strongly suspect that the preference for horn rattles among the Loyal Shawnees is the result of Iroquois influence, particularly the long association of this group with the Mingo Iroquois and their descendants, the Oklahoma Seneca-Cayugas. The cowhorn rattles are made of a section of cowhorn five or six centimeters in length cut from the large end of a cow's horn. These sections are fitted with wooden plugs, top and bottom, through which a waisted handle, about twenty-four centimeters in length, is fitted. Usually BB shot provides the noise.

E.W. Voegelin, in "Shawnee Musical Instruments" states that the Absentee Shawnee women derived their shackles, the leg rattles that they use in providing rhythmic accompaniment in the Leading or Stomp Dance, from their Creek neighbors around 1835. She also notes that the older Shawnees objected to the use of terrapin-shell shackles, which was the only type used by the Creeks at that time, on religious grounds. This, she says, led to the development, among the Shawnees, of leg rattles made of condensed milk cans. (Voegelin "Shawnee Musical Instruments": pp. 468-9). I am personally inclined to take this story with a grain of salt because I have heard other tales, from other tribes, of how "cans" were invented. At the present time both types are worn by Absentee and Loyal Shawnee "shell shaker girls." The condensed milk can type is the more popular of the two, but mainly because this style is both lighter to wear and also louder than the traditional terrapin-shell version.

My informant Alfred Switch manufactures the "can" type of leg rattles as a supplement to his regular income. In 1971 I purchased from him, for use by my daughter, a set of his shackles for which I paid twenty dollars. He told me that he had already sold twenty-eight sets of shackles that year. The women's leg rattles crafted by Switch consist of seven separate stacks of condensed milk cans, four cans to a stack, for each of the wearer's legs, which is a total of fifty-six cans for each pair. The cans are first carefully cleaned and the labels removed. Then each can is perforated with nine vertical rows of nail holes, seven perforations to a row. Through a perforation in the top of each can, which is later soldered shut, a number of small pebbles are added to each can. The cans are then wired together, first in stacks of four cans each. The seven stacks used on each shackle are then wired to heavy pieces of leather. These are equipped with eyelets and laces so that they may be tightly fastened to the outside of the girl's or woman's legs. Usually the "shell shaker girl" (all are termed girls, though many are mature women) pads her legs by wrapping a terry cloth towel around each limb before donning her cans. The shackles are sounded by skillful toe and heel work by the wearer in time with the cadence of the male leader's songs. An experienced shaker can do much to enhance the lead of the male dancer that she follows, producing a noise resembling a drum roll when required, or a neat triplet to mark the end of his song in addition to the usual duple beat (Ch-ch, ch-ch, ch-ch). By the same token an inexperienced or tin-eared shaker can ruin the best singer's lead. For this reason the better leaders prefer to have a woman they know "shake shells" for them.

E.W. Voegelin notes that the messenger men of the Absentee chiefs formerly wore deer hoof kneebands during the Bread Dance. These were worn only with buckskin leggings, never with cloth trousers, and were buried with the man who owned them. Such knee rattles were also once worn by the first and second of the twelve hunters in the Loyal Shawnee Bread Dance. Moccasins to which deer dewclaws were attached were also worn by Absentee Shawnee messenger men (Voegelin "Shawnee Musical Instruments": p. 464). Both knee rattles and "clawed moccasins" have long been obsolete among the Shawnees. One regrets the disappearance of these interesting and unique noisemakers, items of apparel that the Shawnees shared with the Delawares and Oklahoma Seneca-Cayugas. Drake notes that dried deer hooves, which were probably these same knee rattles, were used by Shawnee warriors as a signaling device at the Battle of Tippecanoe: "The Indians advanced and retreated by the aid of a rattling noise, made with deer hoofs, and persevered in their treacherous attack with an apparent determination to conquer or die upon the spot" (B. Drake *Life of Tecumseh and of His Brother the Prophet*: p. 151). These deer hoof signals were probably an Indian adaptation of the snare drum signals then used by white armies. Sleigh bells, the functional equivalent of the earlier deer hoof leg rattles, are still worn by war dancers among the Absentee Shawnees.

An eagle-bone whistle is commonly used by Shawnee Peyote leaders or "Road men" during the midnight water ceremony and morning water call (see W. La Barre *The Peyote Cult*: pp. 50–51: J.S. Slotkin *The Peyote Religion*: p. 25). Such a whistle suspended on a buckskin neck cord was sounded from time to time by one of the dancers in the Absentee War Dance in 1973. Aside from learning that they were formerly used, I secured little information on the manufacture or use of the courting flute or flageolet by the Shawnees. E. W. Voegelin says that such flutes had eight stops ("Shawnee Musical Instruments": p. 475) but an old specimen that I collected has only six.

In 1960 an Eastern Shawnee named Captain, the proprietor of a rural grocery store southeast of Miami, Oklahoma, showed me his collection of hunting horns. They were all well made, highly polished, and he spoke with great relish of their use in calling his dogs during nocturnal coon hunts. All were made of steer horns, about thirty-five centimeters in length. The small end of each was cut off and fitted with a horn or wooden mouthpiece. Such horns are apparently the only musical instrument among the Shawnees that was borrowed directly from the Whites (ibid.: p. 475).

Three different informants mentioned the use of conch shell trumpets, each in a different context. Mary Spoon mentioned that in her youth such trumpets were used as hunting horns, much like the steer-horn bugles that I have just described. Clifton Blanchard, a Shawnee of Little Axe, said that he had heard that such trumpets were used by Shawnee sentries to signal the approach of enemy war parties: "These horns sounded like a buffalo bellowing. It was a signal of danger for the people in the village." Richard Gibson, drumkeeper at the Little River ceremonial ground, remembered that the Absentee Shawnees used to have such a trumpet that was used to call people to worship at the dance ground and to welcome visitors. There was a song that referred to the trumpet, and the trumpet was blown at one point in the song. The song was repeated four times. No details were secured concerning the manufacture of these trumpets. Presumably they were made by grinding away the spire of a large conch shell, such as the Queen conch (*Strombus gigas* L.) to produce a smooth mouthpiece.

FIRST FOOTBALL GAME AND ARBOR DANCE

After the dormant winter season the Shawnee ceremonial year gets under way, with a men-against-women Indian Football Game and "Arbor Dance." This event, which takes place in the latter part of April, is a necessary preliminary to the spring Bread Dance, the first major ceremony of the year. It assembles the faithful to clean up and repair the ceremonial ground and surrounding camp areas and brush arbors (hence the name). Mowing and cleaning up the campground may take several days. On the final day the workers loosen up by playing the first ceremonial football game of the new season. After the evening meal they may dance social dances until midnight.

On the occasion of the first football game and Arbor Dance an important ritual takes place as well, the preparation of the sacred prayer hoop. Unfortunately I have not been privileged to witness this ceremony. Informant Esther Dixon describes the procedure:

> Before the spring Bread dance, just as soon as the twelve women cooks and the twelve hunters have been selected, a prayer hoop is made. A piece of wood [white oak] is cut and bent into a circle. This hoop is then taken into a tent. All of the twelve women cooks come in and seat themselves in a semicircle behind the hoop, which is in the center of the tent floor. The football is placed inside the hoop. Each of the twelve cooks, in turn, ties a small buckskin packet containing a certain kind of seeds to one-half of the circumference of the hoop. These are: (1) red corn; (2) white corn; (3) ordinary squash; (4) native squash; (5) watermelon; (6) cucumber; (7) red beans; (8) brown beans; (9) pumpkin; and three more that I can't remember right now. The women then leave the tent and the twelve men [hunters] enter. They tie, to the opposite side of the hoop, four items: (1) a bit of skunk fur; (2) a bit of raccoon fur; (3) a bit of deer hair; and (4) a turkey feather.
>
> Both the cooks and the hunters are now called to the square ground where they whoop. The decorated hoop is placed around the neck of the head man. Later it is hung on a tree as a sacrifice.

Further details concerning the hoop were supplied by Ranny Carpenter, the drumkeeper at Whiteoak:

> The hoop used in connection with the first football game represents the world. It is a prayer to the Creator for abundant crops and game animals. Some of the seeds tied to it by the women are later removed and planted and add to the fertility of all the crops.
>
> The hoop is made from a small, straight, white oak tree, one about nine feet tall, It is shaved down to a thickness about like a man's finger. The small end overlaps and the large end, and this symbolizes growing. The women tie packets of seeds on one side. The seeds are: (1) red corn; (2) white corn or flour corn; (3) squash; (4) small native squash (these have a superb flavor); (5) brown beans; (6) red beans; (7) watermelon; (8) cucumber; (9) pumpkin. The men, in their turn, tie on only four items: (1) skunk fur; (2) coon fur; (3) deer hair; and (4) a turkey feather. The hoop is worn around the neck of the head man.

On another occasion Ranny remarked that the oak wood used in the hoop must be from a tree growing near the ceremonial ground. He related that on one occasion he and Bill Shawnee, who customarily prepared the hoop each year, could not find a suitable white oak tree near the Loyal Shawnee dance ground and therefore secured one on the Seneca-Cayuga territory near Turkeyford, Oklahoma. When this hoop was presented to Frank Bob, the Loyal Shawnee bundle keeper, for inspection, he immediately knew, though he is blind, that the hoop was somehow different.

Both of these accounts relate to the Loyal band. Mary Spoon, when asked about the procedures followed at the Absentee grounds, said that they, too, prepare a hoop of oak wood, but noted that instead of tying packets of seeds to it the hoop is wrapped with kernels of corn which have been pierced and threaded on a string. The hoop is placed alternately over the heads of each of the twelve head women who will cook for the Bread Dance. As each woman is chosen the hoop is placed over her head. She then places it, in turn, over the head of another woman until all twelve have been chosen. The hoop is then employed in the same way to choose the twelve men and boys who will hunt for the Bread Dance. John Ellis, also speaking of the Absentee Shawnee custom, said that different types of wood are used for the hoops prepared for the spring and fall Bread Dances: dogwood for the Spring and white oak for the Fall.

The Loyal Shawnee hoop, once it has been employed in the ceremony, is hung on an elm tree located west of the ceremonial ground. It is left there until it deteriorates (Plate 36). The Absentee hoops are hung from one of the stringers in the singers' arbor at the west end of the ceremonial ground. In 1973 I observed several old hoops hanging from the roof at the south end of the arbor at the Absentee "New ground".

The use of wooden hoops as tribal or world symbols is widespread in North America, particularly among Prairie and High Plains tribes but also in the Southeast. Small wooden hoops are seen in the Creek war chief's headdress figured by Romans (B. Romans *A Concise History of East and West Florida*: p. 64). A Natchez tale collected among the Creeks in Oklahoma mentions a magical hoop tied to a tree limb through which one could see the future. Strings of grapevine hoops were formerly tied on poles surrounding Choctaw graves (J. R. Swanton *The Indians of the Southeastern United States*: pp. 726–7). Among Prairie and High Plains tribes hoops served as both religious symbols, as in the Dakota and Hidatsa Sun dance, and as war medicines (R. H. Lowie *The Religion of the Crow Indians*: pp. 365, 420; W. Wildschut *Crow Indian Medicine Bundles*: pp. 47, 48, figs.

12,13,14). The Shawnee custom of tying seeds to one side of their
prayer hoops and the fur or feathers of game animals and birds to
the other offers one more example of the sexual dualism that is so
important in Shawnee ceremonialism.

The losing side in the men-against-women football game that
takes place on this occasion must provide the wood for the fires at
the Bread Dance (T. W. Alford *Civilization*: p. 58). Shortly after
the first football game and Arbor Dance, the twelve hunters ready
themselves for the hunt. Traditionally each carries only a small
pouch of parched cornmeal as sustenance during the hunt.

Alford (*Civilization*: pp. 56–58) describes the preparations for
the spring Bread Dance:

> One of the most sacred rites of our people was called *Tak-u-wha- Nag-a-way*
> (Bread dance), and I am glad to say that the custom still is followed though not
> with the sincerity and faith that characterized the dances I remember in my
> youth. Our people believed that before they planted a crop or started the
> important work of the new year they should hold a Bread Dance when the Great
> Spirit would be implored to bless the people and give them a bounteous crop and
> a prosperous, peaceful year. Contrary to the white man's idea of religion—
> which seems to require a gloomy countenance when praying for a blessing—the
> Shawnees believed that in order to obtain a blessing they should show a merry
> spirit and a contented countenance. Therefore when we sought a blessing it
> required an occasion when all were gay and cheerful, and we looked forward to
> the spring Bread dance, as our most festive occasion. The Bread dance really
> opened the festivities of spring and summer, when all nature seemed to be
> rejoicing and happy. Not until after this important ceremony would anyone
> venture to plant a crop of corn or undertake any important work.
>
> The time for celebrating the Bread dance was determined as follows: Early in
> the spring when the buds began to swell on the trees, the birds began to sing
> and chatter to their mates, the wild ducks and geese departed for their northern
> homes, the air became soft and warm, the sun rose earlier, the days grew longer.
> Reciting all these evidences of the passing of winter, the chief gave orders to his
> people to make preparations for their festival of the Bread dance. *But even then
> the dance could not be held until after the full of the moon.*
>
> As the Bread dance is considered a religious rite the preparations for the
> dance and festival were under the supervision of the chief of the *Pec-ku-we* clan
> [The *Pekowitha* division] who by virtue of his clan had charge of all matters
> relating to our religion, or to the Great Spirit. There are two standing
> committees, one composed of twelve men, the other of twelve women, who
> actually have charge of the arrangements. These committees are appointed by
> the chief of the *Pec-ku-we* clan for life, or during good behavior. Each group has
> a leader who is appointed by the chief. Two of my sisters, Nancy and Nellie, are
> members of this committee today. Nancy, the elder, is the leader of the woman's
> committee..
>
> Here again we see a great difference between the customs of the white people
> and of our race, because generally only the young white people dance, while the
> presence of the very old members of our tribe is desired at our dances to lend
> dignity and honor to the occasion, and they always take part in the dance.
>
> The committees are designated *nay-na-how-aych-ki* (preparation utterers), or
> *may-yaw-thech-ki* (those in line by birth). When the proper time for the

celebration arrives—it is watched for and recognized by all the people—the chief assembles both of the committees and makes his appointments to fill vacancies if any exist. He then informs them that the time has arrived for them to perform their duties to their people and to the Great Spirit. Very solemnly he repeats to them the tradition connected with the festival, the dance and its proper observance. He sets a date for the twelve men to begin their hunt for the game required for the feasts. Only certain kinds of game should be used for this feast, namely deer, wild turkey, quail or grouse, and squirrel.

After all the instructions are given to the committees the chief opens a ball game that is peculiar to this event, in which the men play against the women, and all the people who have assembled may take part if they so desire. The losing side must provide the wood for the fires at the Bread Dance. As the grounds are brilliantly lighted by bonfires at the time of the dance, which sometimes lasts two nights, the preparation of the wood is no small matter. The game is animated and lively, but whichever side loses undertakes the gathering of the wood cheerfully.

The twelve men begin at once to get ready for the hunt. They set out for three days, not forgetting to take along some of the parched meal which is always carried as an emergency ration. Those who are to get the wood make sure there is enough for cooking the game and to supply the big bonfires which illuminate the grounds for as many nights as the frolic is to continue. All the people gather at the dance ground and camp.

SPRING BREAD DANCE

At present the spring Bread Dance is held on a weekend early in May. Like its autumnal counterpart it gives thanks to Our Grandmother and to lesser deities and asks for future blessings. In the spring ceremonial the Creator is thanked for having brought the people through another winter. She and her grandson, Cyclone Person, the Four Winds, the Thunderbirds, Corn Woman, and Pumpkin Woman are asked for continued favors in the coming agricultural season.

The Shawnee name of the ceremony, Dakwanekawe, translates literally as "Bread Dance." The Bread Dance is actually a whole series of ritual acts and dances of varying degrees of importance. It is definitely the high point of the ceremonial year; a time when old friends get together to feast and visit and when the Shawnees entertain visitors from other tribes. These visitors, Shawnees from other grounds, Delawares, Oklahoma Seneca-Cayugas, Cherokees, Creeks, Kickapoos, Seminoles, Yuchis, Sauks, and others are urged to assist in the "nighttime" or social dances that take place after the evening meal. Attendance at the Bread Dance is also viewed as an affirmation of faith in the traditional Shawnee religion. No traditional Shawnee, if he or she can possibly manage, fails to attend the Bread Dance at his or her ceremonial ground, and Shawnees who reside in distant locales, such as California, try to return to take part.

To give some idea of the slight variations in the procedures followed in the Absentee and Loyal bands, I will describe the spring Bread Dances at two Shawnee grounds, the 1973 performance at the Little River or "New ground" as representative of the Absentee procedure and the performance at Whiteoak that same year as representative of the Loyal Shawnees.

LITTLE RIVER BREAD DANCE

I arrived at the Little River dance ground about 6:00 P.M. on May 18. Most of the families who belong to this ground were already "camped in", and I was informed that the hunters had been out for two days and would return at dawn the following morning. I was invited to eat at Richard Gibson's (the drumkeeper's) camp. As we visited following the meal I noticed that the Queen Bee and the eleven other cooks were busy preparing the fire crane at the fire over which the squirrels would be cooked the following day, since the woman's side had lost the Indian football game. Setting the heavy forked posts was hard work, yet the women were required to do the work unaided by the men. There were also ritual restrictions on the material employed. Instead of the iron chain and hook normally used to hang kettles over a fire, the pot hook at this ceremonial cooking fire had to be of wood and be attached to the crosspiece of the crane with a wrapping of fresh hickory bark. This fire crane was set up north and east of the ceremonial ground proper.

About 8:00 P.M. Richard Gibson brought the drum, which was tied over a small wooden keg, to the arbor at the west end of the ground. Jose Valdez or Dzhonewa, a famous Mexican Kickapoo singer, and other visiting Kickapoo singers began singing "Old Time Forty-Nine) and other social dance songs, and several people, both Shawnees and Kickapoos, danced to the music. These "women's" and mixed social dances were interspersed with generous segments of the Leading or "Ordinary stomp" Dance, with various leaders, both Shawnees and visitors, taking the lead. At midnight drumkeeper Gibson walked to the customary speaker's position in front of the singers' arbor at the west end of the ground, and delivered a short oration. He welcomed the visitors (in English) and then announced that since the following day would be a long and busy one, everyone should rest for the remainder of the night to be fresh for the morrow.

The next morning, just at dawn, Gibson and his second men, carrying the water drum and coconut-shell rattles, assembled at the ground and seated themselves on the singers' bench at the west end, beneath the brush arbor. The twelve women cooks, each carrying her dance shawl and a set of dishes (a cup, bowl, plate, and spoon tied up in a tea towel) assembled east of the dance ground. Shortly after dawn whoops were heard from the woods about one-quarter of a mile southeast of the ground, followed by a volley of gunfire. Richard Gibson now began tapping his water drum in a solemn measured beat. Again the whooping and another volley of shots were heard, this time a bit closer. This was repeated two more times, each time closer to the singers, cooks, and eager spectators assembled at the dance ground. Finally the file of hunters, eighteen men and boys, trotted out of the woods. They were painted with three black marks on the forehead, cheeks, and chin. Each carried a rifle and had a number of squirrels tied to his belt. One youth had killed a large raccoon, whose tail dangled almost to the ground.

The hunters divested themselves of their rifles, piled their game just southeast of the dance ground, and seated themselves on the easternmost log bench on the south side of the dance ground. Richard Gibson, who had been tapping the water drum in slow time while all this was going on, now picked up the tempo and began to sing. The hunters arose and began to dance, single file, in a counterclockwise circle, using a toe-heel left, toe-heel right step. They were shortly joined by the women cooks, who danced in a separate file outside that of the men. After seven songs the men and boys seated themselves on the log bench again. The women now retired to secure the dishes and food, which they placed on the ground before the hunters. When all had been laid out the women left the square and the hunters were invited to crowd around the food and eat, which they did with great gusto. They cleaned up the food in about fifteen minutes and the women retrieved the dishes. Richard Gibson then informed the hunters that they were excused and that those who wished to dance should return, in ceremonial costume, at noon. Any of the first twelve chosen who did not wish to dance in the Bread Dance was asked to inform him (Gibson) so that a substitute could be chosen. The group at the dance ground then dispersed to their various camps, the hunters to wash up and rest, the twelve cooks to clean and cook the game brought by the hunters.

At 1:30 P.M. the people began to assemble at the dance ground once more. Drumkeeper Gibson started off the afternoon's activities by calling the hunters and cooks to assemble from the speaker's position in front of the arbor. He had brought the water drum and coconut rattles and placed them on the ground in the proper position before the singers' log bench. The men were the first to assemble. Attired in their colorful Shawnee shirts, sequined vests, breechcloths, leggings, yarn sashes and moccasins, topped off with a large western-style hat decorated with eagle feathers or a hat roach, they took their seats on the north side of the dance ground. The leader of the hunters, Isaac Gibson, sat furthest west. The other eleven, in order of their selection, sat to his left. Male "volunteer" dancers sat at the west end of the ground under the covered arbor, just north of the singers.

When all of the men were seated a large tarpaulin was spread near the center of the dance ground by two "servants," who were both older men. Upon the tarpaulin a number of smaller white cloths were spread. While this was going on the twelve women cooks, each beautifully attired in native dress, formed a line at a point a few yards southeast of the dance ground. One young lady was dressed in the Creek style, wearing a silver comb at the back of her head with pendant ribbons hanging nearly to her heels together with a loose blouse, numerous bead necklaces, and a full, floor-length skirt. The other women were all dressed in traditional Shawnee costume—the hourglass shaped headpiece with wide ribbon trailer, blouse with large "Bertha" collar, long, full, ribbon-bordered skirt; and moccasins. One woman wore an apron over her skirt and another wore a bugle bead cape. Each carried a number of loaves and/or biscuits of native corn bread wrapped in a white tea towel. At the assembly point each woman or girl unwrapped her bread and tied the tea towel to a branch of a tree nearby. At a signal from drumkeeper Gibson the twelve women and girls marched into the dance area in a single file, led by the chief matron. They circled the tarpaulin in the center of the ground in a counterclockwise circuit and, one by one, each placed her offering of native corn bread on the clean, white cloth. As each deposited her contribution the male hunters and the singers intoned "He-e-e-e-e!" in appreciation and admiration of the women's efforts. Two trips were required to bring in all the bread furnished by these twelve women. I was later told that the first woman cook must make 101 loaves, one of which is shaped like a turtle; the second woman 91 loaves, one of which is large, the others small biscuits; and so on down to the last woman, who only has to prepare eleven loaves. When each of the twelve cooks had deposited all of her bread, other women from various parts of the encampment appeared with their offerings of bread and put it down. Even small girls, obviously scared to death of making a mistake, followed and laid down a small piece or two of the sacred food.

When all the bread had been assembled the two servants carefully arranged it on the north side of the cloth, stacking the loaves to make room. They then went to the sacred cooking fire and secured the cooked squirrels and the raccoon. The hunters had been lucky and had taken 117 squirrels. The meat was placed on the cloth just south of the bread. When all had been neatly arranged and stacked, the servants brought the ends of the uppermost (white) cloths in and over the pile of food so as to almost cover it. Only one loaf of bread, that piece shaped like a turtle, was visible at the top.

The twelve cooks were now seated on the south side of the ground, in the order of their selection, as with the men. Now the two servants left the ground by the eastern door and went to the sacred cooking fire where the squirrels had been dressed and cooked. They carefully dumped the water from the cooking pots onto the cooking fire, extinguishing it, and then returned.

Richard Gibson then tapped the drum a few times to signal the beginning of the dance. The afternoon's dancing was divided into eight parts or episodes, with a rest period of fifteen minutes or so between each part. The alternation or balancing off of male and female shows up clearly in the sequence of dances. The first dance was started by the men, though the women joined in very shortly. The men rose from their seats (leaving their hats behind) and began circling the food in a counterclockwise direction, the twelve hunters first, in order of rank, followed by any male "volunteer" dancers. The women formed a second counterclockwise file outside that of the men. The step of this dance, the Bread Dance proper, is a simple step-pat left, step-pat right, the file of dancers facing in slightly on one song, turning to face slightly outward on the next, and so on. This dance was divided into two rounds or sets, with eight songs to a set.

The second episode involved only the women and girls. As the music began the women formed two ranks in front of the singers, swaying slightly from side to side, and joining in the songs of the men. This dance, considered characteristic of the Shawnees (though also performed by Sauk women) is termed Kokeki or Takokewe in Shawnee and might be termed the "Cluster" Dance in English. After several songs of this type the women, led off by their head dancer, began a counterclockwise circuit of the food, using a simple step-pat left, step-pat right forward progression. This lasted for eight songs.

The third episode involved both men and women again. This time the step was a heavy, measured treading, whole foot left, whole foot right, et cetera, with alternate facings half inward and half outward on alternate songs. The men and women maintained separate files as they circled the food. At the end of each song the men whooped. Wylie Bird Creek, the second of the twelve hunters, led this whooping. He would cry out and the other male dancers would answer. Alfred Switch stated that this dance is the Thothekawe or Buffalo Dance.

The fourth episode involved only the women and girls again, maintaining the alternation of the sexes. It consisted entirely of Kokeki or Cluster Dance songs.

The fifth episode involved both men and women again. Two different steps were employed. For the first eight songs the Buffalo Dance step was used, as in the third episode. The last eight employed a step-pat left, step-pat right, as in episode one. These last songs involved antiphonal whooping.

The sixth episode had only female dancers. They stood in two ranks before the singers for several Cluster Dance songs. This time, however, the women would move a few feet to the right, then a few feet to the left, still facing the singers. The step they used was the same one called *enskanye* by the Iroquois, that is, both toes are lifted and moved to the right, then both heels, in rapid progression, then after moving several feet to the right, the progression is reversed by moving both toes to the left, then both heels, and so forth. After doing this step, back and forth, for several songs while standing in front of the singers, the twelve cooks led the group out and around the food pile in a counterclockwise progression using the same step and facing inward toward the food. This step, which is very exhausting, was performed well by only a few of the women. I had a difficult time securing a native term for this distinctive dance or dance step. Mary Spoon believed that the correct name for it was Pawithekawe or "Dove" Dance.

The seventh episode was the famous Wapikonekawe or Pumpkin Dance. Of all the various dances that make up the Bread Dance, this is undoubtedly the favorite. Men and women who have not joined in the dance up to this point usually rush to join in at least one round of the Pumpkin, both as an affirmation of faith and because they believe they will benefit physically and spiritually from doing so. This dance was led by Delbert Gibson. The Pumpkin Dance involves a rather tricky toe-toe-heel left, toe-toe-heel right forward progression with alternate in-and-out facings as the songs change. As usual in the mixed or "men's" dances, the men formed an inner file, the women a second outer file. When the dancers are on the side of the dance ground furthest from the singers the leader of the male dancers begins an antiphonal chant, answered by his followers, this in counterpoint to the singing and drumming of the musicians.

The eighth and final episode involved the women and girls standing in two ranks before the singers and joining in their songs, much like the ordinary Cluster Dance. In this last set of songs, however, the men would stop at a certain point in the song and let the women finish the phrase. The words to this particular set of songs were obviously very amusing to the participants, and a spirit of high hilarity prevailed. It is undoubtedly to this episode in the Bread Dance that Alford is referring when he writes,

> The women congregate in compact form in front of the singers who continue to sing as they beat a weird, rhythmic music on their tomtoms. The women sing with them, and move with a slight swaying motion of the body, right and left. A certain phrase in the song ridicules the weakness of human nature. This phrase when sung by the men is directed against the women, and when sung by the women is directed against the men (both men and women are singing). In spite of the reticence practiced, murmurings can be heard in the crowd which show their sympathy with the singers. The women exclaim "the women conquer," or the men cry out "the men have conquered," showing a pleasant, friendly rivalry between the sexes. (Alford *Civilization:* p. 60)

This episode ended with the women making a number of counterclockwise circuits around the pile of food using a simple toe-heel left, toe-heel right forward progression, the so-called Beshiwekawe or "Straight" Women's Dance.

The afternoon ceremonies now reached their climax with drumkeeper Gibson stepping forward from his seat at the west side of the dance ground and taking a position near the pile of bread and meat, facing the east. The entire assembly remained perfectly quiet as he delivered the lengthy and moving Bread Dance prayer. Unfortunately I do not have an exact transcription of Mr. Gibson's remarks, but Lilly Ellis later provided a brief summary. He began by thanking all of those present for their attendance. He especially thanked the committees for their work, the women for their offerings of bread and the hunters for the squirrels. He then addressed Our Grandmother, the Creator, asking her for benefits in the coming growing season. Next he mentioned the various animal species, each by name, especially the wolves, placed on earth to help mankind. He continued by addressing corn, pumpkin, squash, sweet potatoes and other food crops, praying for a good crops. He then spoke to the Thunderbirds, asking them for rain but also praying that their lightning should "go around" and not harm the people. Again addressing the Creator he asked that she should make sickness "go around" as well, avoiding the people. Finally he prayed for all the servicemen, asking that they be allowed to return safely from their tours of duty.

Following the prayer the two male servants called all of the young boys in the audience to come into the square and seated them in a crescent formation at the east side so that they might receive a piece of bread during the distribution. The distribution of the food now began. First it was carefully uncovered by the two male servants. These two were then joined by two of the female cooks. The two men now began distributing the bread, the women the squirrel and raccoon meat. The bread was given only to men and boys, the meat only to women and girls. The first loaf of bread, the piece shaped like a turtle which had been on the top of the pile, was given to Isaac Gibson, the head male "hunter." Other hunters received large loaves, as did the singers and volunteer male dancers. The small boys seated on the ground received several biscuits each. As this was going on the squirrels and the flesh of the raccoon were distributed among the women and girls. This ended the ceremonial daytime activities. It was now about 7:30 P.M.

People now retired to their various camps for dinner. Visitors were invited to dine with local Shawnees. About 10:00 P.M. the secular nighttime or Stomp Dances began and continued through the night. The next morning drumkeeper Gibson attempted to organize an Indian football game, an event prescribed for this occasion, but there was no response and the game was cancelled.

WHITEOAK BREAD DANCE

The 1973 spring Bread Dance of the Loyal Shawnees was attended by many more people than has been usual in recent years. There were several Absentee Shawnee visitors on this occasion because neither of the Absentee Bread Dances conflicted with the Loyal Shawnee date.

I arrived at the ground at 2:00 P.M. on 5 May. The pots of beef stew, which at this ground replace the boiled squirrel and other wild game seen at the Absentee grounds, were already bubbling over a fire just outside the northwest corner of the dance ground. Esther Dixon, one of the twelve women cooks, had been given the duty and honor of watching over these pots as they cooked. Attired in her traditional Shawnee dress she watched the pots from a seat on the log bench nearby, now and then stirring their contents.

At 2:30 P.M. three of the women cooks began the ceremonial sweeping of the dance ground. In this sweeping the square is divided into four quadrants by a swept cross symbolic of the sun and the four directions similar to the painting on the ceremonial drumhead. Leaf brooms are employed, and the sweepers pray silently as they work. First one matron swept a path from the west side of the ground to the east side, midway between the two sides, then she swept another path from south to north forming a cross. Then two other women, each with a leaf broom, swept each of the four quadrants, working from the center to the log benches at the edge of the ground.

About 4:00 P.M. the preparations for the dance itself began. Bill Shawnee, the principal singer, carrying the water drum and the two cowhorn rattles, seated himself at the center of the north side of the ground. He tapped the drum to call the people to the dance. The men and boys assembled first. Ordinarily Bill would have been seconded by Ranny Carpenter, the Whiteoak drumkeeper, but Ranny had suffered a stroke and was confined to his bed. Therefore Bill bore most of the burden for the singing. He was assisted by one older man and by a younger man, Jimmo White, the chief of the Loyal band. Both of these second men employed cowhorn rattles, while Bill beat time on the drum. Frank Bob, the blind bundle keeper and priest, sat immediately to the right (west) of the three singers.

Benny Barnes and another younger man were the aides or servants. They were now called to a position directly in front of the drum and asked to select the twelve male dancers. Because the Loyal Shawnees no longer send out hunters prior to the Bread Dance the twelve dancers must be selected at this time. The two aides, acting under instructions from Bill Shawnee, now proceeded to pick the twelve from the men and boys present. Each aide, in turn, would leave the square, select a man or boy, and return with him to a position before the drum. Here the person was asked if he would serve (all agreed to do so) and were then instructed to carry out the dancing in the proper manner. The final lineup included nine Loyal Shawnees, two of whom were small boys; two Absentee Shawnee visitors (Wayne Longhorn and one of his sons); and Edmund Dixon, a white man and the husband of Esther Dixon (who was Shawnee and Delaware and one of the twelve female cooks). Only three of the male dancers wore any vestige of Shawnee costume (Indian shirts) and two of these were the Absentee Shawnee visitors. After being chosen these twelve male dancers were seated in a row on the south side of the dance ground.

After this had been completed Bill Shawnee called the women to come and bring their offerings. The twelve women cooks and some other women and girls assembled at a tent west of the dance ground. A clean white cloth was spread on the ground near the center of the dance area and weighted with stones by the two aides. The women now proceeded to the dance ground. Each entered through the doorway at the west end, made a counterclockwise circuit of the cloth, deposited her offering of bread, then exited again via the west door. As each woman added her store of bread to the accumulation, the singers and older men intoned "He-e-e-e-e!" as a sign of approval and thanks. It required two trips to complete this. Smaller loaves the size of biscuits were piled in the center with the larger loaves at the sides. When all of the bread had been deposited on the cloth the two large kettles containing the beef stew were brought in and placed west of the cloth upon which the bread was piled. Though the edges of the cloth upon which the bread was placed were slightly turned up there was no effort, as at the Absentee grounds, to almost completely cover the bread and protect it from the dust. When all the food was in place the twelve women and girl cooks came into the dance ground again by the west door and took seats west of the singers. Seven wore the characteristic Shawnee woman's costume, though the numerous silver brooches seen at the Absentee dance grounds, and the traditional Shawnee woman's headpiece and moccasins, were not seen here.

When the women were seated a small pouch of red paint was produced and the dancers and singers were painted. Benny Barnes painted the men, Eva Secondline the women. Bill Shawnee, of course, painted the head of the drum. Apparently anyone who wished to be painted was granted this favor, not merely the twelve male dancers and the twelve women cooks.

Next Frank Bob stood up at his place and prayed in the Shawnee language for about fifteen minutes. The singers then began to sing and the women, led by the twelve cooks, rose and began to circle the dance ground in a counterclockwise circuit. They danced in a single file using a simple toe-heel step. The women made four circuits of the ground during this first episode. When the singing ended each of the women, as they passed before the singers, said *N'yawe* (Thanks).

The second episode was begun by the men. The twelve male dancers arose and walked, in a counterclockwise file, to a position directly before the singers. The drummer produced a rapid flurry of drumbeats after which all the dancers whooped. This was repeated three more times. The singers then began a Bread Dance song. The men moved off in a counterclockwise circuit of the ground, single file behind the head dancer. A line of women, led by the twelve cooks, rose and formed a second line dancing beside the men on the outside. As this double file of dancers reached the south side of the ground the music stopped and the men whooped. The music then began again and the dancers moved on around to the north side until they were even with the singers once more, at which point the music again stopped and the men whooped. This entire procedure was repeated three more times, each dance beginning with four antiphonal whoops and with single whoops at the midway point (south side) and at the end (north side). After four complete circuits of the ground the dancers thanked the singers with the customary *"N'yawe"* and proceeded in a counterclockwise direction to their seats.

The third episode involved only the women and girls. It consisted of the Dove Dance, the Shawnee version of the Iroquois Enskanye or Shuffle Dance. Those women who were able, rose on their toes swinging both heels to the right, then, balancing on the heels, swung the toes to the right, and so on in a rapid progression. All of the dancers faced the center of the ground at first, but on a musical cue they turned about-faced to face outward. The song ended when they reached the south side. The whole dance then began again, the end of the second song bringing them up facing the singers on the north side, where it began once more. There were four complete rounds, after which the women resumed their seats. Several of the older women could not manage this difficult and exhausting step and simply sidestepped throughout. Most of the women, even the young girls, were puffing at the conclusion of the dance episode.

The fourth episode involved both men and women and consisted of four more rounds of the Bread Dance, exactly like the second episode described above. The step employed for this dance by the Loyal Shawnees is a simple cadenced walk in time with the drum, left foot forward, then right, the body erect, hands at the sides, the muscles of the arms are not overly tense but neither overly loose.

The fifth episode was the Kokeki or women's Cluster Dance, performed by the women alone. At the beginning the women stood in a cluster before the singers. They sang in unison with the singers for a number of songs, then moved off in a counterclockwise file using a toe-heel step. The women made three rounds of the dance ground before resuming their seats.

The sixth and final round of dancing was the Pumpkin Dance, involving both men and women. Lewis Dick led the file of male dancers in this dance, as had been his custom for a number of years, though he was not one of the twelve "hunters." He prefaced his performance with a short speech in English in which he stated that for reasons of health (his heart condition) this would be his final performance. As danced by the Loyal Shawnees the Pumpkin Dance begins much like the Bread Dance (episodes two and four above). When the two files of dancers have reached the south side of the ground and are facing east the leader of the men's file (in this instance Mr. Dick) turns obliquely to his right and begins a rocking progression, leading with his left leg and then rocking back on his right, leading with his left again, et cetera. At the same time he begins an antiphonal chant, calling out "Whi yo," to which the male dancers reply by yelling "Huh-huh." This antiphonal Whi yo: huh-huh, Whi yo:huh-huh, continues until the heads of both files of dancers are even with the singers on the north side. The whole is then repeated three more times. For his 1973 performance as leader of the Pumpkin Dance Lewis Dick was attired in a beaded headband with a single feather at the back, a neckerchief with a beaded rosette slide, a Shawnee "ribbon" shirt, white cloth trousers fringed like buckskin leggings, and moccasins. He carried a turkey wing fan in his right hand.

Following the Pumpkin Dance the venerable priest and bundle keeper Frank Bob rose from his seat and delivered the Bread Dance prayer. It was a most touching act of faith, though marred by the loud and uncouth comments of two white men who seemed oblivious of what was taking place. The prayer was followed by the distribution of food. Unfortunately there was too little Indian corn bread for the size of the crowd. In spite of the fact that several of the larger loaves were broken into four pieces, some of the dancers did not receive any bread. The beef stew was distributed to the women and girls from the center of the dance ground where the two kettles stood. Each woman or girl brought a dish or bowl to hold her portion. I was amused to note that a white man, one of the two "good old boys" who had been joking loudly during Frank Bob's prayer, lined up with the women and girls "to get some free soup."

The nighttime dances, which began about 10:00 P.M., were the customary alternation of women's dances and mixed dances with Leading Dance episodes. After midnight the drum was retired and Lead dancing continued until dawn. As the sun was coming up the drum was brought back to the ground and the Drunken Dance, which customarily closes a full night of Stomp dancing, was performed. The only social dance that I observed that I had not seen on previous occasions was the Seneca Dance. It featured a long file of dancers, women only, weaving a serpentine path around the dance ground, much as in the Cherokee Dance. The Cherokee Dance, however, is performed by both men and women. I did not remain to witness it, but I was told that an Indian football game was to take place the following afternoon.

The 1973 spring Bread Dance at Whiteoak was virtually identical with those witnessed in 1969, 1970, 1971, and 1972 except for the fact that on this occasion there were only six episodes of ceremonial dancing instead of the customary eight. In 1973 the dancing was cut short because it was feared that it might rain before the distribution of food. Had there been eight episodes the two additional would have been a repetition of the women's Straight Dance (the first episode in the 1973 performance) and another episode of the Bread Dance proper (the second and fourth episodes in the 1973 dance). These would have followed the fourth episode and preceded the fifth episode of the 1973 performance. At the 1969 and 1970 Bread Dances Frank Bob's Bread Dance prayer in Shawnee was followed by a "sermon" in English, complete with reading from the Bible, delivered by Lewis Dick. In 1971, 1972, and 1973 this was eliminated because of complaints that it was "not Indian" by some older Shawnees.

At Whiteoak, but not at the Absentee grounds, the first episode at the spring Bread Dance is always a woman's dance, emphasizing the fact that this is the beginning of the agricultural season, and such activities are in the hands of the women. At the fall Bread Dance at Whiteoak this is reversed, emphasizing the importance of the male role of hunter at this season of the year. At both Absentee grounds the men lead off both spring and fall dances. Aside from this fact the fall performances of the Bread Dance are identical with those held in the spring except for the content of the prayers and the fact that they are not followed by the football game. The football game is pleasing to the Thunderbirds and hence a rain-bringing ceremony appropriate only during the growing season.

I have noted in chapter nine that the Shawnee female deity, Our Grandmother, the Creator, is credited with originating all of the major Shawnee ceremonies except for the Buffalo Dance. She is thought to descend from her heavenly abode to observe the performance of these rites by her grandchildren, the Shawnees. She is particularly fond, it is said, of the Kokeki or women's Cluster Dance episode of the Bread Dance. Even today, according to Mary Spoon, an extra female voice, that of Our Grandmother, is sometimes heard above the brush arbor joining in the singing of the women. C.F. Voegelin was told that prior to the Civil War two Shawnee men were always stationed in the neighboring forest during the Bread Dance to listen for Our Grandmother singing above the dance, and would later report this to the people (*The Shawnee Female Deity*: p. 15). This was apparently considered a good omen, a sign that Our Grandmother was pleased with her Shawnee grandchildren and had listened to their prayers.

One of the earliest mentions of the belief that the Creator participates in Shawnee ceremonials occurs in J. Johnston's *Account of the Present State of the Indian Tribes Inhabiting Ohio* (I: p. 274):

> This tribe is bitterly opposed to Christianity, alleging that God gave them a dispensation suited to their situation, and that he did the same for whites. They fancy that the Divine Being comes and sings in their religious meetings, and if they do not hear his "still, small voice," they conclude their sacrifice is not accepted.
>
> Before attending treaties, great councils, or any other important national business, they always sacrifice, in order to obtain the good will of the Great Spirit. On a visit to the President of the United States, some years since, having arrived near Wheeling, they retired into the forest, encamped, killed game, and prepared the sacrifice. While singing, they heard, as they believed, the voice of the Great Spirit distinctly. They set forward on their journey with alacrity, anticipating the best success in their business.

Though Johnston gives the impression that the "sacrifice" was an occasional, rather than a seasonal ceremony, it is also quite possible that the ceremony near Wheeling that he describes was a Bread Dance, held there because this party of Shawnees happened to be at that spot at the time of their customary ceremony, not because of the impending visit to the president.

From Shawnees on their reservation in Johnson County, Kansas, Lewis Henry Morgan secured the following account of the Bread Dance in 1859 (*Indian Journals*: p. 47).

> *Bread Dance (Du-qua-na-ga-weh)* This is the dance at the Spring Festival, which they call the Bread dance. They dance a great number of dances at this festival, but this I understand is the principal one. At this time they render their thanks to the Great Spirit for his goodness. It is not for the worship of the Woman Spirit, but the Great Spirit. The ceremonies consist of dancing, speeches and a feast. The hunters at their fall hunts cut out the tongue of every deer they kill, wait a little, then dry it and string it, and these are brought forward on this occasion as a part of the feast. The women have charge of the feast. They are called Ho-ge-ma-wen-gweh, or "chief's Sisters." The word, Blue Jacket says, is nearly equivalent to Queen. I presume they are analagous to the Iroquois Keepers of the Faith, of whom the female portion have charge of the feast, and with the men have charge of the Festival itself. They also have ball and other games at this festival.

Morgan also describes (*Indian Journals*: p. 47) the "Singing and Fasting Festival, Na-ka-mo-weh": "At this festival they commence with a fast which lasts through the day. In the evening they get together and sing all night. It is a form of worship peculiar to the Chilicothe Band. They say that their Grandmother sings with them, and that they can hear her. They allow no impure person at this festival, no woman with child, no person in the menstrual season, no drinking person, or who has drunk within several days. This festival is held but once a year, and that is in the spring." Judging from the native name and the reference to Our Grandmother singing with the participants, likewise the statement that the festival was held only once a year, in the spring, this latter would seem to be merely a garbled account of the spring Bread Dance. The notation that it was peculiar to the Chilicothe band [Chalaakaatha division], however, may possibly indicate that it was a completely different ceremony, that is now completely forgotten by the Shawnees. Neither the Bread Dance nor the "Singing and Fasting Festival" was witnessed by Morgan. He states, in fact (ibid: p. 48): "The Shawnees have abandoned their dances on this reservation, and their tribal organization is but faintly preserved". I find Morgan's comparison, in the Bread Dance account, of the similarity between the Shawnee "Chief's Sisters" and the Iroquois faithkeepers to be very apt.

Spencer (*The Shawnee Indians*: p. 393) quotes his informant Nancy Chouteau concerning the Bread Dance. She mentions that upon their return from the hunt preceding the dance the hunters fire their guns, and men and women go out to meet them. The hunters are then taken off their horses and sent to wigwams to rest.

The most complete account of the Bread Dance in the literature is that of Alford (*Civilization*: 56-60) a portion of which I have quoted earlier. He provides an excellent account of the spring Bread Dance prayers (ibid.: pp. 59-60):

> . . . a prayer is offered by a man versed in the ancient customs and forms handed down from generation to generation by word of mouth, and from time immemorial. This man generally is an orator. He asks the Great Spirit for fruitfulness of the coming season; that the people may be given an abundant crop of corn and beans and pumpkins. He prays for the general welfare of the people, for success in all their undertakings, and voices an eloquent prayer for an increase in game. He then thanks the Great Spirit for the success of the hunters during the past winter, and for all the good things that have come to the people during their lives.

Alford's account would seem to be inaccurate in placing the Bread Dance prayer *before* the ritual daytime dances, and in indicating that the prayer was the only "serious side" of the Bread Dance.

Additional information on former customs of the Loyal Shawnees in connection with the departure and return of the hunters was provided by Esther Dixon: "When the twelve hunters left to hunt before the Bread Dance, it was the custom, years ago, for each of the twelve women cooks to prepare a sack of provisions for one of the men and to saddle his horse. The men would come to the dance ground, take their horse, which was held by the cook of corresponding rank, and mount. When all twelve had mounted up they would whoop and ride off at a gallop. On their return the following Friday they would come in at a gallop again, whooping, and dismount. Again the twelve women would meet them and take their game and skin it and put it on scaffolds."

As is true for Shawnee religion as a whole, there are numerous elements in the ceremonies of other Native American groups in eastern North America that are nearly identical with elements making up the Shawnee Bread Dance, though the total combination of these elements in the Bread Dance is distinctly Shawnee. The positioning of the singers at one side of the dance ground and the custom of employing a single drummer flanked by two seconds or rattle men are common throughout eastern North America. It appears, in fact, in one of the earliest illustrations of American Indian ceremonialism, which is De Bry's engraving after Le Moyne's lost painting of the Victory Dance of the Timucua in 1565 (S. Lorant *The New World*: p. 67). This positioning and arrangement of the singers is still seen among the Creeks, Seminoles, and Yuchis at the present time, as well as among the Iroquois of New York, Ontario and Quebec, and Oklahoma.

The closest parallels to the Bread Dance's display of food in the center of the dance ground and worshipers dancing around this food are found with the Iroquois. E. Tooker (*The Iroquois Ceremonial of Midwinter*: p. 64) notes that the Tonawanda Seneca "Our Life Supporters" ceremony involves, at the end, the women dancing "around the food that has been brought into the longhouse earlier and placed near the women's stove. It is uncovered for this dance." Vegetables, fruits, and melons are likewise ceremonially displayed at the Green Corn Ceremony of the Oklahoma Seneca-Cayugas (Howard "Cultural Persistence and Cultural Change"). The Shawnee name for the ceremony, "Bread Dance" also occurs as an alternate name for the Tonawanda Seneca Harvest Festival. The Harvest Festival is the Seneca equivalent of the fall Bread Dance of the Shawnees (W.N. Fenton *Tonawanda Longhouse Ceremonies*: pp. 145, 155, 160).

The offering of game by the men and cornbread by the women and their distribution at the end of the dance is closely paralleled by the customary proceeding at the Delaware Big House ceremony. Thus, Luckenbach writes: "At the conclusion [of the Big House ceremony] a sacrificial feast is held, for which the deer and bear-meat is provided by all joining in a common hunt, the women furnishing a store of corn-bread. All is prepared, in common, in the house of sacrifice, and there partaken of amid certain ceremonies. For example, the bread is arbitrarily thrown among the guests, and each one catches as much as he can." (L.H. Gipson, ed *The Moravian Indian Mission on White River*: p. 613)

The general form and choreography of the dances making up the Bread Dance are duplicates of, or very similar to those of other eastern tribes. The Shawnee Women's Cluster Dance (Kokeki) has a counterpart in a dance performed by Sauk women at the spring feast of the Sauk Fox clan, likewise in the dance performed by Creek and Seminole women when "blessing" the men's ballsticks prior to a "match" ballgame. The Shawnee women's Straight

Dance (Beshiwekawe) has been observed among the Sauks,
Kickapoos, and Delawares. The Shawnee Dove dance (Pawithe-
kawe) as I have already observed, is the same as the Iroquois
Enskanye or Shuffle Dance.

Finally, the lengthy prayer at the conclusion of the dancing is
an almost universal feature of religious dances in eastern North
America.

12

Spring and Early Summer Ceremonials

FOOTBALL GAMES AND LAST FOOTBALL GAME

Beginning with the football game that is held in connection with the Arbor Dance, and continuing until the latter part of June, a series of ceremonial men-against-women Indian football games are played by the Shawnees. According to Ranny Carpenter, the game is a sacred exercise. It is thought to be pleasing to Our Grandmother and also to the Thunderbirds and is therefore conducive to bringing rain and promoting the fertility of the crops. Because the first game takes place prior to the spring Bread Dance, around the first of May, and the last one during the latter part of June, the season lasts about a month and a half or two months at the most. Other tribes that have acquired the game from the Shawnees, such as the Delawares, Oklahoma Seneca-Cayugas, and Quapaws, may play on into the autumn, but the Shawnees would not think of doing so lest they bring storms and bad weather.

Each Shawnee ceremonial ground has a football field immediately adjacent, and at each ground one person is in charge of the game. At Whiteoak this is Mrs. Ranny (Emmaline) Carpenter, who is also the chief matron of the dance ground. She furnishes the ball that is used throughout the season and is destroyed at the end of the last game. The ball is about eight inches in diameter and three inches thick. The cover is made of two round pieces of buckskin that are sewed together at the edges except for a small opening. The cover is then turned inside out to protect the seam and then stuffed with deer hair, after which the remaining opening is sewed shut.

A description of the last football game of the season at Whiteoak on 21 June, 1969 will indicate the customary procedures. Activities began about noon, with two young men going from camp to camp to gather bets. The men play the women, so the bets consist of comparable items wagered on either of these two sides by individuals. Each person's bet of say, a scarf, is knotted to a comparable bet from the opposite side, and the paired bets are then tied to a long string. When all bets have been gathered the string of bets is suspended between two poles. These were set up, in 1969, at the south side of the ball field, which at Whiteoak begins just northwest of the dance ground and extends for a quarter of a mile to the west. Goals consisted of two sticks about three feet high and the same distance apart set at either end of the field.

The game began about 3:00 P.M. Mrs. Carpenter tossed up the ball at midfield to start the game. Men and boys had to move the ball only by kicking it with their feet, but women and girls could carry and run with it, though the boys and men were free to grab or tackle them to impede their progress or seize the ball. The game is rough and vigorous, though usually played in a spirit of good humor. It is by no means limited to youths, and men and women in their seventies, as well as young children no older than ten or eleven, commonly take part. To score, one side must pass the ball through their opponent's goal from the front side. When this has been accomplished the ball is returned to midfield and thrown up between the center players again. At Whiteoak the women defend the west goal, the men the east one. At the Absentee grounds the reverse is true. Each scoring play earns one point.

The score for the 1969 game was kept by Ranny Carpenter, who sat under a shady tree on the north side of the ball field, about midway between the goals. He used small sharpened pegs, which he stuck into the ground, to keep score. A vertical line traced in the dirt separated the scores for each side. Each peg earned by one side was matched by one on the other side when that side scored, moving away from the scorekeeper until six pegs were in place on either side, after which the direction was reversed. The first side to earn twelve points, or the side which was ahead when the game was concluded in this case, was the winner.

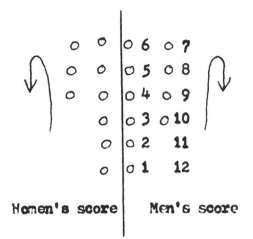

Fig. 8.   Diagram of the scorekeeping of a Shawnee football game

The game lasted about two hours, or until 5:00 P.M. Because this was the last game of the season Mrs. Carpenter took the ball to the center of the field at its conclusion. Uttering a prayer, she slit open its cover at the seam, raised it above her head, and let the deer-hair filling blow away in the breeze. The deerskin cover, however, was retained, as deerskin is now a rare item and cannot readily be replaced.

Everyone now collected his winnings, the men having won the game, and retired to his camp to eat. A night of social dancing followed, commencing at about 8:00 P.M. This consisted of women's Dances and mixed dances interspersed with generous amounts of the Leading Dance.

Accounts of the Shawnee football game in the anthropological literature are few, and provide few details for comparison with present-day procedures. T. W. Alford simply notes (*Civilization*: p. 62): "Another sport that was enjoyed by our people was a ball game which was played early in the summer by both men and women. But after the month of June—as we counted the season— the ball season was closed with a pretty ceremony that put the ball away until the time for the Bread Dance the next spring. All these rules and ceremonies were known to all the people, and they were respected, observed, and kept sacred and inviolate." Spencer's account (J. Spencer *The Shawnee Indians*: p. 393) is even briefer: "The Shawnee football game is played at planting time. It is always stopped before sundown." Briefest of all is Trowbridge's note (C. C. Trowbridge *Shawnese Traditions*: p. 52): "They play also at ball."

Sam Perry, a Loyal Shawnee, told interviewer W. T. Holland about the football game in 1937 (Indian Archives, Oklahoma Historical Society 8: 187): "The men played the women. The women could hold the ball in their hands and run with it, but the men had to kick it. The field is 75 yards long. One person sits at one side and keeps score by setting sharpened sticks in the ground. Eight sticks are prepared for each side. The first side getting eight scores was declared the winner."

Speck (F. G. Speck *Oklahoma Delaware Ceremonies, Feasts and Dances*: pp. 73–78) describes the Delaware version of the football game, noting that the first game was part of a spring prayer and dance "to advance vegetation". This festival closely parallels the Shawnee first football game and arbor dance. Speck notes, regarding this Delaware ceremonial, that "there is reason to trace much of the ceremonial make-up of this festival to the Shawnee with whom the Delaware were, and still are, so closely associated." (Speck *Oklahoma Delaware Ceremonies, Feasts and Dances*: p. 73) He notes the same custom of closing the ball season at the end of June, and the practice of slitting open the ball cover to signify that the season is over, but in a footnote he adds: "Late information states that the ball is not destroyed at the end of the game except when it was conducted upon the principle of the Shawnee ruling which prevailed in Delaware tradition through the influence of this tribe." (Speck *Oklahoma Delaware Ceremonies, Feasts and Dances*: p. 76) Today's Delawares are still divided in their opinion. Some contend that the football should be put away in the spring, following the Shawnee rule, while others insist that this rule does not apply to the Delawares. The Delawares in fact often play the game in connection with their autumn Stomp Dance, and many of the younger Loyal Shawnees join in the game with them.

The spring football games are apparently conducted in much the same way at both the Little Axe "Old Ground" and at the Little River "New Ground"—that is to say the game is played as it is at Whiteoak except for the fact that the men's and women's goalposts are the reverse of their position at the Loyal Shawnee ground. Louis Warrior commented that this difference in the location of the goals is hard to get used to when the Absentees visit the Whiteoak ground. He told an amusing story of an Absentee

Shawnee woman who went visiting at Whiteoak and joined in the football game. She scored a point for the men before she got straightened out on the orientation of the goals.

Spring football games are also still played at the otherwise defunct Sand Hill dance ground northest of Shawnee, Oklahoma. The football used at this ground, according to Mary Spoon, is slightly smaller than those used at Little Axe and Little River.

Lilly Ellis informed me that the Absentee Shawnees have a rule that the last football game of the season must be completed by noon. The Absentees, she said, do not destroy the football at the end of the season as the Loyal Shawnees do, but merely retire it for the year. She was familiar with the Loyal Shawnee practice and added that formerly the Whiteoak ball keeper cut open the seams of the football at the goal where the last point had been scored rather than at midfield as is presently the custom.

The spring football games are great sport and often the occasion of high hilarity, particularly when two of the tribal elders, who on other occasions are models of decorum, struggle for the ball. They are nevertheless integral parts of the ceremonial cycle, and in this respect they rank considerably higher than the nighttime social dances that customarily follow them. Thus, in 1971, drumkeeper Richard Gibson cancelled the Stomp Dance following the last football game at the Little River ground because of the serious illness of his father, though he had authorized the football game itself.

GREEN CORN DANCE (LOYAL SHAWNEES)

Only the Loyal band of Shawnees performs the Green Corn Dance at the present time. If the Absentees ever possessed such a ceremony, no one remembers hearing of it. The ceremony takes place, at the Whiteoak ceremonial ground, some time between mid-July and late August. The Green Corn Dance has much the same form as the spring and fall Bread Dances, though separate and distinct songs are used for the mixed (men and women) dance episodes in two ceremonies. A description of the 1969 Green Corn Dance will serve to indicate the similarity of the rites to the Bread Dance, also the differences.

The activities began about 3:00 in the afternoon. As in the Bread Dance the dance ground was swept clean, in the cross and quadrant fashion, by three women. Next twelve women and twelve men dancers were chosen. In place of the native corn bread and beef stew seen in the Bread Dance, various melons, and other vegetables, together with a large kettle of corn soup, were placed in the center of the dance area, following the same procedure that is employed in the Bread Dance. The musicians, priest or speaker, and men and women dancers were seated in the same positions that they would occupy in the Bread Dance. None of the men wore any vestige of Indian costume on this occasion. Four of the women wore the Shawnee woman's costume, and all twelve women either wore or carried shawls.

When all of the food had been brought in and positioned, and the twelve women dancers had been seated, Frank Bob, the blind priest and bundle keeper, rose and delivered a long prayer. The dancing followed. There were six sets or episodes of dancing, three for each sex. The women danced alone during their episodes but joined the men during the "men's" sets. The format was identical with that of the spring Bread Dance, with the women dancing first, then the men and women together, then women alone, and so on. The first episode began with two renditions of the starting song. The women rose from their seats and began a counterclockwise circuit of the dance ground, using the simple toe-heel left, toe-heel right, single-file progression termed the Women's Straight Dance (Beshiwekawe) by the Shawnees. The third, fourth, fifth, sixth, seventh, and eighth songs were all songs that were associated with this dance.

The second episode began with a fast flurry of drumbeats and four antiphonal whoops led by Jimmo White, present chief of the Loyal band and the head male dancer on this occasion. The dance was identical in choreography with the Bread Dance, the men toe-heeling in one counterclockwise file, the women forming a second file beside them. Four songs, each repeated once, carried the dance, with whooping by the men at the end of the first rendition of each song (at which time the dancers were at the south side of the ground) and again at the repeat (at which time they were back at the starting point, in front of the singers).

The third episode (with women only) began with six songs of the women's Cluster Dance (Kokeki). During these songs the women stood in place before the singers and joined in the songs. The following five songs were women's Straight Dance songs, and as in the first episode, the women danced around the square in a counterclockwise direction.

The fourth episode was like the second, the men and women dancing together, the men whooping four times before each song, then once at the end of the first rendition, and once again at the end of the repeat. Five songs were used, each repeated once.

The fifth episode (with women only) began with three songs, each repeated, of the women's Cluster Dance, then three more, each repeated, of the women's Side Dance or Dove Dance.

The sixth and final episode consisted of five songs of the Pumpkin Dance, with Lewis Dick leading the men's line and starting the antiphonal whooping at the correct point, the south side of the dance area. As in the spring and fall Bread Dances there was a great deal of enthusiasm evident during this episode and cries of "Everybody dance!"

The dancing, which had begun about 4:00 P.M., ended at 6:00 P.M. At its conclusion there was a sermon in English by Lewis Dick, after which the melons, vegetables, and corn soup were distributed. All then retired to their various camps to feast. A night of social dances followed, beginning at 8:00 P.M.

From this above account it may be seen that the Green Corn Dance of the Loyal Shawnees is essentially a junior version of the Bread Dance. It is definitely less highly regarded than the spring and fall Bread Dances. There is much less costuming and the crowd is usually much smaller than that which assembles for the Bread dances. Perhaps the Green Corn Dance was added to the Loyal Shawnee ceremonial cycle as an equivalent to the Iroquois Green Corn, which also involves a display of agricultural produce, and the Green Corns of the various Southeastern groups known to the Shawnees such as the Creeks, Seminoles, Yuchis, and Cherokees. Whatever its origins, the Green Corn has been performed by the Ohio Shawnees, who are now the Loyal or Cherokee Shawnees, for more than 180 years. We have an excellent account of the ceremony, as it was conducted in 1792, from the pen of young O. M. Spencer, who witnessed the festival while he was a captive of the Shawnees in a village on the Auglaize (*The Indian Captivity of O.M. Spencer*: pp. 102-113):

> It was on a pleasant morning about the middle of August, when the ears of corn, grown to full size, were yet in the soft milky state in which they are used for roasting, that the three sons of Cooh-coo-cheeh, with their wives; her daughter, with her husband, Mr. Ironside; Captain Walker and some other Shawnee warriors with their wives, and a few old squaws, in compliance with her invitation assembled at our cabin to celebrate the feast of green corn. This is a festival said to be similar to that of "first fruits" among the Jews . . . when the more wealthy and influential among the Indians of the same tribe, ostensibly to evidence their gratitude to the Great Spirit for his manifold mercies, inviting the members and relatives of their respective families, feast

them principally on green corn variously cooked and entertain them with different games and sports; usually crowning their festivities with copious draughts of "fire water"—either rum or whiskey.

Here, after the usual salutations at meeting, when all were gathered and seated on the grass and the pipe according to custom had several times passed around the circle, a venerable Indian arose and with much solemnity of tone and earnestness of manner addressed them. He spoke (as Mr. Ironside afterward informed me) of the distinguishing favor of the Great Spirit to his red children, the first and most honorable of the human race, to whom he had given the vast country stretching from the sun's rising place in the far east to where it sets in the great waters beyond the Rocky Mountains; extending from the sea of the north to the boundless salt waters of the south; yielding abundantly corn for bread, supplying meat and clothing for their families from the buffalo, the elk, the deer, and every variety of wild game with which the forest once abounded; producing spontaneously the most valuable medicinal plants, furnishing specifics for every disease to which his red children were exposed; of their obligations to him for all these benefits, especially for sending them fruitful showers and now blessing them with an earnest of a good crop of corn, and that they ought to evidence their sense of obligation to Him by gratefully feasting on His bounties there provided for them and by heartily engaging in the manly sports and exercises of the day.

He then spoke of the "palefaces," whome he represented as the first murderers and oppressors; ascribed their own sad reverses to the anger of the Great Spirit for affording these murderers an asylum on their shores; of their duty to exterminate if possible these intruders on their soil, at least to drive them south of the Ohio. He said that their late victories over the whites, particularly their signal defeat of St. Clair, were evidences of the returning favor of the Great Spirit; and concluded by exhorting them to deeds of valor and to conquest of their natural enemies as a certain passport to the boundless hunting grounds in the far, far west, "beyond the vast waters," where the Great Spirit would never "suffer the palefaces" to enter. This speech was listened to by all with deep attention, the auditors improving each deep pause to utter some monosyllable expressive of the various feelings that by turns inspired them; but at the concluding sentence, as if actuated by one sentiment, simultaneously sprang to their feet and uttering a shrill and prolonged whoop, with great animation they commenced their sports.

The first of these was running on foot over a straight course of about one hundred yards, in which the principal competitors were the White and Black Loons, Wawpunnoo, and Captain Walker; Moore [a white captive] not being allowed at the beginning to join in their sports. And here for the first time having an opportunity of witnessing the fleetness of the Indians, I noticed that in running as in walking they turned their toes in, hindering the full forse of the muscles of the leg; and that their movements resembled more the bounding of the deer than the more rapid steps of the whites, whose lower, forward efforts bore them only onward. And I am satisfied that, although from habit continuing to breathe freely, the Indians may run longer at great speed, yet in a short race they are generally less fleet than the whites. Wawpawmawquaw, whose movements were lower and more rapid, won the race; though Moore swore that he could give him twenty steps and beat him in a hundred yards.

In the wrestling that followed Wawpunnoo (brother of the Loons) and Captain Walker, both tall and powerful men, bore off the palm, but in repeated trials with each other, with various success, Walker was acknowledged victor . . .

It being now about noon, the Indians suspended their sports to partake of the splended feast provided by Cooh-coo-cheeh, consisting of boiled jerk and fish, stewed squirrels and venison, and green corn boiled some in the ear and some cut from the cob and mixed with beans, besides squashes and roasted pumpkins. For bread, besides that prepared in the ordinary way from corn meal we had some made of the green corn cut from the cob and pounded in a mortar until it was brought to the consistency of thick cream, then being salted and poured into a sort of mould of an oblong form for more than half the length and twice the thickness of a man's hand, made of corn leaves, and baked in the ashes, was very palatable. The guests did ample justice to the entertainment, eating very heartily out of the wooden bowls in which their dinner was served and which they held in their laps, using their own knives to cut their meat, which they held in their fingers, and the horn, wooden, and pewter spoons of their hostess in eating their succotash; each man and woman as they finished their dinner setting down their bowl saying, "Ooway, nelh, netape hooloo", literally, "I have done; my stomach is full." Having all dined and enjoyed for a few minutes the (with them) great luxury of smoking, a small keg of rum was produced, to the great gratification of the guests, all of whom, both men and women, took a hearty draught; when the men, giving their knives and tomahawks in charge to Cooh-coo-cheeh, arose to renew their sports . . .

. . . The men now formed a circle, within and near the edge of which one of the strongest, lying on his back, held firmly in his hands between his raised knees a piece of rawhide, made soft by soaking and so slippery from greasing as to require a powerful grasp and a strong hand to wrest it from his grip. Following each other at the distance of about three feet, and moving several times around the circle in quick time, with elastic step, sinking alternately on each foot and singing, "A yaw whano heigh, how-wa-yow-wa" in one of their most monotonous tunes, each Indian in succession, giving a loud "whoop-haw," suddenly stooped and firmly grasping the rawhide strove to draw it from the hands of its holder. Failing in this, or drawing it suddenly from his hands, some not infrequently measured their length upon the ground to the no small amusement of the others; but the wresting it from the hands of the holder or raising him by it from the ground erect upon his feet was held to be a proof of superior strength.

Dancing now began, the men moving in an outer and the women in an inner circle, stepping lightly, and rather gracefully sinking with a rocking motion, first on one foot, then on the other, or changing the form, facing each other in lines, sometimes springing up briskly with a sort of galloping motion, at others, with their bodies bent forward slowly raising both feet at once and bringing them down heavily, uttering a "hiegh" at every jump, while an old man, pounding with one stick upon a small drum, sang at the same time slowly or more lively according to the kind of dance, regulating the steps of the dancers, who kept exact time with the music.

It was now the middle of the afternoon and both men and women with the exception of Cooh-coo-cheeh were more than half drunk. Moore had prudently retired with Mr. Ironside across the Maumee, and I had withdrawn to the corn fields; where, however, looking through a small hole in the back of the shed I could without danger witness the movements of the Indians. They now drank more frequently; some dancing singly, others in groups; some singing, some whooping; and some quarreling, until at length "uproar wild and deep confusion reigned." About this time Wawpawmawquaw smarting, probably, under the recollection of the severe falls he had received from Walker, laying hold of him and insisting on another trial of his skill in wrestling, being unfortunately thrown into the fire and severely burned, serving as a signal for bringing the festivities to a close; and in a very short time, staggering off in different directions, all departed to their respective homes.

Spencer's account is most interesting in showing how the Shawnee Green Corn has changed through time while still preserving certain characteristic features. The sports events have been eliminated from today's Green Corn but the prayer, the feast and its typical foods, and the dances are still recognizably Shawnee. It is also interesting to note that liquor, now strictly taboo at all Shawnee gatherings during the sacred daytime ceremonies, was publicly served to all participants. At this time in their history, apparently, strong drink was still so new to the Shawnees that they had not recognized its disruptive effects at public gatherings, though they had learned to gather up the weapons of the warriors to prevent bloodshed.

The remaining historic accounts of the Green Corn are very brief. L.H. Morgan (*Indian Journals*: p. 47) was told that the "Roasting Ear Dance (Ne-pa-na-ga-weh) is held when the corn is ripe." The native name "Ne-pa-na-ga-weh" [Nipenekawe], literally "Corn Dance," which is the same term that is employed today, identifies Morgan's "Roasting Ear Dance" as the Green Corn. Joab Spencer (*The Shawnee Indians*: p. 392) quotes his informant Charles Bluejacket to the effect that no one was allowed to eat corn before Corn Dance. This is a common feature in the Green Corn ceremonies of Southeastern tribes.

In a 1937 interview Sam Perry described the Green Corn of the Loyal band (Indian Archives, Oklahoma Historical Society 8: pp. 176–77). He stated that the great iron kettles used in preparing food for the feasts which accompanied this and other Shawnee dances were kept at the dance ground permanently. This is also a custom of the Oklahoma Seneca-Cayugas and was formerly true of the Wyandots, who cooked a great kettle of corn soup at their "summer picnic", which was probably a degenerate version of the Green Corn ceremony.

In 1937 David Dushane, an Eastern Shawnee, told an interviewer that the Green Corn Ceremony was the last Eastern Shawnee ceremony to be abandoned. It had customarily been held in August. Dushane stated that his band also formerly celebrated a Bread Dance, held in October. (Indian Archives, Oklahoma Historical Society 23: pp. 151–2) Though Dushane did not mention it, he might have added that following the abandonment of their own ceremonies, the more conservative members of the Eastern band became regular participants in the Green Corn of the Oklahoma Seneca-Cayugas (J. Howard "Cultural Persistence and Cultural Change as Reflected in Oklahoma Seneca-Cayuga Ceremonialism": Environment and Culture: The Case of the Oklahoma Seneca-Cayuga") as well as the Green Corn and other ceremonies of the Loyal Shawnees.

RIDE-IN AND WAR DANCE (ABSENTEE SHAWNEES)

Undoubtedly the most colorful of Shawnee ceremonies is the horseback parade or Ride-in of the Absentee Shawnees and its associated War Dance. At one time this ceremony was performed by all five divisions of the tribe but at present it is limited to those Absentees, largely Kishpoko and Pekowitha, who participate in the activities of the Little River ceremonial ground. This form of the War Dance, which the Shawnees share with the Oklahoma and Mexican bands of Kickapoos (but not the Kansas Kickapoos), and the Oklahoma Seneca-Cayugas, and which they shared with the Oklahoma Delawares until 1927 or 1928, should not be confused with the ubiquitous Prairie-Plains derived War Dance now seen at intertribal powwows throughout the country. Instead it is an old Woodland Indian War Dance, that is now set into a religious context with the decline of tribal warfare. A sacred war bundle, the divisional bundle of the Kishpoko, which I have described in chapter ten, is still opened in connection with this dance and certain objects from it are carried or worn by the leading dancers.

The Absentees tend to regard their War Dance as the equivalent of the Loyal band's Green Corn, because both are performed at about the same time of year, at the height of summer when the first crops ripen and are acknowledged with thanks (C.F. Voegelin *The Shawnee Female Deity*: p. 13; John and Lilly Ellis, personal communication, 1974). Like the Bread Dances and the Loyal Shawnee Green Corn, the War Dance is one of the ceremonies given the Shawnees by Our Grandmother. C.F. Voegelin writes (*The Shawnee Female Deity*: p. 16): "At the Men's Dance of the Absentee Shawnee, mounted warriors ride around the dance ground four times just to amuse Our Grandmother who comes to earth for the day with her grandson, Rounded-side, and her little dog."

To show present day procedures, I will describe a performance of the Shawnee Men's Dance (Hileni wekawe) or War Dance (Pethikasenawe kawekawena) that I witnessed in 1970, together with supplementary remarks on the 1973 and 1975 performances to indicate the slight variations from year to year.

LITTLE RIVER MEN'S DANCE

I arrived at the Little River ground at 6:30 P.M. on Friday, 21 August. Several camps had already been set up. George Little Charlie welcomed me and told me I might camp south of the dance ground. After the evening meal I had a long visit with George Whitewater, a well known Kickapoo dancer, whose camp was near mine. He stated that he is one-eighth Shawnee through a paternal grandfather, and that his name, Whitewater, stems from this Shawnee ancestor. He also said that he was to be the head dancer or head warrior for the following day's dance. The head warrior and the four other principal warriors or *waethe* must all be men who have served in the armed forces overseas and who, upon their return, have undergone the four-day ceremony that is required to validate this warrior status. Though there are several qualified warriors among the Shawnees, Whitewater said, many of these do not dance. Therefore, when he was approached by a committee from the Little River ground and asked to dance he had secured the aid of three other Kickapoo men who had undergone the "making of warriors" ceremony to help him: Howard Wapakeche, Ralph Tecumseh, and _____ _____. Because the Kickapoos acquired their version of the men's Dance or War Dance from the Shawnees, validation of warrior status at a Kickapoo ceremony automatically qualifies a man to participate as a *waethe* among the Shawnees as well. George said that the Ride-in or horseback parade would take place about 9:00 A.M. the following morning, but that formerly it began at dawn. We visited until late that night, exchanging stories of our military experiences.

About 9:00 the next morning things began to stir in the camp. Horse trailers began to arrive with the steeds to be ridden in the parade. They had been borrowed or rented from local white ranchers and farmers for the most part. Finally at about 10:30 the men and boys who planned to participate began making up little bundles of dance costume clothing and paraphernalia and rode off on their horses to a spot about 200 yards south of the dance ground. They dressed and painted themselves here, taking about half an hour to do so. The war bundle of the Kishpoko division had been carried to a point near this assembly area, where it was opened and displayed. Only the bundle keeper, the head warrior, and his four assistants were actually allowed to witness the opened bundle. The bundle keeper removed the ancient tomahawk and the four sacred split-plume headdresses from the bundle, and these were distributed to the head warrior and his assistants. This group then returned to the assembly area to finish dressing and painting. When all the warriors had finished dressing in their dance costumes the drum was sounded and the group danced for a short time (four songs) at this assembly point in the woods.

The dancers then mounted up and rode toward the camping area and dance ground. The mounted warriors numbered seventeen mounted men and boys in all. George Whitewater and another Kickapoo warrior were in the lead. Richard Gibson, the Shawnee drumkeeper, followed. He carried a water drum, tied over a small keg, braced on the left-hand side of his saddle. Three of the dancers one of these being George Whitewater wore roach headdresses. Two others were bareheaded but wore the split-feather plumes from the sacred bundle tied to scalp locks at the top of the head. George Whitewater wore two of these feather tufts tied to the spreader of his roach headdress. Tom Sloan, an older Shawnee, wore a headdress resembling the Iroquois gastoweh, consisting of the top of a man's western-style straw hat punched up into a domed shape with a beaded band at the front and two eagle feathers loosely attached at the top. Richard Gibson, the singer, wore a western-style hat with a decorated pheasant feather at the side. He and two other older men wore traditional Shawnee ribbon shirts, but most of the men and boys were either bare chested or wore dark blue vests decorated with sequinwork. Yarn sashes and blue cloth breechcloths decorated with ribbonwork, beadwork, or sequinwork were worn by most of the men and boys. Blue cloth leggins, Shawnee or Kickapoo moccasins, and bells completed the costumes of the dancers. Sleigh bells were worn at both knees and ankles by several dancers, and a few had strings extending from the waist to the ankle as well. The dancers were painted in various styles, most with two or three slashes of red paint across either cheek. One of the horses was painted with red circles around its eyes and had bells attached to the upper forelegs. All in all, the group presented a most warlike and festive appearance.

The group circled the camp four times, riding two abreast in a counterclockwise direction, singing to the beat of the water drum all the while. They followed a circular path laid out just outside those camps next to the dance ground. At the completion of the fourth circuit the warriors dismounted, at the southwest corner of the dance ground, and their mounts were taken and led away by women and small boys. The warriors remained at the west end of the dance ground where four other dancers in costume who had walked to the square joined them.

Now the War Dance itself began. The three principal singers sat on a log bench under the arbor at the west end of the ground. The principal singer, Richard Gibson, sat in the center, his water drum resting on a block of wood. The two seconds or assistant singers flanked him on right and left. They did not use coconut-shell or other rattles, as in the Bread Dance but one, Alfred Switch, had a sleigh bell in his fist that he shook to mark time. The singers faced east and the dancers arranged themselves in a rough crescent formation facing them. Each warrior danced as an individual unit, improvising to the music, much as in the familiar powwow style of war dancing. Rapid alternations of toe and heel served to ring the knee and ankle bells. Now and then a dancer would swoop low and then quickly rise to full height. For the most part they danced in place, but now and then two or more would move in a counterclockwise oval circuit in the area between the musicians and the main body of dancers. This was especially true of the head warrior and his four assistants. One of these always carried the ancient tomahawk from the war bundle. The total effect of this type of War Dance is quite different from the Prairie-Plains War or Grass Dance. It might best be described as having a more tense or "nervous" quality.

Whooping marked the end of certain of the songs. I recognized three distinct types of song, each of which elicited a separate type of dancing: (1) "Straight" War Dance songs, during which the dancers toe-heeled in place or moved forward or backward; (2) "trot" songs, characterized by a slow, measured beat of the drum, the dancers "trotting" by hopping from the ball of one foot to the ball of the other; and (3) Fast or "Double-step" songs, like straight War Dance songs but much faster.

Shortly before noon the recital of war exploits by the head warrior and the principal warriors began. Each, in turn, would take the tomahawk from whoever was carrying it at the time, step directly in front of the singers, and indicate his desire to speak. He would then describe, in Kickapoo or Shawnee, some exploit in his military career, gesturing with the tomahawk or his arm. All the dancers would whoop at the end of the speech. The warrior would then take a plug or two of tobacco from a small paper sack that had been placed at the right foot of the principal singer. This he would give to some honored old man sitting among the spectators. This older man would then rise and join the dancers in two dance episodes. The two renditions (one song, repeated) following a war speech were always very fast and spirited "double-step" songs, ending with the dancer's whooping. This recital of war exploits with its attendant dancing continued until shortly after the noon hour, at which time the supply of tobacco in the paper bag was exhausted. During the latter part of the morning dance, while this was going on, a semicircle of women, dressed in traditional Shawnee costume, had formed behind the men. These women did not dance actively but merely stood in place bouncing slightly on their heels in time with the music.

At this point in the proceedings a number of watermelons were brought to the southwest corner of the dance ground and piled up just outside the log seats. The dancers were informed that these melons were for them and that they should adjourn for the noon meal. The singers thereupon began the dismissal procession song. The dancers formed a single file, led by the head warrior with the principal warriors immediately to his rear and the remaining men and boys behind them. The women dancers formed a second file outside that of the men. The two files now danced one counterclockwise circuit of the dance ground using a simple toe-heel left, toe-heel right progression. When the warriors reached the area of the watermelons they whooped and rushed at them. Each warrior who secured a melon raised it high above his head and dashed it to the ground. Other warriors snatched at the broken pieces, greedily dug out the hearts with their hands, and devoured them, leaving the meat near the rind to go to waste. The obvious intent of this bit of action was to demonstrate the fearsome attitude of warriors and their "don't give a damn" spirit. Small children in the area scurried away with squeals of terrified delight.

Now the women spread a canvas tarpaulin on the ground just south of the dance ground and over it placed a white tablecloth of slightly smaller size. Coffee, iced tea, fried bread, several meat dishes, fruit, cookies and cake, also plates, cups and spoons, were arranged on the tablecloth by the women. The warriors and singers seated themselves cross legged around this food and dined al fresco. This was clearly a "ceremonial" feast not deemed of sufficient quantity for the manly appetites of the dancers, most of whom had been fasting since the previous night. At its conclusion, therefore, each of the dancers was invited to a more ample repast at a table in one or another of the various family camps.

About 2:00 P.M. the dancing resumed. The famous Mexican Kickapoo singer Jose Valdez, or Dzhonewa and two Kickapoo seconds took over the singing for the first hour. The same three types of song used in the morning's dancing were used here, but also a fourth type, identified by George Whitewater as Kickapoo "Wolf" songs. These resembled the Trot songs but involved a great deal of change in rhythm. There was some private grumbling by certain dancers concerning this type of song being used in the War Dance. George Whitewater attributed the use of this type of song by Dzhonewa to the man's part-Comanche ancestry, which is the usual Kickapoo explanation for nonstandard behavior (Cf. F.A. Latorre and D.L. Latorre *The Mexican Kickapoo Indians*: 83). Dzhonewa's singing seemed more spirited than that of drumkeeper Richard Gibson, and his songs were definitely longer. Dzhonewa was relieved, at about 3:00, by Alfred Switch, a Shawnee singer. About this same time women began to join in the dance once more, forming two ranks behind the men on the south and north sides of the ground. They simply stood in one spot, moving up and down in an almost imperceptible manner. At 3:30 P.M. the sky became cloudy and rain began to sprinkle, and by 4:00 it was raining hard. The dancers were all thoroughly soaked and the ribbonwork and sequinwork on their costumes was ruined, but the dance continued without pause.

At 4:15, drumkeeper Gibson informed head warrior Whitewater that it was time to begin the closing series of war speeches. Again, as in the morning's dance, the head warrior and each of the four principal warriors, in turn, brandished the war-bundle tomahawk and recited a deed. After doing so each took tobacco from the bag at the head singer's foot and gave it to an older man. There was a great whoop at this point and the entire group, including the old man thus honored, danced vigorously to two fast songs. After each had done this there was the dismissal procession, as at noon, but this time in a driving rain. Following this the dancers returned to the brush arbor at the west end of the ground where the split-feather plumes worn by the head warrior and the principal warriors were carefully unfastened from the wearer's heads. This ended the War Dance proper. There had been some attempt to protect the sacred headdresses during the last half hour of dancing by providing each of the dancers who wore one with a cardboard box, which he held inverted over his head as an improvised umbrella. I also noticed the bundle keeper hurriedly run to the woods, where the sacred war bundle lay open, with a fifth box to protect it.

By 6:00 the afternoon rain had passed and the sandy soil of the dance ground was dry enough for use. At this time there was a "special event," a Turkey Dance by the women of the camp, assisted by Caddo-Delaware visitors. Joe Bedoka, a Caddo-Delaware from Anadarko, was the principal singer for this dance, which lasted for almost an hour. Following it everyone retired to one or another of the family camps for supper. At 8:00 a night of social dancing began with Joe Bedoka singing a round of "Old Time Forty-Nine" songs. Leading or Ordinary Stomp Dances followed and continued through the night.

Performances of the Men's or War Dance seen in 1973 and 1975 were virtually identical with the 1970 performance. One novel feature that I noticed during the afternoon dancing on both of these occasions was a "charging of the drum" by the dancers. This took place during one of the sets of Trot Dance songs. At the beginning of the song the dancers would be distributed, as usual in a rough crescent formation some distance east of the dancers. During the song they would gradually approach the singers, as if stalking an enemy, and when the song ended they would be in a tight cluster around the head singer. There were many more men and boys in both 1973 and 1975, thirty on the former and thirty-five on the latter occasion, and several more dancers joined in the afternoon dancing on both occasions, including several older Shawnee men and a number of Kickapoo visitors. In 1973 Bill Johnson, a Shawnee, appeared wearing only a breechcloth over swimming trunks, ankle bells, and moccasins. His face and body were vividly painted in red to compensate for his lack of costume pieces. On his chest he sported a design of human handprints, made by rubbing red paint on either hand and then pressing the painted palm on his bare shoulders.

An important addition not seen in the 1970 dance that was, I was told, a regular feature of the War Dance was a closing prayer.

In both 1973 and 1975 when the last tobacco had been given out to
the older men, Sam Creek, the head warrior, led the dismissal
procession. Instead of going out, however, the dancers performed
another set of Straight War Dances facing the west. Then Sam
Creek instructed them to turn and face the east. He then stepped
forward from the group to the speaker's position (as in the Bread
Dance) and, facing the east, delivered a long prayer, fully one half
hour in length. Its content was apparently very similar to the
Bread Dance prayer, for at its conclusion many of the dancers
shook his hand and murmured *"N'yaweh!"* ("Thanks") This
concluded the afternoon War Dance. I suppose that this feature
was eliminated from the 1970 War Dance because of the rain. In
both 1973 and 1975 a Creek-Seminole style Buffalo Dance
followed the War dancing, together with a Creek-Seminole Long
Dance and several Leading Dance episodes. These were led by
Harry Bell, a Seminole, and his Seminole and Creek assistants,
though the Shawnees and Kickapoos joined in as well. Like the
Turkey Dance that followed the 1970 dance, this was only an
added attraction and not an integral part of the Shawnee
ceremony. Again, on both occasions, supper and a night of social
dancing followed these daytime activities.

Additional information regarding the Shawnee Men's or War
Dance as performed at present and in the past was gained from
informants. John Ellis, a member of the Little River ground,
stated that an Arbor Dance is always held the Wednesday
previous to the weekend of the Ride-in and War Dance. It is on this
occasion that the "official" announcement of the forthcoming
War Dance is made. There is the customary refurbishing of the
brush arbors during the day, hence the name, and a night of social
dancing following. Ellis compared this Shawnee Arbor dance to
that which the Yuchis stage prior to their Green Corn Ceremony.

The costuming of today's War Dancers is somewhat standardized, but their dress in times past was considerably more varied.
Richard Gibson recalled an old Absentee named John Snake who
was noted for his beautiful and elaborate dress in the War Dance.
Snake customarily wore a long turkey-beard roach headdress
together with a braided leather head harness. Often he wore a
beaded buckskin shirt and leggings together with a beaded
shoulder bag, the last item of this type among the Shawnees.
Sometimes he would wear a leopard-skin bandolier instead of this
shoulder bag. He invariably carried a long cane whistle that he

sounded during the dance. This whistle, Gibson said, came from a sacred bundle. The last time John Snake danced, however, he dressed in the style of an old-time Shawnee warrior, naked except for his breechcloth, roach headdress, and moccasins.

Several informants recalled that the horses ridden in the horseback parade were more elaborately decorated in times past. Mary Spoon recalled eagle feathers tied in the tails and forelocks of the horses, and shortly before her death in 1975 she gave me two beautiful beaded tassels to be attached on either side of a horse's headstall during the Ride-in. Mrs. C. O. Davis, a Delaware women who attended many Shawnee War Dances as a girl and young woman, remembered that the riders sometimes worked clay into their horses' manes to make them stand up and "look fierce." Cody Mack mentioned that as a boy he had been given a special "medicine paint" to be used by himself and his horse during the Ride-in. For himself this consisted of two horizontal red lines at the corner of each eye with three blue dots in between, and for his mount a red handprint on the right side of the horse's rump and a blue handprint on the left side.

In chapter ten I noted that a small image of a human being in full Shawnee costume is a part of the contents of the Kishpoko bundle. It is probably this item, or another like it, to which Morgan refers, stating, "Some of them in ancient times used idols made of wood" (Morgan *Indian Journals*: p. 47). Anthropologist Carol Rachlin said that she had seen a small wooden image, in a small basket, carried in the Ride-in by chief Little Jim. Mary Spoon confirmed that the image was displayed during the parade but said that it was carried in the hand of the head warrior or war chief.

The performance of the War Dance has apparently been an annual summer event among the Absentee Shawnees for more than a century, for Alford writes: "About the middle of August the chief of the Kis-pu-go clan, who had charge of all matters relating to war, held a war dance. We called that I-la-ni-wag-a-way (man dance, or brave dance). In this dance the music was louder and more of a martial nature, when war whoops took the place of the softly crooned songs of the dance described above [Bread Dance]. This dance was somewhat official, but often was followed by other dances for frolic only, until the end of the season," (*Civilization*: p. 62).

The wearing of the four sacred plumes from the bundle by

selected warriors seems to be a feature of some antiquity as well. Under the title "A Religious Custom" Spencer (*The Shawnee Indians*: pp. 393-8) quotes the following, apparently a garbled account of the Shawnee War dance, by Nancy Chouteau, a Shawnee woman who had seen it as a girl: "Another religious practice they had, which was observed once a year, I think, was as follows: The women carried wood and made a big fire. At midnight the chief brought out a mysterious bundle and took from it some great long feathers. The men dressed themselves in these (putting them in their hair was the usual custom) and sang. If while they were singing they could hear 'the Mother Spirit' sing, that was a sign the world was not coming to an end that year " (Cf. also J. Spencer "Shawnee Folk-lore": pp. 322-3).

No longer a feature in today's Shawnee War Dance is the war pole, though it was apparently standard in the late eighteenth and early nineteenth centuries: "If war was decided upon, a dance was held for luck and to get the warriors in the mood and spirit. To prepare for the ceremony a war pole was cut, and its bark removed; it was then painted black with diagonal stripes of red paint. One end was sharpened and set into the ground, while at the top end a number of scalps were fastened. Some of the Indians painted their faces black with red around the eyes; others reversed this color scheme. All wore feathers in their hair. The dance began with the "fell war whoop." They went around the pole, "writhing their bodies and distorting their faces in a most hideous manner." (D. L. Smith "Shawnee Captivity Ethnography" : p. 34, based upon C. Johnston *A Narrative*: pp. 50-51 and H. Brackenridge *Indian Atrocities*: p. 65) It was formerly the custom during the war speeches for a warrior to strike this war pole prior to speaking, thus indicating how he would strike the enemy in the coming battle, or how he had done so in battles past. This custom is still recalled by the Oklahoma Seneca-Cayugas in their Sun or War Dance, a cognate of the Shawnee Men's Dance. In it a man will rap loudly on the rafters of the Longhouse with a special cane provided for this purpose before making a speech and presenting a gift of candy, oranges, or watermelon to the dancers (Howard "Cultural Persistence and Cultural Change": p. 26). This custom was still remembered by George Whitewater and acknowledged to be "the old customary way". He said that he had thought of reviving it in the Shawnee and Kickapoo War Dances when he made his war speeches. He has not done so, however, because he is of short stature and cannot reach the rafters of the dance arbor even with the added arm length provided by the tomahawk that he carries at this time.

The War Dance is at present performed only by the Absentee Shawnees of the Little River ceremonial ground, but formerly it was common to all Shawnee divisions. It persisted until the late 1930's at the Sand Hill ceremonial ground northeast of Shawnee, Oklahoma. Alfred Switch, who still assists with the singing at Little River, is a member of the White Turkey band and formerly danced in the War Dance there. His War Dance songs, some of which are slightly different from those used at Little River, he learned from his father (Plate 17) who in turn had them from Alfred's grandfather. Switch recalled that the War Dancers of the White Turkey band, such as his father, wore only moccasins, breechcloth, and feather ornaments in the hair. His father, he said, always wore two eagle feathers attached to his scalplock. He would begin growing this scalplock in the spring and it would be about eight inches long by August, when he danced in the War Dance.

Bill Shawnee, the principal singer for the Loyal Shawnees, said that the Loyal band had once performed the War Dance, and he said that he still knew the songs. He was, in fact, a war dancer himself when a youth.

Another site for War Dance performances was the now-defunct Spybuck ceremonial ground near Sperry, Oklahoma. Several Shawnee and Delaware informants recalled attending War Dances at this ground in the period between 1910 and 1938. Freddie Washington, a Delaware of Wann, Oklahoma, recalled the Ride-in and war speeches that characterized these Shawnee War Dances, in which he sometimes joined. Nora Thompson Dean, said that at the Spybuck ground the riders circled the ground only once in the Ride-in before dismounting to dance. Nora remembered that the singers were seated on the north side of the ground, but Freddie Washington remembered them at the west end.

It seems evident that the Men's Dance or War Dance, in essentially the same form in which it is performed by the Absentee Shawnees today, was once fairly widespread in eastern North America. How much of this distribution can be credited to diffusion from the Shawnees is a matter for conjecture, but they seem to have played a major role. This Woodland of type War

Dance is still danced by the Oklahoma and Mexican bands of
Kickapoos (though not by the Kansas Kickapoos). Both Shawnee
and Kickapoo informants agree that the Kickapoos acquired the
dance from the Shawnees, though the Kickapoo dance lacks the
Ride-in feature.

The Oklahoma Seneca-Cayuga Sun or War Dance, though it
has acquired some special features, is basically the same
ceremony as the Shawnee Men's Dance (Howard "Cultural
Persistence and Cultural Change": pp. 25–26) and the same is
undoubtedly true for the War Dance of the New York, Ontario, and
Quebec Iroquois. The Oklahoma Seneca-Cayugas, for whom the
dance has become a weather-controlling ritual, perform the dance
twice annually: once during the latter part of April and again in
August immediately following their Green Corn Ceremony.
Alfred Switch and Bill Shawnee often traveled to Turkeyford to
assist in the singing. The Oklahoma Seneca-Cayugas, though
they retire to the woods to dress and paint, march or dance on foot
to the Longhouse at the beginning of the dance. Earlier Iroquois
practice, however, may have involved a horseback Ride-in as a
regular feature. J.V.H. Clark (*Onondaga*: p. 66, quoted in E.
Tooker *The Iroquois Ceremonial of Midwinter*: p. 166) describes
such a Ride-in by about thirty young braves preceding the
Onondaga War dance.

The old Delaware War Dance or *Ilawkan* ("Men's Dance"),
performed for the last time in 1927 or 1928, was undoubtedly a
close relative of the Shawnee Men's dance: "During the War
Dance the men would ride in on horses. The singers used a water
drum and were placed on the north side of the dance area. During
the dance men would periodically stand and recite deeds of valor.
This was called *Pekendma*. Only one woman was ever allowed to
Pekendma. Her name was Ollie Buffalo and she was said to have
killed an enemy" (T. Stewart "Oklahoma Delaware Women's
Dance Clothes": p. 21). Nora Thompson Dean, the Delaware
informant quoted in the above account, attended the 1973
performance of the Shawnee War dance at Little River and
recognized two of the Shawnee War Dance songs as identical with
those of her tribe.

Particularly interesting in view of the close connections
between the Shawnees and the Creeks during the period of the Red
Stick War was the statement of my Creek informant, Ira Bird
Creek, in 1971. Bird Creek, a member of the Creek town known as

Muddy-water, said that he had witnessed a "Buffalo dance", actually a War Dance, at his town ceremonial ground in the 1930's. Bird Creek described the dance as similar in every respect to the Shawnee War Dance at Little River, which he has observed on a number of occasions. The Creek Dance involved two of the main dancers carrying sacred objects, probably from a war bundle, consisting of a pipe and a war club. The dancers danced in a rough crescent formation facing the singers. The dance, Ira said, has not been performed since that time. Could this be the "Dance of the Lakes" supposedly introduced among the Creeks by the Shawnees in 1811? (see R. S. Cotterill *The Southern Indians*: p. 174; T. S. Woodward *Woodward's Reminiscences of the Creek, or Muscogee Indians*: p. 95) Seekabo, a Shawnee lieutenant of Tecumseh, stayed behind with the Creeks to confirm Tecumseh's teachings and promulgate the new war songs and the "Dance of the Lakes" which the great Shawnee leader had introduced (T. A. Nunez, "Creek Nativism and the Creek War of 1813–1814" Pt. 1: p. 8). This would seem to be very possible in view of the statements by Absentee informants to the effect that Tecumseh had a special involvement with the Kishpoko war bundle, and added the French-style trefoil tomahawk to its contents. Another possibility, however, is the Loyal Shawnee Buffalo Dance, to be described in the following chapter, which is also attributed to Tecumseh by some Shawnees.

13

Ceremonies of Late Summer and Autumn

DEATH FEASTS

Feasts in honor of the spirits of the dead are practically universal in eastern North America, and the Shawnees are no exception to the rule. The Loyal Shawnees generally observe their feast for the dead on the weekend following their Green Corn Dance, which means it generally occurs a week or two before their annual Buffalo Dance. In 1969 it took place on 9 August, in 1971 on 31 July. The Absentee Shawnees also observe their death feast at this season.

Mary Spoon described the custom as practiced at the present time by the Absentees: food is prepared as if for a group of living people. It is put out on a table in one room of the house and a person delegated to perform the task then addresses the spirits. The spirits are told that their relatives in the world of the living think of them fondly and wish to honor them with food prepared especially for them. The person may also ask the spirits not to return to bother the living, especially if a ghost resembling a deceased relative has been observed in the vicinity, or if a person has been consistently dreaming of a deceased family member.

The light in the room is then extinguished and the food is left exposed for some hours in the empty room. It is thought that during this time the spirits of the dead come and partake of the food. Generally the spirits, because they are not flesh and blood, eat only the "spirit" or essence of the food, leaving its material substance behind. It is perfectly permissable for the family members, when they come back to the room and turn on the light, to eat the food. It is thought, however, that the food will have lost all its nutritive value. Sometimes, according to Mary, it is observed that not only the "spirit" but also some of the substance of the food is gone. For example, the level of coffee in a cup will be lower when the family returns.

In some variants of the death feast, according to Mary Spoon, a speaker addresses the spirits after the family has returned as well as before. The death feast is a family-oriented ceremony rather than a public ritual, as evidenced by the fact that it is often carried on privately by individual Shawnees who have married into other tribes and moved away from Oklahoma. Claude Medford Jr. notes that Wilbur Dirt, a Shawnee who married Lilly Abbey of the Texas band of Koasati, observed the annual death feast on the Texas reservation: "He would have Lilly prepare a feast for the dead people at a certain time of the year, set a table, put bowls of food on the table, serve the plates and leave the room."

In regard to the death feast, which he calls the "ghost feast," C. F. Voegelin (*The Shawnee Female Deity*: p. 15) writes:

> The beneficiary of a ghost feast is primarily the spirit of the dead to whom food is offered; the obligations of the feast giver are quite intricate and include the offering of appropriate food and drink, as for example whiskey to the spirit of one who was a drunkard during life, as well as the inheritance of obligations of deceased feast givers. The relation between the feast giver and Our Grandmother is indirect, through the spirit recipient who dwells with the Creator. When an old woman was on her deathbed, she said to her children, "Whenever you raise anything you enjoy, prepare me a dry roasting ear with meat, simply cooked, and the Creator will help you, through me, to get along in this world."

The Oklahoma Seneca-Cayugas observe an annual feast of the dead in a manner very similar to that of the Shawnees (Howard "Cultural Persistence and Cultural Change as Reflected in Oklahoma Seneca-Cayuga Ceremonialism": p. 27) They generally observe the feast while they are still encamped for their annual Green Corn Ceremony, but after its conclusion. Following an address to the spirits, which takes place in the longhouse, they return to their family camps and place food on tables outdoors before their tents, where it is left exposed overnight. As with the Shawnees, they are free to consume the food the next morning but say that one derives no nourishment from it.

Closely related to the death feast is the Shawnee First Fruit ceremony, concerning which C.F. Voegelin writes (*The Shawnee Female Deity*: p. 15):

The former First Fruit ceremony is still preserved by some individuals who set out, cooked, the first corn, beans, squash, melons, etc., of the season for Our Grandmother to taste. This she does during the night, and the next morning those who set the food out eat it. Opinion is divided as to whether the Creator comes down to every feast. The common way for her to receive food from feasts given in her worship is by means of the spirits, those who are dead, who eat in her behalf except at the ghost feast which is not given in worship of the Creator but directly for the benefit of the dead. In order to nourish the Creator, the feast must be specifically in her honor, and certain types of food must be prepared, or at least some foods which are especially nourishing food. Since buffalo are no longer available and other feasts are frequently neglected nowadays, the Creator is hungry, an unhappy condition which reflects on the Shawnee. Reasoning here is somewhat circular: because the Shawnee are poor, the Creator is hungry; because the Creator is impoverished, the Shawnee are poor.

BUFFALO DANCE

The Buffalo dance (Thothekawe, Pethothekawe) is performed as a separate ceremony only by the Loyal band of Shawnees. Until a few years ago it was customarily held on the Monday following the Saturday of the Green Corn Dance. Of late, however, several weeks may intervene between the two. The reason for this postponement is the difficulty experienced by younger Shawnees in getting away on a Monday workday, and the fact that there are other Indian events on the July and August weekends. Therefore the Buffalo Dance now takes place in late August or even early September (in 1969 on 6 September, in 1971 on 28 August, in 1973 on 8 September).

The Buffalo Dance is the only major ceremony of the Shawnees that is not credited, in terms of its origin, to Our Grandmother. Accordingly it does not take place inside the sacred precincts of the ceremonial ground like the Bread dances and the Green Corn Dance but rather in an open area just south of it. There are two versions of how the Loyal Shawnees acquired the ceremony. The first is cited by C. F. Voegelin (ibid.: p. 13):

The Buffalo Head Dance forms an addendum to the Green Corn Dance of the Cherokee Shawnee. It is not given by the other Shawnee bands and is exceptional in being the only annual ceremonial dance which Our Grandmother did not create; it has, nevertheless, taken on the general pattern and spirit of the divinely created dance. It was originally a war dance given to Tecumseh (*circa* 1800) by his guardian spirit, a buffalo. Those who perform it nowadays, all kin of Tecumseh, are conscious of its secular origin but say that their purpose in performing it is to worship Our Grandmother. Prayer to the Creator is especially for plants which buffalo, now nonexistent, find nourishing. The ceremony is paradoxical in many ways and is interesting in this connection as demonstrating implicitly the extent to which the annual ceremonial dances are felt to be occasions for worshipping the Creator.

Two of my informants, Lewis Dick and Bill Alec, subscribed to this story that Tecumseh had introduced the dance, and affirmed that its performance is still directed by Tecumseh descendants. Ranny Carpenter, however, traced its origin not to Tecumseh but to a priest-shaman of mixed blood named Daugherty. Ranny's origin legend for the Buffalo Dance, which he gave in essentially the same form in 1969 and 1971, follows:

THE ORIGIN OF THE BUFFALO DANCE

Many years ago, when the Shawnees were living near present Kansas City, there was a medicine man, a mixblood like myself, named Daugherty. He had only one eye. He had been blessed by many spirits and was known as a great healer by his people. There were many such healers in those days. They were like saints.

At this time a party of Shawnee hunters, young men, left the village and went out on the plains after buffalo. When these young men did not return at the expected time, this man Daugherty went out alone seeking them. He came to the buffalo country and spent many days looking for the missing party, but failed to find them.

As he was traveling alone over the prairies, he was approached by a white (albino) buffalo bull with a black beard. We Shawnees believe that every species of animal or bird life has its own chief, and this is always a white animal or bird. The buffalo bull that appeared to Daugherty was slightly smaller than the average buffalo, but was nevertheless the boss of all buffalo. This white bull with the black chin approached Daugherty in a belligerent manner, tossing its horns and pawing the earth with its hooves. Daugherty was alone and caught out in the open, so he gave himself up for dead, but the buffalo bull did not harm him. It came so near to him that he could put his hands on its head. Daugherty did this [a Shawnee motion indicating that one is asking for a blessing] and the white buffalo bull spoke to him, saying: "I have been watching you for some time, and I see that you have a good heart. You are interested not in yourself but in your people. The Buffalo people, of whom I am the chief, have decided to give you a blessing. From now on, when you want something, you may call upon me."

At the time, Daugherty refused the gift. He did not call upon the white buffalo but prayed to the Creator instead. Many years passed, and Daugherty became an old man. At this time the white buffalo bull appeared to him again. Daugherty was hunting on the bluffs overlooking the Missouri when the white bull approached him. This time the buffalo spoke to him as follows, "I am returning to the spirit world whence I came, but first I want to show you something. Tomorrow you must prepare yourself and come with me. I will meet you here." This time Daugherty decided to accept the offer. He returned to the village and dressed himself in his finest clothes. He told his relatives that he was leaving on a journey, perhaps for the last time. The next morning he went to the spot designated by the white buffalo bull, on the bank of the Missouri. Some of the people from the village followed him at a distance to see where he was going, as they were concerned about him. The Missouri was swollen and almost over its banks at this time.

The white buffalo appeared as it had promised and told Daugherty to follow it. It then walked to the river, plunged in, and disappeared under the surface. Daugherty followed, and he too was seen to disappear beneath the waves. The people watching thought that he must have drowned, but decided to keep watch at the spot for a time [because they knew he had power].

Four days later he reappeared out of the water at the place where he had gone in. Those who had been watching noticed that he was dressed as a Buffalo dancer. On his head he wore a buffalo cap with horns. His body was naked except for a breechcloth, and he was painted with bluish colored mud. He told the people that he was well and that the white buffalo bull had taken him to the spirit abode of the buffalo. Here the buffalo people had feasted him and taught him the Buffalo Dance. When he had learned the songs and the procedures of the ceremony the white buffalo bull told him, "You must now return to your people and teach them how to sing these songs and perform this dance. In this way they will secure blessings from the buffalo people." He was then carried back to the place where he had entered the river by the white buffalo and emerged once again. When he returned to the village he taught the dance to his people and we have performed it ever since.

Ranny Carpenter's origin legend for the dance, regardless of any historical value it may or may not possess, is extremely interesting in its resemblance to other tribal origin legends, particularly those of the Central Algonkian tribes, which account for the origins of certain of their bundle ceremonies. The mention of the white buffalo as the "boss" or chief of the Buffalo people echoes an old and widespread Shawnee and Delaware belief. E. W. Voegelin (E. W. Voegelin, C. Rafinesque, C. F. Voegelin, and E. Lilly *Walum Olum*: p. 191) notes: "Many tribes hold that each of all the different species of animals has its own chief. This animal chief is usually larger than an ordinary animal, or pure white, or both." The same idea was expressed by Mary Spoon in 1971: "Now and then we see a bird or animal that is like others of its kind but is completely white. We Shawnees say that these white animals are the chiefs of their species. Once we saw a white bluejay out front [of her house] here. I suppose he was the chief of the jays.":

At the time of this writing I have witnessed three performances of the Loyal Shawnee Buffalo Dance. All were very similar to one another, therefore my description of the 1971 dance may be regarded as typical.

LOYAL SHAWNEE BUFFALO DANCE

I arrived at the Whiteoak ceremonial ground about 2:00 P.M. on 28 August 1971. In visiting at the various camps I learned that Bill Grass, a Sauk Indian married to a Shawnee, had been selected as the head dancer for this year's Buffalo Dance. Another adult dancer planning to participate was Bob White, a well known

Oklahoma Seneca-Cayuga ritualist of part-Shawnee background. Bob had served as the head Buffalo dancer the previous year. Another man of mixed Shawnee, Delaware, and white descent was the third adult dancer. The remainder of the dancers, about twelve, were all small Shawnee boys.

The dance was held, as is customary, on a flat grassy spot a few yards south of the ground used for the other ceremonial dances. In the center of this area, by way of preparation for the Buffalo Dance, a fire crane consisting of a stout horizontal pole supported at either end by forked posts about five feet high, had been erected. From this, by means of chains and hooks, two large iron kettles of corn mush were suspended. One, I was told, was sweetened and the other was both unsalted and unsweetened. Cloth covers were tied over both to keep out the dust raised by dancing and insects. West of the fire crane, at the edge of the area to be used in the Buffalo Dance, a canvas was spread upon the ground as a seat for the "Buffaloes," the costumed male dancers. Folding chairs were set up for the women dancers and volunteer male dancers on the north, south, and northwest of the Buffalo Dance area. The singers sat on folding chairs on the north side, which was their usual position in regard to the dance ground in the Loyal band.

At 5:00 P.M. the men and boys who were to be Buffaloes retired to the south edge of the camping area to paint themselves for the dance. Until a few years ago, according to Ranny Carpenter, they went to the creek to do this, but at present they merely use a washtub of water to mix the blue mud that they used as body paint. All of the dancers stripped to the waist before painting. On their chests they painted the design of a bison's head. The nipples of the breasts served as the "eyes" of the bison in each case. Blue-grey mud scooped up from the ground mixed with water from the washtub was used for this painting.

In addition each was painted, at the outside edge of either eye, with red paint. This part of the painting was identical with that used in the Bread Dance. I noted three designs: a single red line extending out from the corner of the eye, three lines radiating from the corner of the eye, or two parallel lines drawn out from the corner of the eye with three red dots in between. This red paint was applied by Bennie Barnes, a young ritual assistant. Barnes carried the same bead-decorated buckskin bag of red paint that is customarily employed in the Bread Dances. Barnes and another young assistant (who were not costumed as Buffaloes) were also

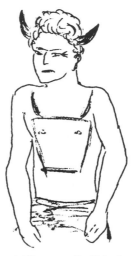

Fig. 9.   A Shawnee Buffalo dancer

painted with red face paint; as were the three singers Ranny
Carpenter (rattle man or second), Bill Shawnee (head singer and
drummer), and Bill Alec (second). Every singer had a single line of
paint extending out from the corner of each eye. As head Buffalo
dancer Bill Grass, in addition to his painting, wore a headdress of
bison hide with horns attached at either side that I had loaned to
him for the occasion. Once painted, the Buffaloes waited at the
edge of the camp.

As the Buffaloes were completing their painting, the singers
began the first set of songs. These were songs of the Women's
Cluster Dance. As they began, a number of women and girls rose
from their chairs and assembled facing the singers, joining in
with the singing from time to time as is customary. The women
wore shawls but otherwise were not dressed in Indian costume.
After several Cluster Dance songs Bill Shawnee changed to
Women's Straight Dance songs, and the women formed a single
file and began a counterclockwise circuit of the fire crane. After a
few rounds of this the music again changed, this time to the Dove
Dance or Women's Side Dance. A few of these songs ended the first
episode, and the women resumed their seats on various folding
chairs opposite the singers.

Now the Buffaloes led by Bill Grass and Bob White, marched to
the dance ground and seated themselves on the canvas at the west

edge of the dance area. After a short while they all stood and walked in a single file, counterclockwise, around the fire crane and positioned themselves in a row before the singers, facing them. Now Bill Grass, the head Buffalo whooped four times to signal that the bison were ready and on the fourth whoop the other Buffaloes whooped as well. The singers now began a set of Buffalo Dance songs, and the Buffaloes began to dance, using a simple toe-heel left, toe-heel right step, the dancers in a single file behind their horned leader, moving counterclockwise around the fire crane. They stomped a bit harder than in the Bread Dance, to imitate bison bulls. Some supernumerary dancers, including the famous Creek singer Netche Grey, joined the male Buffaloes at this time. These volunteer male dancers were not painted. They joined in at the end of the file of Buffaloes. When the male dancers were about halfway around they were joined by a file of women dancing on their right. These women represented bison cows, and used the same step as the men. At each change of phrase in the song and likewise at the end of each song the men and boys whooped. At the end of the episode both men and women walked around the fire crane one more time, and as they passed the singers each intoned *"N'yaweh"* (Thanks!) then they resumed their seats. The costumed Buffaloes always sat on the canvas at the west edge of the dance area, not in chairs.

Three more episodes of Women's Dances, alternating with three more sets of the Buffalo Dance followed, making eight sets in all. Each episode of Women's Dances was followed by an episode of Buffalo Dance in which both men and women participated. Midway during the last Buffalo Dance episode Eva Secondline, one of the matrons at the Whiteoak ground, untied and removed the cloth cover from the kettle of unsweetened mush hanging from the fire crane. This was a signal for the male Buffaloes to dip their hands into the kettle for a taste of mush, mush being a favorite food of bison according to Shawnee belief. The women dancers, as buffalo cows also tried to crowd in and secure a handful or spoonful of this mush, but the male Buffaloes would, in the manner of the species, attempt to prevent this by butting them with their heads, or pushing them away with their shoulders. Often two bulls would converge on a hapless cow to prevent her access to the kettle. The cows in turn would sometimes attempt to duck in quickly and secure some mush, and then escape, but they were usually blocked off by the wary bulls. In a spirit of high hilarity mixed with frustration they would sometimes smear mush on the faces and bodies of the men who were trying to block their escape. These pranks ended the afternoon's dancing.

When things had quieted down a bit after the final Buffalo Dance episode the venerable Frank Bob rose from his chair and delivered a short but moving prayer appropriate to the occasion. Following the prayer paper plates were produced and each buffalo was given a plate of sweetened mush by Eva Secondline. When all of the costumed male dancers had been served the supernumerary male dancers, the women dancers, and a young girl dancer were served, in that order. When all of the dancers had been served others present who had not danced were allowed to help themselves to the remaining mush in the kettles. It was now about 7:00 P.M., and everyone retired to the various family camps for the evening meal.

The night of social dancing began about 9:00. In addition to numerous episodes of the Leading or Ordinary Stomp Dance there were episodes of Women's "Straight" Dance, Dove Dance, Face Dance, Cherokee Dance, Go Get 'em Dance, Stirrup Dance, and the Shawnee or Bear Dance. These dances continued until 2:00 A.M. the following morning.

The exact sequence of dance episodes in the Buffalo Dance itself may vary from one performance to the next. In 1969 the sequence was the same as that just described. In 1970, however, my notes indicate this sequence: (1) Buffalo Dance, men and women; (2) Women's Straight Dance; (3) Buffalo Dance, men and women; (4) Women's Cluster Dance; (5) Women's "Straight" Dance; (6) Buffalo Dance, men and women; (7) Women's Cluster Dance, followed by the Women's "Side" or Dove Dance; and (8) Buffalo Dance, men and women, with the customary battle for the mush.

Additional information on the Loyal Shawnee Buffalo dance, as performed in the period just after this group of Shawnees emigrated to the Indian Territory (1869) is provided by Sam Perry in a 1937 interview. (Indian Archives, Oklahoma Historical Society 8: pp. 189-190):

> The Buffalo dance, as celebrated in the early days, followed within a few days after the Green corn dance. The Green corn dance was usually held the latter part of August, and a few days later came the Buffalo dance.
> Hunters were sent out to kill buffalo for use in the feast. Shawnee hunters rode alongside the running bison and aimed their arrows just back of the shoulder. The bison meat, once it was brought back to the camp, was prepared by the women. The Buffalo dance itself began late in the afternoon, so dancing and eating would continue all night, [the people] stopping at intervals to eat and rest.

The buffaloes were fat by the first of September or the end of August. Later, when bison became unavailable, beef from cattle was used in the Buffalo dance.

Speck (F. G. Speck *Oklahoma Delaware Ceremonies, Feasts and Dances*: pp. 67–69) describes the Buffalo Dance ceremony as it was formerly performed by the Delawares. It is virtually identical with the Shawnee dance. He in fact notes that: "the Delawares . . . still participate in the Buffalo Dance when they visit the Shawnees . . . " Speck's account mentions kettles of hominy rather than mush, and notes that men sometimes used a mussel-shell spoon, rather than their bare hands, to secure hominy at the climax of the dance (Speck ibid.: p. 69). This feature was also described, as part of the Shawnee Buffalo Dance, by Mrs. C. O. Davis, a Delaware woman who used to attend the dances at Whiteoak in the 1920s. She recalled seeing only wooden spoons, though she had heard that shell spoons were used at an earlier period.

The Oklahoma Seneca-Cayugas formerly performed the Buffalo Dance in the same form as the Shawnees and Delawares (J. Howard "Environment and Culture: The Case of the Oklahoma Seneca-Cayuga" Pt. 2: p. 12) and the New York Seneca Buffalo dance seems to have been identical as well (A. Parker *Parker on the Iroquois* p. 125). Parker (ibid.: p. 67) includes a native drawing of the Seneca Buffalo Dance which shows the kettles of mush as in the Shawnee version.

In 1967, at the Nebraska Winnebago centennial powwow, a Buffalo Dance, led by a Winnebago named Smith, was performed as an exhibition dance one afternoon. It involved a file of male dancers, led by Mr. Smith, executing a stamping toe-heel step and following a serpentine progression around the dance arena. Smith wore a buffalo-hide cap with attached horns and from time to time he would lean forward and imitate a buffalo bull, shaking his horned headdress and pawing the ground with his toe. Later Smith told me that the Winnebagos had secured their Buffalo Dance from the Shawnees many years ago. He was obviously proud of the dance and commented, "We have the *real* Buffalo Dance, the *Shawnee* Buffalo Dance."

Other tribes apparently admired the Shawnee Buffalo Dance as well, once such being the Seminoles. Swanton's diagram of the Chiaha Seminole ceremonial ground in 1912 (J. R. Swanton *Social Organization and Social Usages of the Indians of the Creek Confederacy*: p. 293) has a spot outside the square ground labeled "Where the Shawnee Danced the Buffalo Dance at the preceding

Busk." Which group of Shawnees were involved or what form the
dance took, are unfortunately not indicated.

Alfred Switch said that the Absentee Shawnees have a Buffalo
Dance, but it is incorporated into the Bread Dance. The Buffalo
songs, he says, are used during the third episode (the second of the
mixed men and women dance). He also commented that the
Pekowitha division of the Shawnees used to have a separate
Buffalo Dance at the time they had a settlement northwest of the
city of Shawnee, Oklahoma. This Buffalo Dance was performed at
night and only men danced. No kettles of mush figured in this
dance. Switch, who is a singer, maintained that the songs used by
the Absentees in the Buffalo Dance episode of the Bread Dance,
and formerly in a separate Buffalo Dance, were and are the same
as those used in the Loyal Shawnee Buffalo Dance.

PEACH SEED DICE GAME AND FALL BREAD DANCE

At all three of the Shawnee ceremonial grounds the ceremonial
season closes with the fall Bread Dance. Because this dance is
held at the end of the agricultural season, which is the harvest
time, and at the beginning of the hunting season, its emphasis is
slightly different from that of the spring Bread Dance. Now it is
the male role, as hunter, instead of the female role as gardener,
that is at the fore, and while the spring Bread Dance has as its
immediate objective a plea for plentiful crops, the fall dance is a
prayer for good hunting. The autumn dance, however, also serves
as a thanksgiving for a bountiful harvest. Alford (T. W. Alford
Civilization: p. 62) puts this nicely, stating, "Early in the
fall . . . the dance was held that closed the season for dances
until the next spring. This was somewhat similar to the spring
Bread Dance, except that it took the form of a thanksgiving
ceremony, when a prayer of gratitude was offered to the Great
Spirit, and an earnest petition for an abundant game season."

In both the spring and the fall Bread Dances the male and
females roles are neatly balanced off. At the two Absentee
ceremonial grounds the performance of the fall Bread Dance,
except for the prayer, is identical with that of the spring dance. At
Whiteoak however, there is a slight change in the order of the
dance episodes. Here a mixed Bread Dance episode, led off by the
twelve male "hunters" begins the traditional cycle of eight
episodes, the exact reverse of the procedure at the spring dance. As

Bill Shawnee commented, "This is the man's time of year, so the men lead off." The sequence of dance episodes at the 1972 fall Bread dance at Whiteoak, then, was: (1) Bread Dance, men and women; (2) Women's Side or Dove Dance (Pawithekawe); (3) Bread Dance, men and women; (4) Women's Cluster Dance (Kokeki), followed by the Women's Straight Dance (Beshiwekawe); (5) Bread Dance, men and women; (6) Same as (4), above; (7) Pumpkin Dance (Wapikonekawe), men and women; and (8) Same as (4) above.

In spite of the slightly different emphases in the spring and fall Bread Dances, the prayers at the two are remarkably similar. An excellent reproduction of a fall Bread Dance prayer delivered in 1933 is given by C. F. Voegelin (*The Shawnee Female Deity*: pp. 13-):

Well, now all of you, my sisters and my brothers, you must come close around here to our seats, you must listen. That's the place we are coming to. For that reason, the one who is called paapoothkwe created our lives for us. That, to repeat, is why you (addressing Creator) created us, for us to pray to you at this season. For that again you must have pity. You created for us the Corn Person, and another thing (addressing Pumpkin), you, Pumpkin Person, you should lie still and grow beautifully. For that also you (addressing Creator) have pity. Our Corn Person (addressing Creator) you created to produce more food. And another thing, Earth Person, you (addressing Earth Person), the Creator created you to be still and hold us on your lap for eternity. You must grow out well and settle down with a green head. For that also you (addressing Creator) have pity. Now all of you around here who are sitting down and facing us (addressing the winds), my grandfathers, carry us along slowly. For that reason the Creator created you when you go by at all times, you North Wind Person. Now also you, Summer Man, that's why she created you so that you could carry along heat for your grandchildren in that way as you slowly pass along. Because of that again (addressing Creator) you have pity. And all of you, Tree Men, you who are standing up growing and producing for us. And also you, Water Person, what I am asking you is to be still as you lie down floating along. Because of that also (addressing Creator), you must have pity. All of you Thunderers, my grandfathers, you all quietly bring water and sprinkle for us at the places where we live, as you go slowly around. But because of that again (addressing Creator), you must have pity. Also you, you Cyclone Man, you take pity on us out here where all of us are created. Because of that also (addressing Creator), you must have pity. That is a pitiful way in which I am supplicating you, my grandfathers and my grandmothers. Because of that also (addressing Creator), you must have pity. Now also you (addressing fire in center of dance square), you who are Fire Person, and you (addressing tobacco), Old Man, you witnesses whom the Creator created for us, you are carrying us along, you are working for us in that you take up there our message, the prayers of your grandchildren. Now from here on, give our life some more (an addition to the things already possessed and mentioned) for eternity, as you create for us. Because of that also, you must have pity.

Because (addressing spectators) she created us and took pity on us that way, we pray to her when the time comes for us to give a dance and pray to her at that place up there. In that way we make her feel good, as we are being interesting to the one who created us. She said that she would feel good over there if she saw her grandchildren having a lively dance and prayer. Because of that also, (addressing Creator) you must have pity. That's why too (addressing spectators) that if she is forgotten by her grandchildren for eternity paapoothkwe says, "I will feel badly." If she finds only the tracks of insects on our dance-ground at such a time, she would not hear her grandchildren praying to her any more. What she would do next would be to come and discard us in some way that would be frightful for us.

And also you young men and my sisters, you must respect this way in which we pray. It might be better even for the time being if you did not get drunk. And also, you must not speak the white man's language. After the dance nothing that you want to do will be harmful.

That's all that I am able to say to you this evening. All of you, my sisters and now also our brothers, tonight we must borrow the way our relatives dance [referring to the Leading or "Ordinary Stomp" dance, which the Shawnees attribute to the Creeks]. But that's the way you must all stay with it, all of you, everybody who stays over here [referring to the fact that the members of the local ceremonial ground must continue dancing throughout the night, JH]. That's how we must try to dance until morning. Then let's go home. That's the last part of what I tell you who are around here.

Though somewhat longer, this prayer is essentially the same as that given at the 1974 fall Bread Dance at Whiteoak by Chief Jimmo White. As his predecessor had done forty-one years earlier, Chief White addressed the various powers by name and asked for good health and long life for all, after which the meat and cornbread were distributed.

A special feature preceding the fall Bread Dance at all three Shawnee grounds is a ritual dice game played by shaking marked peach stones in a wooden bowl. The Bowl dice game is the functional equivalent of the Football game that precedes the spring Bread Dance. Because the men-against-women Football game, connected with rain-bringing and fertility, would not be appropriate in the autumn, the Bowl dice game is substituted. As in the Football game, the two sexes are opposed, and the same rule that operates in connection with the Football game in the spring applies to the Bowl dice game in the fall: the losers, either the men or the women, must provide the firewood to be used in the forthcoming ceremonies. All twelve male hunters and all twelve female cooks must participate in the Bowl dice game or they cannot dance in the Bread Dance.

Six peach stones, which are symbolic of the six name-group phratries of the Shawnees, are the dice. They are filed and sanded smooth, then painted blue on one side and red on the other. Either fifty or one hundred sticks are used as counters, the number is decided upon prior to play. The men and women form two groups, facing one another. Between the two teams is a folded blanket, and upon it is a large wooden bowl with steep sides and a flat bottom. The six dice are placed in this bowl. Two persons, one male, one female, play at a time. Each player in turn, kneeling on the ground, grasps the bowl at either side and jolts it slightly on the folded blanket. This causes the dice to "jump" an inch or two into the air and fall again.

The score is determined this way: if all six red sides or all six blue sides turn up simultaneously the player scores five points for his or her side. If the player turns up five sides of one color and one of another, he or she gains one point. Any other combination than the two noted above scores a point for the opposite side and the opposing player is allowed to shake the bowl. Each player shakes the bowl until he or she has lost five points, regardless of how many points he or she has won. At this point another player from that person's side takes his or her place. The game continues in this way until either the men or the women have won all fifty (or one hundred) of the counting sticks. The game begins exactly one week before the fall Bread Dance. It may last only a few hours or as long as two or three days. Enormous enthusiasm is generated during the game. A lucky player making a series of scoring plays is encouraged by the shouts of his or her teammates, while disappointed groans accompany one who "goes out" immediately without scoring. Each side has a spokesman constantly busy selecting new players to replace those who are forced out.

The preceding description applies to the game as played at the two Absentee grounds. At Whiteoak, according to Bill Shawnee, the dice are made of coffee beans, but otherwise the game is identical.

According to John Ellis the Absentee Shawnees, at one time in the past, allowed their Bowl dice game to lapse for a number of years. It was then decided to revive it, but no one could remember how many dice were used (the neighboring Kickapoos and Sauks use nine stones, which could have been a possible source of confusion). A council was held to determine the number, and various persons offered opinions as to the correct number of peach stones. Finally a young man asked permission to speak. He said, "I am much younger than many here, but I believe the correct number is six." He then told of searching for peach stones of the right sort from a wild peach tree. He was able to find only six, though he looked carefully. This number, six, was therefore accepted as correct.

The Bowl dice game with many variants is widespread in North America. The form played by the Shawnees is most similar to that of the Iroquois, who also generally employ six (though sometimes eight) peach stones. The Shawnees, in fact, commonly play the game with the Oklahoma Seneca-Cayugas at Turkeyford, Oklahoma. The Oklahoma Seneca-Cayugas play the game as the fourth and final sacred rite in their annual Green Corn ceremony, a custom formerly observed by the Wyandots as well.

Today, among the Shawnees, the Bowl dice game employing six peach stones is played only in connection with the fall Bread Dance. Formerly it was played at other seasons as well, merely for amusement, for Trowbridge (C. C. Trowbridge *Shawnese Traditions*: p. 51) writes, "They have also the game of bowl. In which they use six plumb stones white on one side & black on the other. These are put in a bowl and thrown up—when they fall the black side counts & the white passes unnoticed. This game is described in Chippeway games." A very similar game, but one not employing a bowl to shake the dice, is described by Thomas Ridout, who witnessed it during his captivity in 1788 (M. Edgar *Ten Years of Upper Canada in Peace and War, 1805-1815*: p. 358): "If we encamped at an earlier hour than usual, or remained a whole day in one place, which we were obliged sometimes to do on account of the rain (this being a remarkably rainy spring), the Indian young men and women amused themselves at a game of chance played by sitting in a circle, holding a blanket open in the centre, in which a certain number of bits of wood, black on one side and white on the other, were thrown up, and according to the number of black or white sides which fell uppermost, the game was reckoned." This is apparently the same game noted by Trowbridge (*Shawnese Traditions*: p. 51): "They have a game resembling dice. It is played with pieces of horn shaped like a button, which are thrown up and when they fall all the spots are counted. Six of these pieces of horn are used & the game is concluded when one of the parties has counted fifty."

In recent years the Absentee Shawnees have adopted a version of the bowl dice game from the Kickapoos. This version employs seven bone dice, two of which are animal (turtle) effigies and five of which are round disks. The upper or smooth side of these dice is

left its natural white color, the underside is painted red or blue.
The score in this game, which is purely a secular amusement, is
computed thus:

Two turtles white, all others blue: 20 points
Two turtles blue, all others white: 20 points
One turtle white, all other pieces blue: 10 points
One turtle blue, all other pieces white: 10 points
All pieces blue or all pieces white: 8 points
One round piece blue, all other pieces white: 5 points
One round piece white, all other pieces blue: 5 points
Two round pieces blue, all other pieces white: 2 points
Two round pieces white, all other pieces blue: 2 points
One turtle and one round piece blue, all others white: 2 points
One turtle and one round piece white, all others blue: 2 points

Twelve points wins a game. Penny-ante gambling often accompanies this version of bowl dice. Until the death of her daughter
Frances in 1971, Mary Spoon frequently sponsored dice games of
this type at her home near Tecumseh, Oklahoma These were
attended by Shawnees, Kickapoos, Sauks, and Seminoles, friends
and relatives of Mary.

SHAWNEE PEYOTISM

The Peyote religion is not a part of the traditional ceremonial
cycle of the Shawnees, yet no discussion of Shawnee
ceremonialism would be complete without mention of it. The
Peyote religion has adherents in all three Shawnee bands and
does not seem to militate against traditional ceremonialism in
any way. The leaders at all three ceremonial dance grounds, in
fact, are also Peyotists and attend Peyote meetings (ceremonies)
regularly during the fall, winter and early spring when the
traditional Shawnee ceremonial cycle is dormant.

In the 1930s E. W. Voegelin assembled the following information concerning the introduction of Peyote among the Shawnees.

The Shawnee Jim Clark received peyote from the Comanche in the late
1890's. Informants say the Shawnee have had peyote as a plant for a long time,
using it to keep from getting tired on the march, for moistening the mouth when
dry-camping and to relieve hunger. The first Absentee Shawnee meeting was
held by the Scotts in 1900, under the tutelage of the Kickapoo. John Wilson was
among the Shawnee about 1894, and George Fourleaf (Delaware) brought
peyote to White Oak from Mexico about 1898. Ernest Spybuck got his moon
from the Delaware near Dewey, while the Panthers are said to use the Yuchi
manner. The majority of the Shawnee, however, use the standard Kiowa-
Arapaho moon. Some Shawnee liken the leader's staff to the staff in the Green
Corn Dance, and there is a legend of getting power from peyote which some say
was not peyote but another plant which preceded it. (W. La Barre *The Peyote
Cult* 119-120, quoting E. W. Voegelin's *Shawnee Field Notes*)

The Shawnees have in the past practiced both of the two major types of Peyote ritual, the Big Moon (Cf. V. Petrullo *The Diabolic Root*: pp. 87-117; La Barre *The Peyote Cult*: pp. 151-161; J. J. Mathews *The Osages*: pp. 740-758) and the Little Moon or Basic Plains rite (Petrullo *The Diabolic Root*: pp. 46-63; La Barre *The Peyote Cult*: pp. 43-53; J. Howard "Half-Moon Way": pp. 1-24). Both "fireplaces" or types of ritual involve the participants sitting up all night at the meeting place praying, ingesting fresh or dried peyote (*Lophophora williamsii*) or a "tea" made from it, singing a particular type of song associated with the religion, and performing other ritual acts. The principal difference between the two rituals is the inclusion of a much larger number of forms derived from the White man's church in the Big Moon form. Both rituals have been described at length elsewhere, therefore I will not offer additional description here.

Although E. W. Voegelin seems to imply that John Wilson or "Moonhead," the famous Caddo-Delaware Peyote missionary, and George "Fourleaf" [Falleaf] were responsible for the introduction of the Big Moon rite among the Loyal Shawnees (La Barre *The Peyote Cult*: pp. 119-120) my informant Bill Tyner credited Jack Thomas, an Anadarko Delaware (see Petrullo *The Diabolic Root*: pp. 110-111) with bringing the Big Moon ritual to Whiteoak. Bill said that his father formerly conducted Big Moon meetings. Among the Absentee Shawnees, Earnest Spybuck, who secured his "moon" or ritual from the Delawares near Dewey, ran a modified Big Moon ritual (La Barre *The Peyote Cult*: p. 158). The Big Moon ritual is now obsolete among the Shawnees.

The Little Moon or Basic Plains ritual came to the Absentees in 1900 from the Kickapoos. It reached the Loyal Shawnees through John W. James, commonly known as Jimmy John, who was a Yuchi. He had learned it from the Cheyennes, who in turn had received it from the Comanches (Petrullo *The Diabolic Root*: pp. 71-72). By the 1930s, according to E.W. Voegelin (La Barre *The Peyote Cult*: p. 120) the Little Moon ritual was already practiced by the majority of the Shawnees. Little Moon ritual leaders at present include Bill and Alfred Tyner and Rufus Squirrel among the Loyal Shawnees and the Gibson brothers among the Absentees. Until his death in 1973 Ranny Carpenter was also a Little Moon leader. Afred Tyner has built a structure similar to a Navaho hogahn near his home in Dewey, Oklahoma, for use as a "Peyote church"; but most Shawnee leaders employ a Plains

Indian tipi as their "Peyote temple". I have attended three Shawnee Peyote meetings, one at Alfred Tyner's home in Dewey (before he built his hogahn), one at the country home of Louis Warrior near Bixby; and one led by Richard Gibson near the Yuchi squareground by Kellyville, Oklahoma. All three were standard Little Moon rituals and were held in tipis.

The Shawnees have now practiced the Peyote religion long enough for it to have become well integrated into their culture. They have, in the process, developed some uniquely tribal interpretations of various elements in the ceremony. Several of these are noted by E.W. Voegelin. The leader's staff, according to her, was called the "walking stick of the old" by some Shawnee informants, but the red horsehair tassel at the top was said to symbolize the roach headdress used in the War Dance (La Barre *The Peyote Cult*: p. 67). Elsewhere she writes that "Some Shawnee liken the leader's staff to the staff in the Green Corn Dance", a reference which is unclear to me since I know of no staff used in the Green Corn, although it also indicates the syncretization of Peyote with the traditional ceremonial cycle (La Barre *The Peyote Cult*: p. 120).

In reference to the "ash-bird," a symbol fashioned in the embers of the sacred fire by the fire-boy in the morning, we read: "Tom Panther, a Shawnee leader, called the ash-bird 'a holy bird; it drinks as well as we do of the holy water [some of the ritual water that is poured on the ash-figure in the morning] and it gets alive a little when people drink, and from then on is lively until morning" (ibid.: p. 71). We are also told that "The martin [scissortail flycatcher?] is said to be the Shawnee peyote bird, as indicated perhaps in the 'scissors-tail' shape of some ashes (ibid.) The term "road man" used in reference to the leader of the peyote ceremony seems to have considerable antiquity among the Shawnees (Voegelin, Rafinesque, Voegelin, and Lilly *Walum Olum*: p. 150), though the use of the term is quite common among other peyote using tribes as well.

Certain Shawnees regularly visit the "Peyote gardens" near Laredo, Texas, in order to secure supplies of peyote buttons. In the past some Shawnees acquired the power to cure on these visits (La Barre *The Peyote Cult*: p. 57-58):

> You can get power by visiting the peyote patch in Texas, and telling it at evening that you want help to cure people and get medicine. You sprinkle tobacco there. The next morning, when the Morning Star comes up, the person goes to the patch where he put the tobacco and when he comes close he hears a

rattler rattling. If he has nerve enough to go over there, likely he does not find a snake there, but just something to scare him. If he does find a snake there, he grabs the rattlesnake (which is coiled up on top of the medicine) and takes it off and then he picks one peyote button from that place. Then he goes to another bunch and picks another button . . . Perhaps at the fourth spot where he picks his fourth button, the snake is there again and he must remove it. . . . Jim Clark related this defying of a rattlesnake to the obtaining of another powerful herb in the old days.

Although the Peyote religion is well integrated into contemporary Shawnee culture, the Shawnees are still well aware of its non-Shawnee origins. Thus, even though they have developed their own interpretations for some of the elements, as noted above, and have composed Peyote songs in their own language, no Shawnee has dared alter in any basic manner the form of the ceremony. According to Bill Tyner, his uncle Webb once considered some modifications that would have made the ceremony more congruent with other Shawnee ceremonials. Once at a Peyote meeting he carefully broached the subject asking the other Shawnees present: "Why should the staff always go around in a clockwise manner? [the direction in which the staff and drum are passed in the Basic Plains peyote ritual]. When no one present could cite a reason other than the fact that this was the way the Shawnees had been taught by their Plains Indian mentors, Webb continued, stating that he had experienced a divine vision in which the Creator herself had instructed him that henceforth the staff should move around the tipi in a counterclockwise direction [the Shawnee ritual progression and the line of movement in all Shawnee dances]. He added to this "divine commandment" argument the observation that "bean vines grow this way [counterclockwise] so this must be the right way," this is a conventional justification employed by the Creeks and other Southeastern tribes to explain the counterclockwise progression of their dances. Webb was dissuaded from making this radical change, however, by the others pointing out to him that perhaps his "divine vision" was really a communication from the Evil Spirit or Devil, disguised as the Creator. This last recalls the Shawnee Prophet's initial "false" vision, which he subsequently disavowed (P. Radin *The Winnebago Tribe*: pp. 70–71). The incident is very interesting in that it demonstrates the typical Shawnee pattern of cultural innovation based upon a prophetic vision but the equally typical rejection of such innovation by asserting that not all visions truly stem from the Creator.

According to Bill Tyner during the peyote ceremony, most older Shawnee peyotists address their prayers, to Kokomthena, Our Grandmother, and to other lesser deities. Tobacco, Fire, Water, and Eagle, all important Tipwiwe or Truth-Bearers in traditional Shawnee religion, function in the same way in the Peyote religion. In addition Peyote and Cedar function as Truth-Bearers for Peyotists. Though Bill told me this, he hastened to add that *he himself* does not pray in this manner but instead prays to the Supreme Being whom he identifies with the Christian God through Jesus. Bill, incidentally, does not attend traditional Shawnee ceremonies, only Peyote meetings.

A typical Shawnee peyote prayer, transcribed by E.W. Voegelin, is quoted in La Barre (*The Peyote Cult*: p. 81):

> My prayer is that of a pitiful man. And also these people here, visitors, I wish my creator to answer my prayer to take pity on those visitors. They came to my daughter's meeting for some good reason to learn something about my daughter's meeting. So each of us give blessing, and bless the water that was brought in this morning. So let our friendship purify it, that we might drink this water, to give us long life, and a better life; and I ask our father to bless all my children, and my wife, and all of us who are in this meeting tonight. I am glad my friends came here to help me with my prayer tonight, my daughter's birthday meeting, and we thank thee for this food she brought in, that our friends who are going to eat this food, that they might feel better from now on in everyday life. We ask in the name of Jesus, Amen. (He then cried ceremonially at the finish of the prayer; a few tears ran down his cheeks.)

The praying at a Peyote meeting is quite different from the dignified prayer at the Bread Dance or other traditional Shawnee ceremonial. The speaker's voice usually becomes louder as he proceeds, earnest and quavering with emotion as he stretches out his hands toward the Grandfather Peyote resting on the altar and the fire, now and then raising his eyes to the smokehole above. Sometimes his speech is wholly interrupted by broken sobbing as he cries out for the pity of the supernaturals.

The psychological difference between Peyotism and older Shawnee ceremonies is evident in the music as well. Mathews (*The Osages*: p. 754) speaking of Osage Peyote songs, puts his finger on this difference as well as anyone when he says, "They are nervous songs with quick tempo directed through Chief Peyote to a Creator who seems to be busy with the petitions of the Heavy Eyebrows [Whites]. They are prayer songs that pluck the sleeve of the Creator, not the ancient prayer songs of men pre-eminent, upon whom *Wah-Kon-Tah* [God] focused his attention as they hunted and fought and mated and danced and fasted."

SHAWNEE PARTICIPATION IN THE CREEK GREEN CORN

On 4–7 July 1974 I attended the annual Green Corn or Busk Ceremony at Cedar River Tulsa squareground, a Creek ceremonial ground near Holdenville, Oklahoma. In another work (J. Howard *The Southeastern Ceremonial Complex and Its Interpretation*: pp. 103–119) I have described the sequence of ceremonies which takes place at this ceremonial ground, which is one of the strongest among today's Creeks. Among the many visitors at this Green Corn ceremony, the high point of the Creek ceremonial year, were Bill and Henry Johnson, both prominent members of the Absentee Shawnee "Old ground" near Little Axe, and their families. It is common for Creeks and Shawnees to visit each others' ceremonies, and I would not bother to mention the attendance of a small number of Shawnees at this particular Creek Green Corn were it not for the fact that *as Shawnees*, Bill and Henry Johnson were accorded special treatment by town chief Barney Leader and other Creek officials at Cedar River Tulsa.

Because they were Shawnees the Johnson brothers were seated in the northern bed or arbor at the ground (also occupied by members of the Deer, Potato, and Alligator clans of the local Creeks). They participated in the entire sequence of Green Corn rituals with the Creeks, such as dancing the Feather dance, "taking medicine," et cetera. When it came time for the ritual "scratching," an important Green Corn rite, Bill and Henry were scratched in a different manner than the local Creeks, again because they were Shawnees. This meant that in addition to the customary scratches on arms and legs, both men were scratched in an X across the chest. Henry later informed me that this was the "old Shawnee way" and that it was more difficult, yet also more beneficial, than the usual Creek form.

Both men were obviously quite familiar with Creek Busk procedures, and during the "nighttime" social dances that followed the main ceremonial day, 6 July the brothers sang for a performance of the Shawnee Bear Dance which was incorporated into the sequence of Creek dances on this occasion. The attendance of these prominent Shawnees at a Creek ceremony and the fact that *as Shawnees* special treatment was accorded them undoubtedly reflects a long tradition of Shawnee-Creek ceremonial interaction.

14

"Just For Fun": The Nighttime Dances

Following each of the major Shawnee ceremonies and football games there is a night of social dancing. Most Shawnees distinguish these as their "nighttime" dances, as distinct from their ceremonial or "daytime" dances. Usually the crowd at the dance ground swells enormously in the evening when these dances begin. Many younger Shawnees, who seem to have little interest in the ceremonialism of their tribe, regularly appear for the nighttime dances, which are defined as "just for fun" rather than as an obligation. Especially popular with the young people are the episodes of the "Leading" or "Ordinary Stomp" Dance. Most younger Shawnees can "lead" (sing for) at least one or two rounds of this dance, and expert leaders from other tribes such as the Creeks, Seminoles, Yuchis, Caddo-Delawares, and Kickapoos at the two Absentee grounds; and the Cherokees, Quapaws, Oklahoma Seneca-Cayugas, and Oklahoma Delawares at Whiteoak, are usually on hand to help out the local crew.

The position of the nighttime or social dances as a part of Shawnee ceremonialism should not be misunderstood. While it is quite true that these dances are of a secular nature, they are nevertheless considered an integral part of the whole ceremonial occasion, and like the daytime dances they are thought to be pleasing to Our Grandmother, the Creator. Thus a Bread Dance, Green Corn Dance, or War Dance is not considered a total success unless the locals and visitors in the assembled crowd are able to provide enough song leaders and dancers to continue the dancing through the night and past sunrise the following morning, when the "Morning" or "Drunken" Dance closes the program. I can vividly recall the late Ranny Carpenter, with tears in his eyes, shaking hands with each of us who had stayed awake to participate in the nighttime dances following the 1970 fall Bread Dance at Whiteoak. On this occasion Ranny proudly recounted that this was the one-hundredth year that the "fire" had burned at the Whiteoak ground. I also recall being chided on a number of mornings when sleep had overtaken me sometime after midnight and I had failed to last out the night. Alford (T.W. Alford *Civilization*: 60-61), who terms them "frolic" dances, clearly indicates the position of the nighttime dances in Shawnee thought: "At dusk the frolic dance begins and is continued throughout the night; when men and women dance together, as they sometimes do, the formation is one behind the other. The music for this part of the dance is much faster and louder than for the sacred or ceremonial dance following the prayer. The dance usually closes at sunrise, and each family goes hon.e with a glorified feeling of having appeased the Great Spirit. The dances that follow the Bread Dance, such as the Green Corn Dance, are for frolic and fun. Each has its own set of songs and customs, but they are not considered obligatory."

Ideally the pattern for the nighttime dances is: (1) two men, usually the same two who have served as "aides" during the ceremonial dances that afternoon, gather wood and kindle a fire in the dance ground to provide illumination and warmth for the dancers. At the two Absentee grounds one fire is built near the center of the ground. At Whiteoak the fire is located a few feet west of the halfway point, east and west, and sometimes a second fire is built the same distance east of it. (2) As soon as the fire is burning brightly, the musicians, with water drum and rattles, appear and take their places. They sit in the same places where they sat during the daytime dances. They start off the evening by singing for various women's dances and mixed dances. (3) After about one-half hour of this, some of the older local men lead a few rounds of the Leading Dance. (4) is followed by another women's dance or a mixed dance, and then more episodes of the Leading Dance, this time with younger men as leaders. This pattern of women's or mixed dances alternating with episodes of the Leading Dance continues until midnight or one or two o'clock. (5) The drum is then retired and from this time until dawn one episode of the Leading Dance follows another with only short intervals in between. (6) At dawn or shortly thereafter the drum is returned to the dance ground and the "Morning" or "Drunken" dance concludes the dancing. (7) Breakfast is served at the individual camps, and if it is spring, a men-against-women football game is played beginning around 10:00 A.M.

It is easy to lose one's self in the enjoyment of the dancing at the nighttime dances, but in 1970 I managed to maintain my scientific detachment in order to record the exact sequence of social dances following the fall Bread Dance at Whiteoak. Though each occasion at each ceremonial ground is unique, this sequence may be regarded as fairly typical.

Beginning at 9:00 P.M. there followed 1. One episode of Women's Straight Dance (using "Nighttime" songs), 2. One episode of Leading Dance, 3. One episode of Women's Straight Dance (women alone) going into one episode of the Face-to-face dance (mixed men and women), 4. One episode of Leading Dance, 5. One episode of Cherokee Dance, 6. One episode of Leading Dance, 7. One episode of Raccoon Dance, 8. Two episodes of Leading Dance, 9. One episode of Shawnee Dance, 10. One episode of Leading Dance, 11. One episode of Face-to-face Dance, 12. Three episodes of Leading Dance, 13. One episode of Quapaw Dance, 14. One episode of Leading Dance, 15. One episode of "Bringing" or "Go Get 'Em" Dance.

It was now midnight and the drum was retired. A steady series of Leading Dance episodes followed, continuing until 4:00 A.M., at which time there was a four-hour lull in the activities. Although theoretically the "Morning" or "Drunken" Dance should not be performed unless the dancing has continued through the entire night, 4:00 was considered close enough to dawn so that it could take place. Therefore at 8:00 A.M. the singers, Ranny Carpenter and Bill Shawnee, brought the drum back to the dance ground. The few dancers who were still awake reassembled, and the Drunken Dance was performed. At its conclusion the singers and dancers shook hands all around, wished each other well, promised to see each other again the following spring, and then returned to their various individual camps to wash up and breakfast.

As Alford notes, each social dance has its own set of songs and customs. Many of the dances seem to be of respectable antiquity, being listed by Trowbridge, writing in 1824, or Morgan, writing in 1860. Some of them, particularly those with animal or plant names, were probably of a semi-religious nature at one time, dedicated to the spirit of the animal or plant named (such as Raccoon, Fish, Bear, Horse, Corn, or Bean). Others, judging from their titles, are borrowings from other tribes (like the Cherokee, Quapaw, or Seneca). Still others are secular versions of the sacred dances employed in the Bread Dance, using special nighttime songs (Women's Straight Dance, Women's Side or Dove Dance, Women's Cluster Dance). The characteristics of each of the various dances making up a night of Shawnee social dancing follows:

WOMEN'S STRAIGHT DANCE
(BESHIWEKAWE)

The choreography of the Women's Straight Dance is identical with that of the dance of the same name used in the daytime ceremonial of the Bread Dance (and, at Whiteoak, in the Green Corn Dance). The women, in a single file, circle the dance ground in a counterclockwise direction using a toe-heel left, toe-heel right, step. The songs used to accompany the nighttime performance are different from those used during the day. The Women's Straight Dance is often used to begin the nighttime series. It sometimes follows directly after a series of Women's Cluster Dance songs.

WOMEN'S CLUSTER DANCE
(KOKEKI, TAKOKEKI, SHIKOKEWE)

Trowbridge writes of the Women's Cluster Dance, the most characteristic of the Shawnee women's dances, (C. C. Trowbridge *Shawnese Traditions*: pp. 49–50) "Tuhkoakaawāā [Tahkokewe] —is a dance exclusively performed by women. It is danced for amusement only. This peculiarity and the custom of the women to join the man in singing are its only characteristics. The dancers form in a line fronting the man who sings, and they join him in singing, a kind of prelude, which continues some minutes, when they commence, the man singing alone, and dance around in a circular manner." Trowbridge would seem to be in error in stating that the dance is performed for amusement only, for since at least 1850, the dance has been an important part of the daytime dances at every Bread Dance and the Loyal Shawnee Green Corn Dance. It is also, however, performed as a nighttime dance on occasion, sometimes, as Trowbridge notes, leading directly into the Women's Straight Dance. On at least one occasion it was performed as an incidental daytime dance by Shawnee women attending the Sauk Veteran's Powwow at the Ed Mack farm, near Shawnee, Oklahoma. I suspect, because he notes the women singing, that it is the Women's Cluster Dance that Thomas Ridout witnessed at a Shawnee village on the Wabash in 1788 (M. Edgar *Ten Years of Upper Canada in Peace and War, 1805–1815*: p. 359): "Towards evening there was a dance of young women before the council-house, to the beat of a drum and their voices." The same dance, with the same songs is used by the Creek women to "conjure" the ballsticks of their men prior to the men-against-women football game.

-I have mentioned in my description of the Bread Dance that at the Absentee ceremonial grounds the women sometimes execute a side-to-side progression during one set of Cluster Dance songs, moving a few feet to the right, then a few to the left, all the while in two ranks facing the singers. In doing this they used the step of the Women's Side or Dove Dance, described below, and its reverse.

WOMEN'S "SIDE" OR DOVE DANCE (PAWITHEKAWE)

Like the two preceding dances, this is a secular nighttime version of the dance of the same name used in the daytime ceremonial of the Bread Dance (and at Whiteoak, in the Green Corn Dance). It is the same dance as that called the "Women's Shuffle Dance" or Enskanye by the Iroquois. A line of women and girls, facing the center of the dance ground, proceed in a counterclockwise direction around the fire. The step, which is done well by only a few women and girls, is executed by balancing back on the heels and swinging the balls of the feet forty-five degrees to the right, then balancing on the toes and balls of the feet and swinging the heels of both feet to the right, and so on, in rapid succession. Those women who are too old, and those girls who are too fat or too clumsy to perform the step properly simply side-step to the right.

It may be this dance that O.M. Spencer saw at the Green Corn he witnessed in 1792. At any rate he described the dancers: " . . . with their bodies bent forward slowly raising both feet at once and bringing them down heavily, uttering a "hiegh" at every jump . . . (*The Indian Captivity of O.M. Spencer*: p. 112).

The Shawnee women ordinarily do not execute the step of this dance with the grace and speed of Iroquois matrons in the New York and Ontario longhouses. A part of the greater expertise of the Iroquois women, however, can be credited to the fact that they dance on the smooth boards of the longhouse floor rather than on the packed earth of the Shawnee dance ground, and many of them wear leather-soled "white-women" shoes rather than buckskin moccasins. The wooden boards and slippery-soled footwear enable Iroquois women to fairly glide around the hall, apparently without effort, appearing to move a few inches above the floor. Most of the Shawnee women whom I have seen are usually puffing after one circuit of the dance ground in this dance.

LEADING DANCE OR ORDINARY STOMP DANCE

The term "Stomp Dance" is used by the Shawnees, Delawares, Creeks, Seminoles, Yuchis, and Cherokees in two ways. In its more inclusive sense it refers to the entire set of nighttime dances performed at a ceremonial ground. Thus a ceremonial ground is often referred to as a Stomp Ground. In its more restricted sense it refers specifically to the dance called the Leading Dance by the Shawnees and Delawares (*Nikanikaki* in Shawnee); *Obunga-hadzho* or "Crazy Dance" by Muskogi-speaking Creeks and Seminoles; also *Satkita-obunga*, "Common Dance"; *Diʒsti* or "Mixed" Dance by the Cherokees; and *Tsebenbene-shti* by the Yuchis. The Shawnee and Delaware name for the dance refers to one man leading both the dance and its musical accompaniment, hence *Nikanikaki*, "Leading Dance." When speaking English a Shawnee may refer to it simply as "Stomp" or "Ordinary Stomp."

Concerning this dance form, undoubtedly the most popular of Shawnee dances, Trowbridge writes (*Shawnese Traditions*: p. 50): "Neekauneekauwāā [Nikanikawe]—The leading Dance. This is also a dance for amusement, in which the men and women intermingle. The leader sings the musick and dances around in a ring, his followers shouting at the end of the tune or rather at intervals." The "shouting at the end of the tune" to which Trowbridge refers is the antiphonal response of the file of dancers to the short song phrases of the leader.

To begin an episode or "round" of the Leading Dance the man selected to lead, followed by his assistants, enters the dance area and begins to walk around the fire in a counterclockwise direction. Other experienced male dancers who can "answer" Leading Dance songs now separate themselves from the crowd of spectators and fall in at the end of the file. When a few men have joined and "broken the ice," women and girls also join and soon a long file of dancers, men and women interspersed, are walking slowly around the center fire. Inexperienced dancers and small fry join at the end of the line. It is considered very bad form to crowd in at the head of the line after it has formed, and it is particularly bad etiquette to take a place between the leader and his first, second, or third follower. After glancing over his shoulder to determine that sufficient dancers have joined the group to make a good showing (at least fifteen or twenty) the leader begins his introduction. This is a low, throaty, shout "Yu-wooooo!" to which the men and boys in the line following answer in unison with a cry "Yu-wooooo; Hi!" The leader then shouts another introductory vocable, and is answered, and still another. When he comes to the vocable "He-hie," he begins the cadenced shuffling trot or "stomping" that is the basic step of the dance, followed by the others.

Before his introductory songs are completed, another important functionary emerges from the crowd and takes her place directly behind the leader, pushing in between him and the man following. This is the "shell-shaker girl," who provides most of the rhythmic accompaniment for the dance. Often she is the wife or teenage daughter of the leader, though not invariably. On the outside of the lower part of her legs, from knee to ankle, she wears the traditional "shells" or leg rattles from which the shell-shaker girl takes her name. These are made of either terrapin shells or condensed milk cans fastened to heavy leather or cloth pads. By a skillful combination of toe and heel action she produces the characteristic duple beat of the dance. Small perforations in the terrapin shells or milk cans serve to amplify the sound of the gravel inside, which can easily be heard above the singing of the dancers. If more than one shell-shaker girl joins the dance, the additional women space themselves behind the second, third, or fourth men in the line, with the sexes alternating.

Once the shell-shakers have joined the dance, the leader has nearly finished with his introductory songs or shouts. Now he begins with what might be termed the Leading Dance songs proper. Formerly, according to some older informants, these songs followed one another in a prescribed sequence. This may still be the case with the Creeks, Yuchis, and Seminoles, especially with older leaders. Among the Shawnees, however, leaders simply string together a sequence of their favorite songs that are known to be familiar to their seconds, who must be able to answer them.

The usual pattern of these songs is a short phrase, which is rather low in pitch, with an equally low-pitched but somewhat shorter answering phrase. This is repeated two or three times. Then the same phrase, or a different one, is sung at a higher pitch and is echoed by a higher pitched answer. There is then a slightly lower pitched lead phrase and answer. These last two phrases and their answers may be repeated, after which the leader returns to his original low-pitched phrase, and so on. Often, but not invariably, a cry of "Whiii!" by the leader, echoed by the dancers, signals the end of a song.

Often the pattern of the dance is an unvaried shuffling trot in a counterclockwise direction, flat left foot followed by flat right in quick succession. Once the dance is well under way, however, some leaders introduce variations in both step and figure. For example, on the second or third song the leader usually turns ninety degrees to the left and sidesteps to the right, at the same time holding his arms out over the fire and waving his hands up and down as if performing a gesture of supplication. Apparently all of the male dancers are supposed to follow him in this, though only a few at the head of the line actually do so. Again a leader, when he has really "warmed up" may remove his hat and wave it from side to side over his head, rock back on his heels, and tread in place or even back up for a short interval. If he is in a gay mood he may wind the entire line of dancers into a tight serpentine coil, then reverse and uncoil again, or meander in a zig-zag pattern.

Sometimes figures from the quadrille are introduced, such as the leader and his shell-shaker girl forming a bridge with their arms and the next couple, after passing under this bridge, forming a bridge in turn, until the last couple must dance through a veritable tunnel of raised arms. One good Eastern Shawnee leader observed at the Oklahoma Seneca-Cayuga Green Corn in 1959 used a trick song in which, at a certain point, the dancers were supposed to reverse directions. By slightly altering the musical cue, however, the leader had people "jumping the gun" and reversing willy-nilly, much to the hilarity of all present.

To end the dance, the leader sometimes employs a series of short songs or shouts much like the introduction, gradually speeding up the tempo to indicate that the conclusion is near. Finally, having built up the speed to a furious climax, the leader raises his right arm high above his head and with a sharp cry of "Whiii!", concludes the performance. Sometimes, anticipating the ending, he has wound the whole group into a tight spiral of moving bodies and dust. With the end of the episode the dancers drift to their seats for a breather before the next leader and his assistants take the center of the square for another ten or fifteen minutes of action.

The Leading Dance is undoubtedly the most popular song and dance form among the Shawnees and other Northeastern and Southeastern tribes now resident in Oklahoma. Many individuals, younger Shawnees and visitors from other tribes, attend Shawnee ceremonials solely for the purpose of participating in the Leading Dance, arriving shortly after the evening meal or even later. The Shawnees also attend the dances of the Creeks, Yuchis, Seminoles, and Caddos in the same manner, avoiding the daytime dances and participating only in the Stomp episodes. The appeal of the Leading Dance to teenage youth among the Shawnees and other Eastern tribes is comparable to the popularity of the Forty-nine dance among Prairie and High Plains youths. The dance requires no special costume or expertise, and is compelling in its rhythm and songs, yet it allows for the expression of individual talent by the men and boys as leaders or "seconds" and by the women and girls as shell-shakers. In addition it is certainly in part a symbol of "Indianness" for Indian youth who seem to know little else of their culture. A young Ponca, himself an excellent Stomp leader, once commented disgustedly to me, "All those Shawnee kids are good for is Stomp dancing."

In the past, according to several informants, each leader had his own "string of songs," many of which had Shawnee words and were of his own composition. These "word songs" frequently announced the identity of the leader, and which ceremonial ground he was from, boasted of the quality of the dance leaders from his settlement, and then went on to make sly proposals to the local women indicating that he was "footloose and fancy free." Esther Dixon recalled that when she was a very small girl she was punished by her father for innocently learning and singing around the house some of his songs of the last type. Other "word songs" were of a more serious nature. The Creeks, for example, are said to have a series of songs, so long that it requires two episodes of the dance to complete it, which tells of the "Trail of Tears," the removal of the Southeastern tribes during the period from 1832 to 1839, naming many of the stopping places en route to the Indian Territory. Still other songs tell of incidents in battles of long ago.

Today most of the songs are standardized. There are about thirty songs, in varying combination, carrying 90° of the dancing. Only older leaders, such as Bill Shawnee, still employ word songs to any extent. Creek, Seminole, and Yuchi leaders still use word songs quite regularly but are careful to make certain that they have "second men" who can answer their lead phrases.

It is probably futile, at present, to speculate on the origins of the Leading Dance. One commonly held theory, however, can be rejected out of hand. This is that the dance is of African origin and was introduced by escaped negro slaves to tribes in the Southeast. The basis of this theory is a fancied resemblance of the vocal style of the Stomp Dance songs to African music (such as the negro "wail"). The early and wide distribution of the Leading Dance (from New Brunswick to Florida and the Atlantic to the Mississippi in the early nineteenth century), plus the fact that no African culture has any musical form closely resembling it, would negate this theory. Many Blacks *did* learn the idiom from Southeastern Indians in the antebellum period and there are still good leaders, who are Indian-Negro mestizos, in Oklahoma. The antiphonal style may even have entered Afro-American music via the Stomp Dance. In this connection one thinks of orchestra leader Cab Calloway with his famous "Hi de hi de hi: Ho de ho de ho." To infer African origins for Stomp Dance variants performed by Passamaquoddies, Senecas, or Ojibwas in the early nineteenth century, however, borders on the ridiculous.

Another theory, one sometimes advanced by the Shawnees themselves, is that they learned the dance from the Creeks subsequent to their arrival in the Indian Territory. The listing of the Leading Dance as a Shawnee form by Trowbridge in 1824 would seem to give the lie to this theory as well, though Creek influence on the Shawnee Leading Dance has undoubtedly been strong, and the Creeks may very well have introduced the practice of wearing shackles or leg rattles by women in the dance.

The theory that is most acceptable to me is the one advanced in chapter seven, namely, that the Leading Dance originated as a method by which members of a war party warmed up prior to their day-long jog toward the enemy country, circling their stacked arms, hence the Iroquois name for the dance, "Standing quiver" (W.N. Fenton *Songs From the Iroquois Longhouse*: p. 31).

FACE-TO-FACE DANCE

The choreography of the Face-to-face Dance is identical to the

Raccoon Dance, though the music for the two, according to Bill Shawnee, is slightly different.

The dance is begun by the men, who form a single file moving counterclockwise, using a simple toe-heel left, toe-heel right, step. During the second song the men form into pairs, and pairs of women enter the dance, inserting themselves between the pairs of men and dancing backwards. On musical cue the pairs of women and pairs of men reverse; with the men now dancing backwards. The same pattern continues throughout the dance.

CHEROKEE DANCE (KATUWA WEKAWE)

The name of the Cherokee Dance is derived from the old Cherokee name for themselves, *Kituwa*. Of the dance Morgan (L. H. Morgan *The Indian Journals, 1859–62*: p. 15) writes: "Cherokee Dance, Ka-tu-wha-na-ka-wa, Dance of the _____ by women alone." The Cherokee dance is still a great favorite of the Shawnees today. Music is provided by three singers, one with drum, two with rattles, who sit at one side. The women begin the dance. They form a single file, holding hands, and begin a counterclockwise progression around the fire, using a simple walking step. After a few songs the head singer cries out "Get in there boys!" and the men join the dance, spacing themselves alternately between the women. The dancers now follow a serpentine course around the dance area and even outside it. The leader of the dance is always a woman. At Whiteoak, until she suffered a stroke in 1971, Mary Squirrel could usually be counted upon to lead this dance, as well as the nighttime performances of the Women's Straight Dance. Now her daughter, Anita Valliere, often leads it in her place.

It is apparently to this dance that Alford refers when he writes (*Civilization*: p. 61):

> In some dances—frolic dances—the men and women join hands to form a circle, but not side by side, as white people do. A man holds his hand out behind him which is taken by a woman with a handkerchief or cloth in her hand. She in turn extends her other hand behind her, which is taken by another man. In this dance a young woman is permitted to select the brave she wishes to dance with, by simply taking her place behind him.
> When she extends her hand, if it is bare—not protected by the handkerchief—it is an indication that he will be acceptable to her as a lover or perhaps a husband. If he likes her looks or is impressed with her personality, he is at liberty to make further advances. But always there is great reserve and little mention is made of affection, if indeed any at all.

Though he seems to be speaking of the Cherokee dance, because he mentions the two sexes joining hands while in a single file, Alford is in error when he states that the woman takes her place behind the man of her choice. The Cherokee dance is always begun by a file of women, hence the men would take their places after the dance was under way. The custom regarding the use of the handkerchief is now obsolete, though a girl may still indicate her interest in a man by entering the Leading Dance directly behind him.

Curiously enough this dance, known as the Cherokee Dance by the Shawnees, is known as the Shawnee Dance to the Yuchis. Speck (F.G. Speck *Ethnology of the Yuchi Indians*: p. 128-9) describes the Yuchi performance thus:

> The Shawnee Dance *Yoncta cti*, is said to have been borrowed from the neighboring Shawnee, with whom the Yuchi are very intimate. It is a very picturesque and animated dance, indeed, a general favorite. Only the drum is used, one man beating it while several others sing. A line of women filed out from one corner of the square holding hands, led by a Shawnee girl beautifully dressed. Very soon the men from the different lodges came in between each pair of women and took their hands. The whole line of alternating men and women holding hands, then wound round and about the square-ground imitating the movements of a serpent. The song syllables as remembered, consisted of *ya na na we he'* repeated over and over. At intervals announced by a whoop the dancers all faced right about and continued in that way until the next whoop.

RACCOON DANCE

Bill Shawnee says that the Raccoon Dance came to the Shawnees from the Senecas. It seems identical in choreography with the Face-to-face Dance, which Bill identifies as an old Shawnee dance. The dance is started by the men, who form a single file moving in a counterclockwise direction. The step is a simple toe-heel left, toe-heel right. During the second song the men form into pairs, and pairs of women enter the dance between the pairs of men, dancing backwards. On musical cue the pairs of men and women reverse, with the men now dancing backwards and the women in a forward direction. This pattern continues throughout the dance. As is the case in all of the dances described above except for the Leading Dance, music is provided by a head singer, who keeps time with a water drum, and two assistants with rattles. The dance appears to be identical with the Iroquois Raccoon dance in its choreography (G.P. Kurath *Iroquois Music and Dance*: p. 24-5)

SHAWNEE DANCE, ALLIGATOR DANCE, FISH DANCE (LAMETHAKAWE), AND BEAR DANCE (M'KWA WEKAWE)

All four of these dances are identical in their choreography at the present time, yet each has its own distinctive songs. All four begin with a single file of women circling the fire using a toe-heel left, toe-heel right step. On the second song the men join in the dance, forming a second file of dancers on the outside (right hand) of the women's file. Each man in the right-hand file is paired with a woman in the left. The dance continues in this manner until, on musical cue, the two sexes cross, with the men moving to the left, and the women moving to the right side. The dancers keep to this pattern for a while, and then the two sexes change sides again, and so on.

Nora Thompson Dean (Delaware) and Eva Dick (a Loyal Shawnee) both stated, in regard to the Fish Dance form, that the crossing and recrossing of the dancers symbolize the movements of a school of fish, who pass and repass one another in this manner. The Iroquois, who perform a slightly different form of Fish Dance that also involves the passing and repassing of the couples, assign a like symbolism (Kurath *Iroquois Music and Dance*: p. 69).

The Fish Dance and Bear Dance are both listed by Morgan (*Indian Journals*: p. 77). Of the former he writes: "Fish Dance, Na.ma.tha.ka-wa. Men and women. The women enter the dance at their pleasure. None but a female relative can dance with a man. A woman not a relative is not allowed to do so. This is the Iroquois Fish Dance in form, but I do not know as it must be a relative." Of the Bear Dance he notes simply (*Indian Journals*: p. 77): "Bear Dance, M-qua-ka-we. Men and women. Used in the Bread Dance." The Bear Dance is not used in the daytime dances of the Bread Dance at the present time at any of the three Shawnee ceremonial grounds. Bill Johnson and his brother Henry commonly sing for a performance of the Bear Dance at the all-night Stomp Dance that follows the Creek Green Corn at Cedar River Tulsa square ground, near Holdenville, Oklahoma. The Creeks are well acquainted with the dance but they acknowledge it to be a Shawnee introduction.

Many of the Central Algonkian tribes have, or once had, a Shawnee Dance (*Shawanoge, Shanoge*) somewhat resembling the dance described above but not involving the crossover feature.

These include the Ojibwa (F. Densmore *Chippewa Music II*: pp.
126-30, 234-7), Plains-Ojibwa (J. Howard *The Plains-Ojibwa or
Bungi*: pp. 114-5). Menomini (A. Skinner *Associations and
Ceremonies of the Menomini Indians*: p. 212; F. Densmore
Menominee Music: pp. 52-6), Fox or Meskwaki (T. Michelson *The
Autobiography of a Fox Indian Woman*: pp. 329, 343 note 35; G.
Young Bear *History of the Mesquakie Indians*: pp. 227-8), Miami
(C. C. Trowbridge *Meeārmeear Traditions*: p. 59), and Prairie
Potawatomi (A. Skinner *The Mascoutens or Prairie Potawatomi
Indians, Part I*: pp. 227-8). Today, with most, it is an incidental
exhibition dance performed at powwows to vary the program; but
formerly it was a separate dance, held at night, that often was
used as a vehicle for honoring the spirits of the dead, for ritual
adoptions, curing of a minor sort, and exchange of gifts.

Skinner writes of the Menominee version (*Associations and
Ceremonies of the Menomini Indians*: p. 212) "This sacred
rite (*Cawanokau* or *Tcipai'cimun*, ghost dance) is performed in
honor of the dead and is said to have been borrowed from the
Shawnee at an ancient time when they lived near the Menominee.
It is held a year or more after the death of some person, when the
relatives prepare a feast and invite their neighbors to attend . . .
It is thought that he (the dead) responds and is happy with those
present." The following account, from a mimeographed program
of the Meskwaki or Fox tribal powwow in the 1950's (Young Bear
History of the Mesquakie Indians: p. 1) is representative of accounts purporting to explain the acquisition of the dance by Central Algonkian groups: "3. The Shawnee Dance—In some remote
past, the Shawnee Tribe of Indians, desiring to establish a permanent peace with the Mesquakies, gave them their own tribal
sacred dance. The Mesquakies accepted this dance from the
Shawnee, and as long as they participate in this beautiful dance,
the peace and friendship of centuries remains."

As performed by the Ojibwas, Plains-Ojibwas, Menominees,
Foxes, and Prairie-Potawatomis, the Shawnee Dance consists of a
counterclockwise circling of the dance area by pairs of dancers
using a toe-heel left, toe-heel right step.. Sometimes a Plains-style
War Dance drum is used for powwow performances of this dance
but a Woodland-style water drum seems to be the preferred
instrument. The songs of this dance are interesting in their
frequent changes of tempo. To certain songs of the dance the
dancers back up a few steps, then go forward again on musical

cue. At a Prairie Potawatomi performance of this dance, held near Mayetta, Kansas, in 1959, the dance was interrupted at midnight and James Kagmega, a tribal ritualist, delivered a moving prayer addressed to the "spirits of the night."

In my opinion this "Shawnee dance" of the Central Algonkian tribes may very well be the "certain dance . . . introduced simply for amusement" by Tecumseh and the Prophet to various northern tribes that is mentioned in the Forsyth letter (E.H. Blair *Tribes of the Upper Mississippi Valley Region and Region of the Great Lakes*, Vol. 2: p. 277).

QUAPAW DANCE

In the Quapaw Dance alternating pairs of men and women circle the fire using a toe-heel step. The women dance backwards, facing the men. At each change of phrase in the song the men pass the pair of women just ahead of them and move on to the next pair. In this way each pair of women and each pair of men has the opportunity to dance with each other pair of the opposite sex as the dance continues.

The name indicates the tribal origin of this dance, which is known to both the Loyal and Absentee bands of Shawnees. It is rarely performed at the present time, but is not obsolete.

THE BRINGING OR "GO GET 'EM" DANCE (NATOLEKIWEKAKI)

Concerning this dance Trowbridge (*Shawnese Traditions*: p. 50) writes: "Nauleteeweekāūwaa (*Naletiwikáwe*)—The bringing dance. Like the preceding [the Moving Dance] this is danced for amusement. An old man seats himself with a drum and begins the musick. Another catches hold of a female by her dress and gives her a slight twitch. He begins to dance and she follows him. So they go on, and others join them. Each man bringing his partner. If a young man chooses to go in a wigwam and give the usual sign to a young woman, she is obliged by custom to follow him, even if she have retired to bed."

Though clearly the same dance as that described by Trowbridge, the "Go Get 'Em" Dance as it is performed today includes several features not noted by him. At the beginning of the dance those women and girls intending to dance form in a cluster or rank before the singers. The male dancers at the same time arrange themselves in a single file, following the leader. This leader takes his followers in a counterclockwise circuit of the fire, using a toe-heel left, toe-heel right step, at the same time beginning an antiphonal chant that is answered by the other male dancers following him, much as in the Pumpkin Dance episode of the Bread Dance. When the men have completed one complete circuit of the fire and have come up behind the women, each man, including the leader of the men, picks one or two women or girls by touching her or them on the shoulder. The women so chosen step out from the cluster of women and turn to their left. The man who picked her (them) now puts his hands on her (their) shoulders and steers her (them) into position behind the leader of the file of dancers. The whole process now begins again, but this time the women who have been chosen are guided or "driven" around the circle by the men, who take up the antiphonal chanting as they move out.

Again, when they have made another circuit of the fire, each male dancer releases the woman or women chosen the first time around and selects others, usually, but not invariably, the same one or two selected the first time around plus one additional one. Now, driving or steering two or more women or girls each, the men start a third counterclockwise circuit. The dance proceeds in this manner until all of the women have been selected by a man. Each time around each male dancer "goes and gets" one or more additional female, whom he then guides by dancing behind her, in this way acquiring a sizeable harem before the dance is ended.

HORSE DANCE (SEWEWEKAWE)

Mary Spoon identified this dance as identical with the Bringing or "Go Get 'Em" Dance that I have just described. Morgan (*Indian Journals*: p. 77) enters it as tenth in his listing of Shawnee dances: "Horse Dance, M-sa-wa-wa-ka-wa" but supplies no additional information. The identification of the Bringing Dance with the Horse Dance would seem to be eminently logical as the male dancers "drive" the women as one would a team of horses in both. Bill Shawnee, however, insists that the two dances are distinct from one another. If so, the difference lies in the music, not in the choreography, which is identical for the two dances.

MOVING DANCE

Trowbridge describes the Moving Dance, which is also known as the Corn or Bean Dance: (*Shawnese Traditions*: p. 50):

"Naunemeekāūwenau [*Nanemikawena*] The Moving Dance. The leader in this dance carries a gourd and the others carry rattles. The men and women join in this dance promiscuously and in the music also. It is danced for amusement only and derives its name from the slowness of the motion of the dancers who are thereby enabled to keep very close to each other and to make their motions so exactly correspond as to give the dancers the appearance of one body." Morgan (*Indian Journals*: p. 77) learned of this dance from his informant Kahl-we or Blue Jacket. He writes: Bean Dance, M-sko-che-tha-ka-wa This is danced with joined hands from the head to the feet of the dancers (sic). Men and women [take part]. This dance, though sometimes called the Corn Dance should not be confused with the ceremonial daytime dance series of the Loyal Shawnees known as the Green Corn Dance (Nibenekawe). The Moving Dance, Corn Dance, or Bean Dance is strictly a secular, nighttime social dance. It corresponds to the Iroquois Corn or Bean Dance, the Delaware Bean Dance, and the Caddo Bell Dance. Present day Shawnee names for the dance are *Naminakaki* "Moving Dance; *Taminakaki* "Corn Dance" and *Miskotsithakawe* "Bean Dance".

The Shawnees perform this dance in the following way: A single file of dancers, men and women alternating, headed by a male leader, proceeds in a slow, treading toe-heel progression counterclockwise around the fire. The leader, who carries a coconut shell (Absentee Shawnee) or cowhorn (Loyal Shawnee) rattle beats the rattle, which is held in his right hand, in the palm of his left, and begins one of the characteristic songs of the dance. This is answered by those following. The songs of this dance, which are very slow in tempo, are antiphonal but differ from the Leading Dance songs in that the leader sings a number of musical phrases before the dancers, cued by the second man in line, answer with the characteristic *haii, haaa* response. Once the file of dancers are all in step and properly spaced out behind the leader, he may elect to take them in a fantastic zigzag course, wind them into a spiral, unwind them, lead them out of the dance ground into the camping area, and so on. A favorite leader for this dance at Whiteoak is Bob White (an Oklahoma Seneca-Cayuga of part-Shawnee descent), who is a natural clown as well as a skilled singer and ritualist. Bill Shawnee was also a good Bean Dance man. Among the Absentees Richard Gibson, at the Little River or "New" ground, often leads the dance.

In all of the tribes that perform this dance (New York and Canadian Iroquois, Oklahoma Seneca-Cayugas, Delawares, Loyal Shawnees, Absentee Shawnees, Absentee Delawares, and Caddoes), the songs are nearly identical. Knowing some New York Seneca Corn Dance songs, I had no difficulty seconding Joe Bedoka, a Caddo-Delaware Bell Dance leader. The Moving Dance (Bean or Corn Dance) is usually performed only once during a night of social dancing. The Caddo Bell Dance, probably derived from the Absentee or Anadarko Delawares, derives its name from the fact that a single sleigh bell, held in the hand of the leader, is substituted for the coconut shell or cowhorn rattle of the Shawnees or for the gourd rattles of the Delawares.

SENECA DANCE

I have seen the Seneca Dance only once, at the nighttime dances following the 1972 spring Bread Dance at Whiteoak. It featured a file of women, holding hands, weaving a serpentine path around the dance ground. It was identical with the Cherokee Dance in its choreography except for the fact that the men were not called to join in the dance. Its name indicates its derivation from the Oklahoma Seneca-Cayugas, who commonly join the Loyal Shawnees in their ceremonials at the Whiteoak dance ground.

STIRRUP DANCE

In the Stirrup Dance the participants start out in two files, a file of men on the right, a file of women on the left, both moving counterclockwise using a toe-heel left, toe-heel right step. There must be exactly the same number of each sex. On the second song each woman or girl pairs up with the man on her right and assumes the "stirrup" position, placing her arm around his neck or on his shoulder and her right foot on the top of his left foot, which represents the stirrup of a saddle. The couples now continue in their counterclockwise circuit of the fire, each couple attempting to synchronize its movements as well as possible considering the awkward stance. On musical cue the couples must twirl in place, which is even more difficult. The dance proceeds in this fashion until its conclusion. Like a three-legged race at a picnic, the efforts of the couples, often grossly mismatched in terms of height and age, are the object of considerable merriment. The dance is only rarely performed at present, but it is not obsolete. At Whiteoak its performance is often initiated by those Oklahoma Delawares who usually attend Loyal Shawnee dances.

OLD TIME FORTY-NINE DANCE

This dance, as a nighttime Shawnee dance, is limited to the two Absentee ceremonial grounds. The singers stand near the center of the dance ground, but well away from the fire. They employ a "dry" Plains-style drum, which some of them hold up at waist level by means of rawhide loops attached to the drum frame. The dancers, men and women mixed, in no particular order, form a small circle around the singers, executing a step-left, drag right up to left, step, moving in a clockwise direction. As additional dancers join in the dance they form additional concentric circles around the singers. The singers also pivot slowly in place as they sing, the hub of a giant wheel of dancers. From time to time the women dancers, on signal from the head singer, who holds his drumstick aloft, carry the song for a while.

Absentee informants state that this dance came to the Absentee Shawnees from the Kiowas and Comanches. The name "Old Time Forty-Nine" distinguishes the songs of this dance from those of more recent composition used in the Forty-Nine dance by High Plains tribes.

ROUND DANCE

The Round Dance, too, is limited to the Absentee Shawnees as a nighttime Shawnee dance. It was seen at the Absentee "Old" ground following the spring Bread Dance in 1971 and following the spring Bread Dance at the Little River or "New" ground in 1973. In its choreography it is identical with the Round Dance commonly seen as a powwow feature in Oklahoma, namely a step-left, drag right up to left, step in a clockwise direction, with the dancers facing the center of a large circle. The songs, however, are somewhat different and seem to represent an earlier stage in the evolution of the Round Dance form. The Shawnees have possessed the dance long enough to have changed the positioning of the singers from the center of the dancers to the side of the ground.

MORNING DANCE (WAPANEKAWE)
OR DRUNKEN DANCE

This dance customarily ends a night of social dancing. It cannot be performed, however, unless the dancing has continued uninterrupted thoughout the entire previous night. For its performance the ceremonial drum, which is retired sometime between midnight and two o'clock, is returned to the dance

ground. The singers take their positions at the north (Loyal
Shawnees) or west (Absentee Shawnees) side of the ground,
seating themselves on the log benches. The dancers form a rank or
cluster facing them as the dance begins. At first the dancers
simply stand in place, now and then joining in the chorus of the
song. After the first song, the head singer calls out, "Come and get
me," and some of the women dancers come and take hold of the
drum, pulling the head singer to his feet. His seconds rise as well,
and now the whole party begins a slow counterclockwise
progression around the dance area, most of the dancers dancing
backward followed by the singers who dance forwards. All
employ a simple toe-heel step. Some of the songs are of a jesting
nature, similar to some of the songs of the Women's Cluster Dance
songs used in the Bread Dance, and there is much shaking of
fingers by the women at the men.

One name for the dance, Wapanekawe ("Morning Dance"),
refers to the time of the dance's performance, the dawn of a new
day. The other name, "Drunken Dance", is in my opinion a
misnomer. Speck (F.G. Speck *Ethnology of the Yuchi Inidans*: pp.
129–130; *Ceremonial Songs of the Creek and Yuchi Indians*: p.
204) indicates that among the Creeks and Yuchis drunkenness
and considerable licentiousness between the sexes were
associated with this dance, but I have never observed such
behavior among the Shawnees, Delawares, nor for that matter
among the Creeks or Yuchis. It is true that some of the dancers, as
a result of having danced throughout the night and having
imbibed a few too many six packs of beer, appear somewhat the
worse for wear. Most, however, are completely sober, though in
high spirits.

Densmore's Seminole informants were probably closer to the
truth than Speck when they told her that (F. Densmore *Seminole
Music*: p. 148): " . . . intoxication was not connected with the
dance but . . . people acted without restraint, behaving like
drunken men." Or in the words of her Creek interpreter (Densmore
loc. cit.) "It is the same as though children or anybody was happy
and capered around." "Exhilaration" would be a much better
description than "drunken" for the spirit surrounding the dance's
performance. This exhilaration is less the result of alcoholic
beverages than the feeling of achievement at having been able to

continue the social dancing through the entire night, and thus successfully cap off the occasion. The conclusion of the dance is often marked by a sentimental shaking of hands all around and wishing one another well until the next meeting.

15

Obsolete Dances and Dance Customs

Several Shawnee dances that are no longer performed are mentioned in the literature or were vaguely recalled by my informants. For most of these detailed descriptions are lacking. To add depth to our picture of Shawnee ceremonialism, and for purposes of comparison, I shall review this material here.

BIRD DANCE

The Bird Dance may be the Shawnee cognate of the Iroquois Robin Dance. It is now obsolete and was not known to any of my informants. Morgan, our sole source regarding the dance, writes (L.H. Morgan *The Indian Journals*, *1859–62*: p. 77): "Bird Dance, Ga-che-go-pa-the-wa-ka-wa. By women alone. It is a small bird which appears in winter and sings, not a snow bird." No details of choreography are given. Possibly this is the same as the Quail Dance. Another possibility, the Pigeon Dance, is shown in Plate 27, which is a reproduction of a painting by Earnest Spybuck. The Pigeon Dance was identified by Mary Spoon as a Shawnee dance of which she had heard, but never seen.

DANCE FOR THE DEAD

Morgan is our only source for the Dance for the Dead. Of it he writes, (Morgan *Indian Journals*: p. 77): "Dance for the Dead, Lapse-ma-te-wa. Dance on adoption of one in place of deceased" Although none of my informants mentioned a dance of this name nor could recognize Morgan's name for it, the custom of adopting someone to replace a deceased relative is quite common among the

Kickapoos, Sauks, Potawatomis, and Oklahoma Seneca-Cayugas, and was probably common among the Shawnees in the past. Today the Absentee Shawnees often attend and participate in Kickapoo and Sauk adoptions, but I have not heard of their staging such ceremonies in recent years. Such adoptions generally involve a ritual feast, a lengthy series of daytime dances, and then an all-night series of social dances. Often the adoptee is dressed up in a completely new costume resembling the garb favored by the deceased and is thereafter referred to by the family of the deceased using the same kinship term formerly employed in regard to him or her.

In view of Skinner's (A. Skinner *Associations and Ceremonies of the Menomini Indians*: p. 212) statement that the Menominee "Shawnee Dance" was performed in honor of the dead, and that it was borrowed from the Shawnee "at an ancient time"; likewise the association of the Shawnee Dance with adoptions among the Ojibwas, Plains-Ojibwas, Foxes, and Prairie-Potawatomis, it is likely that the Shawnee Dance was the principal dance at Shawnee adoptions in the past. The Shawnee Dance has been described in the previous chapter.

DOLL DANCE

Mary Spoon said that once when she was a small girl she observed a performance of the Doll Dance by the Absentees at Little River. She believed, however, that it was a Delaware family that sponsored and led this performance. From her account, the performance was done in the classical Delaware manner, with various persons taking turns dancing with the dressed-up doll, which was fastened to a tall pole for the occasion. I strongly suspect that the Doll Dance, whenever performed by the Shawnees, was a direct borrowing from their Delaware friends and allies. An excellent description of the Delaware Doll Dance or *Oxta'uskann* is found in F.G. Speck's *Oklahoma Delaware Ceremonies, Feasts, and Dances* (pp. 61–6). The Oklahoma Seneca-Cayuga doll cult, probably borrowed from the Delawares as well, has been described in my monograph on that tribe (J. Howard "Environment and Culture: The Case of the Oklahoma Seneca-Cayuga", Pt. 2: p. 12). A Delaware Doll Dance doll, formerly belonging to Rosie Frenchman (an Oklahoma Delaware) is shown in Plate 51. This doll, which was latter sold to a collector, was the last of its kind remaining in Indian hands in Oklahoma.

FALSE FACE DANCE AND HUSK FACE DANCE

Both the False Face Dance and the Husk Face Dance were limited to the Eastern and Loyal bands of Shawnees, and both have been obsolete for seventy years or more. Morgan is our earliest source on the Shawnee False face dance (*Indian Journals*: p. 77). He writes: "False Face Dance, Path-ka-ka-wa-ka-wa. Dance with false faces and by men alone." The next person to mention the dance is C.F. Voegelin. Voegelin associates, I believe incorrectly, the False Face Dance with the Doll Dance. He writes (C.F. Voegelin *The Shawnee Female Deity*: p. 13): "Formerly the Doll dance, associated with false faces, served in annual worship of the Creator. Each political division had a doll which the Absentee Shawnee called paathkaka, a term reserved by the Cherokee Shawnee for false face. The Doll dances were discontinued before the Civil War, but a Seneca version of the False Face ceremony was subsequently reintroduced to the Eastern Shawnee for a short time."

E.W. Voegelin ("Shawnee Musical Instruments": p. 463) gives a bit more information on the Loyal Shawnee False Face and Husk Face dances: "Among the Cherokee Shawnees the former False Faces and Shuck Faces, when asked to dance on their village rounds, had one man from among the spectators beat on a board with a small stick as they sang their dance songs." She later notes (ibid: p. 467) that: "they [tortoise shell hand rattles] were also carried by Cherokee Shawnee False Face impersonators." and a bit further on, after describing the construction of the turtle shell rattles, further observes (ibid: p. 467): "Such an instrument was not only used by False Faces when they danced, but to purify persons and ward off disease. 'At each house in the village the False Faces rubbed the people, the walls of the houses, the floor under the beds and every other place with their turtle shell rattles. The reason they used these rattles was because there are only a very few varmints which will attack turtle, he's so protected.' " From the above, which is our only information on the Shawnee False Face and Husk Face dances, they would appear to have been identical in both form and function with the well known False Face and Husk Face performances of the Iroquois (see W.N. Fenton *Masked Medicine Societies of the Iroquois*: pp. 397–429, Plates 1–25; G.P. Kurath *Iroquois Music and Dance*: pp. 9–11).

Both the False Face performers, who wore wooden masks, and the Husk Faces, who wore masks or braided and sewn or twined cornhusks, were members of shamanistic or "doctor" societies. The members of the False Face Society were hunters who had met quasi-human beings in the forests, dreamed of them afterwards, and subsequently carved their faces in living basswood trees for use as masks. They were able to cure certain types of illness by blowing hot ashes on the heads of their patients. The Husk or Shuck Faces wore masks representing another class of earth-bound supernaturals who formed a pact with mankind long ago and taught them the arts of hunting and agriculture. The Husk Faces, though they also doctored, were subsidiary to the False Faces proper, and often served as their messengers.

Aside from the name Paathkaka, which is used for both, there would appear to be no connection between the Doll Dance and the False Face performances. All of my informants on the Doll Dance vehemently denied that masks were ever worn in it as C.F. Voegelin implies. I would guess that both the wooden False Faces and the Husk Faces were borrowed by the Eastern and Loyal bands of Shawnees from the Mingo Iroquois, that group of western Iroquois, largely Senecas and Cayugas, who split off from the main body of the Iroquois in the 1740s and 1750s and ultimately became the Oklahoma Seneca-Cayugas. Morgan's discovery of the False Face dance among the Kansas (formerly the Ohio and later the Loyal) Shawnees in 1860, and E.W. Voegelin's securing excellent "memory" descriptions of False Face and Husk Face dances from Loyal Shawnee informants in the 1930s would indicate that these two Shawnee bands may have maintained two masking societies for some length of time. I was able to secure only vague accounts of the False Face Dance from my Eastern and Loyal Shawnee informants. The Oklahoma Seneca-Cayugas still have the False Face Society and Dance, though they are now reduced to using a single wooden mask in their performances.

UNNAMED MASKED DANCE

Mary Spoon commented that her grandfather had told her that the Absentee Shawnees once performed a dance in which the participants wore masks made of watermelon rinds. The water-melons were carefully cleaned out from one end and the rinds shaved very thin; then eyes, nose, and mouth were cut and the rind was worn over the head by the dancers. Mary's grandfather did not tell her the name of the dance, or when or why it was performed. He merely noted that it had been performed in his youth (around 1850). The occasion for his mentioning the dance was his observing some Indian children making jack-o-lanterns for the white man's Halloween.

The dance mentioned by Mary's grandfather may have been a Shawnee cognate of the Creek and Seminole "Old People's Dance," or Adzhalangi abango, now obsolete, in which masks of bark, melon or gourd rind were worn by the participants. The dancers carried canes and wore old clothing and imitated the gait and mannerisms of elderly people. The dance was usually performed in the fall of the year.

MISINGW IMPERSONATOR

Esther Dixon recalled seeing a masked performer at Loyal Shawnee ceremonials when she was a very small girl. Her description of this masker indicates that he was probably impersonating the Delaware Misingw or Mask Spirit, regarded by that tribe as the guardian of deer and other game and the friend of man. Esther's account may be paraphrased as follows:

> In order to keep the kids out of the Stomp Dances at Whiteoak when I was small, they had a man who dressed in animal hides and wore a wooden mask. It had big eyes, mouth, and small horns at the side. He carried a pouch at his side made of animal hide. This man would come around to each camp about four or five in the evening and the kids would have to give him a pinch of tobacco. Sometimes he would grab your hand as you were giving him the tobacco. We were told that unless we stayed in our beds at our family's camp this creature would get us, and we were terrified of him.
>
> (Question by JH: What did you call this man? From your description of him he sounds like the Delaware Misingw)
>
> I can't remember what he was called. He may have been a Delaware because I think I saw him at a Delaware ceremony once as well as several times at Whiteoak.

It seems likely, in view of the frequent attendance of the Oklahoma Delawares and the Loyal Shawnees at each others' ceremonies, and even the exchange of ritual personnel between the two groups, that the masker observed by Esther was actually a Delaware, the same individual who impersonated the Mask Spirit in the Delaware Mask Dance and just prior to the departure of the hunters on the morning of the fourth day of the Delaware Big House ceremony. If he was not a Delaware, then it can be said with certainty that the character was adopted from that tribe by the Shawnees. The behavior of the Misingw impersonator at Delaware ceremonies was identical with that observed by Esther at Whiteoak.

Speck (*Oklahoma Delaware Ceremonies, Feasts and Dances*: pp. 49–56) describes the Delaware Mask dance ceremony, including the dress of the masker. He notes (ibid: p. 51) that the pouch worn at the side by the masker was used to hold offerings of tobacco given to him. In order to keep children from making so much noise at gatherings, they were told that the bag contained snakes. The Delaware masker carried a snapping turtle rattle in his right hand, which is a feature that is not mentioned in Esther's account. The horns at the side of the mask described by her are not a usual feature. I suggest that she probably mistook the ears of the bearskin cape attached to the wooden mask for horns.

QUAIL DANCE (KWALASOTHE WEKAWE)

This dance is now obsolete but Mary Spoon remembered performing it as a girl. An old man who remembered the dance instructed the women and girls as to how it should be performed, Mary stated. In this dance the women imitated the quail or bobwhite, putting their hands on their hips as they danced.

ROCKING DANCE (NAMENEKAWE)

Concerning this dance Morgan (*Indian Journals*: p. 77) writes: "Rocking Dance, Na-ma-ha-ka-wa. Men and women, a trotting dance." The name of this dance was recalled by Mary Spoon, but she said she had never seen it.

SCRAPING DANCE

The Scraping Dance was not remembered by any of my informants, nor did they recall the characteristic musical instrument used in it. Morgan (*Indian Journals*: p. 77) writes: "Scraping Dance, Lal-ha-ka-wa. They notch a stick and for music scrape a stick along over the notches. This is put over a wood bowl to increase the noise." The description is obviously of a musical rasp, used to accompany the dance. Though at present the musical rasp tends to be limited to a few Southwestern Pueblo groups and to the Utes, who employ it in their Bear Dance, it once had a much wider distribution. It was widely employed by Midwestern and Plains tribes in the nineteenth century. The archeological recovery of notched rib bones indicates an even greater distribution in the prehistoric period. As noted earlier, such notched bones are a characteristic artifact of the Fort Ancient Aspect, a part of which is almost certainly the archeological remains of the Shawnees; hence Morgan's note of the instrument in 1860 is doubly interesting. Groups somewhat similar in culture to the Shawnees who used the musical rasp were the Santee Dakotas, Ojibwas, and Meskwakis or Foxes.

SKUNK DANCE (SEKAKWAWEKAWE)

As his sixth Shawnee dance Trowbridge (C.C. Trowbridge *Shawnese Traditions*: p. 50) lists: "Saakaukwaukauwena [*Sekakwawawena*] Skunk dance. This is danced by women alone. Like the two first described [Women's Cluster dance and Leading dance]." Unless the name of this dance is an obsolete designation for the Women's Straight Dance, as Trowbridge's account suggests, this dance is obsolete. Mary Spoon recalled older people mentioning the dance but said that she had never seen it. Until recently a Skunk Dance was performed by the Creeks, Yuchis, and Seminoles in Oklahoma, but whether this is a cognate of the Shawnee Skunk Dance I do not know.

SQUAT DANCE

This dance seems to be obsolete among the Shawnees, but it was observed as a part of a Kickapoo ceremonial War Dance in 1971. Morgan (*Indian Journals*: p. 77) describes it as follows: "Squat Dance, Na-na-ma-cha-qua-wa. They squat down and shake like a turkey or chicken shakes off the dust, not all at once, but a few at a time."

As observed among the Oklahoma Kickapoos, only young men who were warriors taking part in the War Dance, danced to the Squat Dance songs. One or two at a time, they would jump into the center of the dance area immediately in front of the singers, quickly assuming the squatting position. Remaining in this position they would hop about like birds to the music, or alternately throw out their legs in front as is done in some Russian dances.

SWAN DANCE

The Swan dance (Habethi wekawe) is described by Morgan (*Indian Journals*: p. 77) thus: "Swan Dance, Wa-pa-the-wa-ka-wa. Men and women. Two men side by side and occasionally a woman." The Swan dance as a feature of Shawnee nighttime or social dances is now obsolete. Those Absentee Shawnees who participate in Pan-Indian powwows, such as Ed Mack's Sauk Veteran's Powwow, have adopted the Fox version of the Swan

Dance, which they say is similar to their own. The Fox version of the Swan dance was brought to their Oklahoma kinsmen, the Sauks, and from the Sauks diffused to a number of the tribes in the vicinity of Shawnee, Oklahoma.

As performed today the dance consists of alternating couples, two women, then two men, et cetera, forming a long line. Two experienced women dancers always lead this double file of dancers, which follows a serpentine path around the dance ground in a general counterclockwise direction. The female dancers, but not the men, imitate the flight of the swan by holding their arms extended at the sides like a swan's wings. All employ a fast running step, but take very short steps. The dance is very effective when done well, and often brings gasps of appreciation from the audience when introduced as a powwow feature. I cannot surmise why such a beautiful dance should have disappeared from the regular Shawnee repertoire.

TURKEY DANCE

The Turkey Dance (Pelewekawe) is twenty-first on Morgan's list of Shawnee dances. He simply lists it together with its native name "Pa-la-wa-ka-wa" *Indian Journals*: p. 77). Morgan's listing of the dance in 1860 is interesting, because both my Loyal Shawnee and Absentee informants indicated that the dance was borrowed from the Caddoes in fairly recent times, around 1920.

On the afternoon of 27 May, 1972, at the Delaware powwow near Copan, Oklahoma, a Turkey Dance was held as an afternoon activity (followed by an Indian football game). The singers on this occasion were Bill Shawnee, Ranny Carpenter, and Bill Grass (a Sauk). Bill Shawnee had a peyote water drum and sat in the center of the trio of singers, flanked by Ranny Carpenter and Bill Grass, who carried cowhorn rattles.

The women dancers were led by Ruby Diebold (an Oklahoma Seneca-Cayuga and Shawnee) and included Alice Weller (a Caddo-Delaware), and Loyce Brown (an Oklahoma Delaware) as well as several other Shawnee and Delaware women. They numbered about twelve. All had brought shawls with them, which they wore when they danced. The dance was in three movements. The first series of songs carried a dance in which the women, in a single file following the head dancer, imitated a turkey's gait, darting each foot forward in turn, then quickly drawing it back before planting it on the ground, with the feet alternating in rapid succession. During the second series the women spread out to some distance, then massed in a cluster in the center of the dance ground. During these songs the women kept their feet together and hopped, at the same time turning their bodies from left to right and right to left. In the third movement the women started out with a toe-heel left, toe-heel right step. After a short while each woman dancer picked a male partner from among the spectators. Each man danced backwards facing his partner. On musical cue the men whooped and changed positions with their female partners, who now danced backwards. This reversing also occurred at the end of each song. The entire dance lasted about one hour and fifteen minutes.

Following the dance I spoke with Ranny Carpenter concerning it. According to Ranny the Shawnees, Oklahoma Delawares, and Quapaws jointly acquired the Turkey Dance from the Caddoes. Victor Griffin, the Quapaw chief, purchased the dance for his daughter Ardena when she was a small girl. Griffin observed that his daughter enjoyed the dance while he and his family were visiting among the Caddoes, so he gave the Caddoes valuable gifts of horses and blankets and was allowed to take the Turkey Dance back to the Quapaw dance ground at the Devil's Promenade, near Quapaw, Oklahoma. Ardena Griffin danced the Turkey Dance most of her life, and was the only woman allowed to wear bells around her ankles when she danced, a symbol of her being the "head turkey." When she became too old to dance she gave a speech, very sad and moving according to Ranny, and turned over the leadership of the dance to someone else, accompanied with many gifts. According to Ranny, Bill Shawnee is the only singer from northeastern Oklahoma who can lead the Turkey Dance songs. He has sung for the Turkey Dance for many years, perhaps since Griffin purchased the dance for his daughter.

I have seen the Turkey Dance performed on two different occasions by the Quapaws. In 1954 I saw a Quapaw woman, who I believe was Victor Griffin's daughter, lead the Turkey Dance wearing the traditional ankle bells which go with the dance. On this occasion she was overcome by the heat (it was 105 degrees) and had to be carried from the dance ground. In 1957 I again observed a Quapaw performance of the dance as an afternoon feature at the Quapaw powwow. On this occasion most of the women were dressed in the Shawnee woman's costume. On both occasions several Shawnee women joined with the Quapaws in the dance, and Bill Shawnee was the main singer. A Caddo performance of the dance was observed at the Caddo dance ground at the Binger "Y" in 1970, and it was identical with the three performances mentioned above. Joe Bedoka (Caddo and Absentee Delaware) was the principal singer on this occasion, and wore an ornament of turkey beards at the side of his hat to indicate this office. On this last occasion several Absentee Shawnee women and girls joined in the dance with the Caddoes.

WAR DANCE BEFORE BATTLE

Morgan (*Indian Journals*: p. 77) lists two war dances for the Shawnees, fourth and fifth in his listing of Shawnee dances. The fourth is described as follows: "War Dance, Hik-ne-pa-wa [Which is danced] Before setting out. Men alone." Of the fifth he states "War Dance, He-len-ne-na-ka-wa [Hileni wekawe] Dance on return. It signifies the dance of the braves." The latter of these two dances may be identified, from its Shawnee name, with the present-day Man's Dance or ceremonial War Dance that is still performed by the Absentee Shawnees and described earlier in this work. But what of the other, now obsolete? Its name was not recognized by any of my informants. It was probably the same as the War Dance that Trowbridge (*Shawnese Traditions*: p. 18) notes: "[It] always precedes their [the warriors] departure from the village." No details of its choreography are given, but one imagines that in its general character it resembled the Hileni wekawe or Man's Dance, and involved such features as the "striking of the post" and the recital of war stories. Its function was probably to recruit additional members for the approaching conflict and to work the emotions of those warriors already committed to a fever pitch.

WOLF DANCE (WHEWHAWEKEWE)

Both Trowbridge and Morgan mention this dance, which is now obsolete. Trowbridge says (*Shawnese Traditions*: p. 50): "M'whuwaakauwaa [*M'whawekawe*]—The wolf dance. This corresponds to the Begging dance of the Chippeways, and is disclaimed by the Shawnees, who say it has been borrowed from other nations." Morgan (*Indian Journals*: p. 77) writes: "Wolf Dance, M-wha-wa-ka-wa. This is a begging dance. Every one is expected to give and when the whole is collected they make a feast." Mary Spoon reported hearing of this dance by name but had never seen it. The Ojibwa Begging Dance, of which this seems to be a variant, is still performed by the Ojibwas of Red Lake, Minnesota, as a feature of their Fourth of July powwow each year. As observed in 1953, 1959, and 1960, it involved a party of about thirty costumed dancers and five singers performing the War Dance before various trading stores and the agency office. At each stop the owner of the store, or in the last case the agency superintendent, presented the group with a supply of candy, oranges, cigarettes, and a few dollars in cash, which they divided among themselves. Densmore (F. Densmore *Chippewa Music I*: p. 168) describes the 1908 performance of the dance, but fails to mention its "begging" feature. She also offers a photograph of the mounted dancers returning to their camp (ibid.: Plate 12).

EAGLE DANCE

In 1936 and 1937 E. W. Voegelin secured a description of a Shawnee Eagle dance that she passed on to Wm. N. Fenton. The reference is unclear but the dance was apparently limited to the Loyal band. Fenton (W. N. Fenton *The Iroquois Eagle Dance*: 203-4) writes:

> The one division held the Eagle Dance separately. It is addressed to Eagle who gave the rite to the Shawnee. Roc carried off a man in a hollow log, and the man beat the bird on the head to get home and institute the dance. Three kinds of eagles are distinguished and associated with directions. A preliminary feasting of birds resembles the Seneca method of luring down birds. Shawnee take the third bird, the bundle is there open, and it is later hung on a pole or tree limb. There was no society of those who had been cured of Eagle sickness, or epilepsy, which is caused by wearing untreated feathers or being bitten by bird lice. No ceremonial friendships arose through the rite. The bundle contained 12 feather coats for the dancers, which recall costumes still used in the Pueblo area, besides tobacco, 4 tail feathers, a raven wing—the doctor's emblem as in the Southeast—a drum hide and stick, and 1 gourd rattle. There were 12 songs, 12 dancers, and women might watch. Dancers crouched and cried like eagles and picked up objects in their mouths like Onondaga dancers, but the dance more nearly resembled Catlin's Choctaw Eagle Dance than the Iroquois variant, since the Shawnee dancers rest squatting. (The Iroquois dancers perch on chairs, although I never inquired what they perched on, if anything, before chairs came to them.) Raven is messenger, bundle chief, and priest, and conducts the ceremony; there is no whooper, but the 12 dancers cry like eagles; and the conductor appoints 4 singers, and the dancers. The tobacco offering is not burned, and pipe passing is absent, and no honored old men present fans and rattles to the dancers. There is no striking post and beater, and recitation of war records belongs to another dance, and no fans are waved in the dance or laid down with special song. Four is the sacred number, circuits are counterclockwise, meetings are held toward spring, and the rite lacks sex and color symbolisms of the Calumet Dance of the Hako type.
>
> In the list of 25 peculiar features of Iroquois Eagle dance but 5 outright

negatives occur in the Shawnee data—absence of pole and beater, friendship, feather fans, and a song for laying them down. No head is passed. Tobacco is not burned but offered dry, and the dancers cry; there is no whooper. Yet Shawnee Eagle dance is sufficiently differentiated from Iroquois to have a special quality of its own.

I would agree with Fenton that the Shawnee Eagle dance, thus described, has a "special quality of its own," and that it more nearly resembled the Choctaw Eagle Dance painted by George Catlin than the Iroquois variant. I am likewise impressed by use of feather costumes by the dancers rather than the "pipes" and gourds of the Calumet Dance of the Hako type or the Iroquois Eagle Dance. This suggests a possible relationship of the Shawnee Eagle Dance (though not, in my opinion, the Calumet Dance of the Hako type or the Iroquois Eagle Dance) to the dancing hawk men of the Southeastern Ceremonial Complex of the Mississippian archeological culture (J. Howard *The Southeastern Ceremonial Complex and Its Interpretation*: pp. 37–45, Figs. 9 and 10).

Another Eagle Dance, performed only by women, was mentioned by Cody Mack, who said that it had died out in the 1930s. In it the women imitated the actions of female eagles by waving their arms as they danced.

STRIKING-THE-STICK DANCE

Fenton describes the Iroquois "Striking-the-stick" dance, noting that it supposedly originated among the Shawnees (Fenton *The Iroquois Eagle Dance*: p. 105):

> Striking-the-stick Dance, which Morgan also marked as obsolete, belongs to the class of fighting songs . . . He-strikes-the-rushes has heard that it originated with the Shawnee when they were allied to the Seneca, and that many of the present songs and dances were derived from them. It was really a war dance performed before the departure and on the return of a war party. Two lines of dancers face each other, advance, and as they meet, they strike their clubs; they pass, turn, and return. The dancers demonstrate how they can fight and scalp. The war pole, which was diagonally striped with red paint, was set up at one end of the place, for a speaker to strike at the end of each song. Today, Striking-the-stick ordinarily follows the War dance . . . . .

The movements that are described in this account strongly resemble the Shawnee ceremonial War or Man's Dance, but the feature of striking clubs together is absent from today's Shawnee War Dance, and so is the use of the war pole, though both may have been present among the Shawnee at an earlier period.

LIZARD DANCE

The Lizard Dance was mentioned by Cody Mack as having died out in the 1930s. It was performed in honor of "giant lizards" that Cody said were quite plentiful in the Little River area early in this century.

GIST'S PUTATIVE SHAWNEE "DIVORCE AND REMARRIAGE" CEREMONY

In 1750 Christopher Gist, a Virginia surveyor, was sent out by the Ohio Company of Virginia to secure the permission of the Shawnees to survey and establish a settlement south of the Ohio, in their hunting grounds. In January 1751, Gist left his surveying party encamped on the south bank of the Ohio and journeyed alone to the Shawnee village of Old Chillicothe. Gist was well received by the Shawnees there and gained their consent to survey ground for settlement on the south side of the river. During his stay in the Shawnee village Gist witnessed (or says that he witnessed) a Shawnee "divorce and remarriage" ceremony (C.A. Hanna *The Wilderness Trail*, 2: p. 152; Cf. also T.W. Alford in W.A. Galloway *Old Chillicothe*: p. 203):

> From Thursday, Jan. 31, to Monday, Feb. 11. Stayed in the Shannoah Town; while I was here the Indians had a very extraordinary Kind of a Festival, at which I was present and which I have exactly described at the End of my *Journal* . . . An Account of the Festival mentioned in my *Journal*:
> In the Evening a proper Officer made a public Proclamation that all the Indians' marriages were dissolved, and a Public Feast was to be held for three succeeding days after, in which the women, as their custom was, were again to choose husbands.
> The next Morning, early, the Indians breakfasted, and after spent the Day in dancing till the Evening, when a plentiful Feast was prepared, after feasting, they spent the Night in dancing. The same way they spent the next two days till Evening, the Men dancing by themselves and then the women in turns round the Fires, and dancing in their Manner in the Form of the Figure 8, about 60 or 70 at a time, the Women, the whole Time they danced, sung a Song in their language the Chorus of which was,
> 'I am not afraid of my Husband,
> I will choose what Man I please.'
> singing these lines alternately.
> The third Day in the Evening, the Men being about 100 in number [danced], some times at Length, at other Times in a Figure 8, quite round the Fort and in and out of the long House, where they held their Councils the Women standing together as the Men danced by them; And as any of the Women liked a Man passing by, she stepped in and joined in the Dance, taking hold of the Man's Stroud whom she chose, and the continued in the Dance till the rest of the women stepped in and made their choice in the same manner; after which the dance ended, and they all retired to consummate.

Alford (in Galloway *Old Chillicothe*: pp. 201-4) notes, charitably, that Gist's account is "probably apocryphal" and points out that a "close search of Shawnee literature and tradition has failed to verify this procedure as a custom of this nation." Gist's purpose in disseminating this patently false account was probably to discredit the Shawnees as moral human beings, and hence to justify the expulsion of these "savages" from their lands by white frontiersmen.

Appendix

Shawnee Music
by
James H. Howard
with Transcriptions of Fourteen Shawnee Songs
by Sandra Wilbur

So far as I am aware, the only extant material that relates to Shawnee music is a short paper by Bruno Nettl ("The Shawnee Musical Style: Historical Perspective in Primitive Music"). Nettl's paper, though brief, is an excellent study by a highly competent musicologist, and I have relied heavily upon it in preparing this appendix.

Nettl notes two kinds of melodic movement in Shawnee music. Most common is a type that he characterizes as "undulating," meaning that one finds both rising and descending movement, but with the end of the song almost invariably lower than the beginning (Nettl "The Shawnee Musical style": p. 279). This is not, however, the cascading movement found in most American Indian music from west of the Mississippi (that is, the Prairie-Plains and the Southwest), a type of melody in which ascending sections are extremely rare. This type corresponds to the second type of Shawnee melody.

Much variety is encountered in the range of Shawnee songs. Some have only a third, fourth, or fifth as compass. Nettl noted this in lullabies and the songs accompanying folktales, which he believed to be an archaic type of melody. Most of the songs have a range of about an octave. A third type has a range of about a twelfth. This last feature occurs in songs that exhibit the cascading rather than the undulating movement (ibid.: p. 282).

As melodic intervals Nettl noted mostly major seconds, a large number of thirds and fourths, and occasional fifths and octaves. There is no evidence of such "chromatic" phenomena as two minor seconds occurring in succession in the same direction (ibid.).

On the other hand, he notes that intervals larger than seconds are usually succeeded by seconds. The final tone in a song is either the lowest or the next-to-lowest tone in the scale. Aside from the undulating and cascading types of melody, clear-cut divisions do not emerge from this analysis (ibid.)

Most Shawnee songs have a pentatonic scale, the tones of which are distributed evenly within the octave in seconds and thirds. Only a few show unevenly distributed scales, such as one empty and one filled tetrachord, which is a type of scale construction that is common to Plains Indian music. Occasionally one finds tetratonic and hexatonic scales, and, in songs of the small range type, ditonic and tritonic scales. In the latter songs, a fourth or a fifth is usually functioning somewhere, either as an interval or as the entire compass (ibid.).

A variety of forms is found in Shawnee music. The overall form is strophic; that is, the entire song is usually repeated several times, sometimes with minor modifications, sometimes exactly. Beloff, in her analysis of my Shawnee tapes, noted three types of repetitions. Phrase repetition is most usual. The introductory phrase (a), for instance, is usually repeated by the singers (*(a) abbc* . . . etc.) A song repeated but without the introductory phrase ((a) abbc,abbc) must be distinguished from the song that is entirely repeated ((a)bbc . . . (a)bbc). The former employs one of the most common types of song patterns whereas the latter seems to be used when the song is generally considered by the singers and/or dancers to be a good one or for other reasons that can be determined only in context.

In examining some of the song patterns analyzed, Beloff observed the following:

Bread Dance (1)	(a)aa$_1$a$_1$a$_1$a$_1$,aa$_1$a$_1$a$_1$a$_1$a$_1$a$_1$ ending
Bread Dance (2)	(a)abca$_1$ca$_2$c
Swan Dance	(a)abb$_1$cdebb$_1$c,abb$_1$abb$_1$cdebb$_1$c
War Dance (1)	abcb,abcb
War Dance (2)	(a)abc, (a)abc
Women's Side Dance	(ax)axbxcxdxbxex, axbxcxdxbxe ending

(x is a short motif that is repeated in each phrase. A number (1,2) with a letter (a,b) means that it is a slightly altered form of the original (a,b).)

Repetition, then, occurs in all songs, and the most usual pattern is the repetition of the song without the introductory phrase. If the other types are looked at closely, they are often slightly altered forms of this basic pattern.

Nettl ("The Shawnee Musical Style": pp. 282–3) notes that a few

songs are strictly isorhythmic (with small modifications), some
repeating a long rhythmic unit, others a short sequence of as few
as five tones. The melodic contour may or may not be similar in
the various rhythmic units. In some songs, on the other hand, a
melodic phrase is repeated and modified at various pitch levels,
with only a general rhythmic, similarity between the different
sections. A few songs, Nettl notes, show a rather interesting type
of alternation between various distinct motifs and phrases (ibid.:
p. 283).

Among the songs that are simplest in range and scale, Nettl
found two types; the songs from folktales tend to be through
composed (a short stanza, progressive in form repeated several
times), whereas the lullabies consist of a short motif of three to six
tones repeated several times and followed by a different one as a
cadence (ibid.). Lengthening of formal units at cadential points is
exceedingly frequent. Songs usually end in a low tone which does
not occur elsewhere in the song and is repeated several times
(ibid.).

As compared with some other American Indian styles, the
rhythm of Shawnee songs is more clear cut and easier to analyze.
In some cases it takes the form of a regular meter, such as 3/4 or
2/4, but also 5/4 and 7/4, and others. Combinations of these are
also found, and modifications of the meter in certain positions
such as cadential. There are usually not more than three different
durational values in a song. In the majority of songs one finds a
development of one or more rhythmic motifs, sometimes giving
the effect of a freer kind of isorhythmic construction. The same
sequence of rhythmic relationship is repeated with changes in the
individual durational values (ibid.).

Most Shawnee songs have only vocables as text. These are
limited in number and appear in peculiar sequences that are fixed
within a particular song. Other songs have meaningful texts that
are supplemented by vocables because the meaningful words do
not always coincide with the tones of a song. The most common
manner is to introduce the text, if there is one, in the modified
repetition of the song, if that is part of the musical form.
Occasionally, however, this order is reversed, the text coming first
and the vocables in the repetition. Song texts vary from a single
word to units resembling in length a moderately long English
sentence. When a text is short it may be repeated in whole or in
part several times within the stanza. Nettl notes that in one

Peyote song the text *hikawilo* is repeated some twenty times (ibid. p. 284). The songs from stories are usually filled with text and contain no meaningless vocables.

Nettl, on the basis of their complexity, has arranged Shawnee song styles in a historical continuum. He believes that the oldest Shawnee songs, on the basis of having a small range, simple form, and two or three tone scales, are the songs from folktales and lullabies. The next oldest group, and the most common type of song, are those with undulating movements, clear-cut rhythmic units, and about an octave range. It is found in the Bread Dance songs, Moccasin Game songs, Bean Dance, and Morning Dance, and a type with which I am not familiar, "Old songs sung in Ohio".

Nettl believes that the songs of the Green Corn Dance, because of their large range, rhythmic complexity, and cascading melodic movement, probably date from shortly before 1800 and show the influence of contact with Southern Plains tribes. With all respect to Dr. Nettl I cannot agree with this conclusion. Several of my Shawnee informants stated that the Green Corn Dance songs and the Bread Dance songs were virtually the same. Wilbur tested this native hypothesis and found that the Green Corn and Bread Dance songs did indeed have many basic similarities, though no two songs were exactly the same. Both types have relatively short phrases, many repeats, and more often than not the entire song is repeated. (Example: (a)abb . . . abb . . . abb . . . pause, repeat of whole song) She recognized some syllable patterns which were the same in both sets and some of the same motifs. Most of the endings are of either of these types.

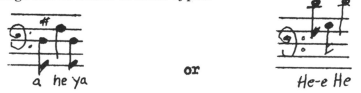

a he ya   or   He-e He

However, it is difficult without analyzing each song to find exactly how they compare on a song to song basis. This would make an interesting project in itself.

Nettl ("The Shawnee Musical Style": p. 279) states that antiphonal singing is confined to the Leading Dance, which he considers to have been borrowed from the Creeks. He is definitely in error on this point, as antiphony occurs in the Pumpkin Dance episode of Bread and Green Corn Dances, the Bringing or "Go Get 'em" Dance, the Horse Dance, and the Moving Dance (also known as the Corn dance or Bean dance). Nettl's error on this point is probably the result of his having worked with recordings made by a single person, and not having seen or heard the songs as performed in a field situation. I have indicated in the main body of this monograph (chapter fourteen) my doubts as to the Leading Dance having been introduced to the Shawnees by the Creeks, though I readily admit that the Creeks may have exerted considerable influence on the Shawnee Leading dance form.

I would definitely agree with Nettl as to the Peyote songs being the most recent addition to the Shawnee repertory. It is unfortunate that the Voegelins' collection of Shawnee songs, the basis of Nettl's analysis, apparently did not contain Buffalo Dance and War Dance songs, as I would enjoy hearing his comments on these two forms.

On the following pages I have included the transcriptions of the five songs accompanying Nettl's paper ("The Shawnee Musical Style": pp. 280–1) plus the fourteen transcribed for me by Mrs. Wilbur. All but the two War Dance songs and the Swan Dance song were recorded at Whiteoak in the years 1969–72, and the singers are Bill Shawnee (head singer), with Ranny Carpenter and (usually) Bill Alec as seconds. The two War Dance songs are from the Oklahoma Kickapoos and were recorded by Edna Snake. I feel justified in including them here in view of the near-identity of this musical form in the two tribes. The Swan Dance song was recorded at the Quapaw powwow at the Devil's Promenade, near Quapaw, Oklahoma. Though Shawnee singers were a part of the group, it is not certain that this is a Shawnee song. A further word of caution should be given concerning the song labeled "Alligator dance." It was transcribed from a tape loaned to us by a friend, and though it is definitely a Loyal Shawnee song, it may be misidentified.

KEY

1) Tones

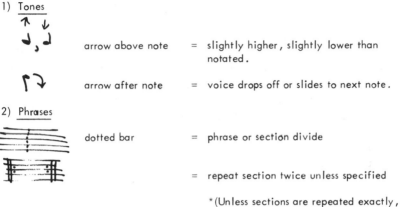

arrow above note = slightly higher, slightly lower than notated.

arrow after note = voice drops off or slides to next note.

2) Phrases

dotted bar = phrase or section divide

= repeat section twice unless specified

*(Unless sections are repeated exactly, I have written them out in full.)

3) Accompaniment

Drum: = eighth note duration with stress on every other beat

= no accented beats except where note is accented ( ).

*(The drum beats continuously throughout each piece using the pattern illustrated at the beginning of the song except where otherwise specified).

4) Text

Pronunciation:

		(as in)
e	=	ate
a	=	hop
o	=	no
eh	=	yet
i	=	key

*The use of the capital letter H is to avoid confusion with the letter n.

Fig. 10. Key to musical notation of Shawnee dance songs

348

Fig. 11. "Lullaby," "Song from Winter Story," and "Pumpkin Dance Song" (*Nettl 1953, p. 280*)

Fig. 12. "Green Corn Dance Song" and "Peyote Song" (*Nettl 1953, pp. 280–81*)

Fig. 13. "Women's Straight Dance Song"

Fig. 14. "Women's Straight Dance Song"

Fig. 15. "Bread Dance Song"

Fig. 16. "Bread Dance Song"

352

*Sung only by lead singer

Fig. 17. "Women's Side Dance Song" and "Swan Dance Song"

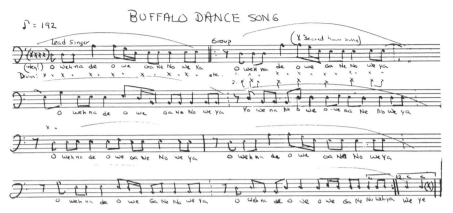

The x's in the beginning, when the song is repeated and at the end indicate the whooping ("Hey") In the beginning of the piece, fast drumming and rattling occurs between each yell. After the song is completed, it is lead and sung again.

x's represent whooping. After the song is completed it is led and sung again, but slightly altered. An additional He-ya (   ) is added to measure (1) and (2); measure six is sung twice, and there is accented drumming in measure 5. The *Ja* is pronounced softly, more like *sha*.

Fig. 18. "Buffalo Dance" songs

Fig. 19. "War Dance" songs

Fig. 20. "Raccoon Dance Song"

Fig. 21. "Go-Get-'Em Dance Song" and "Face Dance Song"

356

*These passages are sung by the dancers, not the lead singer. They can be heard in the background throughout the song.

Fig. 22. "Alligator Dance Song"

Shawnee Syllabary

Pi	Pa	Pe	Po
Fi	Fa	Fe	Fo
Si	Sa	Se	So
Ni	Na	Ne	No
Mi	Ma	Me	Mo
Ki	Ka	Ke	Ko
Wi	Wa	We	Wo
Ti	Ta	Te	To
Gi	Ga	Ge	Go
Li	La	Le	Lo
Hi	Ha	He	Ho
Yi	Ya	Ye	Yo
Qi	Qa	Qe	Qo

Pronunciation Notes

P has the sound of Be (actually the unaspirated p as in English *spin*, JH)

F has the sound of Th

T has the sound of D (actually the unaspirated t, JH)

G has the sound of English J (the sound of z in the English *azure*, JH)

Fig. 23. *Shawnee Syllabary.* The Shawnees, like certain other Midwestern Algonkian speaking tribes (i.e. Sauks, Foxes, Potawatomis, Kickapoos) and the Siouan speaking Winnebagoes, developed their own syllabic alphabet during the latter part of the 19th century, probably as a result of stimulus diffusion from the Cherokees. Once in widespread use, this syllabary is now known to only a few tribal members. The above version, together with the "Pronunciation Notes" (but not the glosses in parentheses) was furnished by Cody Mack.

358

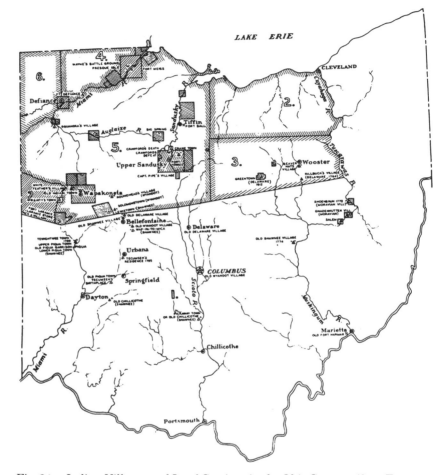

Fig. 24. *Indian Villages and Land Cessions in the Ohio Country.* (from Foreman 1940) Tracts 1, 2, 3, and 5 relate to the Shawnees. Tract 1, an area of nearly 17,000,000 acres, nearly two-thirds of the state of Ohio, was confirmed to the United States in the Treaty of Greenville, in 1795, by the Wyandots, Delawares, Shawnees, Ottawas, Ojibwas, Potawatomis, Eel Rivers, Weas, Kickapoos, Piankashaws, and Kaskaskias. The Indian rights to Tract 2, known as the Connecticut Western Reserve, insofar as they had not been extinguished by the Greenville Treaty, were relinquished by the Treaty of July 4, 1805, made at Fort Industry on the Miami of the Lake. The ceding tribes were the Wyandots, Ottawas, Ojibwas, Munsees, Delawares, Shawnees, and Potawatomis. Indian title to Tract 3 was extinguished at the same time as the preceding tract, and by the same tribal groups, at a cost to the government of a little more than one cent per acre. Tract 5 was ceded to the United States by the treaty of Sept. 29, 1817, at the foot of the rapids of the Miami of Lake Erie by the Wyandots, Senecas, Delawares, Shawnees, Potawatomis, Ottawas, and Ojibwas.

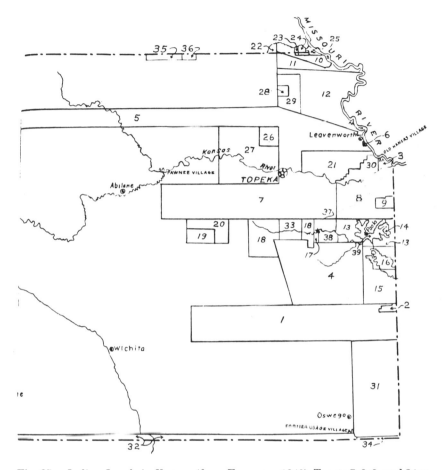

Fig. 25. *Indian Lands in Kansas* (from Foreman, 1940). Tracts 7, 8, 9, and 34 relate to the Shawnee occupancy of that state. Tract 7, consisting of 1,600,000 acres was ceded to the Shawnee Nation in the treaties of Nov. 7, 1825, and Aug. 3, 1831, but was ceded back to the United States in the Manypenny treaty of May 6, 1854, except for Tract 8, of 200,000 acres, retained for their future home, part of which was allotted to the Shawnees and the balance sold to White settlers. Tract 9 is part of sundry small tracts of the above Shawnee land set apart for missionary and church societies. Tract 34, a strip of about twelve sections, was ceded by the Quapaws to the Senecas, mixed Senecas and Shawnees, Quapaws, Peorias, Kaskaskias, Piankashaws, Weas, Ottawas of Blanchard's Fork and Roche de Boeuf, and certain Wyandots, and by them ceded to the United States on Feb. 3, 1867. Figs. 24-25 from Grant Foreman, *The Last Trek of the Indians* © 1946 by Carolyn T. Foreman; renewed 1974 by Mrs. C. Haines Lee. (Reissued 1972 Russell & Russell New York)

Figures and Plates

A NOTE ON EARNEST SPYBUCK,
THE SHAWNEE ARTIST

Plates 20 through 33 are reproductions of watercolors by the lat,
Earnest L. Spybuck, the Shawnee artist. Spybuck was "discovered" and encouraged by the late M. R. Harrington, an
anthropologist working for the Museum of the American Indian,
Heye Foundation. In a short article on Spybuck, Harrington
(1938: 15) notes that Spybuck (1883-1948) was a member of the
Thawikila division of the Absentee Shawnee. Spybuck's school-
ing never extended beyond the Third Reader and as an artist he
was entirely self-taught. Harrington quotes Spybuck as saying
"Mother Earth started me drawing." As a small child Spybuck
made his first drawings of animals on the bare ground with a
stick. Only later did he acquire paper and pencil.

Even better than Indian subjects Spybuck loved to draw
cowboys, livestock, and range scenes. In addition to his Shawnee
series, Spybuck painted ceremonials of neighboring tribes such as
the Delaware and the Sauk. He was a keen observer and possessed
an excellent memory. He usually studied his subject first in the
field and made his drawings later. Occasionally, however, he
sketched directly from nature. Harrington notes that Spybuck at
one time experimented with oils, but that his preferred medium
was still water-colors (1938: 15). Spybuck's paintings are
obviously the work of an unsophisticated and untrained artist, yet
the drawing is good and the general effect pleasing. The detail of
costume and equipment is unusually accurate, hence the
paintings are of great ethnographic value.

Of these plates, all but Plate 23 are in the collections of the
Museum of the American Indian, Heye Foundation, New York
City, with whose permission they are reproduced here. Plate 23
was loaned for copying by the late Mary Spoon.

Ernest Spybuck, Shawnee Indian Artist. Photograph courtesy of the Museum of the American Indian, Heye Foundation

362

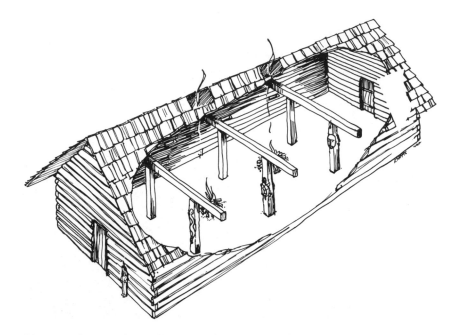

Plate 1   *Shawnee Council House of the Type Used Prior to 1840.* A reconstruction based upon the description of a structure which formerly stood on the farm of Charles Bluejacket in Johnson County, Kansas, by the Rev. Isaac McCoy (1840: 529). A twist of tobacco was tied to the post above the carving of the human face, which was undoubtedly a representation of a Shawnee deity.

Plate 2 *Shawnee Council House Formerly Located in Shawnee Township, Allen County, Ohio.* This Council house is clearly different from the structure pictured in Plate 1 in that it has a door in the middle of one side and no door at the end which appears in the photograph. If, however, there were doors in the two sides which do not show in the photograph the floorplan of this structure would correspond to the layout of the two Absentee Shawnee ceremonial grounds.

Plate 3   *A Possible Tecumseh Portrait.* This painting, now in the collections of the Field Museum in Chicago, and reproduced here with their permission, has been advanced as a portrait of Tecumseh, the famous Shawnee chief, by anthropologist George Quimby (1954: 3). It is part of a collection of paintings obtained by the museum from Emily O'Fallon, a descendant of General William Clark in 1894.

Plate 4 *The Le Dru - Lossing Portrait of Tecumseh* (from Mooney 1896: fig. 58).
This portrait is the one given by Lossing in his *American Revolution and the War
of 1812*, Vol. 3 (1875) p. 283. Lossing gives the history of the portrait as follows:
"The portrait of Tecumtha above given is from a pencil sketch by Pierre Le Dru
. . . In this I have given only the head by Le Dru. The cap was red, and in front
was a single eagle's feather, black, with a white tip. The sketch of his dress (and the
medal above described), in which he appears as a brigadier-general of the British
army, is from a rough drawing, which I saw in Montreal in the summer of 1858,
made at Malden soon after the surrender of Detroit, where the Indian celebrated
that event by a grand feast. It was only on gala occasions that Tecumtha was
seen in full dress. The sketch did not pretend to give a true likeness of the chief, and
was valuable only as a delineation of his costume. From the two we are enabled to
give a pretty faithful picture of the great Shawnee warrior and statesman as he
appeared in his best mood. When in full dress he wore a cocked hat and plume, but
would not give up his blue breech-cloth, red leggings fringed with buckskin, and
buckskin moccasins." Pierre Le Dru was a young French trader at Vincennes in
1808. Though at first glance quite different from the man pictured in Plate 3, a
closer examination and comparison of this portrait with the other reveals a number of points of similarity in the nose, mouth, and eyes of the two visages, and
tends to bear out the validity of Plate 3 as a true portrait of the famous Shawnee
chief. In this portrait, but not in Plate 3, Tecumseh is shown wearing three small
crosses suspended from the cartilage of his nose, and his George III medal which
he had inherited from an ancestor.

366

Plate 5 *The W. Langdon Kihn Portrait of Tecumseh* (from Kihn 1937: Pl. 24). This portrait, though grossly inaccurate in terms of costume detail, has great symbolic value for many present day Shawnees. The print of this painting which appeared in the *National Geographic Magazine*, or reproductions of it in oils or watercolor by native artists, hangs in many Shawnee homes. The picture shows Tecumseh just prior to the Battle of the Thames. Commissioned a brigadier general in the British Army during the War of 1812, Tecumseh led his Shawnees in the capture of Detroit. When his White allies retreated before the Americans under William Henry Harrison, Tecumseh accused them of cowardice. This, perhaps, together with a premonition of his own death, led him to discard his prized British regalia shortly before going into battle on October 5, 1813.

Inaccuracies in the picture are the two feathers in Tecumseh's roach, the failure of the artist to indicate the nose pendants usually worn by him, and the Prairie-Plains style buckskin shirt and leggings.

Painting by W. Langdon Kihn. © National Geographic Society.

Plate 6 *Tenskwatawa or Open Door, the Shawnee Prophet* (from Horan 1972:57) This portrait of the Prophet was painted in Washington by Charles Bird King. Except for the texture of the hairs in the roach headdress this portrait would seem to be quite accurate in terms of costume detail. From *The McKenney Hall Portrait Gallery of American Indians* by James D. Horan. Used by permission of Crown Publishers, Inc.

Plate 7   *Tenskwatawa or Open Door, the Shawnee Prophet, as painted by George Catlin.* Catlin notes that in his right hand the Prophet was holding his "medicine fire" and his "sacred string of beans" in the other. Both of these items were associated with the revitalization movement led by the Prophet. Note that in this portrait the Prophet is apparently wearing the same silver scalplock tube, nose ring, ear-bobs, and wide armbands shown in the earlier Bird King portrait.

Plate 8 *Kishkalwa, a Celebrated Shawnee Warrior and Chief* (from Horan 1972: 465). This chief's portrait was painted by Charles Bird King, probably at the time he led a delegation of Shawnees to Washington. Note the typical Shawnee ear ornaments and nose ring, also the head ornaments, probably indicative of war honors. From *The McKenney Hall Portrait Gallery of American Indians* by James D. Horan. Used by permission of Crown Publishers, Inc.

Plate 9 *Lay-law-she-kaw, He Who Goes Up the River, an aged Shawnee chief.*
This man's portrait was painted by George Catlin, who notes that he was the chief
of his division at the time of Catlin's visit. Note the slit ears. On special occasions
a bunch of arrows or feathers were passed through these orifices and worn as ornaments.

Plate 10   *Pah-te-coo-saw, Straight Man, a Shawnee warrior, as painted by George Catlin*. Catlin notes that Straight Man was distinguished for his exploits in war, and that his facial painting was done in black and red paint.

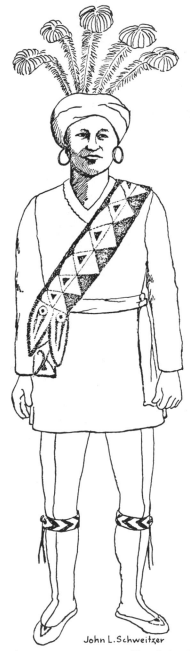

Plate 11 *Shawnee man's costume, ca. 1830*. Sketch by John Schweitzer. The beaded shoulder bag in this sketch is from a specimen in the Masonic Museum, Fargo, North Dakota. Other details of costuming are from a watercolor by Lino Sánchez y Tapia after José Maria Sánchez y Tapia (Berlandier 1969: Plate 12).

Plate 12 *Absentee Shawnee man's ceremonial costume, 1973.* Sketch by John
Schweitzer. This man is shown on his way to the dance ground. Once at the
ground, taking part in the ceremonial dances, he would remove his hat.

374

John L.Schweitzer

Plate 13   *Absentee Shawnee woman's ceremonial costume, 1973.* Sketch by John Schweitzer.

Plate 14   *Wapameepto or "Gives Light As He Walks", better known as Big Jim, chief of the Kishpoko and Pekowi divisions of the Shawnees.* Born in 1834 in Texas, Big Jim died in 1900 in Mexico. Photograph by John K. Hillers prior to 1894, Washington, D.C. Photo courtesy Smithsonian Institution, National Anthropological Archives.

Plate 15   *Tony Wentworth, a Shawnee man*. Photograph taken by J. R. Harrington at Dewey, Oklahoma, in 1910. Note the older style of Shawnee shirt. Photo courtesy of the Museum of the American Indian, Heye Foundation.

Plate 16 *Chief Little Axe, Absentee Shawnee, from a postcard ca. 1930.* The settlement of Little Axe, Oklahoma, is named after this man. Note the old style Shawnee man's shirt with a ruffle at the bottom and the fine beaded leggings and moccasins.

378

Plate 17   *Charley Switch, an Absentee Shawnee chief of the Thawikila division, and his son Alfred Switch, from a postcard ca. 1930.*

Plate 18 *Two Loyal Shawnee rituulists in ceremonial dress, 1969.* The woman is Ranny and Emmaline Carpenter's daughter Beulah, the man is Lewis Dick.

380

Plate 19 *George Richey Sr., a Shawnee mixblood of Red Lake, Minnesota.* Since the various divisions of the Shawnee have moved so often, and for such great distances, there has inevitably occurred a spinoff of personnel over a wide geographic area. Thus we find individuals of part-Shawnee descent in many Northeastern, Southeastern, Prairie, and High Plains Indian tribes, and also among the descendants of White frontier families with whom the Shawnees were in contact at various times in their history. One such is Mr. George Richey. Richey is from an old Indiana family which, although it has been out of touch with any of the recognized Shawnee bands for several generations, still preserves a strong tradition of its part-Shawnee background. Mr. Richey, who is 1/8th Shawnee, came to Red Lake, Minnesota in the 1930's, married an Ojibwa girl, and now has a large family of children and grandchildren. He is a skilled craftsman, and is a well known figure at pow-wows in Minnesota, the Dakotas, and Manitoba.

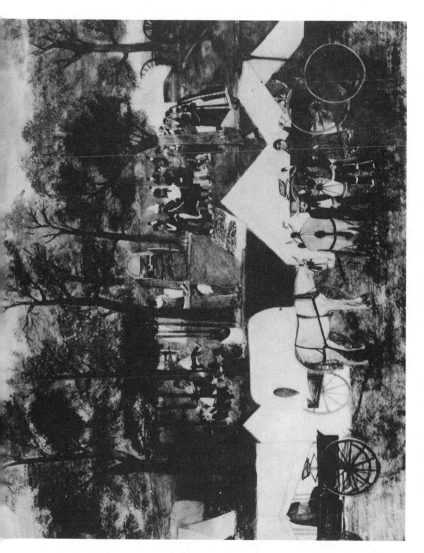

Plate 20 *Pumpkin Dance episode of the Bread Dance, Absentee Shawnees.* Painting by Ernest Spybuck, ca. 1910. Courtesy of Museum of the American Indian, Heye Foundation.

382

Plate 21 *Ceremonial men-against-women Footnote game, Absentee Shawnees.* Painting by Ernest Spybuck. Note the scorekeeper at left. Courtesy of the Museum of the American Indian, Heye Foundation.

Plate 22 Opening the sacred bundle of the Kishpoko division prior to the annual "Ride-in" and Ceremonial War dance, Absentee Shawnees. Painting by Ernest Spybuck. Courtesy Museum of the American Indian, Heye Foundation.

384

Plate 23   *Absentee Shawnee "Ride-in" or Horseback parade preceding the annual ceremonial War Dance.* Painting by Ernest Spybuck, Shawnee artist, ca. 1928. So accurate is this painting in terms of detail that Alfred Switch and Mary Spoon were able to identify individuals and camps in it as follows: The view is from the northeast, looking toward the southwest. From right to left the riders are (1) The man with the war bundle tomahawk is William Little Axe according to Mary Spoon, Little Charley according to Alfred Switch; (2) Second man is John Snake; (3) Third man is Charlie White, a Kickapoo; (4) Fourth man is *Simimi* or Aaron Tyner, a Loyal Shawnee from Whiteoak; (5) Man with drum is Little Jim. The others were not recognized except for the man at the extreme left, who is Little Creek. The camp at viewer's left is that of Nellie Hood, and the camp behind the covered wagon, center left, as that of John Snake. Courtesy Mary Spoon.

Plate 24 *Ceremonial War Dance of the Absentee Shawnees.* Painting by Ernest Spybuck, Shawnee artist. Courtesy of the Museum of the American Indian, Heye Foundation.

386

Plate 25 *Shawnee Leading Dance or "Ordinary Stomp" Dance.* Painting by Ernest Spybuck. Spybuck shows the dance as it was performed in the early years of the 20th century. The fan carried by the leader, at left, is a feature no longer seen. Note the mixture of aboriginal Shawnee garb and "citizen's dress" worn by the dancers. Courtesy of the Museum of the American Indian, Heye Foundation.

Plate 26 *The Shawnee Fish Dance, a "Nighttime" social dance.* Painting by Ernest Spybuck. Courtesy of the Museum of the American Incian, Heye Foundation.

Plate 27 *The Pigeon Dance, a Shawnee "Nighttime" social dance.* Painting by Ernest Spybuck. The Pigeon Dance is now obsolete. Courtesy of the Museum of the American Indian, Heye Foundation.

Plate 28 *Shawnee Turkey Dance.* Painting by Ernest Spybuck. Courtesy Museum of the American Indian, Heye Foundation.

Plate 29 *Shawnee Moccasin game.* Painting by Ernest Spybuck. Spybuck shows, in this painting, a favorite recreation of the old time Shawnees. The time period represented would be 1870–1880. Courtesy of the Museum of the American Indian, Heye Foundation.

Plate 30 *Shawnee Witchcraft (I)*, Painting by Ernest Spybuck. In this painting, the first of a series of four, we see the witch at the bedside of his victim, shooting "witches arrows" into the victim's body by blowing with his mouth toward the victim's chest. He has entered the victim's home in the shape of an owl, a favorite vehicle for witches because of the silent wings of this night flyer, and still carries his owl costume on his left arm. The witch is otherwise naked except for a breech-cloth. The dark rings around his eyes indicate his evil nature. All three occupants of the house, the victim and two other members of his family, have been put to sleep magically by the witch while he performs his nefarious work. Courtesy Museum of American Indian, Heye Foundation.

392

Plate 31   *Shawnee Witchcraft (II)*. Painting by Ernest Spybuck. In this second painting of the series we see that the victim has awakened, and is terribly ill. He is being treated with the contents of the family medicine cabinet by a woman and a man, certainly close relatives and perhaps identifiable as his sister and her husband, but to no effect. Outside the door we see the witch, who has again assumed his owl shape (except for human feet) grinning evilly. The family watch dog, under the effects of the same narcotic-like sleep as the humans in Plate 30, is unaware of the witch's presence.

Plate 32 *Shawnee Witchcraft (III)*. Painting by Ernest Spybuck. In this third scene the victim has been moved out of the family cabin to a tent in the yard where, according to Shawnee belief, he can "breathe easier". The women of the household are brewing native herb medicines over an outside fire. A child wanders disconsolately from tent to cabin and the family dog bays morosely at the moon, sensing the evil in the atmosphere. The witch, now in the form of a black dog with a human face, prowls the premises, gleefully watching his victim's worsening condition. Courtesy Museum of the American Indian, Heye Foundation.

394

Plate 33 *Shawnee Witchcraft (IV)*. Painting by Ernest Spybuck. In this, the fourth and last scene in the series, a sweat doctor has been called in a final desperate attempt to affect a recovery. The doctor has erected a sweat lodge near the cabin and he (seated man wearing only breechcloth) and the victim (reclining figure) are about to enter the sudatory. The witch, however, at some distance from the scene in the woods, is attempting to counter this therapy by evil magic, involving what appears to be a small effigy of the victim, which he manipulates over a small fire. Courtesy of the Museum of the American Indian, Heye Foundation.

Plate 34 *The Loyal Shawnee dance ground as it appeared in 1910.* Photograph by Harrington. Courtesy of the Museum of the American Indian, Heye Foundation.

396

Plate 35 *Loyal Shawnee ceremonial ground near Whiteoak, Oklahoma, 1971.* This view is from the northwest looking toward the southeast.

Plate 36 *Ceremonial hoop, Loyal Shawnees, Whiteoak ceremonial ground,
1972.* This hoop, which is prepared just prior to the spring Bread Dance, has packets of seeds and bunches of animal hair attached to it which are symbolic of the
female and male economic activities and which function as a prayer of Our Grandmother, the Creator, for good crops and abundant game. This picture was taken
with the permission of the ritualists at the Whiteoak ground.

Plate 37 *Loyal Shawnee dance ground officials and dancers, spring Bread dance, 1970.* The man holding the drum is Bill Shawnee, head singer. To Bill's right is Bill Alec, "second" singer. To Bill Alec's right is Frank Bob, bundle keeper and ritual speaker of the Loyal band. To Frank's right is Emmaline (Mrs. Ranny) Carpenter, chief matron of the Loyal Shawnees. To Bill Shawnee's left is Ranny Carpenter, drumkeeper and "second" singer, and to Ranny's left is Lewis Dick (in costume) for many years the leader of the Pumpkin Dance episode of the Bread Dance. View is from the south looking north.

Plate 38 *Loyal Shawnee "cooks" or women dancers performing the Women's Cluster dance.* Spring Bread Dance, Whiteoak, 1970. Note the offerings of food displayed in the center of the dance ground.

400

Plate 39 *Loyal Shawnee women performing the Women's "Straight" dance,*
Loyal Shawnee spring Bread Dance, 1970. First woman dancer is Ruby Diebold,
Oklahoma Seneca-Cayuga and Shawnee, second is Mary Squirrel, Shawnee.

Plate 40 *Distribution of cornbread and meat at the conclusion of the Loyal Shawnee spring Bread Dance, 1970.* View from the north looking south.

402

Plate 41   *Women performing the Women's Cluster Dance at the Loyal Shawnee Buffalo Dance, 1971.* Note the characteristic Loyal Shawnee cowhorn rattle in the singer's hand at left.

Plate 42 *Buffalo Dance episode, Loyal Shawnee Buffalo dance, 1971.* The dancer wearing the horned bison headdress is Bill Grass, a Sauk. Note the "buffalo head" chest painting of the male dancers.

404

Plate 43 *Buffalo Dance episode, Loyal Shawnee Buffalo dance, 1971*. Note the two kettles of mush, the "buffalo food", suspended from the fire crane.

Plate 44 *Women dancing the Cluster Dance, Loyal Shawnee Green Corn ceremony, 1971.* Note the characteristic Green Corn offerings of melons on display in the center of the ground, replacing the cornbread offerings of the Bread Dance.

406

Plate 45 Women's "Straight" Dance episode, Loyal Shawnee Green Corn ceremony, 1971.

Plate 46 *Green Corn Dance episode, Loyal Shawnee Green Corn ceremony, 1971.*

Plate 47 *Shawnee water drum and drumstick.* Drums of this type are used to accompany both ceremonial and social dances. The particular manner in which this drum is "tied" indicates that it belongs to the *Thawikila* division or White Turkey band of Absentee Shawnees. Photo courtesy of the Museum of the American Indian, Heye Foundation.

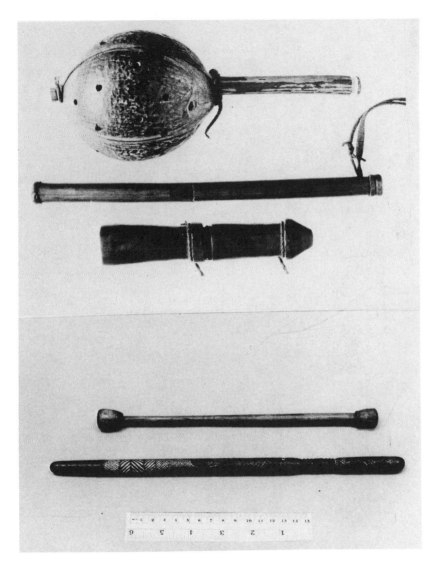

Plate 48   Above: *Coconut shell rattle of the type used to accompany ceremonial and social dance music, War dance whistle, and deer call, all Absentee Shawnee.* Photograph Courtesy of Museum of the American Indian, Heye Foundation.

Below: *Shawnee drumsticks.* Upper stick is an old piece used for many years at the Whiteoak ceremonial ground. Lower stick is a fine example of a Peyote religion drumstick from the Secondine family, Loyal Shawnees of Whiteoak. Note the fine bas-relief carving with white paint rubbed in to bring out the design. Near the center of the stick is a representation of a waterbird (*Anhinga anhinga*), an important Truth-bearer or witness of the peyotists.

410

Plate 49   Above: *Counting sticks for Football game and football.* Counting sticks by Ranny Carpenter, Loyal Shawnee, Whiteoak, Oklahoma, 1969. Football is Delaware, made by Reuben Wilson, Copan, Oklahoma, but is identical with those used by the Shawnees.

Below: *Shell spoon of the type formerly used in the Buffalo dance.* At the conclusion of the Buffalo dance the "buffaloes" dip out unsweetened corn mush from one of two kettles, either with their hands or using a spoon of this type. Specimen shown here is Delaware, made by the late Joe Washington, Wann, Oklahoma, but is identical with those formerly used by the Shawnees.

Plate 50 *Mask, Bearskin suit, pouch, turtle rattle, and cane used by Delaware Misingw impersonator.* According to Esther Dixon the *Misingw* impersonator of the Delawares, or a figure much like him, also appeared at Loyal Shawnee gatherings. Photograph courtesy of the Museum of the American Indian, Heye Foundation.

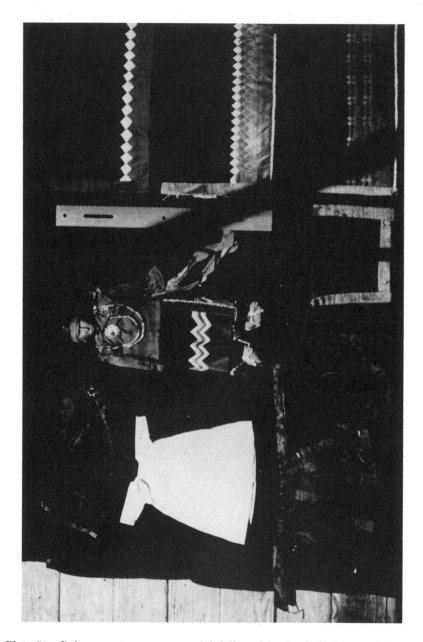

Plate 51 *Delaware otas or ceremonial doll used in the Doll dance, with extra clothing and ribbonwork robes.* This doll, formerly owned by Rosie Frenchman, Delaware of Copan, Oklahoma, is apparently the last of its sort remaining in Indian hands. In the Doll dance it was attached to a long pole carried by the leading dancer. The Shawnees also practiced the Doll dance, which they apparently borrowed from the Delawares.

Plate 52   Above: *Model of one of the foursplit feather "plumes" contained in the Kishpoko division war bundle.* These ornaments are tied to the hair, or to the spreader of the roach headdress, by four selected warriors in the ceremonial War dance.

Below: *Old Shawnee wild turkey tail fan.* This piece dates from the mid-nineteenth century. D. B. Dyer collection, Kansas City Museum, Kansas City, Missouri. Note the "Iroquois embossed" style beadwork on the handle of this fan, a type of beadwork often seen on old Shawnee pieces.

414

Plate 53 *Woman's hair ornament*. The Shawnees share this style with a number of other tribes (Iroquois, Delawares, Miamis, Kickapoos, Sauks, Caddoes, and others). It is worn by the Absentee Shawnee women as a part of their costume at all major ceremonies and was formerly seen among the Loyal and Eastern bands as well. It is attached to the hair at the back of the woman's head and the long ribbons hang down her back to the hem of her skirt. The specimen shown here was made by Mary Spoon in 1972. Entire ornament, with attached ribbon, is shown above. Below is enlarged detail of the upper part. Note that the top of the upper part of the ornament is slightly smaller than the bottom.

Plate 54 *Shawnee man's beaded shoulder bag, early to middle 19th century.*
Shoulder bags of this type, the epitome of Shawnee art in beadwork, became
obsolete by 1880.

Plate 55 A beautiful example of a Shawnee shoulder bag of early 19th century date in the collections of the Linden Museum, Stuttgart, Germany. The bag is of black-dyed buckskin with porcupine quillwork decoration and fringes of metal cones with red-dyed deerhair filler. The shoulder strap is of red stroud cloth with a black ribbon binding. (Photo courtesy Linden Museum, Stuttgart)

Plate 56 *Shawnee man's otterskin turban.* Such turbans, with ribbonwork trim at the top, beadwork and ribbon rosettes, and a golden eagle tail feather erect in a socket at the back of the wearer's head, were commonly seen in the period 1850-1940, but are now obsolete. Made by Mary Spoon, 1971.

418

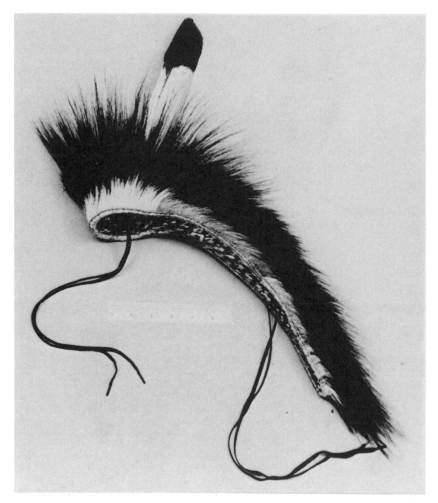

Plate 57 *Roach headdress.* Such headdress are made of fringes of animal hair
sewed tightly together at the base so as to stand erect. A single golden eagle
tail feather is mounted in a bone tube on a flat bone spreader so as to stand
erect and move with the movements of the wearer. Both Shawnees and Delawares always wore only one "center feather" in the roach. Today the roach
headdress is worn by some of the dancers in the ceremonial War dance of the
Absentee Shawnees.

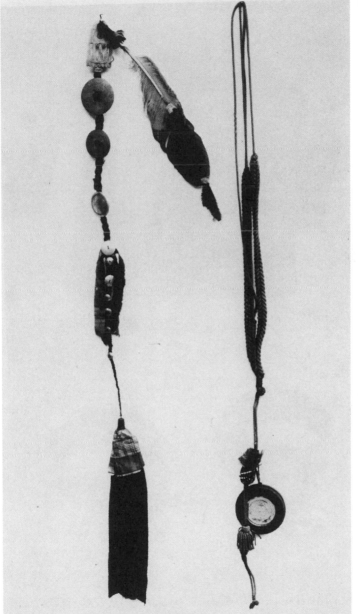

Plate 58   Left: *Elk antler or bone spreader for roach headdress, with attached plume holder, decorated eagle feather, imitation scalplock and hairplates.* The spreader would be worn inside the fringes of hair in the roach headdress (Plate 56) and the scalplock with attached hairplates would fall down the wearer's back.

Right: *Braided bandolier with attached paint bag, mirror, and bone arrow*

Both items would be worn in the *Hileni wekawe* or ceremonial War dance of the Absentee Shawnees. Photograph courtesy of the Museum of the American Indian, Heye Foundation.

420

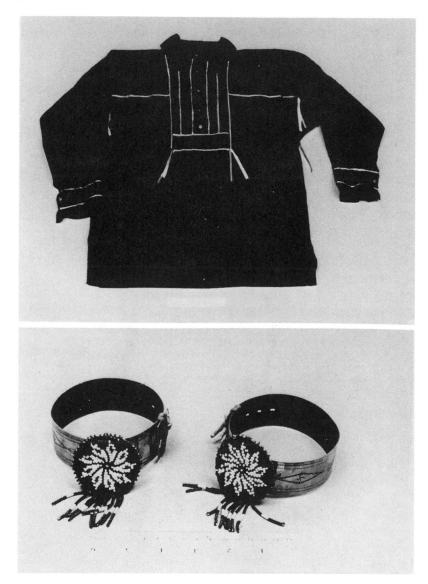

Plate 59   Above: *Characteristic Shawnee man's shirt.* Made by Mary Spoon, 1972

Below: *Man's german silver armbands with beaded rosettes attached.* Rosettes by Mary Spoon, 1972.

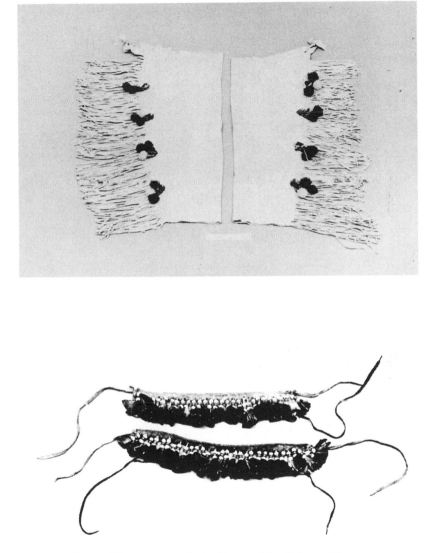

Plate 60   Above: *Shawnee man's leggings of buckskin with yarn pompons.*
Made by Mary Spoon, 1970.

Below: *Model of the now-obsolete deerhoof knee rattles formerly worn by both
Loyal and Absentee Shawnee men as ceremonial regalia.*

422

Plate 61 *Two styles of Shawnee moccasins.* Both pairs are soft-soled and differ only in their beaded decoration. Both were made by Mary Spoon in 1971.
The design on the cuffs of the upper pair is termed simply "leaves", that on
the lower pair "fans". The "fan" design was or is employed by a number of
other tribes as well, including the Iroquois tribes, the Delawares, Miamis, and
Caddoes.

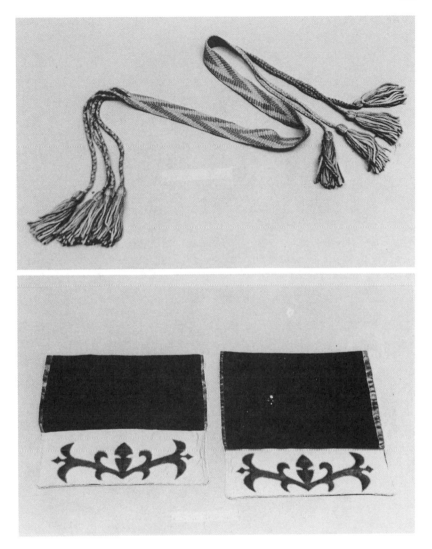

Plate 62 Above: *Creek finger-woven sash or "yarn belt".* Since the Shawnees no longer produce such yarn sashes themselves, they purchase those which they wear as a part of their ceremonial dress from the Creeks, Seminoles, or Yuchis.

Below: *Ribbonwork decorated breechcloth panels.* Made by the late Frances Gokey, Absentee Shawnee, Shawnee, Oklahoma, 1970.

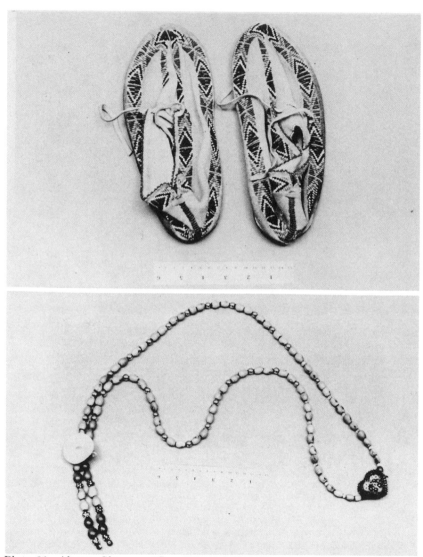

Plate 63 Above: *Shawnee "Peyote" moccasins.* This pair of moccasins, made by Grace Dale, Loyal Shawnee, Whiteoak, in 1968 was intended for wear in the Peyote ceremony. They are a Shawnee copy of the hard-soled footwear of the Southern Plains tribes from whom the Shawnees received the Peyote religion and whose regalia the Shawnees admire.

Below: *Man's bandolier of mescal beans (Sophora secundiflora) and old trade beads.* Absentee Shawnee. Such bandoliers are worn by Absentee Shawnee men both with traditional ceremonial dress in the Bread dance and also in the Peyote ceremony.

References

Abel, Annie Heloise
  1919. *The American Indian as participant in the Civil War.* Cleveland, Ohio: Arthur H. Clark Co.
Adair, James
  1775. *The History of the American Indian.* London.
Alford, Thomas Wildcat
  1934. *Shawnee Domestic and Tribal Life* (in W. A. Galloway, 1934).
  1936. *Civilization.* Norman, Okla.: University of Oklahoma Press.
Askinson, John M.
  1930. *Tecumseh and his times, the story of a great Indian.* New York: G. P. Putnam's Sons.
Bartram, William
  1791. *Travels of William Bartram.* Edited by Mark Van Doren. Reprint. New York: Dover Publications, 1928.
Benndorf, Helga, and Speyer, Arthur
  1968. *Indianer Nordamerikas, 1760-1860.* Deutsches Ledermuseum, Offenbach a.m., Germany.
Berlandier, Jean Louis
  1969. *The Indians of Texas in 1830.* Edited by John C. Ewers. Washington, D.C.: Smithsonian Institution Press.
Blair, Emma H.,ed.
  1912. *Tribes of the upper Mississippi Valley region and region of the Great Lakes.* Vol. 2. Cleveland, Ohio: Arthur H. Clark Co.
Brackenridge, Hugh
  1843. *Indian atrocities: narratives of the perils and sufferings of Dr. Knight and John Slover among the Indians, during the revolutionary war.* Nashville.
Browne, William Hand, et al., eds.
  1883. *Archives of Maryland.* 72 Vols. Maryland Historical Society, Baltimore, Md.
Callender, Charles
  1962. *Social Organization of the Central Algonkian Indians.* Milwaukee Public Museum Publications in Anthropology, no. 7. Milwaukee, Wis.
  1978. Shawnee. In *Handbook of American Indians north of Mexico,* edited by Wm. C. Sturtevant. Washington, D.C.: Division of Anthropology, Smithsonian Institution. pp. 622-635.
Carselowey, James R.
  1938. *Notes on the Shawnee.* (Ms.) Foreman Collection, Indian Archives, Oklahoma State Historical Society, Vol. 88, pp. 160-61.
Catlin, George
  1844. *Letters and notes on the manners, customs, and conditions of North American Indians.* 2 vols. Reprint. New York: Dover Publications, 1973.
Chapman, B. B.
  1946. The Potawatomie and Absentee Shawnee reservation. In *Chronicles of Oklahoma,* Vol. 14, Oklahoma City, Oklahoma Historical Society pp. 293-385.
Clark, Joshua V. H.

1849. *Onondaga; or, reminiscences of earlier and later times.* 2 vols. Syracuse.

Cotterill, R. S.
1954. *The southern Indians.* Norman, Okla.: University of Oklahoma Press.

Crane, Verner W.
1929. *The southern frontier, 1670-1732.* Ann Arbor: The University of Michigan Press.

Culin, Stewart
1907. *Games of the North American Indians.* Washington, D.C.: Bureau of American Ethnology.

Curtis, Edward S.
1930. *The North American Indian.* Vol. 19, pp. 19-21. Norwood.

Densmore, Frances
1910. *Chippewa music I.* Bureau of American Ethnology Bulletin no. 45. Washington, D.C.
1913. *Chippewa music II.* Bureau of American Ethnology Bulletin no. 53. Washington, D.C.
1932. *Menominee music.* Bureau of American Ethnology Bulletin no. 102. Washington, D.C.
1956. *Seminole music.* Bureau of American Ethnology Bulletin no. 161. Washington, D.C.

Downes, R. C.
1940. *Council Fires on the upper Ohio.* Pittsburgh, Pa.

Drake, Benjamin
1841. *Life of Tecumseh and of his brother the Prophet: with a historical sketch of the Shawanoe Indians.* E. Morgan & Co., Cincinnati, Ohio.

Drake, S. G.
1880. *The aboriginal races of North America, comprising biographical sketches of eminent individuals and an historical account of the different tribes, from the first discovery of the continent to the present period.* New York.

Edgar, Matilda
1890. *Ten years of upper Canada in peace and war, 1805-1815, being the Ridout letters, with annotations by Matilda Edgar, also and appendix the narrative of the captivity among the Shawanese Indians in 1788 of Thos. Ridout . . . .* Toronto: William Briggs.

Edinburgh
Scottish Record Office. Dalhousie muniments. (Published in microfilm form, East Ardsley, U.K.: Micro Methods.)

Fenton, William N.
1941a. *Masked medicine societies of the Iroquois.* Smithsonian Institution Annual Reports of the Board of Regents 1940, pp. 397-429, plates 1-25.
1941b. *Tonawanda longhouse ceremonies: ninety years after Lewis Henry Morgan.* Bureau of American Ethnology, pp. 139-65. Bulletin no. 128, Washington, D.C.
1942. *Songs from the Iroquois longhouse: program notes for an album of American Indian music from the eastern woodlands.* Smithsonian Institution Publication no. 3691. Washington, D.C.
1953. *The Iroquois Eagle Dance, an offshoot of the Calumet Dance.* Bureau of American Ethnology Bulletin no. 156. Washington, D. C.

Fenton, William N., ed.
1969. Answers to Governor Cass's questions by Jacob Jameson (ca. 1821-1825). *Ethnohistory* 16:113-39.

Foreman Collection
1937. Foreman Collection, Indian Archives, Oklahoma Historical Society, (Mss.) (Typescript copies of interviews with Oklahoma Indian

informants in 1937. Housed in the Historical Building, Oklahoma City).

Foreman, Grant
1940. *The last trek of the Indians*. Chicago, Ill.: University of Chicago Press.

Forsyth, Thomas
1812. *Tribes of the upper Mississippi Valley region and region of the Great Lakes*. Edited by Emma H. Blair, 2:274-77. Cleveland, Ohio: Arthur H. Clark Co.

Galloway, William A.
1934. *Old Chillicothe*. Xenia, Ohio. The Buckeye Press.
1943. A sacred slab of the Shawnee Prophet.*Cranbrook Institute of Science News Letter* 13: 6-7.

Gipson, Lawrence Henry, ed.
1938. *The Moravian Indian mission on White River, diaries and letters May 5, 1799 to November 12, 1800*. Indianapolis, Ind.: Indiana Historical Bureau.

Goody, Jack
1970. Cousin terms. *Southwestern Journal of Anthropology* 26: 125-42.

Gregg, J.
1905. *Commerce of the prairies*. In *Early Western travels*. Edited by Rueben Gold Thwaites, 20: 342-52 (original edition 1844).

Griffin, James B.
1943. *The Fort Ancient Aspect*. Museum of Anthropology, University of Michigan Anthropological Papers, 28: Ann Arbor, Mich.

Griffin, James B., ed.
1952. *Archeology of eastern United States*. Chicago, Ill.: University of Chicago Press.

Hadlock, Wendell S.
1946. The concept of tribal separation As rationalized in Indian folklore. *Pennsylvania Archaeologist* 16, no. 3, pp. 84-96.

Hagan, William T.
1961. *American Indians*. Chicago, Ill.: University of Chicago Press.

Hamilton, T. M.
1972. *Native American bows*. York, Pa.: George Shumway Publishers.

Hanna, C. A.
1911. *The wilderness trail*. 2 vols. New York and London: G. P. Putnam's Sons.

Harrington, M. R.
1914. *Sacred bundles of the Sac and Fox Indians*. University of Pennsylvania Anthropological Publications, vol. 4, no. 2. Philadelphia. The University Museum.

Harrington, M. R.
1938. "Spybuck, The Shawnee Artist," *Indians At Work*, Vol. 5, No. 8, pp. 13-15.

Harvey, Henry
1855. *History of the Shawnee Indians from the year 1681 to 1854 inclusive*. Cincinnati, Ohio: Ephraim Morgan & Sons.

Hazard, Samuel, ed.
1838-53. *Minutes of the Provincial Council of Pennsylvania*. 16 vols. Harrisburg, Pa.

Heckewelder, John
1876. *History, manners, and customs of the Indian nations who once inhabited Pennsylvania and the neighbouring states*. Rev. ed. Philadelphia: The Historical Society of Pennsylvania.

Hewitt, J. N. B.
1910. Ontwaganha. In *Handbook of American Indians north of Mexico*.

Edited by James Mooney. Bureau of American Ethnology Bulletin no. 30, 2:136. Reprint. Washington, D.C., 1959.

Horan, James D.
    1972.   *The McKenney-Hall portrait gallery of American Indians.* New York: Crown Publishers.

Howard, James H.
    1955.   Pan-Indian culture of Oklahoma. *Scientific Monthly* 18: 215-20.
    1961.   Cultural persistence and cultural change as reflected in Oklahoma Seneca-Cayuga ceremonialism. *Plains Anthropologist* 6: 21-30.
    1965*a*. *The Ponca tribe.*Washington, D. C.: Bureau of American Ethnology Bulletin no. 195.
    1965*b*. *The Plains-Ojibwa or Bungi, hunters and warriors of the northern prairies, with special reference to the Turtle Mountain band.* South Dakota Museum Anthropological Papers, Vermillion, S. D.: University of South Dakota.
    1965*c*. The Kenakuk religion: an early nineteenth century revitalization movement 140 years later. *Museum News*, South Dakota Museum, Vermillion, 26: 1-48.
    1965*d*. The compleat stomp dancer. *Museum News*, South Dakota Museum, Vermillion, 26: 1-23.
    1967.   Half-Moon Way: the Peyote ritual of Chief White Bear. *Museum News*, South Dakota Museum, Vermillion, 29: 1-24.
    1968.   *The southeastern ceremonial complex and its interpretation.* Columbia, Mo.: Missouri Archaeological Society Memoir no. 6.
    1970.   Environment and culture: the case of the Oklahoma Seneca-Cayuga. *Newsletter of the Oklahoma Anthropological Society*, vol. 19, no. 6, pp. 5-13: vol. 19, no. 7, pp. 5-21.

Irving, John Treat, Jr.
    1833.   *Indian sketches taken during an expedition to the Pawnee tribes.* Reprint. Norman, Okla.: University of Oklahoma Press, 1955.

Isaacs, Tony
    Buffalo Dance and Long Dance. On *Songs of the Muskogee* (long-playing phonograph record, no. 3001). Taos, N. M.: Indian House.

Jacobs, Wilbur R., ed.
    1967.   *The Appalachian Indian frontier, the Edmond Atkin report and plan of 1755.* Lincoln, Nebr.: University of Nebraska Press.

Jennings, Francis
    1971.   The constitutional evolution of the covenant chain. *Proceedings of the American Philosophical Society* 115: 88-96.
    1975.   *The invasion of America, Indians, colonialism, and the cant of conquest.* Chapel Hill, N. C.: University of North Carolina Press.

Johnston, Charles
    1827.   *A narrative of the incidents attending the capture, detention, and ransom of Charles Johnston . . . who was made prisoner by the Indians, on the river Ohio, in the year 1790.* New York.

Johnston, John
    1820.   Account of the present state of the Indian tribes inhabiting Ohio. In *Transactions and Collections, American Antiquarian Society* 1.

Jones, David
    1774.   *A journal of two visits made to some nations of Indians on the west side of the river Ohio in the years 1772 and 1773.* Reprint. Sabina Reprints, New York: Arno Press.

Joutel, Henri
    1714.   *A journal of the last voyage perform'd by Monsr. de La Sale, to the*

Gulph of Mexico to find out the mouth of the Mississippi River. Reprint. Chicago, 1896.

Kellogg, Louise Phelps, ed.
1917. *Early narratives of the northwest, 1634-1699*. New York: Charles Scribner's Sons.

Kendall, E. A.
1809. *Travels through the northern parts of the United States in the years 1807 and 1808*. 3 vols. New York.

Kenny, James
1913. Journal of James Kenny, 1761-1763. *Pennsylvania Magazine of History and Biography* 37: 1-47.

Kenton, Edna, ed.
1927. *The Indians of North America*: (Selections from *The Jesuit Relations and Allied Documents: Travels and Explorations of the Jesuit Missionaries in New France, 1610-1791*. Edited by Reuben Gold Thwaites). New York: Harcourt, Brace & Co.

Kihn, W. Langdon
1937. When red men ruled our forest. (A series of twenty-four paintings accompanying Mathew W. Stirling's article America's first settlers, the Indians). *The National Geographic Magazine* 72: 535-96).

Klopfenstein, C. G.
1957. Westward ho: removal of Ohio Shawnees, 1832-1833. *Bulletin of the Historical and Philosophical Society of Ohio* 15: 3-32.

Kuethe, J. Louis
1935. Johnnycake. *American Speech* 10: 202.

Kurath, Gertrude P.
1964. *Iroquois music and dance: ceremonial arts of two Seneca longhouses*. Bureau of American Ethnology Bulletin no. 187. Washington, D. C.

La Barre, Weston
1938. *The Peyote cult*. Yale University Publications in Anthropology no. 19. New Haven, Conn.: Yale University Press.

Latorre, Felipe A., and Latorre, Dolores L.
1976. *The Mexican Kickapoo Indians*. Austin, Tex.: University of Texas Press.

Lewis, Thomas M. N., and Kneberg, Madeline
1958. *Tribes that slumber, Indian times in the Tennessee region*. Knoxville, Tenn.: University of Tennessee Press.

Libby, Dorothy, ed.
1961. Thomas Forsyth to William Clark, St. Louis, December 23, 1812. *Ethnohistory* 8: 179-95.

Liette, Pierre
1962. *The western country in the seventeenth century, the memoirs of Antoine Lamothe, Cadillac, and Pierre Liette*. Edited by Milo M. Quaife. New York: The Citadel Press.

Lilly, Eli
1944. Tentative speculation on the chronology of the Walum Olum and the migration route of the Lenape. *Proceedings of the Indiana Academy of Science* 54: 33-40.

Lorant, Stefan, ed.
1946. *The New World, the first pictures of America made by John White and Jacques Le Moyne and engraved by Theodore De Bry*. New York: Duell, Sloan & Pearce.

Lowie, Robert H.

1922.   *The religion of the Crow Indians.* American Museum of Natural History, Anthropological Papers vol. 25, pt. 2, New York.

Malinowski, Bronislaw
1954.   *Magic, science and religion and other essays.* Garden City, N. Y.: Doubleday & Company.

Margry, Pierre, ed.
1875-1886. *Decouvertes et établissements des Francais dans L'ouest et dans le sud de L'Amerique septentrionale (1614-1754).* Paris: D. Jouaust.

Mathews, John Joseph
1961.   *The Osages, children of the middle waters.* Norman, Okla.: University of Oklahoma Press.

McCoy, Isaac
1840.   *History of Baptist Indian missions.* Washington, D. C.: Wm. M. Morris; New York: S. Rogner.

McDowell, William L., Jr., ed.
1958.   *Documents relating to Indian affairs, May 21, 1750-August 7, 1754.* Columbia, S. C.: University of South Carolina Press.

McKenney, T. L. and Hall, J.
1858.   *History of the Indian tribes of North America, with biographical sketches and anecdotes of the principal chiefs, embellished with one hundred and twenty portraits from the Indian gallery in the Department of War at Washington.* 3 vols. Philadelphia.

Michelson, Truman
1919.   *The autobiography of a Fox Indian woman.* Bureau of American Ethnology 40th Annual Report, pp. 291-344. Washington, D. C.

Miller, Jay
1974.   The Delaware as women: a symbolic solution. *American Ethnologist* 1: 507-14.

Minutes of the Provincial Council of Pennsylvania
1838-1853. *Minutes of the Provincial Council of Pennsylvania,* (16 vols.) Samuel Hazard, ed., Harrisburg.

Mitchell, John
1755.   Map: *A Map of the British and French Dominion in North America,* National Archives, Record group 76.

Mooney, James
1896.   *The Ghost-Dance Religion and the Sioux Outbreak of 1890,* Bureau of American Ethnology 14th Annual Report. Washington, D. C.

1900.   *Myths of the Cherokee,* Bureau of American Ethnology, 19th Annual Report. Washington, D. C.

1928.   *The Aboriginal Population of America North of Mexico,* Smithsonian Miscellaneous Collections, Vol. 80, pp. 1-40.

1959a. "Chowanoc," In: *Handbook of American Indians North of Mexico* (original edition 1910), Bulletin 30, Bureau of American Ethnology, Part I, p. 292.

1959b. "Shawnee," In: *Handbook of American Indians North of Mexico* (original edition 1910), Bulletin 30, Bureau of American Ethnology, Part II, pp. 530-538.

1959c. "Tecumseh," In: *Handbook of American Indians North of Mexico* (original edition 1910), Bulletin 30, Bureau of American Ethnology, Part II, p. 714.

1959d. "Tenskwatawa," In: *Handbook of American Indians North of Mexico* (original edition 1910), Bulletin 30, Bureau of American Ethnology, Part II, pp. 729-30).

Mooney, James, ed.

1910e. *Handbook of American Indians north of Mexico.* Bureau of American Ethnology Bulletin no. 30. Reprint. Washington, D. C., 1959.

Morgan, Lewis Henry
  1877. *Ancient society.* Reprint. Cleveland and New York: The World Publishing Co., 1967.
  1959. *The Indian journals, 1859-62.* Edited by Leslie A. White. Ann Arbor, Mich.

Morgan, Richard G.
  1952. Outline of cultures in the Ohio region. In *Archeology of Eastern United States,* ed. James B. Griffin, pp. 83-98. Chicago.

Murdock, George P. Ford, Clellan S.; Hudson, Alfred E.; Kennedy, Raymond; Simmons, Leo W. and Whiting, John M.
  1950. *Outline of Cultural Materials.* 3d rev. ed. New Haven, Conn.: Human Relations Area Files.

Nettl, Bruno
  1953. The Shawnee musical style: historical perspective in primitive music. *Southwestern Journal of Anthropology* 9: 277-85.

Newcomb, William W., Jr.
  1974. The Walum Olum of the Delaware Indians in perspective. *Bulletin of the Archaeological Society of New Jersey,* Spring-Summer 1974, pp. 29-32.

Nunez, Theron A., Jr.
  1958. Creek nativism and the Creek War of 1813-1814. *Ethnohistory* 5, 1-47; no. 2, pp. 131-75; no. 3, pp. 292-301.

O'Callaghan, M. D.
  1855. *Documents relative to the colonial history of the State of New York, procured in Holland, England, and France by John Romeyn Brodhead, Esq.* Vols. 9 and 10. Albany, N. Y.: Weed, Parsons & Co.

Oklahoma City
  1937. Oklahoma State Historical Society. Indian Archives. Foreman Collection (typescript copies of interviews with Oklahoma Indian informants).
  1938. Ibid. 88:160-61. Notes on the Shawnee [by James R. Carselowey].

Opler, Morris E.
  1972. *The Creek Indian Towns of Oklahoma in 1937.* University of Oklahoma, Papers in Anthropology, vol. 13, no. 1, Norman, Okla.

Ottawa
  Public Archives of Canada. Archives des Colonies (transcripts and microfilm copies of originals in Paris).

Parker, Arthur
  1968. *Parker on the Iroquois: Iroquois uses of maize and other food plants: the code of Handsome Lake, the Seneca Prophet: the constitution of the Five Nations.* Edited by William N. Fenton. Syracuse, N. Y.: Syracuse University Press.

Pearce, Roy H.
  1957. The metaphysics of Indian-hating. *Ethnohistory* 4: 27-40.

Pease, Theodore C., and Werner, Raymond C., eds.
  1934. *The French foundations 1680-1693.* Springfield, Ill.: Illinois State Historical Library.

Perrot, Nicolas
  1911. Memoir on the manners, customs, and religion of the savages of North America. In *The Indian Tribes of the Upper Mississippi Valley Region and Region of the Great Lakes,* ed. Emma H. Blair, 1: 25-272. Cleveland, Ohio.

Peterson, Harold L.

1965. *American Indian tomahawks.* Contributions from the Museum of the American Indian, vol. 19. New York: Heye Foundation.

Petrullo, Vincenzo
1934. *The diabolic root, a study of Peyotism, the new Indian religion, among the Delawares.* The University Museum, University of Pennsylvania.

Ponkilla, Florine L.
1973a. Fry bread. *American Indian Crafts and Culture* 7: 17.
1973b. Blue bread. *American Indian Crafts and Culture* 7: 17.
1973c. Shawnee sour bread. *American Indian Crafts and Culture* 7: 17.
1973d. Fresh cornbread. *American Indian Crafts and Culture* 7: 21.

Potherie, Bacqueville de la
1911. History of the savage peoples who are allies of New France. In *The Indian Tribes of the Upper Mississippi Valley Region and Region of the Great Lakes*, ed. Emma H. Blair, 1: 273-372. Cleveland, Ohio.

Quimby, George I.
1954. Discovered: a possible Tecumseh portrait. *Chicago Natural History Museum Bulletin*, September 1954, p. 3.

Radin, Paul
1923. *The Winnebago tribe.* Bureau of American Ethnology, 37th Annual Report. Washington, D. C.

Rogers, Robert
1765. *A concise account of North America.* Reprint. Johnson Reprint Corporation, 1966.

Romans, Bernard
1775. *A concise history of east and west Florida.* Reprint. New Orleans, La.: Pelican Publishing Co., 1961.

Royce, C. C.
1881. An inquiry into the identity and history of the Shawnee Indians. *American Antiquarian and Oriental Journal* 3: 177-89.

Schaeffer, C. E.
1942. The Grasshopper or Children's War—a circumboreal legend. *Pennsylvania Archaeologist* 12: 60-61.

Schenk, J. S.
1887. *History of Warren County, Pennsylvania.* Syracuse, N. Y.: D. Mason & Co.

Schoolcraft, Henry R.
1854. *Information respecting the history, condition, and prospects of the Indian tribes of the United States.* Vol. 4. Philadelphia, Pa.: Lippincott, Grombo and Co.
1855. Ibid., vol. 5.
1860. Ibid., vol. 6.

Schuyler, Peter
1956. Peter Schuyler to the New York Council, 6 Sept. 1692. In *The Livingston Indian Records 1666-1723, Pennsylvania History* 23: 168-69.

Sipe, C. Hale
1931. *The Indian wars of Pennsylvania.* 2d ed. Harrisburg, Pa.

Skinner, Alanson B.
1915. *Associations and ceremonies of the Menomini Indians,* American Museum of Natural History, Anthropological Papers, vol. 12, pt. 2. New York.
1924. *The Mascoutens or Prairie Potawatomi Indians: part I, social life and ceremonies.* Bulletins of the Public Museum of Milwaukee, vol. 6, no. 1.
1925. *Observations on the ethnology of the Sauk Indians, Part III, Notes on*

Material Culture. Bulletins of the Public Museum of the City of Milwaukee, vol. 5, no. 3, pp. 119-80.

Slotkin, J. S.
  1956. *The Peyote religion, a study in Indian-white relations*. Glencoe, Ill.: The Free Press.

Smith, Dwight L.
  1955. Shawnee captivity ethnography. *Ethnohistory* 2: 29-41.

Smith, Franklin C.
  1946. Pioneer beginnings at Emmanuel, Shawnee. *Chronicles of Oklahoma* 24: 2-14.

Spangenberg, Augustus G.
  1745. Extract des diarii des Br. Josephs u. Mariae vom 26th October 1744 bis zum 28 Febr. 45 st. n.. In *Bethlehem Diarium*, vol. 2 (1744-45), p. 373 (pp. 315-382) Archives of the Moravian Church, Bethlehem, Pennsylvania.

Speck, Frank G.
  1909. *Ethnology of the Tuchi Indians*, Anthropological Publications of the University Museum, vol. 1, no. 1. Philadelphia, Pa.
  1911. *Ceremonial songs of the Creek and Yuchi Indians*. Anthropological Publications of the University Museum, vol. 1, no. 2. Philadelphia, Pa.
  1931. *A study of the Delaware Indian Big House Ceremony*. Publications of the Pennsylvania Historical Commission. Harrisburg, Pa.
  1937. *Oklahoma Delaware ceremonies, feasts and dances.*Memoirs of the American Philosophical Society. vol. 7. Philadelphia, Pa.
  1942. The Grasshopper War in Pennsylvania. An Indian myth that became history. *Pennsylvania Archaeologist* 12: 31-34.

Spencer, O. M.
  1834. *The Indian captivity of O. M. Spencer*. Edited by Milo M. Quaife. Reprint. Chicago: 1917.

Spencer, Joab
  1908. *The Shawnee Indians*. Transactions of the Kansas State Historical Society, vol. 10, pp. 382-402. Topeka, Kans.
  1909. Shawnee Folk-Lore. *Journal of American Folklore* 22: 319-26.

Spoehr, Alexander
  1947. *Changing kinship systems*. Field Museum Anthropological Series, vol. 33. Chicago, Ill.

Stanley, Samuel, and Thomas, Robert K.
  1960. 1950 distribution of descendants of the aboriginal population of Alaska, Canada, and the United States. University of Chicago, Department of Anthropology.

Stewart, Tyrone
  1973. Oklahoma Delaware women's dance clothes. *American Indian Crafts and Culture* 7: 4-13, 18-22.

Stirling, Matthew W.
  1937. America's first settlers, the Indians. *The National Geographic Magazine* 72: 535-96.

Swanton, John R.
  1922. *Early history of the Creek Indians and their neighbors*. Bureau of American Ethnology Bulletin no. 73, pp. 320-87, Washington, D. C.
  1928. *Social organization and social usages of the Indians of the Creek Confederacy*. Bureau of American Ethnology 42d Annual Report, pp. 23-472. Washington, D. C.
  1946. *The Indians of the southeastern United States*. Bureau of American Ethnology Bulletin no. 137, Washington, D. C.

Tanner, John
1830. *A Narrative of the Captivity and Adventures of John Tanner, During Thirty Years Residence Among the Indians in the Interior of North America.* Edited by Edwin James. New York: G & C. H. Carvill.
Thomas, Cyrus
1891. The story of the mound or the Shawnees in pre-Columbian times. Reprinted from *American Anthropologist* 4, nos. 2-3.
Thwaites, Reuben G. ed.
1896-1901. *The Jesuit relations and allied documents, travels and explorations of the Jesuit missionaries in New France 1610-1791.* Reprint. New York: Pageant Book Co., 1959.
Tooker, Elizabeth
1970. *The Iroquois ceremonial of midwinter.* Syracuse, N. Y.: Syracuse University Press.
Townsend, E. B.
1883. E. B. Townsend. Special Agent at Shawneetown, Indian Territory, to Hon. W. Price, Commissioner of Indian Affairs, April 6, 1883. In C. F. Voegelin. *The Shawnee Female Deity.* p. 17.
Trowbridge, C. C.
1938. *Meeār̄meear traditions.* Edited by Vernon Kinietz. Occasional Contributions from the Museum of Anthropology, University of Michigan, no. 7. Ann Arbor, Mich.: University of Michigan Press.
1939. *Shawnese traditions.* Edited by Vernon Kinietz and E. W. Voegelin. Occasional Contributions from the Museum of Anthropology, University of Michigan, no. 9. Ann Arbor, Mich.: University of Michigan Press.
United States Bureau of the Census
1960. *Historical Statistics of the United States, Colonial Times to 1957.* Ser. 2 1-19, p. 756. Washington, D. C.
Voegelin, C. F.
1935. Shawnee phonemes. *Language* 11: 23-37.
1936. *The Shawnee female deity.* Yale University Publications in Anthropology. no. 10, pp. 3-21.
1938a. *Shawnee stems and the Jacob P. Dunn Miami Dictionary, part I, stems in p.* Indiana Historical Society Prehistory Research Series, vol. 1, no. 3, pp. 63-108, Indianapolis, Ind.: Indiana Historical Society.
1938b. Shawnee stems and the Jacob P. Dunn Miami Dictionary, part II, stems in t and č. Ibid., no. 5, pp. 135-67. Indianapolis.
1939. *Shawnee stems and the Jacob P. Dunn Miami Dictionary, part III, stems in k and š and o, with appendix non-initial elements.* Ibid., no. 8, pp. 289-341.
1940. *Shawnee stems and the Jacob P. Dunn Miami Dictionary, part IV, stems in l, m, and n.* Ibid., no. 9, pp. 345-89.
Voegelin, C. F., and Voegelin, E. W.
1935. Shawnee name groups. *American Anthropologist* 37: 617-35.
1944. The Shawnee female deity in historical perspective. *American Anthropologist* 46: 370-75.
Voegelin, C. F.; Yergerlehner, John F.; and Robinett, Florence M.
1954. *Shawnee laws: perceptual statements for the language and for the content.* American Anthropological Association Memoirs, no. 79, pp. 32-46. Chicago, The University of Chicago Press.
Voegelin, E. W.
1939. Some possible sixteenth- and seventeenth-century locations of the Shawnee. *Proceedings of the Indiana Academy of Science* 48: 13-18.
1941. Indians of Indiana. Ibid. 50: 27-32.

1942. Shawnee musical instruments. *American Anthropologist* 44: 463-75.

1944. Mortuary customs of the Shawnee and other eastern tribes. *Indiana Historical Society Prehistory Research Series* 2: 325-444.

Voegelin, E. W.; and Neumann, G. K.

1948. Shawnee pots and pottery making. *Pennsylvania Archaeologist* 18: 3-12.

Voegelin, E. W.; and Tanner, Helen H.

1974. *Indians of Ohio and Indiana prior to 1795*. 2 vols. New York and London: Garland Publishing.

Voegelin, E. W.; Rafinesque, Constantine; Voegelin, C. F.; and Lilly, Eli

1954. *Walum Olum*. Indianapolis.

Walker, Thomas, et al.

1776. *Council, Pittsburgh, Oct. 15, Nov. 6, 1776*. Yeates Collection, Historical Society of Pennsylvania, p. 35.

Wallace, Anthony F. C.

1956. Revitalization Movements. *American Anthropologist* 58: 264-81.

1970. *The death and rebirth of the Seneca*. New York: Alfred A. Knopf.

Warren, W.W.

1885. *History of the Ojibways, based upon traditions and oral statements*. Collections of the Minnesota Historical Society, vol. 5. Saint Paul, Minn.

Washington, D.C.

1755. Library of Congress. Map Division. Carte de la Louisiane [by Nicolas Bellin].

1755. National Archives. Record Group 76. *A map of the British and French dominion in North America* [by Dr. John Mitchell]. Amsterdam, Printed for I. Covens and C. Mortier.

1819. National Archives. Bureau of Indian Affairs. John Johnson to Caleb Atwater.

1861. National Archives. Bureau of Indian Affairs. George A. Cutter to William P. Dole, 4 November 1861.

Weslager, C. A.

1969. *The log cabin in America from pioneer days to the present*. New Brunswick, N. J.: Rutgers University Press.

1972. *The Delaware Indians, A History*. New Brunswick, N. J.: Rutgers University Press.

White, Leslie A.

1939. A Problem in Kinship Terminology. *American Anthropologist* 41: 566-73.

Whitehead, W. A.; Nelson, W.; and Ricord, F. W., eds.

1880-93. *New Jersey Archives, First Series*. Newark, N. J.: New Jersey Historical Society.

Wildschut, William

1960. *Crow Indian medicine bundles*. Edited by John C. Ewers. Contributions from the Museum of the American Indian, vol. 17. New York: Heye Foundation.

Wilson, Charles Banks

1964. *Indians of eastern Oklahoma*. Afton, Okla.: Buffalo Publishing Company.

Winfrey, Dorman H.

1954. Chief Bowles of the Texas Cherokee. *Chronicles of Oklahoma* 32: 29-41.

Witthoft, John

1946. The Grasshopper War in Lenape Land. *Pennsylvania Archaeologist* 16: 91-94.

1953.   The 'Grasshopper War' folktale. *Journal of American Folklore* 66:
        295–301.
Witthoft, John; and Hunter, William A.
    1955.   The seventeenth-century origin of the Shawnee. *Ethnohistory* 2: 42–57.
Woodward, T. S.
    1859.   *Woodward's reminiscences of the Creek, or Muscogee Indians.*
            Montgomery, Ala.
Wraxall, Peter
    1915.   *An abridgment of the Indian affairs contained in four folio volumes,*
            transisted in the Colony of New York, from the year 1678 to the year
            1751. Edited by Charles H. McIlwain. Cambridge, Mass.: Harvard
            University Press.
Wright, Muriel H.
    1951.   *A guide to the Indian tribes of Oklahoma.* Norman, Okla.: University
            of Oklahoma Press.
Young Bear, George
    n.d.   History of the Mesquakie Indians, also Known as the Sac and Fox
            of Iowa, told by George Young Bear. Edited by Jean Kaufmann.
            Mimeographed. Tama, Iowa.

INDEX